# SOCIAL POLICY REVIEW 21

## Analysis and debate in social policy, 2009

Edited by Kirstein Rummery, Ian Greener and Chris Holden

First published in Great Britain in 2009 by

The Policy Press
University of Bristol
Fourth Floor
Beacon House
Queen's Road
Bristol BS8 1QU, UK

Tel +44 (0)117 331 4054
Fax +44 (0)117 331 4093
e-mail tpp-info@bristol.ac.uk
www.policypress.org.uk

North American office:
The Policy Press
c/o International Specialized Books Services (ISBS)
920 NE 58th Avenue, Suite 300 • Portland, OR 97213-3786, USA
Tel +1  503 287 3093 • Fax +1 503 280 8832
e-mail info@isbs.com

British Library Cataloguing in Publication Data
A catalogue record for this book is available from the British Library.

Library of Congress Cataloging-in-Publication Data
A catalog record for this book has been requested.

ISBN 978 1 84742 373 3 hardback

The right of Kirstein Rummery, Ian Greener and Chris Holden to be
identified as editors of this work has been asserted by them in accordance
with the 1988 Copyright, Designs and Patents Act.

Cover design by Qube Design Associates, Bristol.
Front cover: photograph kindly supplied by www.alamy.com
Printed and bound in Great Britain by MPG Book Group.

# Contents

## Part Three: Rescaling social policy

# List of tables and figures

## Tables

## Figures

# List of contributors

**Natasha Cortis** is a Research Associate and Vice-Chancellor's Postdoctoral Research Fellow at the Social Policy Research Centre, and at the University of New South Wales, Australia.

**Howard Glennerster** is Emeritus Professor of Social Policy at the London School of Economics and Political Science, UK.

**Ian Greener** is a Reader in Social Policy at the School of Applied Social Sciences, Durham University, UK.

**Karen Healy** is Associate Professor in the School of Social Work and Human Services at the University of Queensland, Australia.

**Michael Hill** is Emeritus Professor of Social Policy, University of Newcastle, and Visiting Professor at Queen Mary, University of London, and at the University of Brighton, UK.

**Chris Holden** is a Lecturer in Global Health at the Department of Public Health and Policy, London School of Hygiene and Tropical Medicine, UK.

**Professor Ilan Katz** is Director of the Social Policy Research Centre at the University of New South Wales, Sydney, Australia.

**Michael Keating** is Professor of Political and Social Sciences at the European University Institute in Florence, Italy, and Professor of Politics at the University of Aberdeen, UK.

**Hilary Land** is Emeritus Professor of Family Policy at the School for Policy Studies, University of Bristol, UK.

**Ruth Lupton** is a Research Fellow at the Centre for Analysis of Social Exclusion, London School of Economics and Political Science, UK.

**Alexander Masardo** is based in the Department of Social and Policy Sciences, University of Bath, UK. He is currently a Visiting Fellow at the Centre for the Analysis of Social Policy.

**Gabrielle Meagher** is Professor of Social Policy and co-convenor of the Social Policy Research Network in the Faculty of Education and Social Work at the University of Sydney, Australia.

**John Offer** is Professor of Social Theory and Policy at the School of Policy Studies, University of Ulster, UK.

**Martin Powell** is Professor of Health and Social Policy at the Health Services Management Centre, University of Birmingham, UK.

**Gerry Redmond** is a Senior Research Fellow at the Social Policy Research Centre, the University of New South Wales, Sydney, Australia.

**Douglas Robertson** is Head of the Department of Applied Social Science, University of Stirling, UK.

**Kirstein Rummery** is Professor of Social Policy, Department of Applied Social Science at the University of Stirling, UK.

**Peter Selman** is a Visiting Fellow in the School of Geography, Politics and Sociology, Newcastle University, UK.

**James Smyth** is a Senior Lecturer in History at the University of Stirling, UK.

**Paul Stubbs** is a Senior Research Fellow in the Institute of Economics, Zagreb, Croatia.

**Andrew Wallace** is a Research Fellow at the London School of Hygiene and Tropical Medicine, UK.

**Siniša Zrinščak** is Professor of Social Policy in the Faculty of Law, University of Zagreb, Croatia.

# Overview

In this year's *Social Policy Review* (*SPR*) we are pleased to be able to both keep to, and break with, tradition, in the time-honoured fashion that makes social policy as a discipline robust and challenging. We have kept our three-part structure, focusing on developments in the welfare state, a selection of papers commissioned from the Social Policy Association (SPA) annual conference, and a final section on the theme chosen by the editorial team – this year our theme is the issue of the rescaling of social policy and the governance challenges that presents to the welfare state. However, we have also taken the opportunity of the sixtieth anniversary of what many commentators recognise as the 'founding' of the modern welfare state in the UK – the instigation of the Beveridge reforms to tackle the 'five evils' – to commission a series of papers for the first section that take a much broader historical and theoretical overview of welfare developments than our usual annual focus. We hope our readers will find this a particularly useful resource, particularly as the social and economic climates in 2008–09 appear to indicate that the welfare state is about to experience the kind of upheaval we last experienced in the restructuring and rescaling of the 1970s. When our grandchildren come to edit *Social Policy Review 81* in 2068 and reflect on the 120th anniversary of the Beveridge reforms, we trust this edition will prove an interesting marker in the development of welfare policy. We hope this is not misplaced confidence in the enduring significance of the welfare state and social policy.

## Part One: Tackling Beveridge's 'five evils', 60 years on – *Kirstein Rummery*

Past editions of *SPR* have focused on giving readers a considered 'round-up' of contemporary developments in the 'five pillars' of the UK welfare state: social security, employment, education, health and housing. In the past few years the editors have struggled with this structure, as it no longer reflects the complexity of the modern welfare state, nor the contemporary issues it faces. Rather than trying to broaden the scope of this section to include every branch of the modern welfare state, we have chosen this year to take a more thematic, historical and theoretical approach. We commissioned the authors in this section to reflect on contemporary developments in the welfare state in the light of their success, or failure, in tackling Beveridge's 'five evils' of want, idleness, ignorance, disease and squalor.

Michael Hill's chapter looks at the issue of tackling want, 60 years on from the Beveridge reforms. He looks at the way in which the 1948 settlement was a compromised response to want, and the tensions of balancing the objectives of insurance-based and safety-net schemes. His chapter highlights the ongoing tensions experienced by policy makers in trying to tackle want, particularly the impact of feminist and anti-poverty research in highlighting the contested and gendered nature of poverty. He points out how the debate has changed since the 1940s, and looks at contemporary developments in the light of those changes in discourse and policy.

Hilary Land's chapter provides a useful counterpoint, drawing on feminist scholarship to highlight the gendered nature of policy designed to tackle the evil of 'idleness'. She points to the dilemma, unarticulated in the Beveridge reforms but an increasingly important one for policy makers, of how to treat women's paid and unpaid 'work' and contribution to the economy and well-being. She focuses particularly on the challenges posited by the rise in part-time working and lone parenthood, both notable by their absence from serious consideration in the Beveridge model but an increasingly salient feature of the contemporary social and economic organisation of society. Her review of the limitations of the current welfare-to-work policies in tackling 'idleness' points to the continuing challenges facing policy makers.

In looking at policy responses to the evil of 'ignorance', Ruth Lupton and Howard Glennerster's chapter examines the way in which education policy has attempted to tackle the evil of 'ignorance' and promote social mobility, from the perspectives of policy in 1948 and 2008. They point out that the Butler education reforms were among the first raft of legislation which implemented the post-war Beveridge welfare state, and that these reforms were always an uneasy settlement between the public, private and 'third' sector of the welfare state. They discuss how developments in 2008 can be seen as part of the ongoing social and political debate in policy and practice about the role of education in promoting equality of opportunity and social mobility: which of course, is not quite the same as tackling 'ignorance' per se.

In reflecting on the progress made in tackling the evil of 'disease' in the UK since 1948, Martin Powell discusses the way in which the foundation and development of the National Health Service can be seen as an example of a shift from negative (reactive) to positive (proactive) welfare. Policy makers and practitioners have themselves taken the opportunity of the sixtieth anniversary of the foundation of the NHS to review the organisation in the light of the contemporary challenges it faces: these reviews have been mixed in their conclusions about the success in moving from a national 'sickness' service to one that genuinely promotes and provides 'health' to its citizens.

Douglas Robertson and James Smyth have continued the robust tradition of social policy having significant interdisciplinary strengths by drawing on housing studies and historical perspectives to examine how the housing sector's contribution to tackling squalor has changed since 1948, arguing that both a longer historical and a more geopolitical nuanced view is needed in examining developments in this sector. They contrast the experience of Scotland and England, and the competing political discourses, in the development of housing policy, discussing how contemporary policies have been framed by the Beveridge settlement.

Finally, in a timely reminder that anniversaries are both useful and diverting, John Offer's chapter takes an even longer historical view, by examining the impact the Poor Law Commission of 1905–09 has had on contemporary welfare policy. He highlights the importance of continuity and change in the welfare state, and shows how surprisingly contemporary and enduring the issues tackled by the Commission are. We are still debating pensions, and care, and social change and mobility, and how to balance direct provision with other kinds of support to achieve social cohesion and individual well-being. Perhaps our confidence that we will still be debating these issues with rigour in 60 years' time is not misplaced, after all.

## Part Two: Contemporary childcare policy – *Ian Greener*

Part Two of *SPR* is traditionally made up of a selection of papers from the SPA annual conference, which last year was held in Edinburgh. This section keeps with that tradition, but attempts a small innovation in examining a range of issues related to children in social policy. The reasons for this are both deliberate and contingent. The deliberate reason is that there has been an increased emphasis from national governments in considering children, particularly in relation to attempting early interventions to try and move children, particularly from deprived backgrounds, onto trajectories that allow them greater mobility within society. In the UK, Labour's third term in office was originally going to be dominated by the theme of the child, something that has perhaps got rather lost amidst economic crisis and the government's political unpopularity.

The four chapters in this section consider children in social policy from different perspectives, showing the range of work in this area, but also highlighting the very considerable challenges we still face. First is Peter Selman's chapter, which considers the issue of intercountry adoption. Peter's chapter presents an almost bewildering range of statistics and adoption patterns that is both comprehensive and surprising. His conclusions are sobering – that demand for children internationally far outstrips the number of children available for adoption, and that there is significant danger that, where market mechanisms are allowed, this will raise the 'price' of children or lead to prospective parents taking on children, particularly older children, with a range of problems for which they may be unprepared. Despite many intercountry adoptions having positive outcomes for children, it is also an area where trafficking is a significant problem, and raises questions about the implications of market-based reforms.

Ilan Katz and Gerry Redmond's chapter starts off with the observation that, whereas it seems commonplace to assume that children from materially deprived backgrounds often have poorer developmental outcomes than those from high-income families, little research has examined exactly what it is about poor families that links to inadequate parenting, and there is a need to look at other points in the income distribution to bring these factors to light. Based on a study of Australian children, they find that high incomes, but not median or low incomes, seem to be a protective factor for children who score lowly on developmental outcome tests between the ages of four and five. This research carries with it significant implications – that there is an urgent need for families who have children with developmental needs to receive significant material resources for those children to develop to their full potential.

Alexander Masardo's chapter considers an under-researched area of considerable significance – how shared residence is managed in households where the biological parents no longer live together. As I write this, the Children Society's report 'A Good Childhood' is receiving considerable media interest from its suggestion that family break-up, and the consequential absence of fathers from the family home, is a significant factor in damaging the well-being of children. Masardo's chapter compares how shared residence is managed in the UK and France, and concludes that despite attempts, especially in the UK, to create an expectation of shared residence in family break-up situations, there is still a considerable risk of disenfranchising predominantly fathers living apart from their children, and putting in place boundaries that discriminate against this emergent form of family life.

Finally, Gabrielle Meagher, Natasha Cortis and Karen Healy's chapter examines the strategic challenges facing child welfare systems in Australia, England and Sweden. Given the child protection problems faced in 2008/09, especially in England, this chapter is both important and topical. They remind us that the strategic challenges faced in different child welfare systems are very much a function of the way that policy, regulatory and organisational systems intersect, so that the problems of England lead to different patterns of problems compared with those in Australia and Sweden. The Swedish case particularly offers a significant contrast; it is almost unimaginable in the context of child protection in England to imagine a system where accountability is to clients rather than to the state, and where decentralisation is the organisational solution of choice, but given the repeated failings of child protection in England, perhaps it is time for lessons to be learned from abroad rather than blaming individual social workers and imposing ever-greater regulatory burdens.

## Part Three: Rescaling social policy – *Chris Holden*

While the term 'welfare state' suggests that welfare arrangements are primarily organised through the central apparatus of the 'nation state', the contributions to this section engage with processes by which some of the functions of welfare are being reconstituted at other levels or scales. Although much debate among social policy scholars in recent years has addressed this theme by focusing on the ways in which welfare functions are, in some cases, being reconstituted at levels 'above' the nation state, through processes of supra-state regionalisation (exemplified by the European Union) or globalisation, the contributions to this section primarily address the reconstitution of welfare functions 'below' the level of the nation state. However, these are complex processes, and as the contributions by both Keating and Stubbs and Zrinščak demonstrate, processes of globalisation, supra-state regionalisation, or intervention by international agencies, may be pivotal in the reorganisation of welfare functions at the level of sub-state regions or in other ways that challenge the central state. Furthermore, as Wallace demonstrates, the central state itself may be instrumental in attempting to rescale activities at the lowest of levels.

In the first chapter in this Part, Wallace investigates 'the turn to the local' in UK social policy, drawing on the concept of 'governance'. He regards this move towards the self-governance of local neighbourhoods as a genuine, yet contradictory, process. For New Labour, this process of 'localisation' is driven by communitarian ideas that posit the neighbourhood as the unit within which democracy can be revitalised and individuals motivated to act responsibly. Focusing on the New Deal for Communities, he shows how the desire to devolve power to local citizens may fail as a result of particular assumptions about the nature of local spaces and a lack of understanding of how those citizens may wish to utilise opportunities for local governance, or of the structural contexts that help to shape their lives.

In his chapter, Keating discusses processes of regional devolution. The concept of the nation has been important in the development of welfare states, since it has often formed at least part of the basis for social solidarity and a willingness to engage in redistribution. Yet Keating notes that in some cases nations have not in fact coincided with the borders of states. While processes of globalisation seem to suggest the coming of a borderless world in which territory no longer matters, these processes have in fact been accompanied by a 're-territorialisation' as various systems are reconstituted at new scales which, in contrast to the ideal of the nation state, do not always correspond with each other. Keating argues that sub-state regions or nations within states (such as those of the UK) may be a robust basis for social solidarity that challenges the assumption of this role by the central state. This can raise fears of growing inequalities between regions, as well as the spectre of 'the race to the bottom' as territories compete to attract mobile capital and reduce expensive social provision. However, regions may also be spaces for innovation and experimentation in social provision, providing scope (in the best case scenario) for a 'race to the top' as politicians respond to the preferences of citizens.

In the last chapter in this Part, Stubbs and Zrinščak discuss the complex and fluid territorial spaces and identities of South East Europe. While most of these territories share a common social policy legacy from the former Yugoslavia, these arrangements 'have been profoundly destabilised, and subnational, national and regional scales and their interrelationships are still heavily contested' (p 284). The picture is rendered particularly complex by the role of external and international actors in ascribing to various spaces and levels the welfare roles they should play. Stubbs and Zrinščak identify how, as a result of a discourse of humanitarian intervention more suited to less-developed contexts, local structures became subordinated to an international aid apparatus. Furthermore, the multiplicity of external actors, and their lack of coordination, has led to sometimes arbitrary outcomes, with aid often being channelled through non-state actors and a consequent tendency to 'projectisation' and the formation of a parallel system that is poorly integrated with established services. Three social policy areas are examined in detail: labour markets; pensions; and poverty and social exclusion. It is concluded that we cannot understand emergent social policies in the region without understanding the ways in which scale has been socially and politically constructed, through processes that have paid scant attention to questions concerning the optimum scale for different kinds of welfare arrangement.

# Part One

## Tackling Beveridge's 'five evils', 60 years on

# ONE

# Freedom from want: 60 years on[1]

*Michael Hill*

## Introduction

The social security settlement of the 1940s, implemented in 1948, appeared to have the prevention of want as its central focus, inasmuch as its inspiration came from the Beveridge Report (1942). In addressing the issues about freedom from want, this chapter could try to deal with the extent to which poverty was effectively prevented then and now. At the end of this chapter some observations will be included on that, but the achievement of a satisfactory comparison would be very difficult. Moreover, I write as a student of policies rather than as a student of poverty. Beveridge's rhetorical use of the term 'want', though largely synonymous with poverty, has perhaps a slightly looser connotation. Taking my cue from that, I will provide a policy analysis that, influenced by writers like Deborah Stone (1988) and Frank Fischer (2006), gives attention to the discourses that have framed policy making and its leading critiques.

What I will do here will be to consider: what were the characteristics of the 1948 settlement as an approach to the prevention of want; what was problematical about that approach (with the benefit of hindsight); what remain the implications of those problems for social security today and how might we consider (and evaluate) modern approaches to their solution (particularly those encapsulated in very recent government initiatives).

## The 1948 settlement as a response to 'want'

It is appropriate to start from the way in which the Beveridge Report links its rhetoric on the topic of 'want' with its social security proposals. It states:

Abolition of want requires, first, improvement of State insurance, that is to say provision against interruption and loss of earning power. All the principal causes of interruption of loss of earnings are now the subject of schemes of social insurance.... Second, adjustment of incomes, in periods of earning as well as in interruption of earning, to family needs, that is to say, in one form or another it requires allowances for children. (Beveridge, 1942, pp 8-9)

That statement would seem to suggest that the task of preventing want would have been fulfilled by the two pieces of legislation already on the statute book by 1948: the 1944 Family Allowances Act and the 1946 National Insurance Act.

Leaving aside for a moment any questions about the adequacy of the benefits provided under those two proposals, it was evident, even at that time, that those pieces of legislation left gaps in the framework for the prevention of want. Beveridge had recognised that some want would arise where there had been no previous earnings. The concept of social insurance rested on contribution tests, and thus previous labour market attachment. The machinery to fill the gaps in the framework – without more legislation – would have been the continuation of the Poor Law, as modified by measures enacted in 1934 and the early years of the Second World War that set up a national system of assistance for some groups. The final part of the 1948 settlement was, however, the National Assistance Act of that year, which brought the remaining vestiges of the Poor Law into a single means-tested assistance scheme, while passing on the institutional care aspects of the Poor Law to local government.

But clearly 'want' could only really be claimed to have been abolished if the benefits provided under the three schemes recognisably prevented poverty. Here, then, we enter into an area of substantial ambiguity. Those who have studied the process by which (a) Beveridge arrived at his benefit level proposals and (b) the government determined the actual levels of benefits show clearly that what was actually offered was as generous an approach to the prevention of want as the Treasury felt could be afforded (see, in particular, Veit-Wilson, 1992; Lowe, 1993). Veit-Wilson (1992) shows that Beveridge struggled with definitions of poverty, and particularly Rowntree's (1941) definitions of primary and secondary poverty, inclining towards the harsh approach embedded in the former. Glennerster (1995, p 39) sums up the issue bluntly: 'Beveridge was rejected where his own scheme was a muddle or a deception. This was the case in the confusion that surrounded his claim that his benefits would be sufficient to raise everyone above the poverty line'.

This chapter will not try to answer the question posed by the title of John Veit-Wilson's article (1992) as to whether the confused situation in 1948 arose from 'muddle' or 'mendacity' and as to who was responsible for that. Its concern is with the way in which this response to 'want' bequeathed to UK social security a series of problems that, given the continued evidence of poverty today, have been readdressed many times since 1948 and which cannot be regarded as solved. What, then, will be central to this account is that in fact the 1948 settlement embraced two different approaches to the official determination of entitlement (I use that word deliberately here instead of 'want' or even the word often used in official documents −'need') in the schedules implementing the National Insurance Act and those implementing the National Assistance Act. The water was additionally further muddied by the Family Allowance entitlements that could at best be seen as a token response to child poverty.

## National insurance and National Assistance compared

The simplest point about the relationship between National Insurance and National Assistance is that the government chose, at that time, to set the basic level for the latter below that for the former. The weekly National Insurance rate for a married couple was £2.10, the National Assistance rate £2. But then other aspects of National Assistance tipped the balance in the opposite direction to that implied by that simple contrast. That in itself could be seen to indicate uncertainty about what a national minimum might mean. In particular, provision was included within the National Assistance scheme for assistance with rent and some other housing costs. More complicatedly still, National Assistance officers had discretionary powers to contribute to other 'exceptional' costs. Hence, contradictory messages were being sent. In some respects the setting of the basic National Assistance rate below the National Insurance rate implied some notion of less eligibility, yet in other respects the National Assistance scheme seemed to be given the responsibility explicitly to prevent want, charged to take into account some actual expenditure needs.

The setting up of two approaches to entitlement to run parallel with each other in this way established a contradiction in the UK social security system that remains with us to this day. Beveridge had seen

National Assistance as 'for the limited number of cases of need not covered by social insurance' (Beveridge, 1942, p 11). The idea was born of, to slightly mix metaphors, 'the withering safety net' of National Assistance declining in importance as the National Insurance scheme strengthened through the growth of contributions. Yet many people getting National Insurance who had no other resources could also claim National Assistance; the National Insurance scales would therefore have to rise much more than the de facto levels guaranteed by National Assistance for this to happen. Of course, however, certainly Beveridge, and thus presumably the policy makers, had another mechanism to achieve that in mind – the rise of private provisions (particularly occupational pensions).

The reality was a dilemma that came to face every government as it made decisions to deal with annual upgrading of benefit rates. If, in order to buy out dependence on means-testing, the National Insurance rates were increased faster than the National Assistance rates, governments could be accused of disregarding the need to increase the income of the most poor. But if National Assistance rates were increased faster than National Insurance rates, then they could be accused of increasing dependence on means-tests and diminishing encouragement to people to provide for themselves. Paradoxically, of course, the third alternative of moving both rates together attracted criticism from both perspectives, such is the nature of political debate. Today the names have changed – in particular National Assistance was later called Supplementary Benefits and is now living on in a cluster of schemes with different names: Income Support, means-tested Jobseeker's Allowance, Pension Credit, and most recently, Employment and Support Allowances – but the issue of the relationship between the rates lives on, albeit in a form muted by the decline in the availability of social insurance benefits.

Bonoli (1997, p 357) argues that Esping-Andersen's (1990) distinction between regimes in which social insurance is dominant and those where means-testing remains important can alternatively be seen as one between countries where 'Bismarkian social policy ... [is] concerned with income maintenance for employees' and ones where there is 'Beveridgean social policy [which] aims at the prevention of poverty'. But logically, if a Beveridgean social insurance system simply provides a basic minimum then means-testing is unlikely to be eradicated. That is what makes Esping-Andersen's third type of regime (the social democratic one) significant, if only as a reference point for others, combining a national minimum with income replacement benefits that lift many beyond that. The Labour government led by Harold Wilson in the 1960s tried to take the British system in that direction, adding earnings-related additions to sickness and unemployment benefits. There were also efforts, started by the Conservatives in the early 1960s and taken much further by Labour in the 1970s, to add an earnings-related element to pensions for those not in good private occupational schemes. The additions for short-term benefits were abolished by the Conservatives in 1982, who followed this up with a measure seriously weakening the earnings-related pensions scheme. To some degree, the latter has been rescued by Labour since 1997; we return to this below.

## The treatment of women by the benefit system

The notion that National Assistance could provide for people not entitled to National Insurance benefits was important in respect of the treatment of the needs of women by the 1948 settlement. It would be diverging too far from the brief for this chapter to discuss the widely developed critique of the Beveridge Report for treating married women as the dependants of their husbands for National Insurance purposes and therefore only able to get benefits if widowed.

But what is relevant to mention is the divergence in the treatment of mothers affected by family breakdown other than death between National Insurance and National Assistance. Beveridge recognised that these situations posed problems for a comprehensive National Insurance scheme. His report argued that a benefit could be provided to meet circumstances arising from other reasons for family breakdown. However, this was presented as an option, and in practice it was an option that was not taken up. Beveridge saw it as problematical that any proposal for benefits to separated or divorced women would have to be set in a context in which there was a legal system that apportioned obligations in relation to the concept of 'fault'. If the husband were at fault for family breakdown, then the husband should have a continuing obligation to maintain. If the wife were at fault, Beveridge believed that there would be a problem about the state adopting a role as the payer of benefit. His firm commitment to the idea of insurance led him to argue that in this case the system could not be required to pay out where the insured person was herself responsible for her situation. Quite apart from the fact that we now recognise that the concept of 'fault' offers a rather misleading approach to the explanation of much marital breakdown, the fundamental difficulty here is the use of the insurance concept where what would be perhaps more appropriate would be the notion of benefits as 'contingent' on individuals being in a particular situation of need regardless of whether or not it would have been possible to insure against its occurrence. Only in the case of National Assistance was this recognised, but of course in a form underpinned by the means-test. In 1948, the numbers of families involved were small. That was, of course, all to change as marriage breakdown increased and single parenthood outside marriage altogether has also become common.

## The slow abandonment of the 'withering safety net' expectation

I worked for the National Assistance Board in the early 1960s. The Board was a quasi-autonomous agency reporting to the Minister of Pensions and National Insurance, whose activities were seldom in the public eye. The notion that we belonged to a safety net agency designed to wither in importance was widely accepted. When, towards the end of the 1960s, I wrote an article raising questions about some of the discretionary powers of the National Assistance Board, I recall Norman Chester, who had been the secretary to the Beveridge Committee, observing to me that – in effect – he thought that my concerns were unimportant. However, the National Assistance Board was not declining in size and its activities were beginning to be given more attention.

I must confess a lingering attachment to the idea that the safety 'net' of means-tested benefits should 'wither' in favour of more universal benefits. This is a view that has been widely expressed by academic writers on social policy. However, it is quite clear that the perspective of governments, regardless of party, is that mass means-testing is here to stay.

Deacon and Bradshaw (1983, p 98) explore how this came to be recognised in the 1960s and 1970s, saying: 'In few areas of social policy have the hopes and expectations of the 1940s been so totally confounded as in the case of social assistance'. The changing place of National Assistance is well illustrated by the views of two leading social policy academics – Richard Titmuss and David Donnison. Both of them played key roles in the development of the renamed National Assistance system – Supplementary Benefits. Titmuss, in a 1971 article, attacked the growing welfare rights movement for its advocacy of the formal codification of Supplementary Benefits discretionary powers, making it clear that he still saw the solution to the problems that were being raised to lie in the strengthening of universal National Insurance benefits. By contrast, Donnison, who was chair of the Supplementary Benefits Commission between 1975 and 1980, led an extensive exercise to curb discretion and fit the Supplementary Benefits system for a mass role, in which the more demeaning aspects of discretionary powers would disappear, benefit applications could be processed relatively speedily and mechanically, and rights to benefits would not be obscure (see Donnison, 1977).

## The impact of a more effective debate about poverty

The increased focus on the National Assistance/Supplementary Benefits part of the social security system in the 1960s and 1970s was influenced by the emergence of a much more sophisticated debate about poverty. This started in the 1950s, and has been called the 'rediscovery of poverty'. The fact is that, as has already been indicated, the terms of the 1948 settlement rested on a very limited examination of what may really be meant by 'want'. The last of the Rowntree investigations of poverty in York came out in 1951 (Rowntree and Lavers, 1951) and offered a complacent perspective on the achievements of the 1948 settlement. This was challenged by Peter Townsend (1954) as offering an inadequate approach to the measurement of poverty. An important part of his critique involved pointing out how so-called 'primary poverty', embodying what was presented as an 'absolute' definition of poverty, owed more to the calculations of comfortable experts in their studies than to the realities of the life of people trying to live on low incomes.

This led on to a succession of studies questioning the performance of the social security system. Perhaps not surprisingly, since the government saw the National Assistance/Supplementary Benefits system as the central plank in its anti-poverty programme, an easy starting point for these studies was the assembly of evidence that there were many people with incomes even below the National Assistance standard (hence the rhetorical point made in the title of the 1965 book by Abel-Smith and Townsend, which effectively took up this issue – *The Poor and the Poorest*). There were two crucial aspects to this analysis:

- evidence of underclaiming by those who could expect to be entitled to benefits, unaware of their rights or deterred by the stigma of having to prove need;
- evidence that there were families with incomes below the official standards who could not claim National Assistance/Supplementary Benefits because their heads of household were in full-time work.

The former evidence, while from a wider perspective a part of the case against means-testing, had the practical effect of providing a stimulus to the growing 'welfare rights' movement, which aimed to point out people's rights to benefits and to help people make claims. The latter opened up a very different agenda: about the fact that the 1948 settlement had – aside from the limited development of Family Allowances – given little attention to the working poor. The next section explores this.

However, the new poverty experts were only too aware that while using the National Assistance/Supplementary Benefits yardstick as a surrogate definition of poverty enabled them to criticise government in its own terms, the more fundamental question was whether benefits provided using that yardstick actually abolished 'want'; hence, the importance of more systematic studies of poverty, particularly Townsend's *Poverty in the United Kingdom* (1979). Townsend pioneered an approach to the study of poverty that looked at deprivation in terms of the inability to afford a lifestyle taken for granted by others. More recent studies (Mack and Lansley, 1985; Gordon and Pantazis, 1997) lend support to Townsend's argument. They demonstrate the extent to which low-income people lack things that, according to public opinion surveys, are regarded as necessities (see Flaherty et al, 2004, ch 1, for a review of the issues here).

An indirect outcome of the re-examination of what is meant by poverty has been efforts by the European Union (EU) and individual governments including the UK to develop a simple useable measure of poverty in terms of low incomes relative to average incomes. We return to this issue later in the chapter.

## The implications of the 1948 settlement for poverty among those in employment

Logically, responses to the evidence that some people in work were worse off than those on benefits could take the form of efforts to enhance wages or cut benefits. The official position until the introduction of a National Minimum Wage in 1999 was to regard wage levels as a matter for the market, perhaps assisted by the bargaining efforts of trades unions. On the other hand, the National Assistance/Supplementary Benefits regulations contained a provision, echoing the 'less eligibility' principle in the Poor Law, under which benefits for unemployed claimants and their families could be kept below potential earning levels. With the development of a critique of National Assistance/Supplementary Benefits policies this 'wage stop' came under attack and was eventually abolished in 1975.

An alternative to direct wage enhancement is obviously the indirect public subsidy of wages. The only contribution of this kind to the prevention of want among those in work in the 1948 settlement was the small Family Allowance introduced in the 1944 legislation. This was for those families with two or more children. There was no provision to uprate it regularly and it remained frozen at its original level until the 1960s. It was only with its replacement by Child Benefit in 1975 that the principle of regular uprating was established.

Inevitably, campaigners against child poverty (their efforts reinforced by the establishment of the Child Poverty Action Group in 1965) focused primarily on the case for improving Family Allowance/Child Benefit. The universalism of this measure – which is its particular strength inasmuch as it avoids any form of direct wage subsidy or means-testing – has led its opponents to stress its direct cost for the Treasury. Hence, with the recognition of the evidence on child poverty there came a 'centrist' search for more targeted alternatives. It had long been considered undesirable to have public policies that directly subsidised wages – the Speenhamland approach to poor relief, which was officially abandoned in 1832. But then in 1972 the Conservative government led by Edward Heath introduced a means-tested benefit to subsidise families where there was a low-paid full-time principal wage earner – Family Income Supplement. This was the start of the road towards the much more extensive subsidy of low wages (and not just for families) that we have in the tax credit system today.

It should be added that the issues about low wages have become very much more complicated with the emergence of both extensive female labour market participation (characterised by both low wages and often part-time work) and large numbers of female-headed households.

## Long-run and short-run want

Neither the National Insurance system nor the National Assistance system originally paid any attention to the extent to which want might be affected by long periods of time with a low income. The National Insurance benefit rates were the same for all categories of claimants, including pensioners and widows.

The provision within the National Assistance scheme for discretionary extras led to a significant development: as welfare benefits advice developed, an increasing number of long-term claimants secured regular additions to assist with heating and other domestic costs. Hence, when – after the change from National Assistance to Supplementary Benefits

– ways of moving towards more secure entitlements were examined, it was recognised that one option could be to compound the inconsistent discretionary additions into higher rates of benefits for pensioners and for long-term sick and disabled people. Since that time, benefit rates for these two groups have diverged further and further from those for other claimants. This effect is particularly marked now inasmuch as means-tested provision for pensioners is within a separate Pension Credit system rather than in the Supplementary Benefits' successor, Income Support.

There was also some evolution of the National Insurance system away from the 'one size fits all' approach but this was a curious one, with outcomes that remain unsatisfactory to this day. The impact of earnings-related additions was initially to treat most short-term claimants of benefits better than long-term ones. But the crucial change towards today's system came when the Conservatives replaced Sickness Benefit with Statutory Sick Pay, leaving the National Insurance system as only (with some complicated exceptions) concerned with support for the longer-term sick. This then developed into a system with three rates of Incapacity Benefit, according to the length of entitlement, which were changed in 2008 into three rates of Employment and Support Allowances, with some complicated variations in respect of the extent to which either contributions conditions or means-tests apply.

As far as National Insurance pensions were concerned, Beveridge's assumption was that people might make additional private provision for old age, and of course in this respect the availability of a benefit without any sort of means-test encouraged this. Recognition, in the late 1950s, of the divisions arising from the fact that large numbers of better-paid or more secure workers did this but many others could not, led to the development of schemes to enable the latter group to contribute to state-provided additions to basic National Insurance pensions. The complicated history of this development (see Hill, 2007, ch 2) is beyond the scope of this chapter. However, it needs mentioning since the fact that it did not eliminate the problem of poverty in old age for some pensioners has kept the issue of want among pensioners on the agenda.

It is appropriate to end this section with a table that illustrates some of the variations between different claimant groups today (Table 1.1). Bear in mind that it only focuses on some of the simpler examples, involving single claimants without dependants, and does not deal with the additional complications that arise from the fact that some housing costs are met while others are not. Even in this limited form, the table reflects the enormous variation between different categories of beneficiaries. Except in the case of pensions, the distinction (in terms of levels of benefit) between non-means-tested benefits and means-tested ones has effectively disappeared. But there is now a vast difference between the guaranteed minimum for pensioners and that for any other group.

**Table 1.1: Comparisons of basic entitlement levels for single people, 2008/09**

| Benefit | Weekly entitlement |
|---|---|
| Employment and Support Allowance (assessment phase) | £60.50 |
| Employment and Support Allowance (work-related activity group) | Up to £84.50 |
| Employment and Support Allowance (support group) | Up to £89.50 |
| Contribution-based Jobseeker's Allowance for those aged 18-24 (lasts six months) | £47.95 |
| Contribution-based Jobseeker's Allowance for those aged 25+ (lasts six months) | £60.50 |
| Income Support or Jobseeker's Allowance for those aged 18-24 | £47.95 |
| Income Support or Jobseeker's Allowance for those aged 25+ | £60.50 |
| Basic National Insurance pension | £90.70 |
| Pension Credit | £124.05 |

## Contemporary developments

After a long period in which Conservative governments had been unwilling to address the subject of poverty, Tony Blair (1999) proclaimed that the Labour government elected in 1997 had a '20-year mission' 'to end child poverty for ever'. That pledge was followed by the specification of interim targets, and various official indications about how the pledge might be interpreted. Crucial here has been the use by the government of a definition of poverty in terms of income below 60% of 'equivalised' median income. 'Equivalised' here defines a technique to take into account household composition. Both the threshold of 60% of the median and the techniques used to effect equivalisation are the subject of controversy. There are varied views about the desirability of calling this a poverty line. A variation on this used by the EU, for whom it is a useful index for comparative statistics, is to talk of numbers 'at risk' of poverty.

The pledge to end child poverty has been reiterated in various ways, including notably the following from Gordon Brown's speech to the 2008 Labour Party Conference:

> And because child poverty demeans Britain, we have committed our party to tackle and to end it. The measures we have taken this year alone will help lift two hundred and fifty thousand children out of poverty. The economic times are tough of course, that makes things harder – but we are in this for the long haul – the complete elimination of child poverty by 2020. And so today I announce my intention to introduce ground-breaking legislation to enshrine in law Labour's pledge to end child poverty.

Before we look at what this 'ground-breaking legislation' amounts to, it is appropriate to examine what have so far been the characteristics of Labour's overall approach to addressing questions about 'want'. This can best be summed up by reference to a slogan from Blair's introduction to a 1998 Green Paper on welfare reform – 'Work for those who can; security for those who cannot' (DSS, 1998, p iii). In many respects that can now be treated as a distinction between pensioners and younger adults, since significantly, as the figures in Table 1.1 suggest, it is only in respect of the Pension Credit where there has been a serious attempt to bring state-guaranteed incomes up to close to the 60% of median incomes standard. The Child Poverty Action Group (2006, table 1) had produced figures to show how far most benefits fall below that standard. Piachaud's (2007, p 210) trenchant comment on that evidence is pertinent: 'The simple fact is that the social security system comes nowhere near providing the poverty level for those without any other resources'.

The split between thinking about pensions and about income enhancement for adults below pension age is further symbolised by the decision in 2001 to unite the former Department of Social Security with the Department of Employment in the Department for Work and Pensions, indicating expectations of work participation by those below pension age and the playing down of 'security'. Around the same time, tax credits, to extend the subsidy of low wages, administered by an agency of the Treasury, were being moved into a central role in the programme for the prevention of want.

In bringing the story up to date, therefore, two pieces of legislation need to be examined: the 2007 Pensions Act and the 2007 Welfare Reform Act, together with further legislation proposed for parliamentary session 2008/09 and foreshadowed in a 2008 Green Paper (DWP, 2008a).

Since, as already indicated, the centrepiece of the government's response to want among older people is Pension Credit, only a short note is appropriate on the pension legislation. Changes to the rules relating to contributions towards National Insurance pensions, and the restoration of pension uprating in line with incomes (if they rise faster than prices) may be seen – taken together with some rather complex changes to earning-related supplements of the basic pension – as part of a movement towards closing the large gap that (as Table 1.1 shows) has opened up between the basic pension level and the Pension Credit level. This will take a long while and could easily be reversed by future governments. Moreover, even in its proposals for benefit levels after April 2009, the government is increasing the Credit faster than the basic pension.

The government is also seeking to encourage new forms of private pension savings, as before seeing individual supplementation of the basic pension as a key strategy. Details of the implementation of this part of the pension proposals have still to emerge, and it may be commented that the current economic climate is not a favourable one for the encouragement of more saving towards pensions by lower-income workers, let alone the expectation that these savings will be within private – stock market-related – schemes (see Hill, 2007, chs 7 and 8 for a critique of this approach).

Hence, Pension Credit will remain for a long while as the central pillar of government policy. In view of the distinction between policy for the old and policy for the young, one final point that needs noting is that the legislation raises the (pension) age at which that distinction is made, hence even here, issues about 'work and welfare' surface!

An offical short description of the purpose of the Welfare Reform Bill introduced in the November 2008 Queen's Speech provides a very clear indication of the central thrust of the government's approach to the protection of people under pension age from want: 'The purpose of this Bill is to further reform the welfare and benefit systems to improve support and incentives for people to move from benefits into work, and to provide greater choice and control for disabled people' (Directgov, 2008). The next sentence of that document refers to the commitment to eradicate child poverty. However, since it does not connect this to the main statement, the assumption must be that the former is at the core of the anti-poverty strategy. A more detailed reading of the Green Paper explaining the objectives of the legislation (DWP, 2008a) reinforces that view. In other words, the anti-poverty strategy rests primarily on increasing labour market participation. The specific measures are described in the Green Paper as enshrining the 'responsibility to work at the heart of our approach in a simple deal: more support but greater responsibility' (DWP, 2008a, p 12).

Since October 2008, under the 2007 Welfare Reform Act, Incapacity Benefits have been replaced by a three-tier system of Employment and Support Allowances. A low rate of benefit akin to that previously applying to short-term Invalidity Benefit applies for an 'assessment phase' of 13 weeks. During this period the claimant has to undergo a 'work capacity assessment'. On the basis of that, the claimant is then assigned either to a 'work-related activity group' in which, as the name implies, search for work (and related support and training) activities are expected to occur, or to a 'support group' for those who are not expected to do this. The benefits for people in the latter group may be marginally superior.

The further legislation is expected to shift lone parents from Income Support to a modified version of Jobseeker's Allowance, and a similar development is mooted for other carers receiving that benefit. Hence, Income Support will disappear. It is appropriate here to highlight the character of the discourse within which these specific proposals are embedded. The discourse, in respect of this and the introduction of the Employment and Support Allowances, implies that the standard assumption should be that all adults who seek benefits should be regarded as potential jobseekers. The main clear exception is the group of people who are put into the support group for Employment and Support Allowance. As far as lone parents are concerned, the crucial issue is the move away from the longstanding assumption that parents with any children below the minimum school-leaving age should not be required to seek work. Having progressively intensified pressure on lone parents on Income Support with children approaching the teenage years to attend work assessment interviews, the government is now contemplating requiring those with children under 12 to be on Jobseeker's Allowance.

It is important to bear in mind that all of this change is embedded in the context of the central importance given to tax credits. It is also important to note that the changes discussed here are accompanied by various measures that would treat the people targeted by these measures more generously after entry into work, notably through the temporary continuation of some of the Employment and Support Allowances. But this supports the general implication that what is central to the government's anti-poverty strategy is the encouragement of – indeed in some respects the enforcement of – labour market participation.

This labour market participation strategy seems to rest on a view of the labour market that treats the characteristics and attitudes of the potential supply of labour as crucial and gives little attention to the demand for labour. At the time of writing, unemployment is rising sharply, and predictions are being made about a rise to three million people over the next year or two. Since, as has been shown in this chapter, benefits for people out of work remain inadequate for the prevention of want, as defined by various identified poverty levels including in particular the officially favoured one, this event must leave us with considerable doubts about the government's capacity to fulfil it own pledge on child poverty without substantial improvements to benefit levels (see Palmer et al, 2008, for supporting evidence on this).

## Conclusions

This chapter has reviewed the development of social security policy over the 60 years since the 1948 settlement, giving attention to how we got from there to where we are now and to how contemporary policies should be seen in relation to the Beveridge Report's declaration of war on the problem of want. A detailed comparison of absolute benefit levels then and now was contemplated for this chapter, but rejected. In the 1940s, the poverty discourse was very much less sophisticated, and it is hard to compare the complexity of the modern benefit structure with the simplicity of the 1948 model. However, it may be noted that the basic Income Support benefits for single men were then 19.1% of average earnings of male manual workers, and the National Assistance rate was 17.6% (see Parker and Mirrlees, 1988, pp 510-11). An index of wages of male manual workers is not now compiled. Nevertheless it is not irrelevant to note that the modern rate of benefit for single people on Income Support or Jobseeker's Allowance (£60.50) is only 11% of the median full-time gross weekly earned income (DWP, 2008b, table 5.3). Even the Pension Credit is only 22% of that median (DWP, 2008b, table 5.8). These are not very impressive as comments on the situation today.

On the other hand, the system today can be seen as much more comprehensive than the 1948 arrangements. What is particularly significant is the development of the tax credit system. To debate whether this reversion to 'Speenhamland' is a good thing or not would be to go a long way beyond the brief for this chapter. However, it is appropriate to highlight how an employment-based benefit strategy has become so much more central to the modern system for the prevention of want. In the Beveridge Report, the maintenance of a reasonably low level of unemployment was identified as a precondition for a satisfactory social security system, yet on the other hand, Beveridge's model of the employment pattern to obtain in post-war Britain did not include married women in the workforce! It is, then, interesting to note that where the 1948 settlement identified four key groups in need of support – unemployed people, sick and disabled people, older people and widows – the modern system treats all of those groups except older people (including, of course, old widows) as potential jobseekers, but then puts the support of the low-paid employed into a very central role in the income maintenance system.

As Hilary Land notes in her contribution to this book (Chapter Two), while employment has been a central element in government anti-poverty strategy ever since Beveridge, what is exceptional about the modern approach is an expectation of high rates of labour market participation by women as well as men. The policy emphasis is on the *supply* of labour, supported by a combination of training measures and underlying coercion, with little attention being given to *demand* for labour. Two problems follow from that: first, that such a strategy tends to rest on driving down the cost of labour, a solution that may undermine the anti-poverty aspiration; second, that in any case there now seem to be very strong macroeconomic forces pushing unemployment up. Of course, it may be argued that unemployment will before long fall back to the low levels of the early years of this century, but since the global economy is changing and one of the features of the recession is the collapse of a mushroom growth of financial services, there are grounds for questioning that optimistic view. At the time of writing, the government is pushing on with the social security strategy described above, while showing little inclination to consider whether we could be moving into a very different era as far as the maintenance of the remarkably high levels of labour market participation of the beginning of the 21st century is concerned.

**Note**

[1]  I am indebted to two experts on the study of poverty – Jonathan Bradshaw and John Veit-Wilson – for comments on first draft of this chapter. I imagine that they will still think I have failed to do justice to their conceptual and methodological concerns.

## References

Abel–Smith, B. and Townsend, P. (1965) *The Poor and the Poorest*, London: Bell.

Beveridge, W. (1942) *Social Insurance and Allied Services*, Cmd 6404, London: HMSO.

Blair, T. (1999) 'Beveridge revisited: a welfare state for the 21st century', in R. Walker (ed) *Ending child poverty: Popular welfare for the 21st century?*, Bristol: The Policy Press, pp 7–18.

Bonoli, G. (1997) 'Classifying welfare states: a two–dimensional approach', *Journal of Social Policy*, vol 26, no 3, pp 351–72.

Brown, G. (2008) *Speech to the 2008 Labour Party Conference*, http://news. bbc.co.uk/1/hi/uk_politics/7631925.stm

CPAG (Child Poverty Action Group) (2006) *Media Briefing on the Pre-Budget Report*, London: CPAG.

Deacon, A. and Bradshaw, J. (1983) *Reserved for the Poor: The Means Test in British Social Policy*, Oxford: Martin Robertson.

Directgov (2008) *Welfare Reform Bill*, 16 November, www.direct.gov. uk/en/Governmentcitizensand rights/UKgovernment/Parliament

Donnison, D. (1977) 'Against discretion', *New Society*, 15 September, pp 534–6.

DSS (Department of Social Security) (1998) *A New Contract for Welfare*, Cm 3805, London: HMSO.

DWP (Department for Work and Pensions) (2008a) *No One Written Off: Reforming Welfare to Reward Responsibility*, Cm 7363, London: DWP.

DWP (2008b) *The Abstract of Statistics for Benefits, National Insurance Contributions and Indices of Prices and Earnings 2007 Edition*, London: DWP.

Esping-Andersen, G. (1990) *Three Worlds of Welfare Capitalism*, Cambridge: Polity Press.

Fischer, F. (2006) *Evaluating Public Policy*, Mason, OH: Thomson Wadsworth.

Flaherty, J., Veit-Wilson, J. and Dornan, P. (2004) *Poverty: The Facts* (5th edition), London: CPAG,

Glennerster, H. (1995) *British Social Policy since 1945*, Oxford: Blackwell.

Gordon, D. and Pantazis, C. (1997) *Breadline Britain in the 1990s*, Aldershot: Avebury.

Hill, M. (2007) *Pensions*, Bristol: The Policy Press.

Lowe, R. (1993) *The Welfare State in Britain since 1945*, London: Macmillan.

Mack, J. and Lansley, S. (1985) *Poor Britain*, London: Allen & Unwin.

Palmer, G., MacInnes, T. and Kenway, P. (2008) *Monitoring Poverty and Social Inclusion 2008*, York: Joseph Rowntree Foundation/York Publishing Services.

Parker, J. and Mirrlees, C. (1988) 'Housing', in A. Halsey (ed) *British Social Trends since 1900* (2nd edition), London: Macmillan.

Piachaud, D. (2007) 'The restructuring of redistribution', in J. Hills, J. Le Grand and D. Piachaud (eds) *Making Social Policy Work*, Bristol: The Policy Press.

Rowntree, B.S. (1941) *Poverty and Progress*, London: Longmans Green.

Rowntree, B.S. and Lavers, R.G. (1951) *Poverty and the Welfare State*, London: Longmans Green.

Stone, D. (1988) *Policy Paradox and Political Reason*, Glenview, Ill: Scott Foresman.

Titmuss, R.M. (1971) 'Welfare rights, law and discretion', *Political Quarterly*, vol 42, no 2, pp 113-32.

Townsend, P. (1954) 'Measuring poverty', *British Journal of Sociology*, vol 5, no 2, pp 130-7.

Townsend, P. (1979) *Poverty in the United Kingdom*, Harmondsworth: Penguin.

Veit-Wilson, J.H. (1992) 'Muddle or mendacity: the Beveridge Committee and the poverty line', *Journal of Social Policy*, vol 21, no 3, pp 269-301.

# TWO

# Slaying idleness without killing care: a challenge for the British welfare state

*Hilary Land*

Destruction of Idleness means ensuring for every citizen a reasonable opportunity of productive service and of earning according to *his* [sic] service. It means maintenance of employment of labour and our other resources. Idleness is the largest and fiercest of the five giants and the most important to attack. If the giant Idleness can be destroyed, all the other aims of reconstruction come within reach. (Beveridge, 1943, p 43, emphasis added)

The importance that William Beveridge attached to the maintenance of full employment is not surprising. Unemployment had been a major focus of his work both as an academic economist and as a policy adviser since the beginning of the 20th century (see, for example, Beveridge, 1909). The labour exchanges together with unemployment insurance, which, along with other economists, he advocated to facilitate the matching of jobs with those seeking employment, were introduced before the First World War. He was heavily involved in the work of the Unemployment Assistance Board in the 1930s and was all too aware of the problems created by a wages system that took no account of family size and a benefit system that did. (Eleanor Rathbone had converted him to the need for family allowances in the 1920s.) By the 1940s, he had been much influenced by Keynes and governments' crucial role in managing demand to avoid mass unemployment (see Harris, 1977). The experience of two world wars demonstrated that governments did have the capacity to support mass employment. While few argued for continuing such a high level of government intervention in the economy in peace time, there was greater acceptance that governments should and *could* plan the economy in order to minimise unemployment levels.

The coalition government's White Paper *Employment Policy* published in 1944 stated: 'The government accept as one of their primary aims and responsibilities the maintenance of a high and stable level of employment after the war' (White Paper, 1944).

Over the following decades, the balance of responsibility for both the problem and the solution to unemployment shifted between the government and the individual, with more emphasis placed on the actions of unemployed individuals themselves. In this chapter, first, the resulting changes in the meanings of 'idleness' and 'unemployment' will be briefly described. Second, the huge shift in the responsibilities of wives and mothers in relation to the labour market, both ideologically and in practice, will be discussed. It is no accident that Beveridge used the male pronoun when discussing unemployment. He was very clear that, once married, a woman's responsibilities lay primarily in the home. He was less clear about the responsibilities of the mother without a husband. His ambivalence over whether to categorise her first and foremost as a mother or as a worker was widely shared inside and outside government. This persisted in the post-war years although the position of women, both married and unmarried, in the labour market changed dramatically. These changes were both the cause and the consequence of changing attitudes about whether or not mothers *should* be in employment outside the home. Beveridge also did not know how best to include in his scheme 'domestic spinsters', that is, single women not in employment because they were caring for an elderly parent or another relative needing care. He put them in the same category as childless single women and expected them to be active in the labour market. The final section of the chapter will explore the consequences of the government's attempts since 1997 to turn 'the welfare state from being essentially passive to profoundly active … [and to] … create a system that promotes a work culture rather than a welfare culture, rewards responsibility and ensures no-one is left behind' (DWP, 2008a, p 19). The British male breadwinner–dependent housewife model is now being replaced by an individual citizen worker model. Since the 1986 social security reforms, couples in receipt of means-tested benefits have been able to decide who is the main breadwinner and the benefits are paid to that person. (Previously only 'involuntary' role reversal was recognised.) In practice, most couples choose the man to be the claimant and from November 2008, once they no longer have young children, the partner will be expected to be active in the labour market until aged 65 unless they are in receipt of Carers Allowance. This puts them on a par with lone mothers who will no longer be able to claim

Income Support once their youngest child reaches 12 years of age, falling to seven years of age in 2010. In other words, it is expected that most wives and mothers capable of paid employment will combine this with their activities in the home. Only then are they perceived to be both responsible and 'productive'. Failure to be so without good cause may result in a reduction of benefit. This is a very different perspective from that of Beveridge 60 years ago.

## The prevention of idleness

> Maintenance of employment doesn't mean easy times for all: it is the chance for all of productive work and release of energy from paralysing fear. (Beveridge, 1943, p 51)

Beveridge was very clear that unemployment could not be completely abolished because, at the very least, there would be frictional unemployment. In costing the National Insurance and Assistance schemes contained in his report in 1942 (Beveridge, 1942), he assumed an overall unemployment rate of 8.5%. Two years later, in his report *Full Employment in a Free Society* (Beveridge, 1944), he revised this down to 3%. He explained that low levels of short-term unemployment were manageable:

> A certain amount can be properly dealt with by unemployment insurance, by giving a man an income while he is doing nothing. But to give a man an income while he is doing nothing – not for a few weeks or even a few months, but for years and years – is an entire misuse of the whole idea of unemployment insurance. (Beveridge, 1943, p 87)

He therefore proposed that after a certain time (normally six months but shorter for young single people), they would have to attend a training centre. 'Payment of unconditional cash benefits is satisfactory for only short periods of unemployment; after that idleness even on an income, demoralises' (Beveridge, 1943, p 103). Failure to accept an offer of work in order to maintain his family could result in a man being sent to prison. Both these features were incorporated and implemented in the post-war social security system.

Beveridge also proposed that the unemployment insurance scheme should be used at the macro level of the economy as a system to contribute towards stabilising demand and thus maintaining employment levels. Therefore, during times of higher unemployment, National Insurance contributions should be reduced and, at times of low unemployment, increased. He also suggested that industries with high injury rates should pay higher contributions in order to encourage them to improve safety levels. Neither of these proposals was implemented. (A similar proposal was recently made by Grieve Smith, 2008.) As government economic policies shifted from being underpinned by Keynesian demand management theories to an emphasis on monetarist supply-side economics, the government's approach to managing unemployment changed. The school-leaving age was raised to 16 years in the early 1970s and training schemes for young people as well as for long-term unemployed people increased as unemployment levels rose. These schemes, Robert Leaper (1991, p 70) later argued, 'seem to suggest that unemployment is mainly a mismatch of people to jobs and that it can all be solved by training and re-training'. The labour market was changing and in contrast to the 1950s there were fewer full-time jobs that school-leavers could go straight into without any qualifications.

In the 1980s, with supply-side economics in the ascendant, at the macro level of policy, higher unemployment levels were justified as being a price worth paying for reducing wage inflation. In 1984, the unemployment rate peaked at over 12%. Expenditure on social security benefits was not seen as a way of stabilising demand but as a burden on taxpayers, which was in danger of stifling the enterprise and initiative on which the economy depended. The social insurance and assistance schemes were reviewed in the mid-1980s and both eligibility criteria were tightened and benefit levels were cut so that unemployed people would be discouraged from allegedly pricing themselves out of the labour market. Equality between men and women in the social insurance scheme in line with the 1978 Equal Treatment European Community (EC) Directive was achieved by levelling benefit entitlements *down*. Additional allowances for dependent wives disappeared from the contributory benefit scheme and widows' pensions were reduced. Youth unemployment was dominant in the debates about unemployment because the entrance to the labour market of the large cohort of young people born when the numbers of births in Britain peaked in 1964 coincided with the recession of the early 1980s when the numbers of unemployed people exceeded three million. Young people's eligibility for benefits when unemployed was reduced. Lone mothers, however, did not attract particular attention until the *end* of the 1980s.

## Women's work in the home

Beveridge was very clear that men's responsibilities to be productive should be fulfilled primarily by engaging in paid employment. Their entitlement to benefits therefore depended on their relationship to the labour market. In contrast, women's entitlements were dependent on their marital status, that is, their relationship to a man. Marriage was a very clear contract: in return for care, sexual and domestic services, a married man had to maintain his wife (at a standard determined by him) provided she remained sexually faithful. (Until 1978, a single act of sexual infidelity by his wife absolved a man of this responsibility, although he continued to be responsible for the maintenance of his children.)

In his plan for social security, Beveridge (1942, p 53) explained that housewives would be treated as 'a distinct insurance class' who upon marriage undertook 'to perform vital unpaid service'. A married woman was expected to rely on her husband's earnings and contributions for a (lower) pension when he retired. The minority of married women in paid employment (Beveridge assumed one in eight, based on the 1931 Census) who chose to contribute in their own right would receive lower benefits than their brothers or single sisters when sick or unemployed. Maternity benefit, however, was to be paid at a *higher* rate not only for the sake of the mother and baby's health, but also because 'In the next thirty years housewives as mothers have vital work to do in ensuring the adequate continuance of the British race and of British ideals in the world' (Beveridge, 1942, p 53).

Birth rates had fallen in the inter-war years and although the number of births in 1941 was the highest since 1928, there were widespread doubts that this signified a lasting change in the downward trend. This mattered because as Winston Churchill said: 'If this country is ... to survive as a Great Power that can hold its own against external pressure, our people must be encouraged by every means to have larger families' (cited by Beveridge, 1943, p 210). In 1944, a Royal Commission on the Population was appointed to advise the government. However, by the time it reported in 1947 (Royal Commission on the Population, 1947), the birth rate had become less of an issue. The annual number of births had continued to rise and the successful development of the nuclear bomb meant that military strength no longer depended solely on sheer force of numbers. For the first five years of the national insurance scheme, women were paid a higher maternity benefit than the benefit received when they were sick or unemployed.

Widowed mothers remained within the social insurance system and, for the first time, divorced, separated and never-married mothers could claim means-tested National Assistance without being required to register for employment. In the early 1960s, this requirement was also dropped for single women caring for an adult dependant (Beveridge's domestic spinsters) and then for lone fathers 10 years later. Following the abolition of the obligation on parents to maintain co-resident adult children and grandchildren in the 1948 National Assistance Act, an unmarried mother was entitled to claim National Assistance in her own right even if she was living with her parents (as most did at that time). Cohabitation with a man, however, continued to extinguish a woman's claim to means-tested assistance until changes were made in the 1980s to bring the social assistance scheme into line with the 1978 Equal Treatment EC Directive.

## Women in the post-Second World War labour market

The years following the end of the Second World War were characterised by a labour *shortage*. There were many reasons for this. First, the welfare state itself increased the demand for labour. By 1951, there were one and a quarter million people employed in education, health, welfare and charitable services compared with three quarters of a million in 1931 (Rosenbaum, 1970, p 6). Contrary to Beveridge's earlier assumptions, the higher birth rate was sustained throughout the 1940s and by 1951 there were 1.2 million more children under 15 years in Britain than there had been in 1941. Moreover, the raising of the school-leaving age to 15 years in 1947 had removed 380,000 boys and girls from the labour market as well as increasing the demand for teachers. Second, British foreign policy, in particular rearmament policies and involvement in the Korean War, kept the numbers in the Armed Forces high. By 1950, there were over 700,000 men and women in the Armed Forces and this was projected to increase by a further 150,000 by 1952. National Service was introduced and continued until the beginning of the 1960s. This removed nearly all young men from the labour market for two to three years during their late teens. Third, the low number of births in the inter-war years was reflected in the size of the cohorts of new entrants to the labour market throughout the 1950s. The official unemployment rate remained below 2%.

Evidence from government surveys found that women, especially older women, wanted to stay in or return to employment. The number of married women participating in the formal labour market had increased fivefold during the Second World War to 2.5 million. After the war, the government appealed to 'women who are in a position to do so to enter industry ... To encourage this these [undermanned] industries will need to adjust their conditions of work to suit, as far as possible, the convenience of women with household responsibilities' (White Paper, 1947, pp 27-8).

The government continued the practice started immediately after the war of recruiting doctors, nurses and hospital cleaners from the Commonwealth countries. Winston Churchill himself went to Jamaica in 1945 to appeal to Jamaicans to come to Britain because their 'Mother Country' needed them. Even Enoch Powell, who later made alarmist predictions about the consequences of high numbers of black immigrants, recruited nursing staff from the British West Indies when he was Minister of Health at the end of the 1950s.

The welfare state itself created jobs predominantly for *women*. Four out of five workers ranging from manual to professional employees in the health, education and welfare services were women in 1951. The marriage bars, which over the previous half century in Britain had given employers, both in the public and private sectors, the right to require women to resign from their job on marriage, had been abolished (in 1944 for teachers and in 1946 for civil servants). At the same time, equal pay had been studied by a Royal Commission, which published its report in 1946 (Royal Commission on Equal Pay, 1946). Although the government was not prepared to take action in the private sector, it accepted a commitment to introduce equal pay for equal work in the public sector. Equal pay was introduced in teaching and the civil service in the 1950s.

The high post-war marriage and birth rates were sustained through the 1950s and the demand for health and education services, in particular, increased. Although the social insurance and assistance schemes continued to be based on the male breadwinner–dependent housewife model, and the Government Actuary, as Beveridge had done earlier, continued to underestimate (by half) the growth in married women's employment throughout the 1950s, the issue of the employment of married women and mothers could not be avoided by policy makers elsewhere in Whitehall.

## The rise of part-time employment

The expanded welfare state included universal healthcare free at the point of use and free primary and secondary education for all children. The *care* of children and of frail or disabled adults remained residual services to be provided by the state only when the family failed to provide care or was absent. After all, the male breadwinner–dependent housewife model was based on the assumption that the responsibilities of women as wives and mothers included the care of children and other members of the family needing care. In this context, the theories of maternal deprivation of the psychologist and childcare expert, John Bowlby, outlined in his book *Maternal Care and Mental Health* (Bowlby, 1951) were very influential in Britain. For three decades they were used to legitimate official policies based on the belief that preschool children needed to be cared for at home full time by their mother, who was 'not free, or should not be free to take employment' (Bowlby, 1951, p 85). Once the children were in school aged five, their married mothers could work part time. Lone mothers, on the other hand, could be expected to work full time, placing their children in a day nursery once they were three years old (Bowlby, 1951, p 91). Attitude surveys during this period found that these views were widely shared by men and women (Klein, 1960). Only one in six mothers (including lone mothers) with a preschool child were employed in 1959 and, of those, half of them worked part time. Ten years later, while 40% of women thought that mothers with a school-age child could take paid work, only 5% thought that those with preschool children should do so (Hunt, 1968). Although free part-time nursery *education* for three- and four-year-olds increased from the 1970s and now over 90% of children in these age groups use it, full-time formal day*care* for preschool children was and still is treated differently. Full-time day nursery provision stalled until the late 1990s.

In the early post-war years, part-time employment was unusual, with part-time workers accounting for fewer than one in 20 of the working population. The 1951 Census found that among the seven million women in the working population, 830,000 worked part time. Four out of five of these part-time workers were married. During the Second World War, women with children under the age of 14 years had not been *required* to engage in paid or voluntary work to the extent that their childless sisters were, although many did so. Some of the married women's domestic 'duties' were lightened not only by the absence of husbands serving in the Armed Forces, but also by the development of factory canteens and civic restaurants. However, the social services, to the surprise of the policy makers to whom the caring work of single women was invisible, 'far from being reduced in war-time had to be expanded … there was an assumption inside and outside Government Departments that the normal services available for civilians could be curtailed and, indeed, when war broke out a good many of them were at first cut' (Ferguson and Fitzgerald, 1954, p 7). The home help service, which had been introduced at the end of the First World War, only provided care for women during their confinement and local authorities were encouraged to develop domestic help services for the care of sick or older people. The school meals service expanded and the evacuation of children from the large cities to the countryside enabled mothers in some urban areas to work outside the home more easily. Day nursery provision increased from a very low base and only ever provided for a minority (10%) of preschool children (Williams, 1945, p 104). Part-time jobs were created only when, later in the war, full-time workers became unavailable. It was widely held that many jobs were best done full time except in the retail and catering trades (Williams, 1945, p 106). The government committee that was established in 1952 to consider the employment of older people concluded in its *Second Report* that part-time work was unpopular with employers, who 'seem to regard part-time schemes of any sort as both complicated and uneconomic' (National Advisory Committee on the Employment of Older Men and Women, 1955, p 20).

In the face of continuing labour shortages, particularly in the public sector, together with an unwillingness in principle to develop childcare services, which would compete with scarce staffing resources needed for school-age children, the government developed policies to make part-time employment more attractive both to employers *and* to married women as well as continuing to rely on migrant labour from the Commonwealth, particularly for full-time jobs. By the beginning of the 1960s, the numbers of part-time employees had more than doubled to nearly two million, representing 10% of the working population. During the 1960s, the government continued to exhort employers, particularly in the public sector, to create more part-time jobs in order to attract married women. Primary schools were given quotas to fill with part-time teachers. Similar pressures were put on the National Health Service (NHS) and, by the end of the 1960s, half of all women employed in the NHS worked part time. When a selective employment tax was introduced in 1967 to encourage the more productive use of labour, especially in the service sector, there were refunds for those who employed part-time workers. By the beginning of the 1970s, one in six workers was employed part time. Change was uneven across the UK and the question of full-time daycare and nursery education remained controversial. These developments assumed that women's wages were a supplement to the family income. Lone mothers, who really were alone, receiving no maintenance and no help from the family with childcare, faced great difficulties.

At the beginning of the 1970s, a Conservative government introduced Family Income Supplement (FIS) for 'families with small incomes where the breadwinner is in full-time work and there are dependent children' (Family Income Supplement Bill, Clause 1). Families included a single woman with children even if she was living in her parents' or another relative's household and, for the first time in the British means-tested benefit system, parity between one- and two-parent families was established. In other words, the level of benefit paid was determined by the number of children, not the number of parents. This feature was carried over into Family Credit, which replaced Family Income Supplement in the reforms of the mid-1980s, and then into the Working Tax Credit in 2003. By this time, parents with children only had to work 16 hours (rather than 30 hours as in the original Family Income Supplement scheme) to be eligible to apply for Working Tax Credit.

During the early 1970s, evidence emerged that not only was the educational level of lone mothers (and the fathers of their children) lower than that of married mothers but also that the educational achievements of their children were lower than those living with two parents. The argument that daycare and nursery education could be presented *both* as a means of making it possible for lone parents to work full time *and* to compensate for inadequate parenting began to surface. Twenty years later, these arguments were central to the case for New Labour's national childcare strategy, which through the Childcare Tax Credit gave priority to encouraging lone mothers into the labour market, at least part time, by enabling them to pay for the childcare they needed; extended free part-time nursery education to all three- and four-year-olds; and created the Sure Start programme to improve the life chances of the children living in the most deprived areas. By this time, part-time employment was even more prevalent, accounting for more than one in four employees. The majority were still women with caring responsibilities.

## Lone mothers: work or welfare?

Until the early 1980s, lone mothers' economic activity rates were higher than those of married mothers and the majority were in full-time paid employment (see Kiernan et al, 1998, ch 6). Widows were entitled to pensions based on their husband's contributions and in 1964 the limit on what they could earn without a reduction in that pension was removed. Unmarried mothers usually lived with their mothers, who could therefore share childcare. Apart from widows, lone mothers rarely became council house tenants until the end of the 1970s because local authority housing departments gave priority to two-parent families and they had no responsibility for housing homeless families until the 1977 Housing (Homeless Persons) Act. Local authority day nursery places declined after the Second World War but until child abuse was rediscovered in the early 1970s, lone parents' children had priority and accounted for the use of half of the available places. The minority of lone mothers dependent on National Assistance, less than one in five in the early 1960s, were encouraged to move into employment. Dennis Marsden's (1969) study of these mothers living on National Assistance in the mid-1960s found evidence that official expectations of lone mothers were different depending in part on the number and ages of the children, the reason for their lone motherhood and the extent to which the fathers of their children were willing and able to support them. Younger unmarried mothers with only one or two children faced the most pressure (Marsden, 1969, p 77). Evidence from another study, conducted in 1963, was consistent with this and has a contemporary ring. The researchers reported:

> Sometimes quite strong official pressure is brought to bear to make the mothers go out to work. The following story gives one example of such pressure. A mother with two children who was their sole supporter refused to go to work because she did not believe in letting her children come back to an empty house. The National Assistance Board supported her reluctantly until the children were 8 and 9 and then brought her before an Advisory Committee who told her she was battening on the State and mollycoddling her children. She was extremely distressed but held out. (Yudkin and Holme, 1969 [1963], p 77)

The annual reports of the National Assistance Board also provide glimpses of the support that the Board officers or members of the local advisory committees provided. These ranged from helping to make childcare arrangements, supplying clothing, providing a grant to cover a deposit on a bicycle to overcome transport difficulties, to finding an actual job. Members of these committees, which were abolished in the early 1970s, were all volunteers.

During the 1970s, there was some evidence that lone mothers were being pressured to take up employment but most of the accusations of harassment of lone mothers by officers of the Supplementary Benefits Commission, which had replaced the National Assistance Board in 1966, involved the application of the cohabitation rule (Streather and Weir, 1974, pp 25-7). In other words, in determining a woman's entitlement to benefits the state still took much more interest in her relationship to a man than her relationship to the labour market.

During the 1970s, although the numbers of lone mothers dependent on means-tested benefits increased so that by 1979 there were more than twice as many as in 1966, the official view was that lone mothers should be able to *choose* whether or not to take up paid work. In its final report before it was abolished by the new Conservative government, the Supplementary Benefits Commission wrote:

> We stress that our support for better working opportunities for lone parents is not based on the view that they *ought* to be supporting themselves. Many lone parents believe that it is better to concentrate their efforts exclusively on the difficult and important task of bringing up children single-handed, and they are entitled to do that. Thus it is important to raise benefits to a level at which lone parents do not feel compelled to take a job to support their families. Freedom of choice should be the aim. (Supplementary Benefits Commission, 1980, p 12, emphasis in the original)

Ten years later, however, lone mothers were in the limelight. At the end of the 1980s, Mrs Thatcher suddenly woke up to the growing numbers of lone mothers on means-tested Income Support (the successor to Supplementary Benefit) (see Kiernan et al, 1998). Many were young, lacked any educational qualifications and few were receiving any support from the fathers of their children. As her Minister for Social Security said later, fatherhood had become 'inadvertently nationalised' (Peter Lilley, BBC Radio 4, *World at One*, 6 March 1993). The issue of their relationship to the father(s) of their children was the first consideration and only after the spectacular failure of the 1991 Child Support Act to get maintenance from the fathers of their children did their relationship to the labour market move up the policy agenda in the 1990s. The scene was set for a change in how lone mothers' obligations to take up employment were perceived. However, the-then Conservative government saw no reason to change the official view expressed at the time of the previous major review of the social security system: 'Daycare will continue to be primarily a matter of private arrangements between parents and voluntary resources except where there are special needs' (Under Secretary of State at the Department of Social Security, Commons Debate, 18 February 1985, col, 397). It was not until 1997 that an incoming New Labour government made a commitment to developing a national childcare strategy. By this time, one in three of all children in Britain were living in poverty compared with less than one in ten, 20 years earlier. Those living in 'workless' households were most vulnerable to poverty. Moving at least one parent from benefit into employment became a strategy for reducing child poverty. The expansion of childcare provision was integral to the achievement of this aim.

In 2003, a Working Tax Credit system was introduced to target support on poorer working families. Childcare subsidies in the tax credit system became available to mothers (or fathers) in employment. Half the beneficiaries are lone mothers and their economic activity rates have increased to 57%, which is still below the rate (70%) of partnered mothers (ONS, 2008). It is well below that in the 1950s and 1960s. However, the system favoured the one-earner couple family because it created disincentives for the second parent (usually the mother) from taking up employment. In other words, it favoured the male breadwinner model where mothers have low-earning partners. This is in contrast to the introduction of independent taxation in 1990, which removed the tax penalty on the higher-paid married woman. More recently, getting more *parents*, especially lone parents, into employment is now regarded as 'the most sustainable route out of poverty' (DWP, 2008a, p 87) and this now means mothers, with or without husbands or partners, as well as fathers.

## The limitations of welfare-to-work programmes

> We have to ensure that the welfare system helps people to help themselves rather than encouraging dependency. Cash transfers alone will not encourage this personal responsibility. (DWP, 2008a, p 105)

Beveridge would not have disagreed. He wrote: 'Income security is so inadequate a provision for human happiness that to put it forward by itself as a sole or principal measure of reconstruction hardly seems worth doing' (Beveridge, 1943, p 103). However, he did not consider that taking paid employment was the *only* way of exercising personal responsibility, at least for women. In particular, he would not have described mothers at home as 'passive' or 'idle'. For example, noting that men's working hours on average had declined since the beginning of the 20th century, thus increasing their leisure time, he advocated day and night nurseries, not so that mothers could take up paid employment but so that they could enjoy more leisure from time to time, free of their domestic 'duties'. (It is interesting to note that 25 years earlier, one of the leading Fabians, Sidney Webb, advocated not only a minimum wage but also a legally enforced national minimum of leisure and recreation; Webb, 1919.)

The government's welfare reforms set out in the White Paper *Raising Expectations and Increasing Support: Reforming Welfare for the Future* published in December 2008 (DWP, 2008b) are based on the assumption that 'work is the best form of welfare' and therefore, as the Prime Minister explained in the White Paper's Foreword, the benefit system should help all 'to develop their skills, make the most of their talents and build a better life for themselves, their families and their communities' (2008b, p 5). Beveridge would not have disagreed with this but, as already discussed, he did not restrict valued contributions to those made in the labour market. As the government's own Social Security Advisory Committee commented in its response to the preceding Green Paper on welfare reform (DWP, 2008a), by equating work with paid employment, the government 'appears to ignore the important and complex social and economic role of unpaid work by carers in all its many guises' (SSAC, 2008, p 8). The White Paper acknowledges the value of those caring full time for *adults* and, along with those with severe disabilities themselves or children under the age of three years, they will be the only claimants who will not be *required* either to prepare for or to actively seek paid employment. The services that could replace some of the invaluable care of adult carers do not exist and would be very expensive to develop rapidly so this exception is as much (if not more) a practical and financial one rather than one of principle. However, the White Paper has rendered childcare provided by parents and grandparents (mainly mothers and grandmothers) invisible and not counting as an essential and valuable contribution to society. The proposals in the White Paper are based on the assumption that the provision of formal childcare services, once the child has reached the age of six years, enables mothers to take paid employment and access to part-time nursery education between the ages of three and five means that mothers of these young children can prepare to return to the labour market. However, this oversimplifies the situation of many mothers, especially lone mothers.

First, while it is true that the number of formal childcare places has doubled since 1997, formal childcare is not available and affordable to all parents, especially those with more than two children. (The Childcare Tax Credit pays nothing extra for third or subsequent children.) The availability and reliability of childcare for older children or those with health problems is still inadequate (see the Daycare Trust's response to the Green Paper cited in DWP, 2008b, ch 8). Claimants responsible for a child with a disability or health problem will be required to prepare for or seek employment unless they are in receipt of Disability Living Allowance on the child's behalf at one of the higher rates. However, formal childcare for such children is scarce and expensive. In any case, minor health needs such as requiring a special diet or regular medication are often sufficient to exclude a child from an afterschool scheme. Lone mothers are more likely to be responsible for a child with health problems than a partnered mother. The suitability of the formal childcare available will be judged by the officials, not the mother.

Second, the White Paper is completely silent on the importance of *informal* childcare provided by the wider family (mainly grandmothers) and friends, which has *grown* alongside the increase in formal provision. (In 2007, nearly 40% of mothers in paid employment depended either fully or partly on informal childcare.) In the discussion of the decision to require the partners of those in receipt of Income Support, Jobseeker's Allowance or Employment and Support Allowance to seek work, many of whom will be older women, the possibility that they might be caring for a grandchild, if 'only' to fetch the child from nursery or school, is not even mentioned. Will the care of a grandchild be an acceptable reason for not seeking employment?

Third, in preparation for return to paid work, claimants with children must be prepared to engage in training and/or voluntary work as soon as their youngest child is three years old. This is in order to build up confidence and acquire skills that are relevant to labour market activities. Failure to do so may result in a cut in benefit. The experience of voluntary work can indeed be a helpful stepping stone into paid work and many lone mothers want to engage in training and further education (Guillari, 2007) but there is no acknowledgement that the experience of caring in and of itself develops skills and expertise that are essential for many occupations, and not only those to which women are attracted. Instead, the experience of motherhood and running a home on a tight budget is assumed to deskill women. Beveridge at least acknowledged motherhood positively in his social insurance and assistance schemes although, as Barbara Castle said as she introduced her reforming Social

Security and Pensions Bill in 1975 in the House of Commons, married women were treated as second-class citizens entitled to third-class benefits. Beveridge also noted that caring, in general, fostered highly desirable attitudes, observing that 'women had the habit of working not for pay but for service, in their homes: they never related the amount of their effort to what they were going to get by it for themselves' (Beveridge, 1943, p 39). While men did the same in times of war, he wanted these attitudes towards giving service to be encouraged and fostered in civilian life – for men as well as for women – by encouraging voluntary involvement in their local communities.

The current welfare-to-work reforms therefore do little to value time spent on caring more highly or to understand that valuing care and carers means much more than providing formal childcare or adult care services. A recent study of mothers returning to employment when their children started school concluded:

> The most dramatic change is when a child starts school, with the sudden provision of 'free' childcare during school hours, which, according to standard models of labour supply, should encourage mothers to extend their hours by reducing the average cost of care. Yet reality may not be so simple: suitable childcare to cover the remaining hours may not always be available or may create too many complexities in differing and irregular arrangements. In addition a child starting school brings a new involvement in school life for the parent as well as the child, potentially generating new responsibilities for mothers outside the formal labour market. (Brewer and Paull, 2006, p 10)

The current welfare-to-work programmes for mothers and other carers may not be as successful as the policy makers hope, not only because of the economic climate in which they are to be introduced but also because they are based on a far more limited understanding of 'care' than Beveridge had. In addition, they are taking place 'in the face of social arrangements which often continue to take for granted the flexibility of a mother's time' (OECD, 1999, p 16).

Claimants with children (but not the carers of adults) will be able to move into part-time employment supported by the tax credit system, which requires parents with a child aged under 12 years to work only 16 hours a week. However, this does not guarantee an escape from 'in-work' poverty for families with children. The development of part-time jobs described above has indeed helped women to combine their family 'duties' and the demands of paid work and the majority of women now stay in the labour market for most of their working lives. However, they have paid dearly for this method of reconciliation. Part-time employment in Britain has always carried lower pay, less security and fewer opportunities for training and promotion. The gender pay gap between men and women working full time has narrowed since the introduction of the 1970 Equal Pay Act but the gender pay gap for women working part time (under 30 hours a week) has remained high and is the highest (46%) in the European Union (EU) (Manning and Petrongolo, 2005), despite the various EC and EU Directives seeking to reconcile employment and family needs. The 'long hours' culture that has developed in Britain over the past 25 years has further entrenched workplace norms, which disadvantages those (mainly women) who work shorter or flexible hours or take leaves, even though more of these are now paid. At the time of writing, the UK government was still insisting on opting out of the EU Directive limiting maximum hours of work to 48 hours a week.

Reconciling paid work and care has also become more difficult in other ways. Travel-to-work times have increased and the majority of married women in paid employment no longer work within a 15-minute journey to work as they did in the 1960s (Hunt, 1968). In addition, the majority of primary school children are now escorted to school by an adult. The working day, including time spent travelling, has become longer and more complex even for those employed part time. As a result, recent research (Scott, 2008) suggests that although by 2002 only two in five men and fewer than one in three women agreed that 'it is the husband's job to earn the income and the wife's to look after the children', a growing proportion, including more highly paid mothers with husbands or partners, are finding the combination of paid work with their caring and other 'domestic duties' more stressful and less desirable (Carvel, 2008).

The more fundamental issue is that the gendered division of labour embodied in the male breadwinner model on which the post-war social security system was based still affects the way not only paid work but also *time* is structured and valued (Lewis, 2004). What is needed is what feminists have called 'an ethic of care' (see, for example, Tronto, 1993; Sevenhuijsen, 1998) to inform a wide range of public and social policies in order to recognise and value care as a public good. *All* children and adults needing care should be entitled to receive good care as citizens in their own right and not just because their carers are needed in the labour market. On these wider issues the current welfare-to-work reforms are silent.

**References**

Beveridge, W. (1909) *Unemployment: A Problem of Industry*, London: Longman Green.

Beveridge, W. (1942) *Social Insurance and Allied Services*, Cmd 6404, London: HMSO.

Beveridge, W. (1943) *Pillars of Security*, London: Allen & Unwin.

Beveridge, W. (1944) *Full Employment in a Free Society*, London: Allen & Unwin.

Bowlby, J. (1951) *Maternal Care and Mental Health*, Harmondsworth: Penguin.

Brewer, M. and Paull, G. (2006) *Newborns and New Schools: Critical Times in Women's Employment*, DWP Research Report 308, London: The Stationery Office.

Carvel, J. (2008) 'Two into one won't go: Cambridge survey shows new doubts over working mothers', *The Guardian*, 28 October, www.guardian.co.uk/society/2008/aug/06/equality.gender

DWP (Department for Work and Pensions) (2008a) *No One Written Off: Reforming Welfare to Reward Responsibility*, Cm 7363, London: The Stationery Office.

DWP (2008b) *Raising Expectations and Increasing Support: Reforming Welfare for the Future*, Cm 7506, London: The Stationery Office.

Ferguson, J. and Fitzgerald, H. (1954) *Studies in the Social Services*, London: HMSO.

Grieve Smith, J. (2008) 'Tax cuts are needed fast', *The Guardian*, 17 November, p 13.

Guillari, S. (2007) *Proofed for Parents by Parents: Participatory One Parent Proofing: The Findings*, Bristol: Single Parents Action Network.

Harris, J. (1977) *William Beveridge: A Biography*, Oxford: Oxford University Press.

Hunt, A. (1968) *A Survey of Women's Employment Report*, London: HMSO.

Kiernan, K., Land, H. and Lewis, J. (1998) *Motherhood in Twentieth Century Britain*, Oxford: Oxford University Press.

Klein, V. (1960) *Working Wives*, Occasional Paper No 5, London: Institute of Personnel Management.

Leaper, R. (1991) 'Idleness', *Social Policy and Administration*, vol 25, no 1, pp 63-72.

Lewis, J. (2004) 'Individualisation and the need for new forms of social solidarity', in T. Knijn and P. Komter (eds) *Solidarity Between the Sexes and the Generations*, Cheltenham: Edward Elgar.

Manning, A. and Petrongolo, B. (2005) *The Part-Time Pay Penalty*, CEP Discussion Paper 679, London: London School of Economics and Women and Equality Unit.

Marsden, D. (1969) *Mothers Alone*, Harmondsworth: Penguin.

National Advisory Committee on the Employment of Older Men and Women (1955) *Second Report*, Cmd 9628, London: HMSO.

OECD (Organisation for Economic Co-operation and Development) (1999) *A Caring World: The New Social Policy Agenda*, Geneva: OECD.

ONS (Office of National Statistics) (2008) *Social Trends 2007*, No 38, London: The Stationery Office.

Rosenbaum, M. (1970) 'Social services manpower', *Social Trends 1970*, No 1, London: HMSO.

Royal Commission on Equal Pay (1946) *Report*, London: HMSO.

Royal Commission on the Population (1947) *Report*, Cmd 7695, London: HMSO.

Scott, J. (2008) *Women and Employment: Changing Lives and New Challenges*, Cheltenham: Edward Elgar.

Sevenhuisjen, S. (1998) *Citizenship and the Ethics of Care*, London: Routledge.

SSAC (Social Security Advisory Committee) (2008) *No One Written Off: Reforming Welfare to Reward Responsibility – The Response of the Social Security Advisory Committee*, London: SSAC.

Streather, J. and Weir, S. (1974) *Social Insecurity: Single Mothers on Benefit*, Poverty Pamphlet 16, London: CPAG.

Supplementary Benefits Commission (1980) *Annual Report 1980*, Cmnd 8033, London: HMSO.

Tronto, J. (1993) Moral Boundaries: A Political Argument for an Ethic of Care, London: Routledge.

Webb, S. (1919) *The Necessary Basis of Society*, Fabian Tract No 159, London: Fabian Society.

White Paper (1944) *Employment Policy*, Cmd 6527, London: HMSO.

White Paper (1947) *Economic Survey for 1947*, Cmd 7046, London: HMSO.

Williams, G. (1945) *Women and Work*, London: Nicholson and Watson.

Yudkin, S. and Holme, A. (1969) (first published 1963) *Working Mothers and their Children*, Stamford, CT: Sphere Books.

# THREE

# Tackling ignorance, promoting social mobility: education policy 1948 and 2008

*Ruth Lupton and Howard Glennerster*

## Introduction

In this chapter, we reflect on education policy in 2008 in the light of the events and debates of 1948. We concentrate on events in England, although contrasts with the devolved policies of other parts of the UK also feature in our analysis.

1948 was a quiet year in the war on ignorance, with Butler's Education Act already four years old. Moreover, rather than embodying a clear set of post-war 'ideals', education policy reflected an uneasy post-war settlement hammered out after bitter pre-war divisions between church and non-church schooling and other unsettled arguments.

Some things were clear. A public opinion poll conducted by the Ministry of Education in 1945 found that the strongest public support was for the raising of the school-leaving age and for 'everybody to have an equal chance' (Gosden, 1976, p 341). The coming of free secondary and university education with scholarships and maintenance grants was seen as a means to that last ideal. Two other ideals were woven into the 1944 Act: that the state's responsibility should extend to preparing all of its citizens for employment and to provide them with the intellectual capacity to be fully participating citizens. In practice, economic pressures and employers' objections meant that neither of these goals was implemented. Education also reflected the same implicit 'deal' with the professions that characterised the National Health Service (NHS) and other parts of the post-war settlement. Enlarged state involvement in funding and organisation would be matched by professional freedom. This involved both the freedom to practise with minimal state interference and day-to-day control by professionals over their own working lives.

Yet on the issue of school structures there were divisions. The non-conformists and the Left in the Labour Party had only reluctantly accepted that church schools should receive state funds, missing the opportunity to establish a single, local authority-governed state system. Many in the Labour Party also opposed the tripartite structure of grammar, secondary modern and technical schools that was being thrust on local education authorities by their own government. These disputes reflected a wider disagreement within the party about what secondary education was (Barker, 1972). For the old Fabians, education was the way to ensure that able working-class children would rise through the ranks of an elitist but unequal society, hence the role for grammar schools. For others, schools were part of the means by which society could be equalised. This drove the belief in common schooling, the view that the proper role for schools went beyond academic learning to building a society in which people learned to respect one another in a society made up of different but equally respected talents.

2008 was also a relatively quiet legislative year for education in England. The major New Labour reforms in England were now in place. These included the expansion of the specialist school programme and the introduction of state-funded academy schools run at arm's length from local authorities, the expansion of the school workforce, the enhanced fee funding of universities and the focus on adult learning through the Skills for Life Strategy. Increases in education spending had slowed somewhat (Sibieta et al, 2008). Gordon Brown had restructured the central department the year before. This integrated school-based education within a new, broader, Department for Children, Schools and Families (DCSF). Universities and adult learning responsibilities now came within a Department for Innovation, Universities and Skills (DIUS). Both were beginning to bed down.

However, four significant developments in education policy in 2008 do stand out:

- the introduction of the Education and Skills Act, which will ensure that by 2013 all 17-year-olds, and by 2015 all 18-year-olds, are in some form of education and training;
- the debate over national tests in England, followed by the abolition of Standard Assessment Tests (SATs) at age 14;

- a package of measures – the National Challenge programme – that would simultaneously expand the academies programme and bring major new investment to low-attaining schools;
- the publication of the new Conservative plans for schools (Conservative Party, 2008a) that set the framework for the likely next government.

At least superficially, these developments reflect some continuities with the ideals and policies of the post-war period. The extension of universal compulsory education to 18 actually goes further, bringing to fruition an unfulfilled goal of the 1944 Act. However, they are also reminiscent of the debates of the post-war period, this time rearticulating them in terms of social mobility.

## Extending universal education

Ball (2008a, p 62) argues that notwithstanding halting, patchy and incomplete implementation, 'it was in the field of education that a commitment to universalism first became embedded in state policy', with schooling becoming formally accepted as a social right in the late 1900s. The 1944 Act established universal free secondary education with the school-leaving age initially set at 15. The Act's goal of raising the school-leaving age to 16 was not achieved until 1972.

The proposals in the 2008 Education and Skills Act have been widely reported as raising the school-leaving age to 18, although this is not quite true. The 2008 legislation should ensure that by 2013 all 17-year-olds, and by 2015 all 18-year-olds, will be in full-time education or training, or be participating in training in accordance with an apprenticeship contract, or be working full time but with arrangements for 'guided learning' equivalent to 280 hours over a one-year period. Duties are laid upon young people, their parents, employers and local authorities. January 2008 also saw the publication of 'World Class Apprenticeships': a plan to extend and improve the apprenticeship system such that every suitably qualified young person could be offered an apprenticeship place (DIUS, 2008). The government expects that within the next decade, one in five 16- to 18-year-olds will be taking an apprenticeship, a significant expansion of the system. Apprenticeships will be brought into the national qualifications and credit framework, with national certification and a system of support and mentoring for both employers and apprentices.

While these changes in themselves do not deal with the crucial issue of parity of esteem between academic and vocational qualifications that has dogged English education since 1944, the 2008 legislation does represent an application of universalist principles. In large part, it enacts the provisions of the 1944 Act that all young people were to be required to maintain their education and training until they were 18. Those not at schools were to be given day release from work to receive not just training but also a general education: a responsibility of the county colleges that was never implemented despite the Crowther Committee's later recommendation that it should be (Ministry of Education, 1959). Thus, despite a common view that New Labour has retreated from a universalist model of social policy (correct in some ways), it will have presided over an extension of education both upwards to 18 and downwards to three, together with an extension of the school/care day.

As in other areas of New Labour welfare policy, entitlements are linked to responsibilities and backed by some coercion. The 2008 Act proposes a duty on young people to attend education or training, which may be reinforced by an attendance notice, breach of which can lead to the imposition of a fine. Parents may also be asked to sign parenting contracts to help their offspring to fulfil their duty of attendance, and local authorities may apply to the courts for the imposition of Parenting Orders, including a requirement to attend guidance or counselling.

The enforcement elements of the Act suggest that the government anticipates difficulties in securing the participation of those who are not currently in any form of education. They also reflect its failure to encourage much more voluntary staying on despite the introduction of Education Maintenance Allowances, and other programmes designed to raise aspirations and widen participation in higher education, such as Aimhigher. In 2007, the proportion of 16- to 18-year-olds in education or training had reached its highest ever level (78.7%). However, this represented only a 1.9% increase over that of 1997. The so-called NEET group (those not in employment, education or training) was higher than when New Labour came to power, hovering stubbornly around 9–10%.

The NEET group have been a longstanding focus of New Labour social exclusion policy, given their increased risks of crime, unemployment and social exclusion (SEU, 1999). Requiring this group to participate in education may be an investment that will yield wider benefits. However, it is by no means clear how far enforced training will change their social or employment histories without tackling the deeper structural causes of their predicament (see Colley and Hodkinson, 2001, for a similar critique of New Labour's earlier approaches to this problem). Moreover, the 1944 Act (section 43(1)), placed a requirement to continue to prepare these young people for 'the responsibilities of citizenship'. There is no modern equivalent in the latest legislation, even if 'citizenship' carries a rather different meaning today.

## School accountability and professional responsibility: the debate over testing in England

A second significant development in 2008 was the debate over testing and assessment in England, ignited by a report in May from the House of Commons' Children, Schools and Families Committee (House of Commons, 2008a), and followed by an announcement in October that SATs for 14-year-olds in England would be abolished.

Standard Assessment Tests in English, mathematics and science were introduced in 1995 by the Conservative government. From that date, or soon after for some protesting schools, these tests were taken by all school children at state schools in England aged 7 (Key Stage 1), 11 (Key Stage 2) and 14 (Key Stage 3). They were seen as a necessary accompaniment to the National Curriculum, which was finally introduced by the Conservative 1988 Education Reform Act but which had been under deliberation for some years previously and was supported by the-then Labour opposition. The very idea that the state would set a National Curriculum and use regular pupil testing to hold teachers to account would have been foreign to those in the education world of 1948, for whom the curriculum was very much the preserve of teachers. Even an attempt in the early 1960s by the Ministry of Education to set up a mere Curriculum Study Group was seen off by the profession. The eventual introduction of the National Curriculum represented a fundamental change to the 'hands-off' approach to the curriculum the Ministry of Education had followed in the 1940s and before.

The contrast between the consensus of the 1940s and the consensus of the 1990s and beyond arose from the convergence of three rather different political forces. One was an increasingly widespread concern with the so-called 'progressive' approach to teaching, or 'a retreat from the basics' – a worry that schools and teachers were somehow running beyond the limits of the acceptable. The 'scandal' of the William Tyndale school (Gretton and Jackson, 1976) and the publication of the Black Papers (Cox and Dyson, 1969) set in train a process of rethinking in the Department of Education and a shift in political attitudes that challenged the freedom of the teaching profession. Some of this supposed freedom was perhaps spurious, at least for those preparing students for external exams, while there was a left-wing as well as a traditionalist view that there should be some democratic control over the curriculum.

A quite different strand of ideas sprang from the view that competition should be used to raise standards of public provision. If schools were to compete for custom, and hence funds, parents would need good information on a school's quality and regular exam results related to a common basic curriculum would provide that. This view lay behind the Conservative marketisation of education in the 1988 Education Reform Act and has survived into the New Labour period. Different again was a social-democratic concern that schools were failing poor children especially badly. Rutter et al (1979), and the large body of school effectiveness and school improvement research that followed during the 1980s and 1990s, argued that while much poor achievement might be caused by children's deprived home backgrounds, much was also the fault of schools and the ethos within them. The view gained currency that teachers set low expectations for children in deprived areas for understandable but false reasons, and thus that setting expectations against a national set of standards, combined with a robust regime of inspection, targeted support and threats of closure for the lowest-attaining schools, would raise poor pupils' achievements. This reasoning lay behind the Blair government's enthusiastic pursuit of this policy. Thus, politicians had decided, for differing reasons, that it was their duty to challenge the profession's freedom to set the school curriculum and the ethos within their schools – a freedom the profession had been granted, and took for granted, in the 1940s.

The introduction of SATs was followed by a significant improvement in average results and a particular increase among the lowest-performing schools and the most disadvantaged pupils, albeit amid media controversy about whether this was in part a result of allegedly easier examinations (Lupton et al, 2009). This followed several decades of stability, if not decline, in English pupils' mathematics performance, for example, and wide disparities between the performance of the highest- and the lowest-performing schools. There is also some evidence from England and abroad that competition and good information on schools' performance does raise standards in the lowest-performing secondary schools (Levačić, 2004; Hoxby, 2006). It is difficult to assign the striking improvements in SAT scores entirely to spurious effects and even critics of SATs do not do that (Tymms, 2004). On the other hand, many have argued that this 'performative' regime in education, with SATs a fundamental part of its architecture, has transformed education for the worse, redefining the meaning of teaching and learning (Ball, 2003), narrowing the curriculum, gearing learning only to the test and causing schools to focus on certain pupils at the expense of others in order to raise their achievement marginally to reach expected levels (Gillborn and Youdell, 2000).

In both Scotland and Wales, these latter arguments have apparently proved convincing to politicians and there have been far-reaching moves to dismantle the testing regime. Scotland decided to drop SATs altogether after it achieved devolution. Universal testing has been replaced by testing samples of pupils in a sample of schools every year. Children are tested more frequently on a wider range of subjects than in England, and individualised pupil progress is monitored by teachers tracking pupils' progress, moderating their judgements by discussions with teachers in other local schools. They can also use online 'national assessment' tools, which their pupils take to check how far the teacher's judgements are out of line with national standards. However, the results are not published. Wales has taken a similar route since 2005. Teachers must produce an assessment for each child, based on their own observation and judgement, and in relation to national targets at the end of Key Stage 1. Tests for Key Stage 2 at age 11 were ended in 2005 and teacher assessments replaced them. Since 2007 teachers have been able to draw on optional national assessment materials. Teacher assessment also applies at Key Stage 3.

In England, a partial retreat from SATs was signalled in 2005 when tests for seven-year-olds were replaced by teacher assessments built up from their all-round knowledge of the child, although this does include a test of a child's basic skills. In 2007, it also began to pilot 'single-level tests', which could be taken at any time a pupil was ready, rather than at the end of a Key Stage. However, tests have remained the central part of the school accountability framework.

In 2008, this element of SATs came under fire from the House of Commons' Committee for Children, Schools and Families. Having taken evidence from a wide range of experts including representatives of the teacher unions, the Committee argued that the use of tests for school accountability purposes was leading to a 'serious distortion of the education experience of pupils' (House of Commons, 2008a, p 39):

> A variety of classroom practices aimed at improving test results has distorted the education of some children, which may leave them unprepared for higher education and employment. We find that 'teaching to the test' and narrowing of the taught curriculum are

widespread phenomena in schools, resulting in a disproportionate focus on the 'core' subjects of English, mathematics and science and, in particular, on those aspects of these subjects which are likely to be tested in an examination. Tests, however, can only test a limited range of the skills and activities which are properly part of a rounded education, so that a focus on improving test results compromises teachers' creativity in the classroom and children's access to a balanced curriculum. (House of Commons, 2008a, p 3)

The Committee also took the view that unless testing for pupil assessment was de-coupled from testing for school accountability, the same problems would beset the new single tests. More emphasis should be given in publicly available information on school performance on the wider activities of schools, as indicated by their Ofsted reports, while assessment for formative and diagnostic purposes should not form part of a national accountability system but be left to teachers, supported with appropriate professional development and assessment tools. 'In our view,' the Committee said, 'a brighter future for our education system as a whole lies in a recognition of the professional competence of teachers' (House of Commons, 2008a, p 87).

In its response (House of Commons, 2008b), the government endorsed the important role of teachers but firmly rejected the view that the accountability and assessment purposes of teaching were incompatible. It was somewhat surprising, therefore, that in October 2008, Ed Balls, the Secretary of State for Children, Schools and Families, announced a new accountability system for schools based on an, as yet unclear, 'report card' system and the abolition of SATs at age 14 (Balls, 2008). He also announced the establishment of a small panel of educationalists, including two headteachers, to investigate among other things how to guide schools in limiting 'teaching to the test' at Key Stage 2 and how to develop a national-level sampling approach at Key Stage 3. The announcement followed long delays in the marking of the 2008 SATs by the American company employed to administer them, providing an administrative as well an educational reason for their abolition.

These moves can hardly be regarded as an abandonment of the market rationale for SATs. Indeed, the importance of SATs in enabling parental choice and the accountability of individual schools to central government has been reaffirmed. The Secretary of State's argument is that tests at age 11 are still needed because there is no other nationally uniform information available on a primary school's performance (Balls,

2008). Many suspect that the changes that have been made are only a response to government's embarrassment over the 2008 marking delays. However, even if this is the case, these developments do reflect a partial return to professional responsibility and teacher autonomy, particularly in identifying and supporting pupils who are falling behind. In a very small way, and without any structural change to a system of strong central accountability, the teaching profession has won back a little ground.

## Markets, social mobility and equality: school structures under Labour and the Conservatives

The third policy area in which there has been considerable activity in 2008 is that of school organisation. First, the government injected a new momentum into its academies programme through the announcement of new funding, as part of a package of measures (the National Challenge) to raise achievement in the lowest-performing schools. Second, the Conservative Party, likely, it then seemed, to be the next governing party, published its new policy for schools (Conservative Party, 2008a). This was, perhaps, the most important education policy initiative of 2008. It could set the path for education policy in the coming decade.

Academies, first introduced in 2000, have been a core element of New Labour's commitment to a mixed economy of welfare that replaced the notion of a powerful local state as the education provider. Academies are brand new schools, with state-of-the-art facilities, provided mainly in disadvantaged areas and often as a replacement for existing low-performing schools. They are state-funded but independent, backed by a sponsor who must make an initial contribution to the provision of the school, and who can then appoint the majority of the governing body, employ staff and determine admissions. Links with sponsors were intended to give each academy a distinctive feel and provide distinctive opportunities, for curriculum specialisation, mentoring or business links. This input from private, higher education or third sector organisations was one of the main distinctive features of academies, seen as a key tool in raising aspirations and standards and thus enabling students from disadvantaged areas to close the gap on their more advantaged peers. The government argued that 'Sponsors challenge traditional thinking on how schools are run and what they should be like for students. They seek to make a complete break with cultures of low aspiration which afflict too many communities and their schools' (www.standards.dfes. gov.uk/academies/what_are_academies/?version=1).

However, the existence of academies outside the local authority system prompted concerns that they would cream off more advantaged pupils, leading to a more segregated and less equal system. Moreover, given the fact that some of the initial sponsors were from fundamentalist Christian organisations, and in conjunction with the government's encouragement of faith schooling more generally, they have reinvigorated the 1940s debate over the desirability of incorporating faith schools within the state system.

As schools opened for the 2008/09 school year, there were approximately 130 academies, with another 50 due to open in September 2009 and 55 more in September 2010. The new 'National Challenge' programme, aimed at 638 schools not achieving the government's target that 30% of 15-year-olds should achieve five A*-C grades at General Certificate of Secondary Education (GCSE) level including English and mathematics, allocates £195 million (half the total funding) for academies. This suggests that organisational 'solutions', rather than extra ongoing support, will be the fate of many of these schools. In fact, the government estimates that nearly one third of the National Challenge schools (more than 200) will be replaced with academies, and the new funding allows for an extra 75 academies in all by 2010. By this time, roughly one in ten secondary schools, far more in urban areas, will have academy status. The removal of at least a tenth of schools from local authority control marks a very significant break with the post-war welfare model.

Unsurprisingly, given the continuity between New Labour's policies and those that it inherited from the Conservatives in 1997, and given Conservative support for the controversial 2005 White Paper (DfES, 2005), recently announced Conservative policies embody many of the same principles as New Labour's. Entry of new schools to the state education marketplace and parental choice are the core principles. The Conservative Party (2008a) document envisages a major extension of academies. It prefigures a significant long-term shift in the state's role from being the dominant provider of schools to being merely a funder of free schooling. These new entrants to the education market will, it is argued, promote innovation, extend choice and sharpen competition between schools. This will, it is claimed, drive up standards in state schools more generally. New entrants will not have to provide capital funding for the new schools. If they cannot do so the state will, so long as the plans seem worth funding. Current restrictions on entry will be relaxed. If the schools are set up in poorer areas they will get the extra funding that any local authority school would get with a similar intake.

Conservative plans aim to create nearly a quarter of a million 'new academy' places over a 10-year period. Alternative providers are listed as 'charities, trusts, voluntary groups, philanthropists and cooperatives on behalf of parents' (Conservative Party, 2008a, pp 36-7). Non-state schools, funded by the state, would be a growing and significant part of the educational future.

The model, used as an exemplar, is that of Sweden. There a new independent sector has been created, more or less from scratch, in the past decade and a half, and now provides schooling for 15% of the population, mainly in larger urban areas. The original Swedish Conservative reforms were modified by later Social Democratic governments. Independent schools must not charge fees, or select on academic, social or ethnic grounds *and* they must meet standards set by the state. If they fulfil these conditions, they can receive the same level of current funding as a state school. But they do not receive state capital support. In this respect, the British Conservative scheme is more generous.

For the Conservatives there is little new here, and perhaps merely a move to the middle ground as policies advocated by previous administrations have been dropped. David Cameron's party has backed away from previous policies that entailed giving state scholarships to certain pupils to attend fee-paying independent schools (the Assisted Places Scheme) and from Friedman-inspired 'top-up vouchers' that would have enabled all or some parents to become eligible for state help in attending private schools. On the other hand, traditionalist values are evident in a raft of *dirigiste* proposals. Primary schools will be pressed to follow the phonics model for teaching reading. The mathematics and science national curriculum will be revised. School children will have to wear school uniforms, or at least schools will be encouraged to ensure they do. As Ball (2008b) has commented, it is unclear how new freedoms for teachers and greater enjoyment and experiment in learning, which are also advocated, are going to be promoted through these means.

Our central point here, however, is that there now seems to be a consensus between the parties, or at least the party leaderships, that the state school system should consist of a range of providers, offering different products, and operating within an educational marketplace. Diversity appears to be valued by both parties, as a model that enables experimentation and individualisation, as well as a product of a choice-based system in which new and different providers are key to enabling choice and providing the competition that will drive up standards. Individual consumers are to choose what is best and most appropriate for their children. There is little here either about the social goals of schools or their role in making society more equal. Rather, the ideal is that the provision of a range of good but different schools should enable everyone to construct their own routes to educational success. This will enable even the least advantaged to become socially mobile.

Social mobility is currently high on the political agenda (Cabinet Office, 2009). Social mobility in the UK grew following the 1944 Act but then declined again through the 1980s as it did in some other countries, although it has since stabilised (Blanden and Machin, 2007). Education is seen as a key driver. Former Secretary of State, Ruth Kelly, was quite explicit: 'I see my department as the department for life chances ... I see it as my job to boost social mobility' (Kelly, 2005).

For Lord Adonis, a key architect of the 2005 White Paper (DfES, 2005) and champion of academies, the function of academies in the state system is to enable individual social mobility, just like the grammar schools were supposed to do:

> My vision is for academies to be in the vanguard of meritocracy for the next generation in the way that grammar schools were for a proportion of the post-war generation – providing a ladder, in particular, for less advantaged children to get on, and gain the very best education and qualifications, irrespective of wealth and family background, but without unfair selection at the age of 11. (Adonis, 2008)

In this sense, the post-war debate seems to have been resolved, with both parties moving to some common ground. However, this would be to paint too simplistic a picture. This debate still represents one of the major divisions within the Labour Party. A backbench revolt over the 2005 White Paper came close to bringing down the Blair government, notwithstanding Conservative support. Labour backbenchers have also established a campaigning group – the Anti Academies Alliance. The parallel with the rebellious group of Members of Parliament (MPs) who opposed grammar schools and the 11-plus in the 1940s is close.

There remain significant differences, however, between the parties in their approach to educational inequality. In a surprising move, the Conservatives decided to challenge New Labour during 2008 over its record on inequality. Following a series of parliamentary questions on the government's record on closing social class attainment gaps, Shadow Secretary of State for Children, Schools and Families, Michael Gove, produced a document entitled *A Failed Generation* (Conservative Party, 2008b), detailing New Labour's ostensible[1] failures in this respect.

The theme of a large and widening attainment gap was also picked up in the Conservative Party's policy document (Conservative Party, 2008a, p 13). However, the document is notable for its absence of any specific policies to address this problem and for the rather select use of international comparison to make the policy case. It is worth noting that both Belgium and the Netherlands have operated a similar funding system to the Swedish one for most of the period since the Second World War (Glennerster, 2009). But they have not applied the same strict non-selective social and academic selection rules. Indeed, these countries evolved their system of funding precisely to legitimate separate schooling for their different religious and social/language groupings in their countries. In addition, in Belgium, academic cream-skimming resulted (Vandenberghe, 1996). The Conservative Party document does not suggest that it sees limiting social and academic selection as a major objective or a problem. Comparisons with Swedish educational success do not help much. Sweden did better on reading in the recent Organisation for Economic Co-operation and Development (OECD) PISA study (OECD, 2007) compared to the UK. It did slightly better for mathematics, although neither differs significantly from the OECD average, and the UK did better in science. Sweden has a closer range of academic outcomes. But it had done better on these kinds of measures long before this policy was adopted.[2] It had a long tradition of comprehensive education and is a much more egalitarian society to begin with.

By contrast, New Labour under Gordon Brown and with Ed Balls as Secretary of State for Children, Schools and Families has stepped up its focus on 'closing the gap', and attempted, at least in part, to limit academic and social selection. Since 2007, the academies policy, while expanded, has also been softened in a number of ways. New academies have to follow the National Curriculum in the core subjects of English, mathematics, science, and information and communication technology, but they now have flexibility beyond this. Academy sponsors are required to set up an endowment fund to be spent locally on countering the effect of deprivation on education. Universities are encouraged to sponsor academies. These measures are accompanied by a strengthening of the school admissions code, and measures to enable lotteries for the choice of pupils to enter oversubscribed schools. 'Banding' children to ensure a mixed intake, as the Inner London Education Authority used to do, is also permitted.

Furthermore, while the National Challenge may be seen as a Trojan horse for the academies programme, it will also provide support for disadvantaged schools. A specialist adviser for each school will support the school and oversee a tailored package of assistance. Funding of £120 million will be available for leadership, teaching, learning and study support. This will supplement the already wide range of initiatives in place to tackle educational disadvantage, such as full service extended schools, support for individual children through programmes such as learning mentors and learning support units, and an increasingly redistributive school funding settlement (Lupton et al, 2009).

2008 also saw the extension of the successful London Challenge programme to two further areas: Greater Manchester and the Black Country, as City Challenge (not to be confused with National Challenge). Consistent with New Labour's market policies, City Challenge ignores the 'elephant in the room' in urban school systems: the very uneven distribution of children between schools, founded on residential social segregation and exacerbated by school admissions practices. According to Tim Brighouse (2007, p 77), former Commissioner of London Schools and leader of the London Challenge programme, it was made abundantly clear by ministers from the outset that the issue of admissions was strictly 'off limits'. However, City Challenge is a significant development in tackling disadvantage not only because it operates at the level of the conurbation rather than the individual school or even local authority, but because it incorporates a social structural response incorporating the provision of key worker housing for teachers, measures to improve teacher recruitment to difficult areas, and additional support for management and leadership, alongside the more typical initiatives that focus on the quality of teaching and learning in the classroom. It is a broader view of school improvement than we have hitherto seen.

## Conclusion

Reflecting on the policies and debates of 60 years ago, we can see that much of the territory on which policy is made has shifted substantially. Local authorities, the powerful main agents of education policy in the later 1940s, have a much less prominent role, and the teaching profession more constraints (albeit perhaps with a minor shift beginning to occur). Central state control of curriculum and assessment goes widely unchallenged, and a mixed economy of public, private and voluntary provision in which parents are active choosers is accepted and promoted by both main political parties. Moreover, education has moved from being seen as a policy world all on its own, and is now fully integrated in many ways with the wider social and urban policy agenda.

However, the central debate over the structure of schooling and the role of universal state education remains. For a period during the 1960s and 1970s, social equality became central for many in the education profession and for many Labour politicians. Educational institutions could change society and the way people related to one another, although many on the Left and Right saw this as naive (Cox and Dyson, 1969; Ford, 1969). New Labour has laid more stress on 'equality of opportunity' and the importance of education in achieving it. It has also talked about the importance of a 'knowledge-based economy'. This has rested on the argument that Britain's high level of inequality, and low levels of social mobility, arose in large part because its economy had come to adapt to the low level of skills in its labour force. The long-run cure for inequality and low social mobility thus lay in 'education, education and education'.

Yet different competing notions of the role of education are to be found implicit in politicians' statements. One is that which was largely dominant in 1944: that there is a hierarchy of positions in society. The best talents are needed for the socially and economically important jobs and it is education's task to sort children efficiently and fit them into these positions. An alternative view is that the structure of the economy itself is importantly shaped by the human capital content in the labour force. A very long tail to the distribution of human capital will attract money capital and hence produce an economy structured to produce goods and services that demand a large number of low-skilled people. Change that distribution of human capital and the structure of the economy will be different. Esping-Andersen (2007, 2008), for example, claims that this strategy is what helps to explain the Scandinavians' more equal distribution of income. The key lies not only, or even mostly, in the education system but at the preschool stage. To change the 'quality of children', as he puts it, requires free universal and high-quality childcare from the age of two and spending more, substantially more, on children with disadvantages in school. Human capital will change the structure of the economy. When the structure of opportunity in society has thus been made more equal – the rungs of the ladder are closer – then social mobility will follow. Whether this will turn out to be equally naive is a matter for debate.

There are reflections of the latter view in current policy under Gordon Brown and Ed Balls: not just in the policies of 2008 but in the extension of daycare and 'wrap-around' school extension policies, positive discrimination in the allocation of funding to disadvantaged schools, Every Child Matters, and perhaps even the creation of the Department for Children, Schools and Families. But it goes nowhere near as far as the Scandinavian strategy – our daycare is not free, for example. Whether these attempts to create social mobility can be successful within the framework of an educational market is also contestable.

**Notes**

[1] Many of the claims in the document are based on inaccurate data or analysis, which substantially weakens the Conservative case (Crace, 2008).

[2] See www.iea.nl for further details.

**References**

Adonis, A. (2008) 'Academies and social mobility', Speech to the National Academies Conference, London, 7 February, *www.standards.dfes.gov.uk/academies/software/Andrew_Adonis_Speech_feb08.doc?version=1*

Ball, S.J. (2003) 'The teacher's soul and the terrors of performativity', *Journal of Education Policy*, vol 18, no 2, pp 215-28.

Ball, S.J. (2008a) *The Education Debate*, Bristol: The Policy Press.

Ball, S.J. (2008b) 'Staggering backwards to the future: Conservative Party education policy', in J. Cruddas and J. Rutherford (eds) *Is the Future Conservative?*, London: Soundings.

Balls, E. (2008) 'Announcement of changes to school accountability sytem', 14 October, www.dcsf.gov.uk/pns/DisplayPN.cgi?pn_id=2008_0229

Barker, R. (1972) *Education and Politics 1900-1951: A Study of the Labour Party*, Oxford: Oxford University Press.

Blanden, J. and Machin, S (2007) *Recent Changes in Intergenerational Mobility in the UK*, London: The Sutton Trust.

Brighouse, T. (2007) 'The London challenge: a personal view', in T. Brighouse and L. Fullick (eds) *Education in a Global City: Essays from London*, London: Institute of Education.

Cabinet Office (2009) *New Opportunities: Fair Chances for the Future*, London: Cabinet Office.

Colley, H. and Hodkinson, P. (2001) 'Problems with "Bridging the Gap": the reversal of structure and agency in addressing social exclusion', *Critical Social Policy*, vol 21, no 3, pp 337-61.

Conservative Party (2008a) *Raising the Bar, Closing the Gap: Policy Green Paper No 1*, London: Conservative Party.

Conservative Party (2008b) *A Failed Generation: Educational Inequality under New Labour*, London: Conservative Party.

Cox, C.B. and Dyson, A.E. (eds) (1969) *Fight for Education: A Black Paper*, London: Critical Quarterly Society.

Crace, J. (2008) 'Is inequality worse than ever?', *The Guardian*, 26 August, www.guardian.co.uk/education/2008/aug/26/schools. socialexclusion

DfES (Department for Education and Skills) (2005) *Higher Standards, Better Schools for All: More Choice for Parents and Pupils*, Cm 6677, London: The Stationery Office.

DIUS (Department for Innovation, Universities and Skills) (2008) *World Class Apprenticeships: Unlocking Talent, Building Skills for All: The Government's Strategy for the Future of Apprenticeships in England*, London: DIUS.

Esping-Andersen, G. (2007) 'Sociological explanations of changing income distributions', *American Behavioral Scientist*, vol 50, no 5, pp 639-57.

Esping-Andersen, G. (2008) 'Investing in children and their life chances', in A. Espina (ed) *Estado de Bienestar y Competitividad: La Experiencia Europea*, Madrid: Fundacion Carolina.

Ford, J. (1969) *Social Class and the Comprehensive School*, London: Routledge & Kegan Paul.

Gillborn, D. and Youdell, D. (2000) *Rationing Education: Policy, Practice, Reform and Equity*, Buckingham: Open University Press.

Glennerster, H. (2009) *Understanding the Finance of Welfare* (2nd edition), Bristol: The Policy Press.

Gosden, P.H.J.H. (1976) *Education in the Second World War*, London: Methuen.

Gretton, J. and Jackson, M. (1976) *William Tyndale: Collapse of a School or a System?*, London: Allen & Unwin.

House of Commons (2008a) *Testing and Assessment: Third Report of Session 2007–08*, Children, Schools and Families Committee, HC 169-1, London: The Stationery Office.

House of Commons (2008b) *Testing and Assessment: Government and Ofsted Responses to the Committee's Third Report of Session 2007–08*, Fifth Special Report of Session 2007–08, HC 1003, London: The Stationery Office.

Hoxby, C.M. (2006) 'Do vouchers and charters push public schools to improve?', in P.E. Petersen (ed) *Choice and Competition in American Schools*, Lanham, MD: Rowan and Littlefield.

Kelly, R. (2005) 'Education and social progress', London, 26 July, cited in A. Dyson, K. Kerr and M. Ainscow (2006) 'A "pivotal moment": education policy in England 2005', in L. Bauld, N. Clark and T. Maltby (eds) *Social Policy Review 18*, Bristol: The Policy Press.

Levačić, R. (2004) 'Competition and performance in English secondary schools: further evidence', *Education Economics*, vol 97, no 4, pp 477-94.

Lupton, R., Heath, N. and Salter, E. (2009) 'Education: New Labour's top priority', in J. Hills, T. Sefton and K. Stewart (eds) *Towards a More Equal Society? Poverty, Inequality and Policy since 1997*, Bristol: The Policy Press.

Ministry of Education (1959) *15 to 18*, Report of the Central Advisory Council for Education, England, London: HMSO.

OECD (Organisation for Economic Co-operation and Development) (2007) *PISA 2006: Science Competencies for Tomorrow's World*, Paris: OECD.

Rutter, M., Maughan, B., Mortimore, P. and Ouston, J. (1979) *Fifteen Thousand Hours: Secondary Schools and their Effects on Children*, London: Open Books.

SEU (Social Exclusion Unit) (1999) *Bridging the Gap: New Opportunities for 16–18 Year Olds*, London: The Stationery Office.

Sibieta, L., Chowdry, H. and Muriel, A. (2008) *Level Playing Field? The Implications of School Funding*, Reading: CfBT Education Trust.

Tymms, P. (2004) 'Are standards rising in English primary schools?', *British Educational Research Journal*, vol 30, no 4, pp 477-94.

Vandenberghe, V. (1996) *Functioning and Regulation of Quasi-Markets*, Louvain-la-Neuve: Catholic University.

# FOUR

# Beveridge's giant of disease: from negative to positive welfare?

*Martin Powell*

## Introduction

The 60th anniversary of the National Health Service (NHS) gives an appropriate time to reflect on progress in conquering Beveridge's (1942) giant of disease. After Bevan, Beveridge is often regarded as a parent of the NHS (coming sixth in the *Health Service Journal*'s 'Diamond' list of the most important people in the 60 years of the NHS; *Health Service Journal*, 30 June 2008). However, Beveridge's role in creating the NHS was limited. As Scrivens (1991, p 27) points out, although a comprehensive health service was a central feature of the post-war reconstruction programme, Beveridge made little reference to its specification.

There are two main ways of defining health: the positive approach, where health is viewed as a capacity or an asset, and the negative approach, which emphasises the absence of specific illnesses, diseases or disorders (Baggott, 2004, p 1). The famous 1948 definition by the World Health Organization of 'a state of complete physical, mental, and social well-being and not merely the absence of disease or infirmity' (www. who.int/about/definition/en/print/html) clearly stresses the positive (if rather utopian) view. Giddens (1998, p 111) claims that when Beveridge famously declared war on want, disease, ignorance, squalor and idleness, his focus was almost entirely negative. He said that we should speak today of 'positive welfare' to which individuals themselves and other agencies besides government contribute – and which is functional for wealth creation. The guideline is investment in human capital wherever possible, rather than the direct provision of economic maintenance. In place of the welfare state, we should put the social investment state, operating in the context of a positive welfare society. Positive welfare would replace each of Beveridge's negatives with a positive: in place of want, autonomy; not disease but active health; instead of ignorance, education, as a continuing part of life; rather than squalor, well-being; and in place of idleness, initiative (p 128). However, Giddens is incorrect in that – at least on paper – the NHS has always been concerned with positive health, but has been concerned in practice with negative health: talking positively but acting negatively. Recent years have seen claims that the NHS is focusing upstream (Hunter, 2008) but, as we shall see, this represents something of a 'Groundhog Day' in that similar claims have been made throughout its history.

This chapter presents a review of recent activities in the NHS, but in the context of a wider focus on positive health, and stresses the importance of implementation and evaluation of existing policies rather than a sole focus on new policies. It will focus on the English NHS, but issues such as the 'market', prescription charges, long-term care, waiting lists and hospital car parking charges continue to pose questions about intra-UK health system divergence (Greer and Rowland, 2007; Greer and Trench, 2008; Hunter, 2008, pp 83-7; Jervis, 2008).

## NHS: positive or negative health?

The view that health status is influenced by factors outside a curative health service is not new (see, for example, Fraser, 2003, ch 3). As Scrivens (1991, p 28) points out, prevention was the popular theme of the day in the period running up to the creation of the NHS. In 1938, a British Medical Association report argued that 'the system of medical service should be directed to the achievement of positive health and the prevention of disease no less than to the relief of sickness'. This was drawn on for Beveridge's (1942, para 301) Assumption B, which saw comprehensive health and rehabilitation services for prevention and cure of disease and restoration of capacity for work, available to all members of the community. Fox (1986, p 104) writes that, according to Beveridge, the goal of health policy was the attainment of positive health. Timmins (2001, p 22) points out that Beveridge's future wife, Jessy Mair, urged him to concentrate on 'prevention rather than cure' and the 'education of those not yet accustomed to clean careful ways of living'.

The Coalition government White Paper, *A National Health Service* (Ministry of Health, 1944), advocated a comprehensive health service, with the real need being to bring the country's full resources to bear upon reducing ill-health and promoting good health in all of its citizens (p 5), and discussed health centres (p 30) as well as agencies outside the NHS such as factory medical inspection; 'works doctors'; the school medical service, and environmental and preventive services in school and industry (p 10).

The 1946 NHS Act states that 'It shall be the duty of the Minister of Health ... to promote the establishment ... of a comprehensive health service designed to secure improvement in the physical and mental health of the people ... and the prevention, diagnosis and treatment of illness' (cited in Harrison and McDonald 2008, p 15). Bevan (1946, col 509) stressed the importance of prevention: 'If we can get a stream of healthy people attending the health centre, it becomes a health centre: but if we merely have morbid cases going to a health centre, it becomes a morbid centre'.

However, it was hardly surprising that the 1948 NHS was essentially a national hospital service or a national illness service rather than a national health service (Klein, 2006, p 6). The 'rise of modern medicine' or 'the age of optimism' was associated with the drugs or therapeutic revolution, and post-war medical achievement was built on the twin pillars of antibiotics and steroids (Le Fanu 2000, p 192). This broadly continued despite occasional nods towards a wider and positive notion of health. For example, the Department of Health and Social Security (DHSS, 1976, p 47) claimed that prevention and health was 'Everybody's Business': 'we need to interest individuals, communities and society as a whole in the idea that prevention is better than cure'. According to the Royal Commission on the NHS (1979, pp 9-12), one of the objectives of the NHS was 'encouraging and assisting individuals to remain healthy'. The Thatcher Conservative government endorsed a range of screening, promotion and education measures, commissioned an inquiry into public health that led to changed elements of public health administration including the appointment of directors of public health in each health authority who were required to produce an annual report on public health, and struggled with a range of issues from BSE/CJD to HIV/AIDS. The Major Conservative government produced *The Health of the Nation* strategy (DH, 1992) with targets for coronary heart disease and stroke, cancer, mental illness, accidents, HIV/AIDS and sexual health (Klein, 2006).

## New Labour and positive health

The New Labour government appointed a Minister of Public Health, introduced a new anti-smoking strategy including a ban on tobacco advertising, and proceeded with the creation of an independent Food Standards Agency. It commissioned the Acheson Report on Inequalities in Health (Acheson, 1998) – the 'child of Black' – which produced 39 main recommendations ('the 39 steps'). The government published Green and White Papers on public health (DH, 1998, 1999), which set targets to reduce disease and illness on the four areas of cancer, heart disease and stroke, mental illness and accidents. While the Green Paper rejected health inequalities targets, the White Paper set the first health inequalities targets for England. *The NHS Plan* (DH, 2000) contained a slim chapter buried deep in the plan that was devoted to improving health and reducing inequalities (Hunter, 2003, p 64).

In 2000, the-then Secretary of State for Health, Alan Milburn, argued that 'the time has come to take public health out of the ghetto' (cited in Hunter, 2003, p 36). In 2002, he stressed the importance of public health, improving health and reducing health inequalities, and that for too long the health debate in Britain had been focused on the state of the nation's health service and not enough on the state of the nation's health (cited in Hunter, 2003, p 159). Before a somewhat astonished audience at the Faculty of Public Health Medicine, Milburn claimed that the time had come to 'put renewed emphasis on prevention as well as treatment so that we develop in our country health services and not just sickness services. It is time for a sea change in attitudes' (cited in Hunter, 2003, p 2). He assured the House of Commons Select Health Committee that *The NHS Plan* (DH, 2000) was of equal status to *Saving Lives* (DH, 1999) (cited in Hunter, 2003, p 74).

Public health continued to feature in New Labour's second term. The Wanless Reports (2002, 2004), commissioned by the Treasury, argued that the future growth of health expenditure could be curbed through public health measures, particularly those aimed by changing individual lifestyles. The White Paper *Choosing Health* (DH, 2004) focused on the various causes of ill-health, although the key strategy stressed the importance of providing information and support to enable individuals to make healthy choices for themselves.

## 2007–08: refocusing upstream?

New Labour has brought in a large number of diverse health policies. The Department of Health (DH, 2005) outlines four mutually reinforcing reform streams: transactional; demand-side; supply-side; and system management and regulation. These are examined in this section. In addition, the Darzi reports, the 60th anniversary of the NHS, the NHS Constitution, and the change of Prime Minister and Secretary of State are added to the mix. The section ends by examining the two themes highlighted earlier: implementation and evaluation of existing policies, and the notion of refocusing upstream.

### Transactional reforms

The main reform ensuring that 'money follows the patient' is the misnamed 'payment by results' (PBR), which is more accurately termed 'payment by activity'. This is an evolving tariff-based system. Financial rewards for quality will be introduced in the future. In a 'simple overlay to PBR', payments to hospitals will be conditional on the quality as well as the quantity of care (DH, 2008a, pp 41-2). The Audit Commission (2008) states that PBR – one of the government's key NHS modernisation reforms – has helped hospitals to be more business-like but has not yet increased NHS efficiency significantly.

### Demand-side reforms

Demand-side reforms include choice, voice and commissioning. Choice has become very important in the NHS in recent years (Greener and Powell, 2008, 2009; Powell and Greener, 2009). The most obvious instrument is the 'Choose and Book' system, which provides choice of hospital (including private hospitals) rather than other dimensions of choice. In particular, choice at level of hospital means that patients do not know whether Dr Jekyll or Mr Hyde will be carrying out their operations. Moreover, although a 'national' policy, it has not yet been universally implemented. Some 46% of patients recalled being offered a choice of hospital for their first outpatient appointment, and 88% of patients offered choice were able to go to the hospital they wanted, with hospital cleanliness and low hospital-acquired infection rates the main factor in choice of hospital (DH, 2008b). In little over 12 months this has resulted in the number of patients opting for private hospitals rising tenfold to over 3,500 a month (BBC news, www.bbc.co.uk,

2 December 2008, 'Patients going "private" on NHS"). However, a broader 'personalisation' will be the 'cornerstone of public services' (DH, 2008c). 'User-driven public services' include individual or personal budgets and direct payments, which entail giving patients financial control over the health and social care services they receive, so that they can direct the support or services they get. The government has stated that by 2011 it intends to make personal budgets available to all people receiving publicly funded adult social care (DH, 2008c; PASC, 2008, pp 9–10). These policies have been evaluated (Glendinning et al, 2008; Hatton et al, 2008). Gordon Brown (2008) claims that future NHS reforms such as direct payments and individual budgets will move beyond 'choice' towards 'personalisation'. The final Darzi Review (DH, 2008a) stated that patients with long-term health conditions will be offered personal health budgets in a national pilot from early 2009.

In contrast to the fast-moving area of choice, voice appears to have stalled. In recent years, the government has unveiled a rapid parade of acronyms linked with voice or 'patient and public involvement' (PPI) – ICAS (Independent Complaints Advocacy Service), PALS (Patient Advocacy and Liaison Services), PPIF (Patient and Public Involvement Forum), CPPIH (Commission for Patient and Public Involvement in Health), OSC (Overview and Scrutiny Committee) – culminating in the delayed LINKS (Local Involvement Networks) (Harrison and McDonald, 2008, ch 5; Greener, 2009). In addition, governors and members are meant to run Foundation Trusts (FTs). According to Gordon Brown (2008), citizens will have more 'voice':

> I want to see 3 million foundation trust members by 2012 – up from 1 million today – and give them an even greater say in the workings of their trust.... we will also explore the ways of improving the legitimacy and accountability of primary care trusts and of the commissioning decisions they make on behalf of their local communities.

In the same speech, the ever-generous Prime Minister promised to empower the user *and* the professionals (see DH, 2008a). New guidance from the Department of Health (DH, 2008d), drawing on the Darzi report (DH, 2008c) the Operating Framework for 2008/09 (DH, 2007a), 'world-class commissioning' and the NHS Constitution (DH, 2008e), urged PCTs to engage better with the public and patients to achieve 'real involvement'.

Primary Care Trusts must embrace 'world-class commissioning' (DH, 2007b, 2008f, 2008g), which, according to Hunter (2008, p 100), is a 'vacuous phrase devoid of all useful meaning'. Practice-based commissioning, which has a remarkable similarity to the Conservatives' general practitioner (GP) fundholding (Greener and Mannion, 2006), continues to be rolled out, but the desire that most practices would be engaged in practice-based commissioning by 2008 looks optimistic (Hunter, 2008, p 76; see DH, 2008h for latest position).

## Supply-side reforms

Supply-side reforms are concerned with replacing the 'monolithic' NHS with provider plurality, including FTs and private and social enterprise providers. All members of the 'NHS family' are subject to regulation and inspection.

According to the House of Commons Health Select Committee (2008), FTs have proven strengths. They have performed well financially and in terms of routine NHS process quality measures (HCC, 2008). However, as FTs were selected from the best-performing NHS Trusts, it is not clear whether this performance is linked with FT status. Moreover, they have made little contribution towards delivering more NHS care outside hospitals, and have been slow to innovate and generate greater public involvement. To some extent, FTs' slowness to innovate and invest has been seen as a failure on the part of PCTs to provide strategic guidance. It is 'unfortunate' that the world-class commissioning programme has lagged behind rather than predated the FT programme.

Independent Sector Treatment Centres (ISTCs) were heavily criticised by the House of Commons Health Select Committee (2006). In order to encourage market entry, the first wave of ISTCs were paid irrespective of the volume of activity, but the planned programme was reduced in 2007 (Hunter, 2008, p 69; Lister, 2008, pp 235-6). However, if the ISTC programme slowed down, it was full speed ahead elsewhere. In 2008, Care UK was awarded the first Alternative Provider Medical Services (APMS) contract to operate a GP practice in the UK, in Barking and Dagenham, and then in City and Hackney (MIS, 2008, pp 214-19; see also the discussion of the Darzi report below).

## System management and regulation reforms

The publication *Developing the NHS Performance Regime* (DH, 2008i) introduces the concept of 'challenged' organisations, building on the concept of Financially Challenged Trusts introduced under the 2007/08 Operating Framework. There will be three stages of escalation and intervention – 'underperforming', 'seriously underperforming' and 'challenged'. Mirroring earlier 'name and shame' policies (target/command-and-control policies, according to Le Grand, 2007, pp 23-30), the NHS Chief Executive will publicly designate organisations as 'challenged' and subject them to intervention at board level. Under 'challenged' status, the strategic health authority may impose temporary appointments, initiate action to suspend or remove members of the Board and agree a 'turnaround' plan (DH, 2008i, p 40). Where recovery is not feasible, the organisation will be 'under directions' and may lead to closure and asset disposal; franchising by the independent sector, NHS or FT; or acquisition by another NHS body (2008i, p 46).

The current Health and Social Care Bill will set up a new Care Quality Commission (CQC) (DH, 2008i, p 17). The main responsibilities of the CQC are to:

- register health and social care providers;
- carry out periodic assessment of all NHS providers and commissioners;
- carry out special reviews of services;
- carry out investigations into specific organisations where CQC believes that user safety is seriously at risk; and
- carry out gatekeeping and proportionate regulation (DH, 2008i, p 55).

## The Next Steps Review/Darzi reports

In 2007, eminent surgeon Professor Ara Darzi was asked to conduct a 'Next Steps Review' of a vision of the NHS over the next decade. Darzi opened his 2007 interim report (DH, 2007c) declaring that he was a doctor, not a politician (but see Lister, 2008). He gave his vision of a 'world-class NHS' that was fair, personalised, effective, safe and locally accountable. The report stated that the NHS had 'vastly improved' since 1997, but was only about two thirds of the way through the reform programme set out in 2000–02. The report set out a number of immediate steps, including over 100 new GP practices in the most deprived and under-provided parts of the country (p 36), and led to a significant consultation exercise in the NHS.

The final Darzi report (DH, 2008a) was termed by Gordon Brown in its preface a 'bold vision for the NHS' and a 'once in a generation opportunity' (p 2). Many of its themes were closely related to existing policy direction (see Hunter, 2008; Lister, 2008). Darzi advocated an NHS that 'gives patients and the public more information and choice, works in partnership and has quality of care at its heart' (DH, 2000a, p 7). Quality improvement is the 'guiding principle for this Review' (p 8). As Hunter (2008, p 65) puts it, Darzi is concerned with quality improvement rather than getting the numbers right. The report echoed a long line of claims that we need to create an NHS that helps people to stay healthy, that the NHS needs to focus on improving health as well as treating sickness (DH, 2008a, p 9). It went on to say that patients and the public had zero tolerance for variations in access to the most effective treatment (p 43), and promised that steps would be taken to end this so-called 'postcode lottery' for new drugs and treatment (p 44), which appears to be a less ambitious version of the promise of 1997 to end the postcode lottery, with the setting up of the National Institute for Clinical Excellence (NICE). In an apparent 'cut and paste' of earlier New Labour documents, it promised – yet again – to put 'frontline staff in control' (p 59) with 'greater freedom to the frontline' (p 61; compare, for example, Greener, 2009). Change will be locally led, patient centred and clinically driven (p 17). The new elements of the Darzi report include ensuring that payments to hospitals will be conditional on the quality as well as the quantity of care (pp 41-2) and setting up 'polyclinics' (super health centres).

As Lister (2008, p 236) points out, the promise to deliver 100 new GP practices and 150 new polyclinics is linked with the private sector. Some areas such as Heart of Birmingham PCT are trying to 'out-Darzi Darzi' with proposals to press-gang 76 GP practices into 24 franchises, to be run from polyclinics, which could be offered to 'trusted' high-street companies such as Asda, Tesco or Virgin (p 239). Hunter (2008, p 64) sums up the Darzi report by pointing out that, although generally welcomed, there are concerns about what it all means, whether it was necessary at all, since most of what is promised amounts to a reaffirmation of what is already in train, and how far implementation will follow.

## The NHS Constitution

For its 60th birthday, the NHS got ... a Constitution! The interim Darzi report (DH, 2007c) examined the possibility of an NHS Constitution, and it was confirmed in Darzi's final report (DH, 2008a). It is unclear why a country without a written constitution requires an NHS Constitution, and it appears in many ways to be a policy re-tread of John Major's Citizen's Charter.

The draft NHS Constitution was published on 30 June 2008 (DH, 2008e) (with its own NHS Constitution Facebook Group!). It claims that the NHS is there to improve our health, supporting us to keep mentally and physically well, to get better when we are ill and, when we cannot fully recover, to stay as well as we can. However, as we have seen, this is a seriously lopsided three-legged stool. It sets out NHS values (p 1) but these are vague and problematic. For example, the NHS should provide a comprehensive service, available to all, with access based on clinical need but, as we shall see below, this is simply not the case.

It then sets out legal rights and pledges ('will strive to...'), and responsibilities (but unlike areas such as employment, there is little discussion of what will happen if citizens' 'responsibilities' are not met). The document continues that you have the right to seek treatment elsewhere in Europe if you are entitled to NHS treatment but you face 'undue delay' in receiving that treatment (p 2). However, who defines this term? Is it beyond the 18-week target? Compared with waiting times in many parts of Europe and in the UK private sector, it could be argued that even a month or two in pain might be considered an 'undue delay'. The cross-border healthcare Directive was adopted by the European Commission in July 2008. However, it may take two years to come into force, and 'small print' terms such as 'undue delay' may have to be clarified in court (MIS, 2008, pp 268-9).

If 'clinical need' is what your doctor says you need, then there are many cases where people do not get access to expensive drugs because they are not (yet) licensed in the UK, or because NICE has deemed them not cost-effective. Moreover, 'postcode prescribing' still exists. The issue of co-payments or 'top-ups' has also recently come to light. For example, cancer patients who top up their care with a drug not available on the NHS were forced to pay for the rest of the NHS treatment. Media reports resulted in 'Cancer Czar' Professor Mike Richards' review on co-payments (DH, 2008j). The government accepted all 14 of Richards' recommendations, and put out proposals for consultation. 'Top-ups' will be allowed under strictly regulated conditions, which would avoid a 'two-tier' service. However, the insurance industry believes that there is a lucrative market opening up to sell 'top-ups' (BBC news, www. bbc.co.uk, 7 November 2008, 'Distressing top-ups ban lifted; insurance firms eye top-up market'). Earlier media reports indicated that Health Secretary Alan Johnson was expected to declare that NHS rules allowed them all along, and the problem resulted from a 'misinterpretation' by some NHS hospitals (but why was this not clarified earlier and why was the review necessary?). A letter from a patient who subsequently died asked: 'Could you please inform me who is responsible for the decision to force me out of the NHS?'. The answer appears to be that no one was responsible or accountable. Patients who have been denied NHS care because they bought private drugs are suing for the treatment that has been withdrawn (*The Sunday Times*, 19 October 2008). The reason for this situation is that ministers feared a two-tier system that would breach NHS principles. However, in preserving the equity principle, they have broken the 'ability to pay' principle, but affluence rather than poverty is now a barrier to access, denying 'clinical treatment' according to need. Parrot-like repetitions of 'NHS principles' do not help in situations when principles clash. Brown (in the Introduction to DH, 2008e) claims that healthcare is a 'moral right secured for all', but this seems to assume no rationing and co-payments.

## Change of Prime Minister and Secretary of State for Health

The period under review has seen a new Prime Minister and Secretary of State for Health. Lister (2008, p 194) writes that the switch from Blair to Brown brought no slowing of the relentless pace of 'reform' in the NHS, with a continuing commitment to more privatisation and marketisation. Brown (2008) claims that the NHS has been a central priority since June 2008, and that 'the renewal of the NHS will be our highest priority' (another Groundhog Day, as it was 'renewed' in 1997 and 2000) with immediate changes such as 'deep cleaning' of wards, but our ambitions for the future of the NHS can and should go much further. There will be 'even wider and deeper reform', with no 'no-go areas' for reform. However, there appears to be some change in discourse. Brown (2008) tends not to stress the terms of 'choice' and 'consumer'. 'Real empowerment' of patients will come from going further, with the driving force of patients becoming more than consumers – partners in health and healthcare. Patients will have real power and control, and take more responsibility: more than today's new choice of where and when you are treated but a new choice tomorrow – in partnership with your clinician – about your treatment itself. The NHS of the future will offer prevention.

It has been said that, for Alan Johnson, addressing health inequalities is a central – possibly the central – issue for the Department of Health, the NHS and a range of government and adjacent agencies (*Health Service Journal*, 8 July 2008). In Johnson's own words, his principal objectives are to improve the health of the whole population; and to ensure that the health of the poorest improves the fastest (MIS, 2008, pp 8-9; see also next section).

### Improving health and reducing health inequalities: refocusing upstream

Since 1997, a range of policy initiatives have been introduced with the aim of improving health, preventing illness and reducing health inequalities (Hunter, 2003, 2008; AC and HCC, 2008). For example, the smoking ban in England introduced on 1 July 2007 (following the other UK nations) was termed 'one of the most important steps forward in public health for many years' and it is claimed that 'the significance of the law cannot be underestimated' (DH, 2008k). A recent report has concluded that Britain has the toughest smoking controls in Europe (*Daily Mail*, 29 October 2008).

However, while there have been some gains in improving health, progress towards reducing health inequalities has been mixed, with the gap increasing rather than narrowing in some areas (DH, 2007d, 2007e, 2008l; Wanless et al, 2007; AC and HCC, 2008). Looking at the eight public health targets in the 2006/07 health check relating most closely to the *Choosing Health* priorities, 31% of PCTs achieved five targets or more, 42% three or four targets and 27% two targets or fewer (AC and HCC, 2008, p 53). Eighty per cent of PCTs achieved health inequalities targets (AC and HCC, 2008). Moreover, the performance of PCTs in 2006/07 with regard to most of the public health targets was worse than in 2005/06.

Recently, acknowledgement of these problems has resulted in a renewed emphasis on issues of health improvement, health inequalities and well-being (see *Health Service Journal*, special edition 30 October 2008). Health Secretary Alan Johnson, launching a strategy for tackling health inequality in June 2008, claimed that 'promoting health and wellbeing is the raison d'être of the NHS' (Johnson, 2008). Health improvement, health inequalities and well-being indicators are emphasised in the Delivery Agreement of a new health and well-being Public Service Agreement. There is a new performance framework for local authorities and partnerships. Partnership working on health improvement and health inequalities is a major theme of recent policy, with emphasis being placed on the role of Local Strategic Partnerships and Local Area Agreements (see DH, 2007d; AC and HCC, 2008). The 2007 Local Government and Public Involvement in Health Act places duties on both PCTs and local authorities to work together to achieve local people's priorities. There has been a torrent of guidelines, toolkits and tips to improve health and reduce health inequalities (for example, DH, 2007d, 2007e, 2007f, 2007g, 2008f, 2008g; AC and HCC, 2008). This increased relevance is found in the *Commissioning Framework for Health and Wellbeing* (DH, 2007g) and in the impetus to establish world-class commissioning in England (DH, 2008f, 2008g). In future years, there will be an increased focus on commissioning for PCTs, with public health as a fundamental component of the commissioning process. Public health is also an issue for providers: the Healthcare Commission is increasingly focusing on health promotion and improvement measures that provider trusts are able to implement along the patient pathway and with their workforce (AC and HCC, 2008, p 51).

However, a diabetes 'epidemic' may cause the first fall in life expectancy for 200 years. According to government adviser Professor Sir George Alberti, the government has begun to tackle obesity and inactivity but converting good words into action is very difficult. It will take ages to have an effect (*The Independent*, 20 October 2008).

## Implementation and evaluation

Many reviews focus on the 'shock of the new', but implementation and evaluation of old policies are also important. Many accounts take a 'Webbsian' view of social policy, ending the story when the policy reaches the statute book. Matthew Taylor, Chief Adviser on Political Strategy to the Prime Minister from 2003 to 2006 admits that when he started out in the 1980s, he believed that what changed the world was policy, he knew little or nothing about systems and he was uninterested in implementation. However, he emerged from Downing Street with a very different perspective: 'Policy may provide the recipe for successful change, but systems provide the ingredients ..., implementation does the cooking and, however enticing the dish, without clear communication [or spin?] no one will come to dinner' (cited in Timmins, 2008, p 119). He continues that even the advisers and officials who knew their stuff were much better on the destination than they were at charting the journey, and the big-thinking strategists all too often forget that while reform takes place, stuff (such as MRSA) still happens (p 120). Similarly, Simon Stevens (2008) reminds us that proposals are not always implemented: quite a lot of the good stuff from John Reid's 2004 White Paper (DH, 2004) never saw the light of day after the 2005 General Election. And even more of Patricia Hewitt's thoughtful 2006 White Paper on primary and community services (DH, 2006) ended up on the cutting-room floor as deficits and budget crises crowded out the reform agenda.

Many accounts entered the celebratory birthday spirit. According to NHS Chief Executive, David Nicholson, 'the NHS is performing extremely well' (DH, 2008i, p 3). Nationally, 92.78% of December 2008's admitted pathways were completed in 18 weeks or less, 'sustaining the achievement of the target' (www.18weeks.nhs.uk/ content. aspx?path=/measure-and-monitor/current-performance-data/RTT-data-publication), and the NHS was on course to meet challenging targets for reducing rates of healthcare-associated infection. Mortality rates for cancer and cardiovascular disease have been substantially reduced, while access to GP and other primary care services is quickly improving. In its 60th anniversary year, public confidence in the NHS and patient satisfaction with the quality of NHS care are both at their highest level for years. But David Nicholson added that this was no time to be complacent or rest on our laurels (DH, 2008i, p 3); for example at Maidstone and Tunbridge Wells hospital there were outbreaks of C. difficile that led to an estimated 60 deaths (HCC, 2007). According to Alan Johnson, in his Foreword to the Department of Health's *Autumn Performance Report 2008* (DH, 2008m), the NHS has made 'major progress' in achieving its 18-week target, and in halving the number of MRSA infections (but why was it so high in the first place?). Leatherman and Sutherland (2008) write that unquestionably the past 10 years have seen significant changes in quality that have made a real difference to patients and the public. The Healthcare Commission's Annual Health Check (HCC, 2008) shows significant improvements across the NHS, with 42 trusts – over twice as many as the previous year – being rated as 'excellent', and only six (down from 20 last year) being rated 'weak' for both quality and finance. Twenty-six trusts raised their performance for quality of service by two levels on the four-point scale. For the second consecutive year, annual improvement is evident. Mental health trusts performed best; with good performances from acute and specialist trusts; and FTs performing better than non-FTs. For the third year in a row, PCT performance is poorest, but PCTs are assessed against up to 17 targets, while mental health trusts are assessed against one target.

However, Wanless et al (2007) note the recommendation of the 2002 Wanless Report that government should review future resource requirements. The 2002 report outlined three possible spending scenarios for healthcare up to 2022/23: slow uptake (SU), solid progress (SP) and fully engaged (FE), depending on assumptions about the effectiveness of NHS performance and the health status of the population, with FE the most ambitious and resource-efficient and SU the least satisfactory and most expensive scenario. Wanless et al (2007) note that in the five years following 2002, there were unprecedented levels of government investment in the NHS. However, they classify changes in input costs as SU/SP; in resources – investment in staff, premises and equipment – as SP; in productivity as SU; in outputs or activities as SU/SP; and in health outcomes as SU/SP. They conclude that policy is broadly moving in the right direction, and the NHS is now in better shape than in 2002, with a number of major successes, but huge challenges remain.

Timmins (2008, p 15) noted that, according to the National NHS Staff Survey of 2007, almost a quarter of hospital staff, ranging from fewer than 2% in some trusts to over 40% in a handful, said that they would not be happy to have their care provided by their own organisation. David Green of Civitas claims that the NHS has been a triumph of romance over results. He cites the 2006 Staff Survey in which only 42% agreed that they would be happy as a patient with the standard of care provided, and the 2007 Staff Survey in which only 48% agreed that care of patients/service users was their trust's top priority (cited in Timmins, 2008, p 153). The birthday party was also spoiled by the Euro Health Consumer Index, which rated Britain 13th of 31 European countries on six measures of patient satisfaction, and worse than Estonia (Devlin, 2008). Alan Johnson rejected the report on the grounds of 'flawed methodology and old data', preferring to point to a more favourable report by the Commonwealth Fund, which scored Britain highly for 'access' and 'efficiency' (Devlin, 2008).

## Conclusion

The 60th anniversary of the NHS has seen a number of reviews of the service (Appleby and Thorlby, 2008; DH, 2008n; Timmins, 2008). The NHS has clearly changed significantly since 1948, spending about eight times as much per capita in real terms, with more staff but fewer beds. The number of people on NHS waiting lists may have fallen over the last 10 years, but is still higher than in 1948. Moreover, as Appleby and Thorlby (2008, p 15) comment, life and health were also very different in 1948. Although smoking rates have tumbled, no one compiling reports in the early years of the NHS 'could perhaps have predicted a situation of too much food as a threat to public health'. This appears to reinforce the point below that it is too simple to credit – or blame – the NHS for changes in health and well-being.

The NHS does appear to be in better shape than it was in 1997. However, whether 'results' have matched the degree of 'investment' and 'reform' is less clear. Moreover, investment was always going to be less generous in the future, even before the current financial crisis, with the Treasury allegedly eyeing up NHS surpluses. Recent changes from 'deficit to surplus', with the NHS in England running a £500 million surplus in June 2007 in place of the previous year's deficit (Lister, 2008, p 196) may be a warning of future 'boom and bust'.

This period – like recent years – has seen a fast-moving policy agenda. However, a number of potentially far-reaching policy documents – always 'talked up' as the most important in NHS history – need to be closely monitored in terms of implementation and evaluation. The period has also seen the continuation of a number of policy re-treads such as 'cut and pastes' on patient voice and devolution to the 'frontline', 'challenged' status as a reinvented 'name and shame', polyclinics as the 'Sellafield' to health centres' 'Windscale' and 'Groundhog Day' of the importance of a health rather than a sickness service.

Given that one estimate suggests that about 25% of the health of a developed population is attributable to the healthcare system (Harrison and McDonald, 2008, p 165), refocusing upstream appears an obvious strategy. Yet, moving upstream may be as difficult as water-defying gravity. As Wanless (2004, p 23) pointed out, numerous policy statements and initiatives in the field of public health have not resulted in a rebalancing of policy away from healthcare ('a national sickness service') to health ('a national health service'; see Hunter, 2008, ch 6). The de jure ('paper' or 'discourse') health service has always been a de facto sickness service. The initial NHS claims to give high priority to the promotion of health were in reality never more than weakly developed, with spending on prevention still less than 1% of overall NHS expenditure (Hunter, 2003, pp 80-1). It follows that Giddens' (1998) claim to turn Beveridge's negatives into positives is misleading as the NHS has always talked positive but acted negative.

Not only is the devil in the detail, but also the exactitudes are in the implementation. Translating words into action will be problematic due to factors such as inherent difficulty (the limited evidence base), practical politics (long-term health rather than short-term political benefits;

concerns over 'liberty' and the 'nanny state') and a little constituency for prevention.

Klein's (2004) chapter 'Transforming the NHS' in *Social Policy Review 17* reports that the first priority in the Department of Health's 2004 planning framework for the years ahead is to improve the health of the population. In a familiar phrase, the course is to be set towards 'a health service, not a sickness [service]'. He warns that until the day comes when successful health promotion policies (or genetic engineering miracles) ensure that everyone lives to be 101 (that is, no health inequalities!) and then drops dead without ever having suffered a day's illness or disability, most people will probably settle gratefully for an efficient, effective and accessible sickness service (2004, p 66).

## References

AC and HCC (Audit Commission and Healthcare Commission) (2008) *Is the Treatment Working?*, London: Audit Commission.

Acheson, Sir D. (1998) *Independent Inquiry into Inequalities in Health*, London: The Stationery Office.

Appleby, J. and Thorlby, R. (2008) *Celebrating the NHS at 60*, London: King's Fund.

Audit Commission (2008) *The Right Result? Payment by Results 2003-07*, London: Audit Commission.

Baggott, R. (2004) *Health and Health Care in Britain* (3rd edition), Basingstoke: Palgrave Macmillan.

Bevan, A. (1946) *Hansard, Standing Committee on the NHS Bill*, London: HMSO.

Beveridge, Sir W. (1942) *Social Insurance and Allied Services*, Cmd 6404, London: HMSO.

Brown, G. (2008) Speech on the NHS, 7 January, www.number10.gov.uk/Page14171

Devlin, K. (2008) 'Patient survey rates NHS worse than Estonia', *The Daily Telegraph*, 14 November, p 18.

DH (Department of Health) (1992) *The Health of the Nation*, London: HMSO.

DH (1998) *Our Healthier Nation*, London: The Stationery Office.

DH (1999) *Saving Lives*, London: The Stationery Office.

DH (2000) *The NHS Plan*, London: The Stationery Office.

DH (2004) *Choosing Health: Making Healthy Choices Easier*, London: The Stationery Office.

DH (2005) *Health Reform in England: Update and Next Steps*, London: DH.

DH (2006) *Our Health, Our Care, Our Say: A New Direction for Community Services*, London: The Stationery Office.

DH (2007a) *The Operating Framework for the NHS in England 2008/09*, London: DH.

DH (2007b) *World Class Commissioning: Competencies*, London: DH.

DH (2007c) *Our NHS Our Future: NHS Next Stage Review – Interim Report*, London: DH.

DH (2007d) *Tackling Health Inequalities: 2007 Status Report on the Programme for Action*, London: DH.

DH (2007e) *Tackling Health Inequalities: 2004–06 Data and Policy Update for the 2010 Target*, London: DH.

DH (2007f) *Key NHS Interventions to Support the Achievements of the National Health Service Health Inequalities Target*, London: DH.

DH (2007g) *Commissioning Framework for Health and Wellbeing*, London: DH.

DH (2008a) *High Quality Care For All* (final Darzi report), Cm 7432, London: The Stationery Office.

DH (2008b) *Report of National Patient Choice Survey July 2008 and Provisional Headline Figures for September 2008*, London: DH.

DH (2008c) *Personalisation*, London: DH, www.dh.gov.uk/en/SocialCare/Socialcarereform/personalisation/index/htm

DH (2008d) *Real Involvement*, London: DH.

DH (2008e) *The NHS Constitution*, London: DH.

DH (2008f) *Commissioning Assurance Handbook*, London: DH.

DH (2008g) *Achieving the Competencies: Practical Tips for NHS Commissioners*, London: DH.

DH (2008h) *Practice Board Commissioning GP Survey: Waves 1-5 Results (December 2008)*, London: DH.

DH (2008i) *Developing the NHS Performance Regime*, London: DH.

DH (2008j) *Improving Access to Medicines for NHS Patients: A Report for the Secretary of State for Health by Professor Mike Richards*, London: DH.

DH (2008k) *Smoke Free England – One Year On*, London: DH.

DH (2008l) *Health Inequalities: Progress and Next Steps*, London: DH.

DH (2008m) *Autumn Performance Report 2008*, London: DH.

DH (2008n) *Sixty Years of the National Health Service: A Proud Past and a Healthy Future*, London: DH.

DHSS (Department of Health and Social Security) (1976) *Prevention and Health*, London: HMSO.

Fox, D. (1986) *Health Policies, Health Politics*, Princeton, NJ: Princeton University Press.

Fraser, D. (2003) *The Evolution of the British Welfare State* (3rd edition), Basingstoke: Palgrave Macmillan.

Giddens, A. (1998) *The Third Way*, Cambridge: Polity Press.

Glendinning, C., Challis, D., Fernandez, J., Jacobs, S., Jones, K., Knapp, M., Manthorpe, J., Moran, N., Netten, A., Stevens, M. and Wilberforce, M.L. (2008) *Evaluation of the Individual Budgets Pilot Programme: Final Report*, IBSEN (Individual Budgets Evaluation Network), York: University of York.

Greener, I. (2009) *Healthcare in the UK*, Bristol: The Policy Press.

Greener, I. and Mannion, R. (2006) 'Does practice based commissioning avoid the problems of fundholding?', *British Medical Journal*, vol 333, no 7579, pp 1168-70.

Greener, I. and Powell, M. (2008) 'The changing governance of the NHS: reform in a post-Keynesian health service', *Human Relations*, vol 61, no 5, pp 617-36.

Greener, I. and Powell, M. (2009) 'The evolution of choice policies in UK housing, education and health policy', *Journal of Social Policy*, vol 38, no 1, pp 63-81.

Greer, S. and Rowland, D. (eds) (2007) *Devolving Policy, Diverging Values? The Values of the UK's Health Services*, London: Nuffield Trust.

Greer, S. and Trench, A. (2008) *Health and Intergovernmental Relations in the Devolved United Kingdom*, London: Nuffield Trust.

Harrison, S. and McDonald, R. (2008) *The Politics of Healthcare in Britain*, London: Sage Publications.

Hatton, C., Waters, J., Duffy, S., Senker, J., Crosby, N., Poll, C., Tyson, A., O'Brien, J. and Towell, D. (2008) *A Report on In Control's Second Phase*, London: In Control.

HCC (Healthcare Commission) (2007) *Investigation into the Outbreaks of Clostridium difficile at Maidstone and Tunbridge Wells NHS Trust*, London: HCC.

HCC (2008) *The Annual Health Check 2007/08*, London: HCC.

House of Commons Health Select Committee (2006) *Independent Sector Treatment Centres*, HC 934-1, London: The Stationery Office.

House of Commons Health Select Committee (2008) *Foundation Trusts and Monitor*, HC 833-1, London: The Stationery Office.

Hunter, D. (2003) *Public Health Policy*, Cambridge: Polity Press.

Hunter, D. (2008) *The Health Debate*, Bristol: The Policy Press.

Jervis, P. (2008) *Devolution and Health*, London: Nuffield Trust.

Johnson, A. (2008) 'Health inequalities', Speech at the IPPR, 9 June, www.dh.gov.uk/en/News/Speeches?DH_085336

Klein, R. (2004) 'Transforming the NHS', in M. Powell, L. Bauld and K. Clarke (eds) *Social Policy Review 17*, Bristol: The Policy Press, pp 51-68.

Klein, R. (2006) *The New Politics of the NHS* (5th edition), Oxford: Radcliffe Medical.

Le Fanu, J. (2000) *The Rise and Fall of Modern Medicine*, London: Abacus.

Le Grand, J. (2007) *The Other Invisible Hand*, Princeton, NJ: Princeton University Press.

Leatherman, S. and Sutherland, K. (2008) *The Quest for Quality: Refining the NHS Reforms*, London: Nuffield Trust.

Lister, J. (2008) *The NHS after 60: For Patients or Profits?*, London: Middlesex University Press.

Ministry of Health (1944) *A National Health Service*, London: HMSO.

MIS (Medical Information Systems) (2008) *NHS 60: The NHS 60th Anniversary Edition*, London: MIS.

PASC (Public Administration Select Committee) (2008) *User Involvement in Public Services*, HC 410, London: The Stationery Office.

Powell, M. and Greener, I. (2009) 'The healthcare consumer', in R. Simmons, M. Powell and I. Greener (eds) *The Public Service Consumer*, Bristol: The Policy Press.

Royal Commission on the NHS (1979) *Report* (Chair: Sir A. Merrison), London: HMSO.

Scrivens, E. (1991) 'Disease', *Social Policy and Administration*, vol 25, no 1, pp 27-38.

Stevens, S. (2008) 'Opinion', *Health Service Journal*, 10 July.

Timmins, N. (2001) *The Five Giants* (2nd edition), London: HarperCollins.

Timmins, N. (ed) (2008) *Rejuvenate or Retire? Views of the NHS at 60*, London: Nuffield Trust.

Wanless, D. (2002) *Securing Our Future Health*, London: HM Treasury.

Wanless, D. (2004) *Securing Good Health for the Whole Population*, London: HM Treasury.

Wanless, D., Appleby, J., Harrison, A. and Patelet, D. (2007) *Our Future Health Secured?*, London: King's Fund.

# FIVE

# Tackling squalor? Housing's contribution to the welfare state

*Douglas Robertson and James Smyth*

## Introduction

This chapter offers a long-term perspective on the role played by council housing in tackling the 'social evil' of squalor within Scotland. By the mid-1970s, public sector housing – encompassing council, new town and Scottish Special Housing Association property – accommodated fully two thirds of the Scottish population (Gibb, 1989). The proportion of the population housed by the public sector in England, by contrast, was markedly less at just one third (Ravetz, 2001). So public housing in Scotland was on a markedly different scale, with a state housing sector comparable to many countries in the-then 'Eastern Bloc'. Scotland consequently provides the ideal locus to explore the contribution that council housing has made to the post-war welfare state over the last 60 years. But given that the state's role in housing provision pre-dates other welfare state developments, the longer timeframe of this intervention demands proper consideration since it established the immediate post-war ambitions for housing policy. Further, adopting this longer timeframe adds a new dimension to current debates, which see the rapid retreat from the ambitions of the welfare state solely as a response to an overt privatisation agenda, best encapsulated by the Conservatives' 'Right to Buy' legislation of the 1980s. What this chapter argues is that state housing intervention was never primarily focused on eradicating squalor, but rather on housing 'respectable' working-class families. Given the resultant population profile of those accommodated in council housing by the mid-1970s, it was broader societal changes and associated social policy interventions, rather than just privatisation per se, that ensured that private and individual housing responses triumphed over post-war public welfare universalism; thus, the rapid demise of council housing as a mass housing solution. Today, by contrast, council housing provides for the poor and marginalised, a situation that closely fits the dominant pre-1914 conception of who should be accommodated by local authorities. Only through having to respond to the consequences of broader social changes did council housing eventually address squalor. Throughout the chapter empirical material from both Glasgow, as Scotland's largest city, and Stirling, more typical of a smaller town, is drawn on to illustrate the local impacts of national policy.

## Welfare state housing post-1945

Immediately after the Second World War, the Labour government made a commitment to build new council housing, given this was a core part of national reconstruction plans. However, due to a balance of payments crisis, repayment of war debts to the United States, colonial conflicts in Malaysia and East Africa and then the Korean War, housing plans in the immediate post-war period were put on hold (Merrett, 1979). It was not until 1951, when the Conservatives came into office, that housing received significant attention. The prime focus was on tackling overcrowding, which had been exacerbated by the lack of house building during the war years, the 'Blitz Bombings' and what transpired to be a significant and sustained post-war baby boom.

The catalyst for action in Scotland was the 1951 Census, which starkly revealed appalling overcrowding rates. Glasgow in particular stood out, with half the city's houses being either of one or two rooms and almost a quarter of the population living at densities greater than two people per room. Population densities for equivalent English cities, such as Birmingham and Manchester, stood at 48 and 77 people per acre respectively; the Glasgow figure was 163 (Robertson, 1997). Over 90,000 families were registered on Glasgow Corporation's housing list.

The city's severe housing problem ensured that it became the focus for Scottish housing policy. This led to the mass construction of new more spacious family housing, through the construction of large peripheral housing estates composed of standardised four-storey walk-up tenements. Resolving Glasgow's squalid slum conditions was to be left to a later date. In order to increase the output of council houses, the-then British Housing Minister, Harold Macmillan, decided to cut the overall specification. Hence, in Scotland, flats were preferred over houses. However, the Conservatives were the first, if not the only, UK government to meet their stated construction targets of 300,000 starts (new housing) per year (Merrett, 1979).

The move to cheap utilitarian family accommodation had been predicted, and argued against by the influential Scottish Housing Advisory Committee (SHAC, 1944). Its report set down expectations for new family housing. It also contained a strongly worded minority report, written by Jean Mann, a leading light of the Town and Country Planning Association and later Glasgow housing committee convenor. Mann argued for the adoption of 'Garden City' design principles, challenging the report's view that the modern European flat provided acceptable accommodation. In the minds of most Scots at that time, flats equated to slums. This perception had been reinforced by the construction of utilitarian three- and four-storey walk-up 'slum clearance' tenements under the short-lived 1935 Housing Act. Such developments were considered a marked retrenchment from the design and build standards achieved under earlier Housing Acts (Reiach and Hurd, 1945). Early council housing estates, such as Stirling's Riverside, were considered exemplars, whereas the subsequent 1930s developments such as Raploch were thought of as poor and grudging by comparison. So although the immediate post-war Stirling estates of Cornton, Cultenhove and St Ninians were modern flats, they represented the continuation of the much-criticised tenement tradition, rather than providing individual family houses with gardens.

In addition to planning for new housing construction, the Scottish Housing Advisory Committee (SHAC) also examined the possibility of improving older property as a means of helping alleviate shortages. The resulting report predicted the persistence of unacceptable slum conditions and argued that more properties would become slums unless modernisation work was undertaken on better-quality older property (SHAC, 1946). Councils, however, were not keen on providing public monies to improve property owned by private landlords, when the same cash could be used to build new council houses, which they would both own and manage (Robertson, 1992).

So the focus throughout the immediate post-war period was on providing new family accommodation for 'respectable' working-class families. This was also the key group housed by the two other public bodies involved in providing housing – the five New Town Corporations and the state housing agency, the Scottish Special Housing Association. As these bodies focused on providing housing in support of state-sponsored economic restructuring, it was only skilled workers and their families who were housed, not slum dwellers (Robertson, 2001). Given the economic profile of such tenants, the rent charged was higher than equivalent council properties so the quality of the housing provided was higher (Rodger and Al-Qaddo, 1989). Both these bodies were therefore used by government to be exemplars of good design and thus encourage higher standards in council housing.

## Refocusing on slums

With family overcrowding well on the way to being addressed nationally and private sector house builders now significantly increasing their output, only then did housing policy specifically address the slum problem. In 1965, despite the massive council house-building efforts of the 1950s and early 1960s, one third of Glasgow's housing stock remained either one- or two-roomed flats: 40% had no fixed bath or shower, 20% had no internal WC and 40% had no hot-water supply. Moreover, Glasgow still had a very high overcrowding level (more than 1.5 people per room) at 34%, compared with Birmingham and Manchester at 11% and 6% respectively (SHAC, 1968).

As a means of addressing this, Glasgow instigated a major renewal plan eight years earlier, which involved tearing down and redeveloping one third of the entire city (Corporation of the City of Glasgow, 1957). The destruction of the tenements now took on a political imperative, given that they symbolised squalor, poverty and exploitation (Robertson, 1992). Ensuring their replacement by new, clean, warm and dry council houses for working-class families had long been a deeply held political ambition of the city's Labour politicians. However, due to 'green belt' planning restrictions, all new housing was required to be accommodated within the city boundaries through a massive programme of high-density development and, to a lesser degree, via overspill to new and existing towns (Robertson, 2005). Under this latest phase of council house construction, an estimated 25,000 dwellings were built between 1965 and 1970, of which all but 600 were in public ownership. Only now were the slums being systematically cleared to be replaced by high-rise and system-built developments.

## Who was public housing to be for?

Labour's focus on housing the 'respectable' working class can be traced back to the pre-1914 period. In the years before the Great War, housing became a major political issue in Scotland, as the fledgling Labour Party campaigned for local authorities to construct cottage-type properties for 'respectable' working-class families. However, this remained very much a minority viewpoint. The predominant Liberal perspective was that the housing problem was primarily about how to house the poor, who resided in truly squalid conditions, rather than skilled artisans (Smyth, 2000).

Scottish housing was then renowned for its poor condition and severe overcrowding, when compared to England (Rodger, 1989; O'Carroll, 1996). Rapid growth in the early to mid part of the 19th century had created tremendous strains on the existing stock of urban housing. As more and more migrants flooded into the towns and cities, they were accommodated largely through subdividing existing property, rather than building more. The economic upturn from the 1860s onwards produced waves of new tenement construction, a building form favoured because of Scotland's feudal land ownership system, associated longstanding building traditions and the rating system (O'Carroll, 1996). With the scale of construction, the housing problem appeared to resolve itself. The working classes then found themselves being criticised for not being prepared to spend a similar proportion of their income on rent as the middle classes. Further, gaining access to larger properties was thought to make matters worse by encouraging an ingrained tendency to take in lodgers (Census of Scotland, 1871).

Despite substantial evidence to the contrary, the Royal Commission on the Housing of the Working Classes, which collected its evidence between 1884 and 1885, reported that there was no great problem with housing in Scotland (Rodger, 1989). This conclusion partly emanated from the perceived lack of tenant opposition to poor, unsanitary and squalid conditions. The main complaint of tenants prior to 1914 was with the letting system, which demanded yearly contracts, with 15-month commitments, quarterly payments of rent and annual payment of rates (Rodger, 1989). Nonetheless, the desperately poor condition of so much working-class housing could not be ignored given the direct connection between poor housing conditions, illness and mortality (Chalmers, 1930).

Scotland's largest city, Glasgow, became the main focal point for political tension over housing. Major contributions to reform were made by the Church of Scotland and Glasgow Corporation, both of which established Commissions to examine the Housing of the Poor in 1891 and 1902 respectively. The very titles of these Commissions illustrate the shift in emphasis. Where previous concerns had been with the working class generally and specifically the skilled male worker, the focus was now exclusively on the poor. The rationale behind this was twofold: first, as already mentioned, the large number of new tenements that had been recently constructed and, second, the rise in wage rates over the same period, which was calculated to have outstripped rent increases (Glasgow Municipal Commission on the Housing of the Poor, 1904).

At the same time, the Glasgow Municipal Commission recognised that for those workers earning less than £1 per week, it was very difficult to find suitable affordable accommodation. Such workers included male labourers and also most women workers, many of whom earned just seven or eight shillings per week. In addition, the Glasgow Municipal Commission noted that there was a 'large class of poor people who are more or less ineffective, lacking, that is to say, physical, mental, or moral capacity' whose needs were as much to do with being instructed in general cleanliness, as they were with the inability to pay rent (Glasgow Municipal Commission on the Housing of the Poor, 1904, pp 18-19).

While the two inquiries did graphically detail the unsanitary horrors of Glasgow housing, their recommendations still emphasised that it was the responsibility of the poor to address their own situation, and the need for them to change their habits. For instance, a Presbytery of Glasgow report commented that overcrowding was 'not only detrimental to health but to morals', but in the same sentence declared that 'landlords are absolutely blameless' (Presbytery of Glasgow, 1891, p 15).

For its part, the Glasgow Municipal Commission recommended further demolition of unsanitary housing, while accepting an obligation to build replacement accommodation. Given its concern about social distinction, two types of replacement housing were recommended: for the decent or respectable people of the 'poorest class', one- and two-apartment tenement flats under the management of caretakers; for the better section of the second class, an experiment was proposed aimed at those 'who are willing to submit to necessary regulations ... with the view of rehabilitating their characters, and in time qualifying for a better house'. These houses were to be designed by the City Engineer and 'should be of the plainest construction, with indestructible fittings, and should be capable of being quickly and efficiently cleansed' (Glasgow Municipal Commission on the Housing of the Poor, 1904, p 22).

Glasgow's Labour Party was staunchly opposed to such an approach: houses should not be built for the improvident poor but for the 'thrifty, industrious and sober working classes' (Glasgow Municipal Commission on the Housing of the Poor, 1904, p 550). Moreover, Labour was increasingly influenced by the English 'Garden City' movement and called for cottage-style family housing rather than tenements. Thus, John Wheatley, future Housing Minister of the 1920s, called for Glasgow to build its own workers' cottages and let them to families at a rent of £8 per annum (Wheatley, 1913). Wheatley's vision represented a quantum leap forward in working-class housing: spacious family homes comprising four apartments plus kitchen and bathroom, with front and back gardens. These were not the houses the Glasgow Municipal Commission on the Housing of the Poor sought to build, and were for an entirely different social stratum. Put simply, there was no room in Wheatley's plans for the inhabitants of squalid slums (Smyth, 2000).

## Triumph of 'respectablity'

With the establishment of a Royal Commission to examine the housing of the industrial classes (rural and urban) in Scotland shortly before the First World War, Labour's vision became more influential. The operations of the Commission, the most detailed examination of housing conditions ever undertaken within the UK, had been suspended due to the war, but reactivated in 1917. The already desperately bad conditions revealed by the evidence collected before 1914 had worsened due to the inactivity and war disruption. Scottish housing was shown to be in quite an appalling condition in respect of fabric, amenities and size. In 1911, 7.1% of England's stock was one or two rooms; the figure for Scotland was 53.2%. Overcrowding displayed a similar disparity at 9.1% in England and 45.1% in Scotland. Across Scotland, the Commission found 'unsatisfactory sites of houses and villages, ... gross overcrowding and huddling of the sexes together in congested industrial villages and towns, occupation of one-room houses by large families, ... clotted masses of slums in the great cities' (Royal Commission, 1917, p 364).

The Commission's report was published at a time when attention was being focused on post-war reconstruction, and was followed shortly after by the highly influential Tudor Walter Committee Report (Local Government Boards for England and Wales and Scotland, 1918) covering all of the UK, later described as the 'bible' for council housing (Ravetz, 2001). The Commission concluded that private enterprise had completely failed 'to provide anything like a sufficiency of houses, and that in particular they had failed to provide houses of a reasonable standard of accommodation and habitability' (Royal Commission, 1917, p 292). Thus, the majority of the Commission embraced the need for council housing, and rejected the long-held Liberal position on housing reform.

As the immediate fears of political unrest and revolution gave way in the 1920s to disillusion and mass unemployment, retrenchment rather than reform became the order of the day. Nonetheless, the promise of reconstruction could not be totally negated. The Coalition government had won the December 1918 General Election on the promise of better housing, so something tangible had to be offered to the nation and most pressingly to the millions of returning ex-servicemen. The Glasgow Rent Strikes of 1915 had revealed just how combustible housing could be as a political issue, and it was now perceived as the main bulwark against revolution (Melling, 1983).

The resulting commitment to build council houses was expressed nationally in the 1919 Housing and Town Planning Act, and in Scotland via accompanying separate Scottish legislation (Addison, 1922). It is difficult even now to fully gauge the significance of this legislation. Although few houses were built under the legislation, those that were have remained among the very best council houses ever constructed. In addition, the legislation did represent the first, pioneering step into council housing: the notion of publicly owned housing had become a reality.

The quality of the houses built under the 1919 Act partly reflects the idealism of the time: an attempt to make a general reality of the utopianism enthused by the 'Garden City' movement (Ravetz, 2001). Such idealism did not last long, with the building programme effectively abandoned in 1921 and, thereafter, the Conservatives promoted their traditional policy of supporting private building (Addison, 1922). The financing of council housing was achieved through offering local authorities a rent subsidy, and not via the central state acting as loan guarantor. Yet in spite of the Conservatives' stated intentions, their own legislation, the 1923 Housing Act, continued state support for local authorities, albeit at a reduced rate, which resulted in lower-specification houses. This legislation was superseded by the incoming Labour government's 1924 Wheatley Act, which increased the rental subsidy, but did not lead to a reinstatement of the high quality of building and design that emanated from the original 1919 Act. In terms of scale, however, the 1924 Act was the most effective of all inter-war housing legislation, resulting in over half a million new houses (Melling, 1989).

The intended inhabitants for all these early council houses were 'respectable' working-class families, exactly the social group that Labour had championed prior to the war. Archive work undertaken into initial allocations in Stirling's Riverside estate, built under the 1919 Act – one of Scotland's very first council house developments – revealed that most tenants were skilled manual workers, foremen, some managerial grades and a few other white-collar workers including salesmen and teachers. There were also a small number of unskilled workers. The dominance of the working-class family was indicated by the fact that of the initial

52 households only three were headed by women, two of whom were unmarried teachers (Robertson et al, 2008). This evidence challenges some of the urban myths that were spread about the class status of initial tenants; in Glasgow there were reports that middle-class, white-collar workers, even professional people with servants, had secured these desirable properties (Morgan, 1989).

While much of the political power of the various investigations into housing had emanated from descriptions of the most squalid of housing conditions, the needs of the slum dwellers – the poorest, most marginalised and most vulnerable group within society – were ignored. The acting assumption held at that time was that their conditions would improve through 'filtering up', a process whereby the houses vacated by the better off would eventually be taken by the less well off. Unfortunately, such an assumption failed to take account of the reality of life for unskilled and irregularly employed workers.

## Focusing on squalor

Ignoring the squalid slums could not last, however. In the face of persistently high levels of unemployment, the shortlived Labour governments of the inter-war period sought to prove their fitness to govern through maintaining strict fiscal orthodoxy until overwhelmed by the Depression. The new so-called National Government with, in effect, a massive Conservative majority, further embraced retrenchment and in 1933 completely stopped the rent subsidy introduced by the 1924 Act. It did not, however, abandon council housing. Rather the emphasis switched from general needs, housing the 'respectable' working classes, towards a targeted programme of slum clearance. This has usually been interpreted as a marked change in policy, although contemporary studies tended to identify more continuities (Bowley, 1945).

Up to 1934, of the houses built in Scotland, the great majority – 84% – were constructed using subsidy, including the 61% provided by local authorities. The equivalent figures for England were 49% and 31% respectively (Bowley, 1945). The greater use of subsidy was put down to Scottish local authorities' interpretation of the term 'working class in no narrow sense' (Department of Health for Scotland, 1932). As a result, a more middle-class population was being housed, in larger properties, which in turn depressed demand for private housing. Later changes in subsidy arrangements increased the output of houses, but these were built to a far lower standard, thus ensuring that this housing could at long last rehouse slum families.

The first piece of legislation directing local authorities to clear slums was introduced by Labour in 1930, under the Greenwood Act, although this was intended to complement rather than replace the 1924 Act (Ravetz, 2001). This Act demanded that local authorities carry out a slum survey to assess future demand. Evidence from Stirling indicates that to reduce such future commitments only a small proportion of potential slum properties were actually recorded (Robertson et al, 2008). By 1938, Scottish authorities had closed or demolished 55,000 of the 63,000 identified slums, building 40,000 replacement houses, plus another 27,000 that were not specifically tied to the slum programme (Bowley, 1945).

To achieve such growth in output, as mentioned earlier, standards fell. Authorities found themselves in a 'Catch 22' situation, in that to bring rents within the range of most slum families, replacement housing needed to be smaller with poorer amenities. The Department of Health for Scotland would not allow construction below certain minimum standards, but economics forced it to concede, as evidenced by its concerns about the standards proposed in Stirling's Raploch estate, built to house families from the medieval slum, the 'Tap o'Toun' (Robertson et al, 2008). By 1938, only 28% of new council houses had more than three rooms, 61% three rooms and 11% had less, usually two (Department of Health for Scotland, 1938).

Where smaller houses were permitted, while this solved one problem – housing quality – another – severe overcrowding – was never addressed. Again, this is recorded in Stirling, where there was strong public criticism of the council for lowering space and quality standards, drawing the accusation that in Raploch its actions were creating future slums (*The Scotsman*, 8 June 1933). As a consequence of growing health concerns about overcrowding and, in particular, tuberculosis, a further Housing Act was introduced in 1935, the driver here being the persistence of sanitary and health problems caused by overcrowded slum accommodation (Bowley, 1945).

So by the end of the 1930s, council housing was firmly part of Britain's social fabric, being already part of the welfare state. In England and Wales, almost four million houses were built between 1919 and 1939, with just over one million of these being council houses (Ravetz, 2001, p 89). Whereas in England and Wales, 28% of all houses constructed were by the local authorities, and 72% by private enterprise, in Scotland the respective figures were reversed, at 70% and 30% (Rodger, 1989). In all of urban Scotland, only Edinburgh had a preponderance of privately built new homes (O'Carroll, 1996). In Stirling, a relatively wealthy burgh, out of a total of 1,772 houses built between 1929 and 1939, only 115 were by private builders (SHAC, 1943–44). As elsewhere in Scotland, council housing was already well on its way to becoming the predominant housing tenure. Yet, for those who resided in the poorest and most squalid conditions, council housing still largely eluded them. The slum clearance programme had arrived late in the day, and then was curtailed by the war. Tackling overcrowding was also not much of a success given that, if anything, the 1930s council houses merely added to that problem. Properly addressing overcrowding had to wait until the immediate post-war years, by which time the scale of the problem had expanded massively, again ensuring that slum clearance waited decades before it was finally revived. The plans of the welfare state did include the eradication of squalor, but the approach adopted mirrored that of the preceding war years. The focus was on housing the 'respectable' working-class family first and foremost. It was not housing policy per se that lifted the poor out of the slums, rather it was the rejection of council housing by the 'respectable' working class that facilitated the entry of the slum dwellers.

## Demise of council housing

The 1967 monetary crisis, which resulted in the devaluation of the pound and immediate cutbacks in public expenditure, put council housing directly in the firing line (Merrett, 1979). This was the catalyst that brought about the rapid switch from recently revived slum clearance programmes and associated construction of new council houses, to an individualised private home improvement policy. The government chose to portray this switch as a reaction to aesthetic and community concerns about new high-density developments, rather than the inevitable consequence of a major public finance crisis (Dunleavy, 1991; Harloe, 2004a). The 'number game' that had so long characterised housing policy, first in dealing with overcrowding and only latterly for slums, was over. Now, national housing policy would encourage individual home owners, who resided in what had previously been deemed slums, to improve them through the provision of generous improvement grants.

There was another dimension to this change of emphasis. Within England, there had been deep-seated concerns that clearance schemes would start encroaching on what were then termed 'twilight areas', which housed significant minority ethnic populations (Rex and Moore, 1968). Rehousing obligations would have ensured that minority ethnic groups would gain access to new council housing in large numbers for the first time. Given that this was at the same time as Enoch Powell's infamous 'rivers of blood' speech, such a prospect was highly contentious: so the switch in housing policy was welcome.

Such districts were also the locus of a good number of individuals long debarred from accessing council housing, because they did not constitute the traditional nuclear family. Rather, they were single working-age people sharing accommodation, cohabiting couples or those who were considered to be in odd or peculiar family structures. Many of these people had purchased slum property as the only means of securing accommodation. The prospect of imminent clearance had not been in their interest, given that they would receive limited compensation and had no direct right to be rehoused by the local authority. A statutory right to be rehoused, as a result of clearance activities, was not implemented until the 1974 Housing (Scotland) Act.

So although by 1975 council housing had become the dominant provider of family accommodation in Scotland, the whole raison d'être of council housing was about to be questioned. This would see council housing having to adapt to what was a rapidly changing society, and through this allow the squalid slum dwellers, at long last, access to this housing stock.

### Changing demand

Major demographic changes, increasing affluence, rising divorce rates, a weakening of religious mores in relation to family life, plus the influx of minority ethnic groups had a dramatic impact on who was housed within council housing. Between 1911 and 1981, lower birth rates and increased life expectancy, especially among women, brought about a threefold increase in the proportion of people aged 65 and over, while the proportion of children under 15 fell by one third (Ravetz with Turkington, 1995). In 1900, marriages with five or six surviving children were common: by the mid-1930s, under two children had become the norm. In spite of the baby boom of the early 1950s through to 1964, family size continued to fall, sustained by effective contraception.

Another critical factor in explaining these demographic changes was increasing household affluence, in large part explained by increasing female participation in the labour market. The sole 'breadwinner' of the immediate post-war era soon gave way to the 'joint-income household'. This again partly relates to the enhanced control of fertility. It also bears witness to a rapidly expanding labour market, in which female employment became critical. Whereas only 10% of married women were in paid employment in 1931, by the mid–1980s the figure had risen to over 50%.

In addition, there was growing affluence among young people. Whereas in the past they would continue living in the family home until married, increasingly the young set up home on their own, or at least initially with friends. This change put further pressure on the housing system, but until quite recently local authorities resisted housing them. By the 1960s, home ownership had become increasingly accessible to those in secure employment, causing a sustained exodus out of council housing by wealthier tenants. The difficulties in accessing council housing also encouraged young people to pursue a quite different housing career from their parents.

An increasing divorce rate saw women with children become a growing proportion of the population and they quickly became identified as a vulnerable group who needed priority rehousing. This major social change coincided with the decline of the institution of marriage, with substantial numbers of couples opting to cohabit. As a result of the interplay of all these changing demand factors, and with no new supply being added, the council house population steadily altered. With demand from traditional working-class families falling away, other groups started to gain access.

## Allocations

Until the late 1970s, housing management was in its infancy, but quickly became professionalised, bringing with it a belief that local authorities needed to adopt 'needs-based' allocations systems. Thus, long-established local discriminatory allocations practices slowly started to fall away.

Allocations had always been highly political, with local councillors able to influence which particular families would gain access to council housing within their wards. Even if national policies had been more liberal at that time, it is unlikely that non-family groups would have been able to gain access to it. Two official reports into local authority housing allocations practices changed that by raising serious concerns about who was gaining access (SHAC, 1967; Cullingworth, 1969). The basic premise was that given that such housing was a public asset, should not every citizen have equal access to it? Both reports argued the need for councils to develop 'needs-based' systems to ensure that a degree of equity was introduced into the process. Although it took nearly two decades for these recommendations to work themselves through, slowly but surely council housing was opened up to a broader range of clients.

Local authorities' allocation policies, as illustrated above, had always been almost exclusively family focused, reflecting both local and national political priorities. The only non-family group that had received some limited attention were older single women, again reflecting longstanding prejudices about who were 'deserving' cases. Spinster accommodation, for example, had been provided after both world wars, given the number of war widows.

## New groups

Probably the most significant piece of legislation in altering access to council housing was the 1977 Housing (Homeless Persons) Scotland Act. This introduced a statutory duty on local authorities to house homeless families. Local authorities were, in the main, highly resistant to implementing this legislation and used the legal categorisation of whether those presenting as homeless were 'intentionally' rather than 'unintentionally' homeless as a convenient means of denying access (Anderson, 2007). Further, when the homeless were housed it was only in the poorest parts of their stock, thus exaggerating existing social polarisation. Through sustained pressure from homeless pressure groups, further statutory rights for the homeless were added and, eventually, local authorities found it difficult to avoid their responsibilities (Anderson, 2007). The focus on families also altered over time, and thus more single people were housed through these procedures.

One significant piece of legislation in this regard was the 1982 Matrimonial Homes Act, which introduced a statutory duty on local authorities to house both parties in the event of marital breakdown. As this demanded the rehousing of single people, often with child access issues, the provision of a one-bedroom property to the father was insufficient. With this group of single people now gaining access, it became difficult to deny other single people.

Further, as traditional demand fell away, local authorities became desperate to fill vacant accommodation, thus maximising income. Migrant groups from ex-colonial countries eventually started to gain access to council housing, helped by the 1968 Race Relations Act, which outlawed discrimination on grounds of race.

### Rent subsidies

Ensuring access to council housing was all well and good, but whether new tenants could pay the rent was another matter entirely. The introduction of an integrated rent and rates rebate scheme – Housing Benefit – in 1982, represented another marked change in social policy. There had long been a public debate on how council housing should be subsidised. The Left's position was that council housing should be available to all – a subsidised social service – one of 'the pillars of the welfare state' (Malpass, 2005). The Right took the opposing view, challenging indiscriminate state provision. Rather, as a last resort, subsidies should only be made available to those who could not be provided for by the market. After initially trying, and failing, to get all council rents onto a market basis in the early 1970s, the Conservatives set about transferring public subsidy away from the dwelling and the provider of that housing, the council, to the consumer, the individual tenant.

Housing Benefit brought together the previous rent and rates relief arrangements into a single unified system (Kemp, 1985). Rent relief had a long history going back to the Poor Laws, whereby assistance for the poor was again derived through popular notions of who were 'deserving' and who were not. The 'undeserving' received the minimum of help and were forced to earn their keep in the Poor House (or Workhouse in England), whereas the 'deserving' received charity, albeit somewhat grudgingly (Ferguson, 1948). With the introduction of Housing Benefit, that culture altered, in that the full cost of rented housing was paid but only where the applicant met strict means-test requirements. Steep eligibility tapers ensured that those with a limited earned income quickly paid the full costs of their housing.

Throughout the 1980s, rents rose steeply due to the combined effects of subsidy shifts and inflation. Add to this high unemployment, a result of the 1980s' recession, and council housing quickly found itself with an ever-increasing welfare benefit-dependent population. Over time, fewer and fewer tenants paid rent directly from their earned income: the majority became totally reliant on Housing Benefit. Ironically, paying rent for those in low-paid employment became an increasingly expensive housing choice, which encouraged them to look to other housing options.

## Changing priorities and providers

Those long marginalised from council housing had sought housing either in the private market, via renting or 'cheaper-end' purchase, or via charities. Housing associations, traditionally charities, had long tried to house such excluded groups – single working people, physically disabled people, people with learning difficulties and older people. Previously, such groups had been housed in various institutions. Single people, for example, who were not able to stay with relatives or friends were housed in lodging houses or hostels. Although councils had, over the years, engaged in a series of tokenistic housing programmes for single women, with the marked rise in the older population from the late 1960s, sheltered housing projects emerged (Ravetz with Turkington, 1995; Ravetz, 2001). Given that older people corresponded to long-held notions of what constituted the 'deserving poor', they were politically safe to house, albeit in small and often basic accommodation. Housing other special needs groups represented an entirely different proposition, as council officials and councillors, in fearing a tenant backlash, simply refused them.

As councils were viewed as being incapable, unable or unwilling to respond to the needs of such groups, government saw housing associations as the best vehicle for new 'special needs' housing investment. From the 1960s onwards, money was very limited. However, with the 1974 Housing Act, government decided to promote associations as their key vehicles for all future capital housing investment. Local authorities could continue to make a contribution, but they were seen not to need capital investment given that they had a large housing stock that could be used to 'pool' resources if they wanted to develop new housing.

Another legislative change, the introduction of 'care in the community', encouraged the rapid closure of Victorian institutions that had traditionally housed a range of 'special needs' groups. The residents of these institutions required to be rehoused, often in purpose-built accommodation that had appropriate locally based support services. Again associations were key to implementing this ambition, and again these changes reflected broader social changes within society that demanded equality of treatment to all and, therefore, housing services were required to respond.

Within Scotland, as well as associations dealing with single people, disabled people and older people, there emerged new community-based housing associations that specifically focused on dealing with the remnants of the slum clearance programme (Robertson and Bailey, 1996;

Robertson, 1997). Overall, changing social mores saw once-excluded groups being regarded as a priority for new housing investment and, more critically, over time, local authorities were encouraged to respond to their needs by opening up their housing to them.

## Privatisation

The 'Right to Buy' was the Conservatives' flagship privatisation policy. They had long held the view that many of those in council housing were well able to house themselves and had noted that more and more people were buying their own homes. While wealthier tenants had started to move out of council housing and buy their own homes, this was not feasible for those on lower incomes. The Right to Buy changed that. Deep discounting of up to 70% of market value – depending on the type of property and the number of years of tenancy – overnight brought home ownership within the reach of a large numbers of tenants. As rents continued to rise, for those not on benefits, it made economic sense to buy their home.

Labour quickly overcame its initial ideological resistance to the Right to Buy. In fact, Labour had toyed with introducing a similar policy in the mid-1960s (Pimlott, 1992). Both Labour and the Conservatives concurred with the political ambition of creating a property-owning democracy. This immediately 'relegated council housing to the position of second "estate": a complementary but inevitably inferior tenure' (Ravetz with Turkington, 1995, p 64).

Mortgage finance also became easier to secure because of a liberalised mortgage market. Under the 1986 Building Societies Act, banks were encouraged to compete with building societies for this new lending business. One of the Act's stated ambitions was to force lending downmarket, thus encouraging take-up of the Right to Buy. Since 1980, over two million council houses in the UK have been sold (Bramley et al, 2004), and the figure for Scotland alone is now 454,000 dwellings (Scottish Executive, 2006). Given the past focus of council housing on the 'respectable' working class, it is easy to understand its popularity. Within Stirling this has meant that all but four houses of the popular Riverside estate have been sold, but the Right to Buy never took hold in the unpopular and stigmatised Raploch. Sales thus acted to further socially polarise council housing.

## Conclusion

The historical significance of council housing in Scotland is popularly assumed to lie in the 19th-century industrial legacy of poor squalid housing and its association with overcrowding and ill-health. However, as has been shown, those who suffered the worst housing conditions were not the initial beneficiaries of council housing. Through aiming to house the families of skilled workers, the state established subsidised council housing as the norm for most Scottish families. Through meeting this ambition, the original goal of alleviating the atrocious housing conditions of the 'deserving' poor was effectively lost for 50 years. Council housing in Scotland became a sought-after social commodity, one that was closely tied to the power and influence of municipal politics: a reward, not a palliative. Given that the family was the dominant social entity, its pre-eminence was inevitable. That agenda, however, ended abruptly in the late 1960s, by the rapid withdrawal of the 'number game' house-building programme (Harloe, 2004b).

The only break from this focus was in two short bursts, one in the late 1930s and the other in the early to late 1960s. Only then did council housing specifically try to assist the poorest slum dwellers. The housing produced during these two brief phases proved never to be truly popular, but rather socially stigmatised right from the start. Not surprisingly, today's demolition programmes, which are as extensive as those conducted in the 1960s, are focused almost entirely on 1930s slum clearance estates and 1960s high-rise developments. Later substantial capital investment throughout the 1980s by housing associations and via private renovation grants mopped up the remnants of these squalid slums.

Major social, economic and political changes within contemporary society over the last 40 years ensured that the whole raison d'être of council housing altered. Now, it is welfare housing for the poorest and most marginalised within society: ironically those for whom 100 years previously such housing had been planned. The emergence of consumerism from the 1950s onwards and with it individualism, rather than post-war welfare state collectivism, produced a major challenge to the envisaged role and ethos of council housing. Individualism also had a profound influence on civil rights and equality issues, and with accompanying legislation again challenged the previous ways of working. Discrimination on a whole variety of counts was no longer socially nor politically acceptable. As a consequence, within what is now a more socially polarised society, council housing has become the only tenure now open to the marginalised. Council housing has replaced the slums, but at the same time has been abandoned by 'respectable' working-class families who no longer view it as a socially acceptable commodity. But then, does this not mean that council housing has at last matched its original conception?

## References

Addison, C. (1922) *The Betrayal of the Slums*, London: Herbert Jenkins.

Anderson, I. (2007) 'Sustainable solutions to homelessness: the Scottish case', *European Journal of Homelessness*, vol 1, December, pp 163-83.

Bowley, A. (1945) *Housing and the State*, London: George Allen & Unwin.

Bramley, G., Munro, M. and Pawson, H. (2004) *Key Issues in Housing: Policies and Markets in 21st Century Britain*, London: Palgrave.

Census of Scotland (1871) *Census of Scotland*, Report (Volume 1), Edinburgh: HMSO.

Chalmers, A. (1930) *The Health of Glasgow 1818-1925: An Outline*, Glasgow: Glasgow Corporation.

Corporation of the City of Glasgow (1957) *Report on the Clearance of the Slum Houses Redevelopment and Overspill, Development Plan First Quinquennial Review*, Glasgow: Architectural and Planning Department, Planning Division, Glasgow Corporation.

Cullingworth, J. (1969) *Council Housing Purposes, Procedures and Priorities: Ninth Report of the Housing Management Sub-Committee of the Central Housing Advisory Committee*, London: HMSO.

Department of Health for Scotland (1932) *Annual Report of the Department of Health for Scotland*, Edinburgh: The Scottish Office.

Department of Health for Scotland (1938) *Annual Report of the Department of Health for Scotland*, Edinburgh: The Scottish Office.

Dunleavy, P. (1991) *Democracy, Bureaucracy and Public Choice: Economic Explanations in Political Science*, London: Harvester Wheatsheaf.

Ferguson, T. (1948) *The Dawn of Scottish Social Welfare*, Edinburgh: Nelson.

Gibb, A. (1989) 'Policy and politics in Scottish housing since 1945', in R. Rodger (ed) *Scottish Housing in the Twentieth Century*, Leicester: Leicester University Press, pp 155-83.

Glasgow Municipal Commission on the Housing of the Poor (1904) *Report of the Glasgow Municipal Commission on the Housing of the Poor*, Glasgow: Corporation of Glasgow.

Harloe, M. (2004a) 'Social housing – past, present and future', *Housing Studies*, vol 9, no 3, pp 407-19.

Harloe, M. (2004b) *The Peoples' Home: Social Rented Housing in Europe and America*, Oxford and Cambridge, MA: Basil Blackwell.

Kemp, P. (1985) *The Cost of Chaos: A Survey of the Housing Benefit Scheme*, London: SHAC.

Local Government Boards for England and Wales and Scotland (1918) *Report of the Committee Appointed by the President of the Local Government Board and the Secretary for Scotland to Consider. Questions of Building Construction in Connection with the Provision of Dwellings for the Working Classes in England and Wales, and Scotland and Report upon Methods of Securing Economy and Despatch in the Provision of Such Dwellings*, London.

Malpass, P. (2005) *Housing and the Welfare State: The Development of Housing Policy in Britain*, Basingstoke: Palgrave.

Melling, J. (1983) *Rent Strikes: People's Struggle for Housing in West Scotland 1890–1916*, Edinburgh: Poylygon.

Melling, J. (1989) 'Clydeside rent struggles and the making of Labour politics in Scotland, 1900–1939', in R. Rodger (ed) *Scottish Housing in the Twentieth Century*, Leicester: Leicester University Press, pp 54–88.

Merrett, S. (1979) *State Housing in Britain*, London: Routledge & Kegan Paul.

Morgan, N. (1989) '£8 cottages for Glasgow citizens: innovations in municipal house-building in Glasgow in the inter-war years', in R. Rodger (ed) *Scottish Housing in the Twentieth Century*, Leicester: Leicester University Press, pp 125–54.

O'Carroll, A. (1996) 'Historic perspectives on tenure development in urban Scotland', in H. Currie and A. Murie (eds) *Housing in Scotland: Housing Policy and Practice Series*, Coventry: Chartered Institute of Housing, pp 16–30.

Pimlott, B. (1992) *Harold Wilson*, London: Harper Collins.

Presbytery of Glasgow (1891) *Report of Commission on the Housing of the Poor in Relation to their Social Condition*, Glasgow: Presbytery of Glasgow.

Ravetz, A. (2001) *Council Housing and Culture: The History of a Social Experiment*, London: Routledge.

Ravetz, A. with Turkington, R. (1995) *The Place of Home: English Domestic Environments 1914–2000*, London: E & FN Spon.

Reiach, A. and Hurd, R. (1945) *Building Scotland: A Cautionary Guide*, Edinburgh: Saltire Society.

Rex, J. and Moore, R. (1968) *Race, Community and Conflict: A Study of Sparkbrooke*, London: Oxford University Press.

Robertson, D. (1992) 'Scottish home improvement policy, 1945-75', *Urban Studies*, vol 29, no 7, pp 1115-36.

Robertson, D. (1997) 'The packaging and repackaging of housing policy', in O. Källthorp, I. Elander, O. Ericsson and M. Franzén (eds) *Cities in Transformation: Transformation in Cities*, Aldershot: Avebury, pp 289-315.

Robertson, D. (2001) 'Scottish homes: a legacy', in C. Jones and P. Robson (eds) *The Health of Scottish Housing*, Aldershot: Ashgate, pp 110-33.

Robertson, D. (2005) 'Scotland's new towns: a corporatist experiment', in J. Beech, O. Hand, M. Mulhern and J. Weston (eds) *Scottish Life and Society: The Individual and Community Life: A Compendium of Scottish Ethnology, Volume 9*, Edinburgh: John Donald, in association with the European Ethnology Research Centre and National Museum of Scotland, pp 576-604.

Robertson, D. and Bailey, N. (1996) 'Review of the impact of Housing Action Areas', *Scottish Homes Research Report*, no 47, Edinburgh: Scottish Homes.

Robertson, D., Smyth, J. and McIntosh, I. (2008) *'Whaur are you Fae': Neighbourhood Identity in Stirling, Over Time and Place*, York: Joseph Rowntree Foundation.

Rodger, R. (ed) (1989) *Scottish Housing in the Twentieth Century*, Leicester: Leicester University Press.

Rodger, R. and Al-Qaddo, H. (1989) 'The Scottish Special Housing Association and the implementation of housing policy, 1937-87', in R. Rodger (ed) *Scottish Housing in the Twentieth Century*, Leicester: Leicester University Press, pp 184-213.

Royal Commission (1917) *Report on the Housing of the Industrial Population of Scotland (Rural and Urban)*, Edinburgh: HMSO.

Scottish Executive (2006) *The Right to Buy in Scotland: Pulling Together the Evidence*, Edinburgh: Scottish Executive.

SHAC (Scottish Housing Advisory Committee) (1943–44) *Report of Distribution of New Houses in Scotland,* Edinburgh: HMSO.

SHAC (1944) *Planning Our New Homes*, Edinburgh: HMSO.

SHAC (1946) *Modernising Our Homes*, Edinburgh: HMSO.

SHAC (1967) *Allocating Council Houses*, Edinburgh: HMSO.

SHAC (1968) *The Older Houses in Scotland: A Plan for Action*, Edinburgh: HMSO.

Smyth, J. (2000) *Labour in Glasgow 1896–1936: Socialism, Suffrage, Sectarianism*, Scottish Historical Review Monograph, East Linton: Tuckwell Press.

Wheatley, J. (1913) *Eight Pound Cottages for Glasgow Citizens*, Glasgow: Glasgow Labour Party.

# SIX

# The Poor Law Commission of 1905–09: a view from a century on

*John Offer*

## Introduction

On 1 January 1908, the total number of persons in receipt of some form of poor relief in England and Wales was 928,671: 'one out of every 44 persons was a pauper' (Poor Law Commission, 1909a, vol 1, p 31). Behind the figures, within a framework amended in 1834 yet retaining local variations in policy, was a world of interaction yielding decisions about the quality of life for the most vulnerable in society. The Royal Commission on the Poor Laws of the time still signifies as a landmark in social policy with its celebrated division over future policy, where Fabian socialism and a moral and idealist analysis collided. This discussion, however, breaks with tradition by excavating the Commission's own evidence on how *participants* closely involved in the local running and practices of the Edwardian Poor Law themselves *perceived and interpreted* its operation. A new interpretation of the intellectual environment of the Commission's majority and minority reports is then developed.

There was already pressure for a review when Balfour's Conservative government announced the Commission, on 2 August 1905. Coincidence or not, this was one day after jobless workers rioted in Manchester, confirming doubts that the 1905 Unemployed Workmen Bill was a sufficient response to unemployment (Brown, J., 1971; Brown, K.D., 1971; McBriar, 1987, p 178).

The membership was announced on 4 December. Lord George Hamilton (a retired Conservative government minister) was chairman. The 18 other members were:

- the O'Connor Don (an Irish Catholic government adviser on Ireland);
- Sir Henry Robinson (of the Local Government Board [LGB] for Ireland);
- Charles Booth (social scientist and advocate of old-age pensions);
- Sir Samuel Provis (of the LGB for England);
- F.H. Bentham (chairman of the Bradford board of guardians);
- Dr A.H. Downes (Senior Medical Inspector, LGB for England);
- the Rev. Thory Gage Gardiner (from the settlement movement and the Charity Organisation Society [COS]);
- George Lansbury (socialist, and 'labour' guardian at Poplar);
- Charles Stewart Loch (sympathetic to idealist social thought and Secretary to the COS);
- James Patten-MacDougall (of the LGB, Scotland);
- Thomas Hancock Nunn (from the settlement movement and the COS);
- the Rev. Lancelot Ridley Phelps (from the COS, and Fellow of Oriel College, teaching classics and political economics);
- William Smart (economist, University of Glasgow);
- the Rev. Henry Russell Wakefield (London cleric and municipal administrator);
- Helen Bosanquet (writer on social work, an interest shared with her husband, Bernard, an idealist philosopher);
- Beatrice Webb (active, with her husband Sidney, in social research and the Fabian Society);
- Octavia Hill (pioneer in housing management and the COS);
- Francis Chandler (of the Trades Union Congress), added in February 1906.

Following the O'Connor Don's death, the Most Rev. Denis Kelly, Catholic Lord Bishop of Ross, substituted. Ill-health brought Booth's resignation early in 1908. At least six had involvement with the COS, unsurprising given its patronage and twin roles as think-tank and charitable provider. The terms of reference were to inquire into the working of the laws relating to the relief of poor persons and into other means for meeting distress arising from lack of employment, and to consider whether any changes to the Poor Laws, or new legislation for dealing with distress, were advisable (Poor Law Commission, 1909a, p v).

Divisions about policy fostered majority and minority reports on England and Wales, and, separately, on Ireland and Scotland. The minority reports were written by Beatrice Webb (with her husband, Sidney Webb), co-signed by Lansbury, Chandler and Wakefield; Helen Bosanquet and Smart were mostly responsible for the majority report on England. The minority wanted to 'break up' the Poor Law, substituting for generic provision specific services and institutions. Specialist staff would report to specific committees of county and county borough councils (for health, education, asylums and 'pensions'), preventing needs from arising besides simply meeting them. *All* people would have access to provision, with charges for persons able to pay. The unemployed would be the responsibility of central government. The majority favoured retaining a generic service, covering major needs (with accommodation in specialist institutions as appropriate) for people who had lost economic independence. Modified and rebranded as Public Assistance, responsibility would transfer to Public Assistance Committees in county and county borough areas, working closely with Voluntary Aid Councils and Committees.

However, the reports agreed on recommending the abolition of the local boards of guardians of Poor Law unions. (In Scotland, parish councils were responsible; in England and Wales there were 643 unions; in Ireland 159.) General workhouses were to go too, and there were to be new powers of administration established at county and county borough level.

The Commission's divisions, the Poor Law's own fight back, the First World War and subsequent economic depression diluted enthusiasm for reform. Workhouses though became Public Assistance Institutions, and guardians sometimes became regarded as 'defenders of the nation against revolution' (Gilbert, 1970, p 136). On 16 February 1921, *The Times* noted the merits of a system 'which keeps the spenders of public money in such intimate touch with public opinion' (Gilbert, 1970, p 136). In outline, the 1929 reform of local government and poor relief owed something to majority ideas; the 1940s remodelling owed nothing explicit to either majority or minority ideas, although the Curtis Report (1946) on the care of children and the 1948 Children Act in England and Wales had minority-style cores of 'specialist' administration and trained staff.

## Rethinking the Poor Law in the 1900s

The Commission's recommendations are the normal focus in social policy studies. Bypassed, therefore, are its other documents: there are 37 *Appendix Volumes*, 'vast tomes of evidence, relatively unexplored' (Rose, 1985, p 13). In 1909, they moved Bernard Bosanquet to eulogy: 'extraordinarily well worth reading, ... almost a new departure in the procedure of Royal Commissions' (1909, p 126). The principal aim here is to explore how guardians and officials *themselves* interpreted the Poor Law in their evidence to the Commission, on themes from familial care and old-age pensions to everyday perceptions of the workhouse. This material provides, however, missing context in which the normative social theories and recommendations of the reports need to be situated, a subject also discussed. In respect of the *reports*, it has been shown, taking the case of the care of older people as an illustration, that contrasting positive evaluations were placed by the majority on social support rather than purely medical assistance, on guidance and supervision, and on the maintenance of morale and 'character', and by the minority on medical care, on institution-based care, and on surveillance allied with directive intervention in personal lives (Offer, 2006a). However, in the process the reports also *shared* an underlying and structural commitment, in terms of social theory, to 'idealist social thought', broadly defined (Harris, 1992).

To guard against confusion, it must be emphasised that a 'simple' contrast between the minority and majority reports as 'Fabian' and 'idealist' respectively is replaced by an account of *both* of them as fundamentally idealist in terms of the logical features of their social theory, but with differences within that tradition displayed over the means (such as the role of the state) rather than the ends of social policy. Policy and personal intervention were framed as *direct* means to the ideal society, guided by a holistic conception of social life and the concept of the 'general will'. Individuals were taken to constitute a whole such that from its 'interests' or 'will' could be derived lessons about how individuals should live. One important advantage gained by identifying both reports as idealist is that it pinpoints their opposition to a (non-idealist) theoretical approach in which society was regarded as a providential catallaxy (the word derives from Whately's preference, in the first of his *Introductory Lectures on Political-Economy* delivered in 1831 (Whately, 1832), for the name 'catallactics' over 'political economy'), being the spontaneous, socially interacting life of its constituent members, with limited roles for government.

This approach took socially minded individuals, and their capacity to develop virtuous lives in themselves and in others around them with whom they interacted, as the starting point of theory and policy, rather than 'society', conceived of as a superior, holistic level of epistemic and moral reality. Thus, this chapter will also consider, in its fourth section, whether guardians and officials shared an idealist orientation or, as is suggested, thought mostly in countervailing terms, representing a legacy of 'Christian political economics'. Dating from the late 18th century, this was a union of nascent economic thought (or 'catallactics') and natural theology, critical of utilitarian materialist psychology, in which progressive increases in virtue went hand in hand, by providential 'design', with participation in market exchanges (Hilton, 1988; Mandler, 1990; Waterman, 1991; Lyon, 1999). Governments were unable to create virtue or prevent sin, although through impious measures they could hinder virtue and encourage vice. Important contributors included John Bird Sumner (a member of the 1832 English Poor Law inquiry), Richard Whately himself, (chairman of the 1833 Irish Poor Law inquiry) and Baden Powell (Savilian Professor of Geometry at Oxford University). Christian political economics yielded a non-idealist, liberal theory of social life in which social individuals were *ends in themselves*, with non-disabled individuals seeking relief as 'queenly' rational agents, or at least 'lapsed queens', rather than passive or untutored 'pawns' (Le Grand, 2003; Offer, 2006b).

It is important to note that around 1900 the Poor Law in England was emerging from a period since 1871 when some unions adopted a 'crusade' to limit outdoor relief expenditure, urged on by the LGB (outdoor relief to able-bodied people had often continued after 1834 as well as to non able-bodied people). By 1890, the older people getting public assistance had halved since 1870, and the outdoor relief still awarded had halved in its value. A study of Brixworth union in Northamptonshire shows that ratepayers 'exploited the "crusade" ethos, gaining more control over both Poor Law and sanitary administration, to the detriment of the poor' (Hurren, 2005, pp 403-4). Guardians could curb health expenditure since they often held joint office on rural sanitary authorities. In Brixworth in 1889, diphtheria struck, poor drainage and water being the causes. Adverse publicity followed for the LGB: the 'crusade' wobbled. The same decades, however, saw capital expenditure grow on Poor Law infirmaries/hospitals, and on other forms of institutional relief related especially to children. A public general hospital system emerged, outstripping the growth of bed provision in the voluntary hospitals. Social investigations in the 1860s, new medical skills and informed opinion had 'forced the Poor Law bureaucracy to make classification effective' (Pinker, 1971, p 79). In 1885, moreover, the Medical Relief (Disqualification Removal) Act erased the penalty of disenfranchisement (except for the elections of guardians) as the price of receiving Poor Law medical relief, thereby broadening public access. The Poor Law inspector Henry Longley believed that effective treatment in therapeutic institutions by those with knowledge *of* the poor would enable unions to limit outdoor relief to cases where it was an economic use of resources, in a manner demonstrable and comprehensible to the poor (Abel-Smith, 1964, pp 83-100; Williams, 1981, pp 86-107; Lees, 1998, pp 259-93). Although Longley's strategy was, at best, mediated through varying local practices, a pattern materialised where expenditure on an indoor pauper (a recipient of assistance within Poor Law premises) was about three times that on an outdoor pauper (a recipient of assistance in their home), and outdoor relief declined. In 1871, there were 39.1 outdoor paupers per 1,000 population in England; by 1905, that was down to 16.3, with indoor paupers under half that figure throughout the period (Crowther, 1981, pp 59-61; detailed statistics are in Williams, 1981, pp 156-233).

The 'crusade' period was not a hiccup 'along the road to the welfare state', but a resolute and often successful attempt 'to steer society in another direction altogether by effecting a lasting realignment of public and private responsibilities for the welfare of citizens' (Thomson, 1986, p 374). To deem the 'crusade' a mere glitch in the history of welfare provision in welfare historiography is therefore mistaken. 'It helps to explain tensions, on the one hand between the LGB Poor Law and Medical Departments, and on the other hand between Poor Law and sanitary authorities in the regions who were in conflict in many localities' (Hurren, 2005, p 417).

Ratepayers rejoiced over clear targets and tighter financial management, but friction with local public health interests served to antagonise medical interests: the 'crusade' and the policy of 'strict' waned. Beyond doubt, by 1905, guardians and their staff were in changed circumstances, facing a broader franchise, more female guardians, ordinary working people without property elected as guardians, outdoor relief to older people rehabilitated, and unemployment widely accepted as connected with economic factors, not only 'character'. The formation of the National Poor Law Officers' Association was emblematic of movement in power relations, and guardians now contributed to pensions for officers (Crowther, 1981, p 116). Digby's (1978) study of East Anglian unions found discrepant social meanings of the workhouse for those inside and those not 'wise' to it: few poor people directly experienced it. Such remoteness, in Digby's assessment, had produced 'a folklore ... which had small resemblance to the reality of conditions in the workhouse' (1978, pp 162-3). By this time too, officials recognised the social significance of burials and cooperated with the poor; pauper funerals were not necessarily feared (Hurren and King, 2005).

Even to some of its critics, the Poor Law remained acceptable as the basic structure in which any modified social provision would develop. Canon Barnett, committed in London to social reform, had argued in 1883 that a revised Poor Law would 'make the life of England healthier and more restful' (Rose, 1972, p 41). The state, according to the influential New Liberal writer J.A. Hobson (1902 [1996], pp 201–2), could realise its obligations to society once

> our Poor Law has eradicated every element of degradation from its working, and has succeeded in humanizing the conditions of work and life which it affords, so that a self-respecting man or woman who fails to get proper work and wages outside will speedily and willingly have recourse to it as an expedient expressly designed to maintain the standard of public life.

It is widely agreed among Poor Law historians that local relief practices varied substantially between unions. Their *social meanings* are much less well understood, however. How were these practices *perceived* by those involved in them at union level? Evidence in the next section on attitudes within and towards the Poor Law at local level by the middle of the first decade of the 20th century challenges the orthodox accounts of representations of the social meanings of assistance that faced the Commission. Thus, Rose's (1972, p 41) declaration that 'large sections of the working class regarded it with fear and loathing' will appear weakly tethered. Rose also entertained a fatalistic historicism: the Poor Law 'was bound to become increasingly dubious, inadequate and even irrelevant. Its controllers were unwilling to expand into new fields of social action, and even had they done so it is doubtful if the poor would have accepted them' (1972, pp 41–2). Meanwhile, Gilbert (1966, p 109) raced from micro to macro levels in judging the Relief (Schoolchildren) Order of April 1905 as 'destroying forever any vestige of the possibility that the Poor Law guardians would be permitted to take part in the reforms of the next decade', because in some towns 'fathers refused to allow their children to receive the tickets for meals' on discovering they came from the guardians. Middleton, however, accompanied an account of 'continuous attacks' on the Poor Law with insightful recognition of an historical and sociological conundrum: its survival (until 1948) was 'an important social phenomenon not easily explained' (1971, p 294). A plausible 'answer' is that the Poor Law was less detested and vulnerable than critics supposed, as this discussion explores.

## The Edwardian Poor Law in practice

A narrative of how guardians and others reflected on their tasks, not a direct concern of the reports, is one small step towards a nuanced account of the Poor Law in the early 20th century; the material in this case furnished by the Commission's own less familiar publications. The guardians were presumably not 'impartial' witnesses, but that is immaterial here: their own perceptions of their participation in the Poor Law, whether or not 'justified' by some external standard, help to establish the social reality of the time. The record of the examinations of chairs, members and officers of boards of guardians yields a wealth of 'grassroots' experience and interpretative comment. Some witnesses appeared before the Commission in London, others as it visited elsewhere in the UK. Topics covered included:

- the need for specific services as opposed to a generic provision;
- the roles of charity and friendly societies;
- the adequacy of the union as the unit for meeting needs;
- reliance on local finance (rates);
- the calibre of guardians and their utilisation of *Gemeinschaft* local insight;
- the pay, conditions and career prospects for officers;
- the extent and standards of medical and 'social' care;
- the place of institutional rather than 'outdoor' relief;
- administrative pressures generated by the demands of the LGBs;
- 'settlement' as a basis for determining eligibility for relief; and
- the place of guardians as opposed to county councils or other relief authorities in the future.

A focus on children, older people and vagrants recurs, but widows, 'imbeciles' and the seriously ill feature too. Drilling down to this level yields a cornucopia of local experience; its magnitude and diversity, however, permits only a 'sample' of themes and selective demographic coverage, here drawn from the large volumes on the rural unions. The themes explored are perceptions of 'informal care' (in today's lexicon), difficulties of organisation and location, how best to give older people assistance, and attitudes to workhouses and relief. Arguments about social theory and the Poor Law are also discussed.

The attitude of relatives, friends and neighbours to undertaking care, particularly of older people, including relatives' attitude to the legal and financial responsibilities falling on them from kin, is a recurring topic.

The relieving officer of Kington, Shropshire, emphasised in evidence, in July 1907, that outdoor relief to older people enabled them to live with their married sons and daughters untroubled by resentment over their expense (Poor Law Commission, 1910, p 133). Similarly, from Leominster, a guardian, the Rev. Ernest Kevill-Davies, reported that the children of older people were ready to help them and 'act up to their responsibilities' (1910, p 178), the outdoor relief awarded saving ratepayers greater expense. However, the chairman of Church Stretton union pinpointed as a cause of pauperism the 'disregard of parents' needs by grown-up sons', while adding that daughters 'are almost always ready to do their share' (1910, p 160). Charles Booth concluded his interrogation of a district medical officer for the Walsingham union in East Anglia with the observation: 'The parable of the Good Samaritan does not seem to have had its effect in your neighbourhood'. This followed on from the doctor's reports of difficulty in securing nursing help from neighbours, and the saga of a son and daughter who, living in the same village as their parents, but hitherto unknown to him as their parents' doctor and providing no assistance, returned one night to their dead mother and seriously ill father to raid the house, fleeing with furniture and 'the bedclothes from off the old man and the wedding ring from the old woman's hand as she lay dead' (1910, p 249). In Freebridge Lynn too, weakening ties of family, friendship and neighbourliness disturbed the chairman of the union: the virtue of poor people in the district had declined; they had become more selfish, not caring 'to do anything for the aged, as they used to, or for their friends in any way' (1910, p 258). The Rev. Henry Moody, an Ellesmere guardian, also found virtue in decline, complaining that any sense 'of filial responsibility seems almost lost in our union' (1910, p 155). The Rev. Charles Heale of Williton considered that 'care for the old and infirm by their families is dying out' (1910, p 59). However, by contrast, in North Witchford, the kindness of neighbours had impressed the union clerk (1910, p 251).

The doubtful logic of local boundaries caused friction, having evolved apparently haphazardly over centuries. At Thingoe union the workhouse was in nearby Bury St Edmunds, but in a labyrinthine arrangement Bury itself had a separate Poor Law administration and no workhouse of its own – its vagrants were sent to the Thingoe house under, however, Bury's rules. These rules struck the Thingoe guardian under examination, the Rev. James Mahomed, as unsympathetic and draconian. Even the seemingly straightforward matter of physical access to Poor Law facilities could be a stumbling block. Helen Bosanquet, when confronting the chairman of the Freebridge Lynn union with the inaccessibility of its workhouse, elicited the nonchalant reply that it was indeed 'on the road to nowhere.... It is a long way from the station, of course, but if a person wants to go and visit any relation in the union probably their master will lend them a horse and cart to go there' (1910, p 259).

Mahomed, the Thingoe guardian, believed that the guardians' personal knowledge of an applicant's character ensured that outdoor relief to older people was not pauperising (how equitable such decisions might be was not raised). He also welcomed the prospect of old-age pensions: 'when the people have worked hard and done respectably and lived soberly, they should not be left to want in their old age' (1910, p 284). On 9 October 1906, F.E. Elkerton and J.T. White were questioned as representatives of the Association of Workhouse Masters and Matrons. They regarded workhouses as now for inmates unfit for work, mainly the over-sixties, and that non-disabled people should be catered for in other places. They thought that, in practice, the 'character' of these inmates was formed already and indoor relief had little direct effect. In fortifying this statement (in response to Bentham) White observed:

> Our workhouses are, to a large extent, now inhabited by people who − yes I will put it as strongly as that − have a right to be there, if you like to put it that way. Therefore, we think the workhouse to a very large extent now is really an almshouse; it is not a workhouse as it was understood twenty-five years ago, by any manner of means. There is no task of work and there is no deterring influence about liberty; clothing is not uniform to the extent it was, the diet is more liberal, and the whole surroundings of the place are different, even compared to what it was fifteen years ago. Under the trend of public opinion ... the workhouse will be an almshouse.... In many of our country workhouses to-day the conditions of comfort and the conditions of life are such that the great majority of the inmates are leading comfortable and happy lives. (Poor Law Commission, 1909b, p 106)

White wanted more opportunities for older inmates to socialise as they wished, and agreed when Gardiner named it 'the great hardship of the aged poor ... that they never can practically get alone from the moment they go into the house till they go into their coffin' (1909b, p 106). This pattern of practice accords with Digby's (1978, p 81) general claim regarding the evidence of Norfolk guardians and officers that outdoor relief was given whenever possible, and the workhouse was 'the almost exclusive preserve of the aged and infirm (who were unable to look after themselves any longer), the feeble-minded, a few "bad" characters and some unmarried mothers'.

In some unions, apparently, the workhouse and deterrence were seldom connected in the popular consciousness. On 11 December 1906, Dr Cecil Stephens, district and workhouse medical officer for the North Witchford union in Cambridgeshire, informed Downes that the workhouse was less of a deterrent than formerly. The workhouse had got a bad name 'very often, I think, from the fact that the inmates of the workhouse go outside and they are very anxious to get money, and they say how badly they are treated in the workhouse' (Poor Law Commission, 1909b, p 440). Stephens adjudged the odium undeserved, and replied to Booth's further inquiry about deterrence: 'Yes, it is decreasing a great deal, I am sure of that' (Poor Law Commission, 1909b, p 440). Indeed, E.J. Richardson, relieving officer of the same union, concluded his submission in ebullient form: 'the present system of Poor Law relief will take a lot of beating' (Poor Law Commission, 1910, p 509). On the other hand, the Rev. W.H. Macnaughton-Jones, a guardian at Henstead, Suffolk, admitted a deterrent effect and traced it, first, to 'an inherited prejudice from old times, from the Oliver Twist sort of workhouse system', and, second, to older people who 'do not like to go, and will not go, into an institution where they are bound to mix with people that they would not otherwise mix with in life' (1910, p 192).

An Atcham (Shrewsbury) relieving officer, James Heathcote, justified to Booth the entrenched policy tradition there of strictly limiting outdoor relief, but in the process unusually exhibited a minority-style dismissal of older people's own preferences: if admission to the house at an initial stage of infirmity were offered, the person's margin of safety is increased, otherwise after out-relief for a few years they will want to stick to it 'even under their miserable conditions rather than face the bath and the regular conditions of the workhouse' (1910, p 105). Regretting 'experiments ... on elderly people', he still believed that 'second childhood is not an empty term' (1910, p 105): any irony in Gardiner's prompting that this was judged 'from one's own opinion of the standard of life and comfort, and not from theirs' (1910, p 108) was wasted, as Heathcote eagerly agreed.

An Ely guardian, A.J. Pell (whose uncle had adopted the 'crusade' at Brixworth, and himself with prior Poor Law experience in London), questioned by Booth whether guardians took an interest in the theory of poor relief, replied ruefully that they did not (1910, p 240). However, Christopher Harrison, a Yorkshire guardian, magistrate and county councillor, opposed reform. He reported that, in York, personal circumstances and a virtuous character shaped the relief awarded, with no fixed scale used: 'where any poor man, who has been a very hard-working man and is what we term a deserving case, applies to us, we do treat him well and keep him from the workhouse as much as we can' (1910, p 310). In Beatrice Webb's diary entry for 31 July 1907, Harrison's interrogation barely signified: 'hearing five rural experts – the three stupid ones were in favour of the status quo, the two clever ones in favour of the county authority for Poor Law and not against distributing the service among the existing committees' (Webb, 1948, pp 386-7). From a few unions, guardians sympathetic to 'labour' interests appeared as witnesses, fingering low wages as the root of poverty and embracing greater collective bargaining as the remedy. A.J. Murrin, of Newton Abbot, opined that workers had little control over the economic law of supply and demand, and expected the Poor Law to be usurped by a system more 'in consonance with the altruistic spirit of the age and our common Christianity' (Poor Law Commission, 1910, p 41). 'Society', he added, 'owes a debt to the poor people which it can never adequately repay' (1910, p 42). From Atcham, James Kent-Morris attributed pauperism to 'the system which permits the owners of land and capital to exact from the toilers nearly two-thirds of the wealth they produce' (1910, p 89), declaring the workhouse demoralising, and hence no less of an evil than *inadequate* outdoor relief (1910, p 91).

In sessions with critics of the Poor Law and representatives of Poor Law and charitable associations, opinions surfaced more often on social theories and desirable social and economic interventions, drawing in members of the Commission. Sir William Chance was active in the COS, in developing Poor Law administration, and a guardian at Hambledon; he also defended the deterrence principle and championed individual liberty. Chance, with Downes, served on the departmental committee on vagrancy in 1904, and became prominent in supporting Poor Law interests. Under interrogation in London on 15 October 1906, he clashed with Lansbury – asked why a man should be pauperised 'because circumstances which he cannot control overcome him', Chance rejoined that the interests of all individual members of a society mattered, and thus that no man should be encouraged to rely on relief. Not even a record of paying rates should bring an entitlement to relief. The idea of a right to relief from the community might occupy the press and be growing, 'but if you are going to increase the taxes and the rates, you will decrease the possibility of better wages being given' (Poor Law Commission, 1909b, p 130). Likewise, in a written submission, the Bradfield guardians aimed to keep in mind 'not only those who do come on the rates, but those who do not, whether ratepayers or otherwise' (Poor Law Commission, 1910, p 533). Thomas Mackay, Poor Law historian and COS luminary, while lamenting the low wages of widows in London who were rearing children, deftly sidestepped the ambush set by Mrs Webb's invitation to support a minimum wage, retorting that it denied a worker's right to work for less (Poor Law Commission, 1909b, p 237). Phelps established in his examination of the Social Democratic Federation's (SDF) Henry Quelch on 8 October 1906 that 'the deterrent effect of the workhouse is quite independent of the administration and the condition of the workhouses' (1909b, p 67). But the effect involved, insisted Quelch, a loss of 'social *status*' inapplicable in receiving outdoor relief. Phelps leaves in the air the implication that Quelch's admission that outdoor relief trumps thrift and self-respect compromises the SDF's own proposals on reform. Later, Quelch offered Gardiner a holistic perspective on society: 'the welfare of the individual means the well-being of the State' (1909b, p 78). Pressed to clarify, Quelch affirmed the state's duty to 'maintain ... decently' idiots and imbeciles, or 'clear them out of the way', which 'society is not prepared to do' (1909b, p 78).

On 2 October 1906, Beatrice Webb interrogated J.T. Dodd of the Oxford board of guardians. She pursued the line that increased medical surveillance of young mothers on outdoor relief would reduce infant mortality *and* improve character and a sense of responsibility. Dodd emphasised that he was concerned primarily with the health dimension. Webb suggested that it would 'improve the amount of deliberate conduct as opposed to impulsive conduct' in mothers (1909b, p 51), thus improving character. She asserted, unperturbed by Dodd's reservations, that 'I should put character first and health afterwards' (1909b, p 51). Later, Bentham suggested to Dodd that 'the fewer the dependents ... the healthier the state of society', but in his response, Dodd challenged orthodoxy in a rare nod towards idealist social thought: 'We are all dependent upon each other – we all are really. "We are members one of another"; that is the truth of it' (1909b, p 53).

A few other aspects deserve a mention here. At Ellesmere, the union contemplated new provision for older people with better access; Gardiner, though, cautioned that the roads were 'motor-haunted' (Poor Law Commission, 1910, p 147). Also in Ellesmere, the past vice-chairman of the guardians admitted (to Helen Bosanquet and to Charles Booth) that he was unaware that medical relief did not make the recipient a pauper in the sense of 'disfranchising' them (1910, p 140). Indeed, in a number of unions, lethargy and apathy had crept in: guardians were elected unopposed, men and women were unwilling to stand,

and meetings were thinly attended. From Williton in Somerset, Flora Joseph, a co-opted female guardian, reported to Phelps that housing quality for the poor was declining: cottagers were priced out of their homes by people from Bridgwater because they proved more lucrative as 'week-end habitations' (1910, p 70). But Joseph also observed that her fellow (male) guardians were too apt to discuss the crops and read the newspapers at meetings (1910, p 71), and regretted that the office of elected guardian had become an 'appanage' of being elected a rural district councillor, with Poor Law matters misunderstood (1910, p 69). Women guardians, it should be noted, were also elected in increasing numbers from the 1890s. The commissioners often made a point of discovering if a union had women guardians and how men perceived their contribution (usually as constructive; at Williton the vicar drew attention to Joseph's work to improve facilities for children; 1910, p 68). In 1907, the total number of elected female guardians was 1,099, about one in ten guardians in urban unions and as low as one in one hundred in rural unions (Poor Law Commission, 1909a, vol 1, pp 142-3; on the growth of elected female guardians, and the reforms of the governance and administration of the Poor Law associated with the 1894 Parish and District Councils Act, see Hollis, 1987, ch 7).

In the space available in this chapter, only part of the picture can emerge. Nevertheless, it is significant that there is *at least* this part to it. Most of the witnesses discussed here demanded old-age pensions and prided themselves on improvements in accommodation for the aged poor and others. The large majority of *all* the numerous Anglican clergy who were still involved in local Poor Law administration, and who were giving evidence, shared these views. Overall, informal familial care was a central topic and valued highly, but while in some unions it was seen as readily forthcoming, elsewhere its future was concerning. Indoor relief and deterrence was widely raised. Mostly, the view was that people were reluctant to enter the house, but that the reluctance was declining, or at least explicable as based on either 'old' beliefs or personal preference rather than the present administration or conditions. In some unions, anomalous geographical boundaries led to support for reorganisation and a larger (county) unit of administration, but elsewhere this was opposed as removing decisions from localities and officers with detailed understanding of applicants. More generally, it becomes apparent that a pragmatic 'muddling through', but within the parameters of husbanding resources and encouraging Christian virtues, was often the order of the day. Low wages as a problem were widely accepted, but the SDF's emphasis on *society's* needs was exceptional. Beatrice Webb's exchange with Dodd over 'character' is discussed in the next section.

## Social theory and the Poor Law

This discussion has largely sidestepped the detail of the familiar disagreements over policy between the minority and majority groupings on the Commission, but it does now reconsider their apparently conflicting theoretical approaches to interpreting social life. In the Scottish minority report, tensions surfaced, with words used by Bernard Bosanquet, Helen Bosanquet's husband, recycled to malign the (English) majority report. In the Scottish minority report, most destitution is attributed to factors such as sickness, where no 'moral defect' occurs. This claim is an explicit response to Bosanquet's argument, which is quoted, that where there is 'a failure of self-maintenance' there is 'a defect in the citizen character, or at least a grave danger to its integrity', with such cases raising problems that are 'moral' in the sense of 'affecting the whole capacity of self-management, to begin with in the person who has failed, and secondarily in the whole community so far as influenced by expectation and example' (Poor Law Commission, 1909c, p 274). However, Bosanquet was not uncharacteristically advocating allegedly 'individualist' values associated with a crude economic laissez faire. These he questioned. He was raising a different point, about a 'failure' to be an *ideal citizen* (Vincent, 1984; Lewis, 1995, p 8). The 'defect' was to ignore the 'common good' or wider interests when facing situations where it is possible to act deliberately and rationally rather than through impulsive conduct, exactly, however, the distinction we saw *Beatrice Webb herself* insisting on in the previous section (see also Brundage, 2002, p 139). Incapacities themselves could be willed or unwilled, but the quality of the individual response was an ineliminable ingredient. For the majority, voluntary action, with a theodicy based on casework and aided by social therapeutics, tutored citizens to look to wider interests and to control, not succumb to, circumstances. Bosanquet, the COS and the majority reports did *not* attribute destitution to moral inadequacy, unless 'willed incapacity' to work, for example, arose, and then the exercise of the coercive powers of the state were agreed on with the minority reports. They accepted economic and 'environmental' causes of temporary destitution (McBriar, 1987, p 300). Whatever the problem, the majority were seeking preventive, curative and restorative treatment of the *whole person*: on this dimension, indeed, the majority held the minority to be lacking.

It can be claimed, as outlined in the second section, that idealist social thought has an intimate connection with both the majority and the minority reports (Harris, 1992, p 133). In many ways divergent, the Fabian socialism of the minority and the social thought of (key figures of) the majority nevertheless shared the lens of idealist communitarian traditions of social theory stemming from Hegel, Plato and Rousseau. They saw social policy as directly 'empowering' individual wills, giving them 'positive freedom', so that the 'right' choices in life would be made that furthered the 'good society', rather than as doing so indirectly (at best) by enabling individuals to find by choice their own sense of duty and understanding of fulfilment of self and others. Beatrice and Sidney Webb appealed to the holist idea of promoting 'social health' in support of their policies, and, as already indicated, the minority and the majority distrusted unsupervised and untutored familial or 'informal' care (Offer, 2004, 2006a). McBriar (1987, p 174) noted that both sets of reports subscribed to 'an "organic" idea of society', both wished to move from 'a "hedonistic" ethical criterion to a more socially qualitative one', both championed 'the role of the "statesman" and the expert civil servant against demands for "direct" democracy', and that on social structure both endorsed 'a qualified version of the "station and its duties" doctrine'. Whether primacy was accorded to the state or charity as the agency to this end was ultimately a secondary dispute. Loch and Bernard Bosanquet developed a systematic philosophy 'concerning the role of charity in the universal scheme of things' (McBriar, 1987, p 55), whereas the Webbs plumped for the state, while granting to voluntary action 'pioneering' functions that the state would later undertake itself. Non-idealist liberal visions were denied legitimacy *tout court* by both as outmoded and even incoherent 'individualism'. Hobson, among others, feared that the minority schemes of reform especially were weak on accountability, citizen representation and participation – states, he asserted, must be 'democratized as well as socialized' (Meadowcroft, 1995, p 209).

As the previous section showed, to represent the Edwardian Poor Law in its time as increasingly unacceptable or universally 'discredited' (Gilbert, 1970, p 308) is to align prematurely with its intellectual opponents and the verdicts of, particularly, the minority reports. The Poor Law years were not a Dark Age, and to characterise them glibly as about 'laissez faire', 'atomistic individualism' and 'stigma' in effect denies legitimacy to the texture and social meanings of past practices, hindering our capacity to learn from them. Poor Law practice often represented a secularised version of a theory of virtue and moral responsibility descended from the Christian political economics of the first half of the previous century. It would be arbitrary to discount as *passé* theory and practice concerned with personal well-being but *not* idealist, not aimed *directly* at realising a holistic 'good society'. The weakness, *if* such it was, was scepticism over making enhancement of 'positive freedom' a policy aim: why, then, as Chance questioned, strive to be virtuous? Nevertheless, in terms of method, historical and social studies require the bracketing off of later criticisms of its epistemological and moral status: viewing the past through such preconceptions hinders analysis of the Poor Law, with normativity displacing understanding.

It may be added that, interpreted as resource redistribution, Poor Law assistance itself represented a comprehensive pooling of risks coupled with interpersonal redistribution. It was not the bounded contractual entitlement of New Liberal insurance (Johnson, 1996, p 245), and the behaviour expected of individuals was not specified by reference to a reified social holism. Johnson's (1996, p 246) observation, referring especially to systems of finance underpinning policies, that straight lines of welfare development which run 'from the Poor Law to Beveridge are ... an erroneous historical construct' was shrewd. Johnson, though, was referring to Beveridge's National Insurance scheme of 1942; there are continuities from the Poor Law to later *means-tested* benefits (Harris, 2002, p 436). It suited politicians, however, to make more of the changes than reality warranted, and to describe *all areas* of the discarded Poor Law as embodying 'mean-spirited parsimony' (Silburn, 1983, p 148). Reconsideration suggests that this is not the whole story.

## Conclusion

There is more of significance about the Royal Commission than its famous reports; new light is cast on the Edwardian Poor Law by its own store of evidence, itself untouched by the *parti pris* selection of extracts which were made and included to buttress the reports. Revisiting the evidence disinters how local practitioners were experiencing and interpreting the Poor Law, covering themes from familial care and old-age pensions to everyday perceptions of the workhouse, and yields missing context in which the reports themselves can be better understood. If the idea of idealist social thought, broadly defined, was the theoretical core of both reports – regarding people as the direct means to realising the end of a holistically conceived 'good society' – the outlook of those delivering the Poor Law locally seldom represented this social philosophy. *Their* framework was *non*-idealist, conceiving individuals as social beings and capable of virtue, but concerned with those needing assistance to restore their capacity to fulfil *their own projects*, or care in old age.

What of a broader perspective on 1909 a century later? The reports have no echoes in the UK's social services today. Direct responsibility for provision by local government scarcely figures, whittled away to abet financial control by central government and the separation of providers from purchasers, and to curb 'postcode lotteries'. The ascendancy of management was unimaginable in 1909. Voluntary action as a partner to public provision on the model urged by the majority remains a pipedream. Demolition now routinely terminates the physical 'afterlife' of workhouses, commonly as National Health Service (NHS) hospitals. For the 1909 reports themselves, however, oblivion is undeserved. Their astonishing perspicacity means that policy suggestions of today might well be tested against them: a therapeutic dissection of strengths and weaknesses of a close ancestor may well slumber therein.

Everyday anxieties about contemporary policy include the erosion of perhaps already romanticised *Gemeinschaft* professional–service user relationships, raised as an objection to primary healthcare 'polyclinics', and parents evading 'responsibility' as their atavistic teenagers attack each other, and as they themselves neglect their own elderly parents. Such themes had earlier lives within the Edwardian Poor Law, bringing perspective to new/old concerns about today's service users and providers. A truncated or partisan sense of the past cramps our ideas faced with present dilemmas: Edwardian welfare heuristically cradles familiar concepts in unexpected settings, including rights, discretion, equity, desert, justice, well-being, and familial and personal responsibility. Accepting the theoretical variety that they can colonise sharpens thought on modern policy, as well as on the Edwardian Poor Law. Moreover, despite its tarnished image, the Edwardian Poor Law's intrinsic localism and reflexivity came close to capturing an intimate dimension to assistance, adaptable to individual and familial welfare preferences: a goal of contemporary social work and social policy in relating to 'informal care' that remains desirable but perennially elusive (Pinker, 2006, p 16).

## Acknowledgement
The author is grateful to the British Academy for the award of a Small Research Grant, which facilitated the research on which this chapter is based.

**References**

Abel-Smith, B. (1964) *The Hospitals, 1800-1948*, London: Heinemann.

Bosanquet, B. (1909) 'The Majority Report', *Sociological Review*, vol 2, no 2, pp 109-27.

Brown, J. (1971) 'The Poor Law Commission and the 1905 Unemployed Workmen's Act', *Bulletin of the Institute of Historical Research*, vol 44, pp 318-23.

Brown, K.D. (1971) 'The appointment of the 1905 Poor Law Commission: a rejoinder', *Bulletin of the Institute of Historical Research*, vol 44, pp 315-18.

Brundage, A. (2002) *The English Poor Laws, 1700–1930*, Basingstoke: Palgrave.

Crowther, M.A. (1981) *The Workhouse System 1834–1929*, London: Methuen.

Curtis Report (1946) *Report of the Care of Children Committee*, Cmd 6922, London: HMSO.

Digby, A. (1978) *Pauper Palaces*, London: Routledge & Kegan Paul.

Gilbert, B.B. (1966) *The Evolution of National Insurance in Great Britain*, London: Michael Joseph.

Gilbert, B.B. (1970) *British Social Policy, 1914–1939*, London: Batsford.

Harris, J. (1992) 'Political thought and the welfare state 1870–1940: an intellectual framework for British social policy', *Past and Present*, vol 135, pp 116-41.

Harris, J. (2002) 'From Poor Law to welfare state? A European perspective', in D. Winch and P.K. O'Brien (eds) *The Political Economy of British Historical Experience 1688–1914*, Oxford: Oxford University Press.

Hilton, B. (1988) *The Age of Atonement*, Oxford: Clarendon Press.

Hobson, J.A. (1902 [1996]), *The Social Problem*, reprinted by Bristol: Thoemmes.

Hollis, P. (1987) *Ladies Elect: Women in English Local Government, 1865–1914*, Oxford: Clarendon Press.

Hurren, E.T. (2005) 'Poor Law versus public health: diphtheria, sanitary reform and the "crusade" against outdoor relief, 1870-1900', *Social History of Medicine*, vol 18, no 3, pp 399-418.

Hurren, E. and King, S. (2005) 'Begging for a burial: form, function and conflict in nineteenth-century pauper burial', *Social History*, vol 30, no 3, pp 321-41.

Johnson, P. (1996) 'Risk, distribution and social welfare in Britain from the Poor Law to Beveridge', in M. Daunton (ed) *Charity, Self Interest and Welfare*, London: UCL, pp 225-48.

Le Grand, J. (2003) *Motivation, Agency and Public Policy*, Oxford: Oxford University Press.

Lees, L.H. (1998) *The Solidarities of Strangers: The English Poor Laws and the People, 1700–1948*, Cambridge: Cambridge University Press.

Lewis, J. (1995) 'Family provision of health and welfare in the mixed economy of care in the late nineteenth and twentieth centuries', *Social History of Medicine*, vol 8, no 1, pp 1-16.

Lyon, E.G. (1999) *Politicians in the Pulpit: Christian Radicalism in Britain from the Fall of the Bastille to the Disintegration of Chartism*, Aldershot: Ashgate.

McBriar, A.M. (1987) *An Edwardian Mixed Doubles: The Bosanquets Cersus the Webbs*, Oxford: Clarendon Press.

Mandler, P. (1990) 'Tories and paupers: Christian political economics and the making of the new Poor Law', *Historical Journal*, vol 33, pp 81-105.

Meadowcroft, J. (1995) *Conceptualizing the State*, Oxford: Clarendon Press.

Middleton, N. (1971) *When Family Failed*, London: Gollancz.

Offer, J. (2004) 'Dead theorists and older people', *Sociology*, vol 38, no 5, pp 891–908.

Offer, J. (2006a) *An Intellectual History of British Social Policy: Idealism Versus Non-Idealism*, Bristol: The Policy Press.

Offer, J. (2006b) '"Virtue", "citizen character" and "social environment": social theory and agency in social policy since 1830', *Journal of Social Policy*, vol 35, no 2, pp 283-302.

Pinker, R. (1971) *Social Theory and Social Policy*, London: Heinemann.

Pinker, R. (2006) 'From gift relationships to quasi-markets: an odyssey along the policy paths of altruism and egoism', *Social Policy and Administration*, vol 40, no 1, pp 10-25.

Poor Law Commission (1909a) *Report of the Royal Commission on the Poor Laws and Relief of Distress*, 3 vols (the Minority Report is vol 3), Cd 4499, London: HMSO.

Poor Law Commission (1909b) *Royal Commission on the Poor Laws and Relief of Distress: Appendix Volume 111: Being Evidence Mainly of Critics of the Poor Law and Witnesses Representing Poor Law and Charitable Associations*, Cd 4755, London: HMSO.

Poor Law Commission (1909c) *Royal Commission on the Poor Laws and Relief of Distress: Report on Scotland*, Cd 4922, London: HMSO.

Poor Law Commission (1910) *Royal Commission on the Poor Laws and Relief of Distress: Appendix Volume V11: Minutes of Evidence with Appendix, England*, Cd 5035, London: HMSO.

Rose, M.E. (1972) *The Relief of Poverty, 1834–1914*, London and Basingstoke: Macmillan.

Rose, M.E. (ed) (1985) *The Poor and the City: The English Poor Law in its Urban Context, 1834–1914*, Leicester: Leicester University Press.

Silburn, R. (1983) 'Social assistance and social welfare: the legacy of the Poor Law', in P. Bean and S. MacPherson (eds) *Approaches to Welfare*, London: Routledge & Kegan Paul, pp 132-49.

Thomson, D. (1986) 'Welfare and the historians', in L. Bonfield, R.M. Smith and K.Wrightson (eds) *The World we have Lost*, Oxford: Blackwell, pp 355-78.

Vincent, A. (1984) 'The Poor Law report of 1909 and the social theory of the Charity Organisation Society', *Victorian Studies*, vol 27, pp 143-63.

Waterman, A.M.C. (1991) *Revolution, Economics and Religion: Christian Political Economics, 1798-1833*, Cambridge: Cambridge University Press.

Webb, B. (1948) *Our Partnership*, London: Longmans Green.

Whately, R. (1832) *Introductory Lectures on Political-Economy*, 2nd edn, London: Fellowes.

Williams, K. (1981) *From Pauperism to Poverty*, London: Routledge & Kegan Paul.

# Part Two
## Contemporary childcare policy

# SEVEN

# Intercountry adoption in Europe 1998–2007: patterns, trends and issues

*Peter Selman*

## Introduction

Critics have raised many doubts about the movement of children for intercountry adoption, asking whether it is a 'global trade or global gift?' (Triseliotis, 2000), 'a global problem or a global solution?' (Masson, 2001). In this chapter I want to explore this question in Europe, which shares with America the pattern of being a continent with major movements of children between countries – in America from South to North; in Europe from East to West. However, Europe is of particular interest in the context of the enlarged European Union (EU), which contains both receiving states and states of origin.[1] I shall look in particular at the pressures on Romania and Bulgaria to reduce the number of children sent for intercountry adoption in the years preceding their accession in January 2007, which resulted in the ending of international adoptions by non-relatives from Romania in 2005 and a major reduction in the number of adoptions of children from Bulgaria.

One aim of this chapter is to provide the first detailed analysis of the movement of children for intercountry adoption between European countries in the context of the total movement of at least 45,000 children in 2004. The chapter starts with a statement of the countries defined as 'European' and clarification of the identification of these as primarily receiving states or states of origin. There will be a brief consideration of the history of intercountry adoption (ICA) in Europe since the Second World War, a more detailed account of which can be found in a paper presented at the 1996 Social Policy Association conference (Selman 1998), but the chapter will concentrate on the pattern of movement in the first seven years of the 20th century. Data presented in the tables and figures are based on statistics from central authorities of 23 receiving states. Estimates for states of origin are based on information about country of origin in the returns from the 23 receiving states listed in Table 7A in the Appendix as having reliable data (see also Selman, 2002, 2006).

## Countries studied and classification as sending or receiving states

This study is concerned with the movement of children for intercountry adoption to and from European countries. The countries chosen were the member states of the Council of Europe in 2007, with the addition of Belarus as a candidate for membership. This made a total of 48 states for which data were sought.

In order to carry out the analysis, countries were divided into receiving states and states of origin. Where possible, countries have been categorised by their responses to questionnaires sent to all contracting states by the Hague Conference on Private International Law for the 2005 Hague Special Commission on Intercountry Adoption (Hague Conference, 2005) or by ChildONEurope for their study for the European Parliament (Selman et al, 2009). Although many receiving states send some children as well, only Portugal has consistently described itself as 'both a receiving state and a state of origin'. Countries not responding to either questionnaire were classified in accordance with the available data – that is, whether they sent or received more children.

Table 7.1 shows the division of states, which resulted in 24 states being classified as receiving states and 23 as states of origin, with Portugal self-classified as 'both a receiving state and a state of origin'. The statistical analysis of receiving states in this chapter is based on 18 countries, as only limited data were available for Austria, Greece, Liechtenstein, Monaco, San Marino and Slovenia.

The resultant division is, not surprisingly, between the rich and poor countries of Europe (see Tables 7A and 7B in the Appendix to this chapter). The poorest receiving country with adequate data (Malta) had a per capita Gross National Income (GNI) of US$12,250 in 2004. In the richest sending country (Hungary), the per capita figure was US$8,270. The two countries classifying themselves, in their response to the 2005 Hague Special Commission on Intercountry Adoption questionnaire (Hague Conference, 2005), as 'both sending and receiving' – the Czech Republic and Portugal – had figures of US$9,150 and US$10,441 respectively. The states of origin sending most children had a consistently

**Table 7.1: European states[a] and intercountry adoption, 2007**

| Receiving states | | States of origin | |
|---|---|---|---|
| *EU* | *Hague* | *EU* | *Hague* |
| Austria | Yes | Bulgaria | Yes |
| Belgium | Yes | Czech Republic | Yes |
| Cyprus | Yes | Estonia | Yes |
| Denmark | Yes | Hungary | Yes |
| Finland | Yes | Latvia | Yes |
| France | Yes | Lithuania | Yes |
| Germany | Yes | Poland | Yes |
| Greece | No | (Portugal)[b] | (Yes) |
| Ireland | Signed | Romania | Yes |
| Italy | Yes | Slovak Republic | Yes |
| Luxembourg | Yes | **9 (10)** | **9 (10)** |
| Malta | Yes | | |
| Netherlands | Yes | | |
| (Portugal)[b] | (Yes) | *Non-EU* | |
| Slovenia | Yes | Albania | Yes |
| Spain | Yes | Armenia | Yes |
| Sweden | Yes | Azerbaijan | Yes |
| UK | Yes | Belarus[a] | Yes |
| **17 (18)** | **15 (16)** | Bosnia | No |
| | | Croatia | Yes |
| *Non-EU* | | Georgia | Yes |
| Andorra | Yes | Macedonia[c] | No |
| Iceland | Yes | Moldova | Yes |
| Liechtenstein[c] | No | Montenegro[d] | No |
| Monaco | Yes | Russia | Signed |
| Norway | Yes | Serbia | No |
| Switzerland | Yes | Turkey | Yes |
| San Marino | Yes | Ukraine | No |
| **7** | **6** | **14** | **8** |
| **24 (25)** | **21 (22)** | **23 (24)** | **18 (19)** |

Notes:
[a] All the states listed are members of the Council of Europe except Belarus whose application for membership is currently suspended.
[b] Portugal described itself as 'both a receiving state and a state of origin', supplying statistics supporting this definition for the period 2003–07. (The Hague Conference, 2005; Selman et al, 2009), and has been listed (in brackets) under both.
[c] Macedonia (The former Yugoslav Republic of Macedonia) and Liechtenstein acceded to the Convention in 2008 and 2009, with effect from 1 April and 1 May 2009, respectively.
[d] Montenegro became a full member of the Council in May 2007, prior to which it was classified as still part of Serbia, and so is not included in Appendix 7B or in the tables below.

*Source:* Hague Conference (2005, 2009); Selman et al (2009)

lower total fertility rate than the countries to which they sent children (see Table 7B in the Appendix).

## Intercountry adoption in Europe from the Second World War to the Hague Convention

The movement of children from Europe to distant lands has a long history, notably in the 160,000 'child migrants' sent by the UK to Australia, Canada, New Zealand and the US between 1618 and 1967 (Bean and Melville, 1989; Parker, 2008). However, intercountry adoption as a legal phenomenon involving formal agreements between sending and receiving countries is usually seen as developing in the aftermath of the Second World War, 'primarily as a North American philanthropic response to the devastation of Europe in World War II that resulted in thousands of orphaned children' (Altstein and Simon, 1991, p 1), although during the war itself there were movements of children within Europe – for example, from Finland to Sweden (Serenius, 1995) – and the widespread 'adoption' in Germany during the Third Reich of 'a great number of children born to Aryan women in occupied countries and fathered by German soldiers' (Textor, 1991, p 109).

### Adoption from European countries to the US, 1948–91

During the period 1948 to 1962, US parents adopted nearly 20,000 children from abroad. Many of these came from European countries – 3,116 from Greece (influenced also by the Greek Civil War), 1,845 from Germany and 744 from Austria – but there were also nearly 3,000 children adopted from Japan and a new source of adopted children emerged in the mid-1950s following the Korean War, with over 4,000 children adopted from Korea by 1962 (Altstein and Simon, 1991). The peak of 'European' adoptions came in the period 1947–57 when around 70% of children adopted in the US were of European origin (Carstens and Julia, 1995). The number of children adopted from Germany by 'foreigners' worldwide was over 1,000 per year from 1953 to 1962, reaching a peak of over 2,000 per year in the late 1950s (Textor, 1991, p 51). In the next 12 years – from 1963 to 1974 – a further 30,000 children were adopted by US citizens, the majority from Korea but some 20-25% from Europe (mostly from Germany, Italy and Greece but also from England and Ireland). After 1975, the number of adoptions to the US from Europe fell dramatically while the number of children adopted from Asia and Latin America rose (see Table 7.2).

**Table 7.2: US: major states of origin for children granted orphan visas and percentage of the total: selected years, 1948–91 (European states in bold)**

| 1948–62 | | 1967 | | 1972 | | 1982 | | 1987 | | 1991 | |
|---|---|---|---|---|---|---|---|---|---|---|---|
| Korea | 22 | **Germany** | 30 | Korea | 52 | Korea | 57 | Korea | 58 | **Romania** | 28 |
| **Greece** | 16 | Korea | 25 | Canada | 12 | Colombia | 9 | India | 8 | Korea | 20 |
| Japan | 13 | **Italy** | 7 | **Germany** | 7 | India | 7 | Philippines | 6 | Peru | 8 |
| Germany | 10 | Japan | 5 | Philippines | 4 | Philippines | 6 | Guatemala | 3 | Colombia | 6 |
| **Austria** | 4 | **England** | 4 | Vietnam | 4 | El Salvador | 4 | Mexico | 3 | India | 5 |
| **Totals** | | | | | | | | | | | |
| 19,230 | | 1,905 | | 3,023 | | 5,749 | | 10,097 | | 9,008 | |

*Source:* Altstein and Simon (1991, pp 14-16); US Department of State (2007)

By the late 1980s, Europe had become insignificant as a source of children for international adoption. Many of the former states of origin had become receiving states; for example, Germany and Italy were receiving more than 500 children per year and the only European country *sending* children on a significant scale was Poland. It is only in the last 15 years that Europe has once again become a significant source of children for adoption in the US, initially with adoptions from Romania and later from other Eastern European countries, such as Russia and the Ukraine. In 1991, a third of all intercountry adoptees who entered the US were from Romania alone (US Department of State, 2007).

## Intercountry adoption to and from Europe, 1970–94

There was also a movement of children *within* Europe. As late as 1974, a quarter of all intercountry adoptions in the Netherlands involved European children and during the 30 years following the Second World War a total of 576 Greek and 291 Austrian children are recorded as being adopted by Dutch parents (Hoksbergen, 1991). In Denmark, 80% of intercountry adoptions in 1970 involved children from other European countries; 10 years later, only 24 of the 766 intercountry adoptions in 1980 were of European children (Rorbech, 1991, p 128).

In this period, intercountry adoption in Europe became largely about children moving from third world countries and was increasingly seen as a response to the needs of childless couples for whom the availability of young children for domestic adoption had diminished dramatically following the liberalisation of abortion laws in the 1970s. Although substantial numbers of children from overseas were adopted in France,

Germany and Italy, the level of adoption in relation to population size was highest in the Netherlands and Scandinavia, where rates were several times higher than in the US. In Sweden, it has been estimated that during the period 1977–85, out of every hundred children added to its population, two were adopted from abroad (Andersson, 1986). Large-scale intercountry adoption was first seen in Sweden in the 1960s but by the 1970s was well established in the Netherlands and Scandinavia. By 1980, four European countries, Sweden, the Netherlands, Denmark, and Norway, were receiving almost as many children as the US (see Table 7.3); 15 years later they received less than a third of the total in the US and France was receiving more children than all four.

**Table 7.3: Annual number of intercountry adoptions in the US, Sweden, the Netherlands, Denmark, Norway and France, 1970–95, ranked by number in 1975**

| Receiving country | 1970 | 1975 | 1980 | 1987 | 1993 | 1995 |
|---|---|---|---|---|---|---|
| US | 2,409 | 5,633 | 5,139 | 10,097 | 7,377 | 9,769 |
| Sweden | 1,150 | 1,517 | 1,704 | 1,355 | 934 | 895 |
| Netherlands | 177 | 1,018 | 1,599 | 872 | 574 | 661 |
| Denmark | 226 | 770 | 766 | 537 | 473 | 541 |
| Norway | 115 | 397 | 384 | 465 | 519 | 488 |
| France | n/a | n/a | 935 | 1,723 | 2,784 | 3,034 |

Source: Selman (2006)

In the 1980s, the number of adoptions to the US and France rose sharply, while in Denmark, Sweden and the Netherlands, numbers were falling. However, from the late 1980s, the number of children going to the US also began to fall, reaching a low point of 7,093 visas granted in fiscal year 1990. During this period, European countries had been major recipients of children but contributed little in the way of sending children for intercountry adoption. Intercountry adoption in Europe in the 1970s and 1980s was largely about children moving from Asia and Latin America. Kane's study of the 1980s (Kane, 1993) shows that Korea (61,235) alone accounted for about a third of all intercountry adoptions and that, of the other 13 countries sending at least 1,000 children between 1980 and 1989, the only European country was Poland (1,480).

This pattern was then reversed dramatically with the collapse of the Ceausescu regime in December 1989 and the huge wave of adoptions that ensued in the following two years (see Selman, 1998, 2009).

'UNICEF (1999) has estimated that more than 10,000 children were taken from the country between January 1990 and July 1991, when the newly established Romanian Adoption Committee finally imposed a moratorium' (Selman, 2009, p 52). The arrival of 2,594 children from Romania in fiscal year 1991 had boosted the number of orphan visas issued in the US to 8,481, but a year later the number had fallen to 6,472 in 1992, less than two thirds of the number granted in 1987, and many commentators were talking about an end to intercountry adoption (for example, Altstein and Simon, 1991, p 191).

A similar pattern is found in European countries. During the five months from August 1990 to February 1991, 500 or more Romanian children went to France, Germany and Italy and at least 200 to Greece, Switzerland and the UK (Defence for Children International, 1991). Thereafter, numbers fell back sharply. Table 7.4 shows changes in countries sending the most children to France from 1979 to 1994.

**Table 7.4: France: major states of origin, 1979–94 (European states in bold)**

| 1979 | | 1981 | | 1985 | | 1991 | | 1994 | |
|---|---|---|---|---|---|---|---|---|---|
| Korea | 639 | Korea | 478 | Korea | 944 | **Romania** | 688 | Vietnam | 877 |
| India | 168 | India | 256 | Brazil | 225 | Brazil | 504 | Colombia | 328 |
| Colombia | 118 | Colombia | 171 | India | 147 | Colombia | 288 | Brazil | 292 |
| Lebanon | 34 | **Romania** | 145 | Colombia | 173 | India | 122 | **Russia** | 160 |
| **Poland** | 8 | Peru | 34 | Chile | 101 | Chile | 118 | India | 100 |
| **Totals** | | | | | | | | | |
| 971 | | 1,256 | | 1,988 | | 2,872 | | 3,058 | |

*Source:* Mission de l'Adoption Internationale

The rapid growth of intercountry adoption worldwide in the 1980s 'led to increasing concerns about abuses of the practice and the failure of many adoptions to meet the needs of the children involved' (Selman, 1998, p 149). Principles to govern the practice were included in the 1989 United Nations Convention on the Rights of the Child (UNCRC). In 1988, the Hague Conference on Private International Law set up a Special Commission on Intercountry Adoption, which met during the next five years and was attended by more than 65 states, both sending and receiving. The process culminated on 1 May 1993 in the Hague Convention on the Protection of Children and Cooperation in Respect of Intercountry Adoption, which recognised that intercountry adoption 'may offer the advantage of a permanent family to a child for whom a suitable family cannot be found in his or her State of origin', and provided a framework for cooperation between sending and receiving countries to ensure that intercountry adoption was only carried out in the best interest of the child. Fifteen years later, the Convention is supported by 78 states; of the major receiving countries, only Ireland has yet to ratify.

## Receiving states in Europe, 1995–2007

Although the number of children adopted from Romania fell dramatically after 1991, by the end of the decade other Eastern European countries – Belarus, Bulgaria, Russia and the Ukraine – had become important new sources of children, alongside China, and in the US the number of orphan visas rose to 22,884 in fiscal year 2004, while global numbers were estimated at over 45,000 (see Table 7.5). In that year, European sending countries accounted for over 30% of all intercountry adoptions despite a virtual cessation of adoptions from Romania. It is to an analysis of trends in this period that I will devote the rest of the chapter.

From the mid-1990s, the number of children adopted internationally began to rise in all European countries, including those that had experienced major falls in the previous 15 years (see Table 7.5). Throughout the period, France, Italy and Spain accounted for more than half of the total intercountry adoptions to Europe.

Although about half of all children sent for international adoption since 1998 have gone to the US, throughout the period the highest *level* of intercountry adoption (per 100,000 population) has been found in Norway, Sweden, Denmark and (since 2001) Spain and Ireland (see Table 7.6).

The differing levels of intercountry adoption are very striking and merit further examination, especially the dramatic rise in Spain and Ireland (see Table 7.7) and the continuing low rate in the UK, which has been variously attributed to official policies (Weil, 1984), attitudes of professionals (Hayes, 2000), costs (Halifax, 2006), the continuation of domestic adoption in contrast to most of mainland Europe and past experience of sending children to other countries.

**Table 7.5: Number of intercountry adoptions to the US and selected European receiving states, 1995–2007, by rank in 1999**

| State | 1995 | 1999 | 2003 | 2004 | 2006 | 2007 |
|---|---|---|---|---|---|---|
| US | 8,987 | 16,363 | 21,616 | 22,884 | 20,679 | 19,613 |
| France | 3,034 | 3,597 | 3,995 | 4,079 | 3,977 | 3,162 |
| Italy | 2,161 | 2,177 | 2,772 | 3,402 | 3,188 | 3,420 |
| Spain | 815 | 2,006 | 3,951 | 5,541 | 4.472 | 3,648 |
| Sweden | 895 | 1,019 | 1,046 | 1,109 | 879 | 800 |
| Nether-lands | 661 | 993 | 1,154 | 1,307 | 816 | 778 |
| Germany | 537 | 977 | 674 | 650 | 583 | 567 |
| Denmark | 548 | 697 | 523 | 528 | 447 | 429 |
| Norway | 488 | 589 | 714 | 706 | 448 | 426 |
| Belgium | 430 | 450 | 430 | 470 | 383 | 358 |
| UK | 154 | 312 | 301 | 334 | 364 | 356 |
| Ireland | 52 | 191 | 358 | 398 | 313 | 392 |
| **Europe (18 states)** | **10,429 (15)[b]** | **13,716 (17)[b]** | **16,922 (18)[b]** | **19,502 (18)[b]** | **16,561 (17)[b]** | **15,160 (18)[b]** |
| **World total (23 states)[a]** | **22,088 (19)[b]** | **32,913 (22)[b]** | **41,529 (23)[b]** | **45,288 (23)[b]** | **39,742 (22)[b]** | **37,526 (23)[b]** |
| % to Europe | 47% | 42% | 41% | 43% | 42% | 40% |
| % to the US | 41% | 49% | 52% | 51% | 52% | 52% |

*Notes:*

[a] The other states included in the totals are Australia, Canada, Finland, Iceland, Luxembourg, New Zealand and Switzerland – with the addition of Israel and Malta from 1999; Cyprus, 1999–2005 (EurAdopt only) and 2007; and Andorra, 2001–07.

[b] Figures in brackets indicate the number of states for which data were available each year.

*Source:* Statistics provided by the central authorities of the listed states

**Table 7.6: Crude intercountry adoption rates (per 100,000 population): US and selected European receiving states 1998–2006, ranked by rate in 2004**

| Receiving state | Number of adoptions 2006 | Adoptions per 100,000 population | | | |
|---|---|---|---|---|---|
| | | 2006 | 2004 | 2001 | 1998 |
| Norway | 448 | 9.6 | 15.4 | 15.9 | 14.6 |
| Spain | 4,472 | 10.2 | 13.0 | 8.6 | 3.8 |
| Sweden | 879 | 9.7 | 12.3 | 11.8 | 10.5 |
| Malta | 60 | 14.8 | 11.4 | 9.8 | 10.8 |
| Denmark | 447 | 8.2 | 9.8 | 9.8 | 11.8 |
| Ireland | 313 | 7.4 | 9.8 | 9.3 | 3.3 |
| US | 20,679 | 6.8 | 7.8 | 7.6 | 5.8 |
| France | 3,977 | 6.5 | 6.8 | 6.7 | 6.4 |
| Italy | 3,188 | 5.4 | 5.9 | 4.8 | 3.9 |
| Finland | 218 | 4.1 | 5.5 | 4.2 | 3.5 |
| Belgium | 383 | 3.7 | 4.5 | 4.2 | 4.8 |
| Germany | 583 | 0.7 | 0.8 | 1.0 | 1.1 |
| UK | 363 | 0.6 | 0.6 | 0.5 | 0.4 |

Source: Number of adoptions taken from statistics provided by the central authorities of the listed states; Population data from UNICEF (2000, 2003, 2006, 2007)

**Table 7.7: Percentage change in number of adoptions, 1998–2004: selected European receiving states and the US, ranked by increase**

| States | Adoptions 1998 | Adoptions 2001 | Adoptions 2004 | Change 1998–2004 (%) |
|---|---|---|---|---|
| Spain | 1,487 | 3,428 | 5,541 | + 273 |
| Ireland | 147 | 179 | 398 | + 171 |
| Finland | 181 | 218 | 289 | + 59.7 |
| Netherlands | 825 | 1,122 | 1,307 | + 58.4 |
| Italy | 2,233 | 1,797 | 3,402 | + 52.3 |
| **Europe (18 states)** | **13,098** | **14,352** | **19,502** | **+ 48.9** |
| US | 15,774 | 19,237 | 22,884 | + 45.1 |
| Total (23 states) | 31,924 | 36,379 | 45,288 | + 41.9 |
| UK | 258 | 326 | 333 | + 28.7 |
| Sweden | 928 | 1,044 | 1,109 | + 19.5 |
| Norway | 643 | 713 | 706 | + 9.8 |
| France | 3,777 | 3,094 | 4,079 | + 8.0 |
| Denmark | 624 | 631 | 528 | – 15.0 |

Source: Selman (2006)

## The growth of intercountry adoption, 1998–2004

The number of international adoptions worldwide doubled between 1995 and 2004 (see Table 7.5). Between 1998 and 2004, the overall increase was 42% but there was wide variation between receiving countries, with Spain experiencing a rise of 273% and Ireland a rise of 171% (see Table 7.7). In contrast, total numbers fell in Canada and Denmark.

## The decline in numbers, 2004–07

The steady increase in the global number of intercountry adoptions was reversed in 2005 and the decline accelerated in 2006 and 2007, by which time almost all the major receiving countries had experienced a fall in numbers. Overall, there was a fall of 17% across 23 states but there was variation between countries, with the largest decline in Finland, Norway and the Netherlands and a rise in Italy and Malta (see Table 7.8).

**Table 7.8: Changes in number of adoptions, selected receiving states, 2004–07, ranked by percentage change, 2004/05–07 (peak years in bold)**

| State | 2004 | 2005 | 2006 | 2007 | Change 2004/05–07 (%) |
|---|---|---|---|---|---|
| Finland | 289 | **308** | 218 | 176 | – 43 |
| Norway | **706** | 582 | 448 | 426 | – 40 |
| Netherlands | **1,307** | 1,185 | 816 | 778 | – 40 |
| Spain | **5,541** | 5,423 | 4.472 | 3,648 | – 35 |
| Sweden | **1,109** | 1,083 | 879 | 800 | – 28 |
| Denmark | 528 | **586** | 447 | 429 | – 27 |
| Belgium | 470 | **471** | 383 | 358 | – 24 |
| France | 4,079 | **4,136** | 3,977 | 3,162 | – 23 |
| Europe (18 states) | **19,502** | 18,412 | 16,557 | 15,138 | – 22 |
| World total (23 states) | **45,288** | 43,857 | 39,742 | 37,507 | – 17 |
| US | **22,884** | 22,728 | 20,679 | 19,613 | – 14 |
| UK | 333 | **369** | 363 | 356 | – 3.0 |
| Ireland | **398** | 366 | 313 | 392 | – 2.0 |
| Italy | 3,402 | 2,874 | 3,188 | **3,420** | + 0.5 |
| Malta | 46 | 39 | 60 | **64** | + 39 |

*Source:* Statistics provided by the central authorities of the receiving states listed

## States of origin in Europe 1991–2007

In 1991, Romania accounted for 31% of intercountry adoptions in the US. Five years later, Romanian adoptions contributed only 5% but this was more than compensated for by the contribution of Russia in the aftermath of the collapse of the Soviet Union. In the period 1989-91, only two of the 20 countries sending most children to the US were European – Romania and Poland. By 1994, this had risen to six with the addition of Russia, Bulgaria, the Ukraine and Lithuania and in 1997 the total increased to seven, with Russia the most important source of children. In 2003, seven of the top 20 sending countries were European, but three years later in 2006 only Russia, the Ukraine and Poland remained in the top 20. Table 7.9 shows the number of orphan visas issued for children from nine European countries between 1991 and 2007.

There have also been changes in the movement of children *within* Europe. From 2001 to 2004, six of the 10 countries sending most children to Italy were European – the Ukraine, Romania, Bulgaria, Belarus, Russia and Poland; by 2007, this had reduced to three: Russia, Poland and the Ukraine. A similar pattern is found in Spain (four to two) and France (three to two) (see Tables 7.10a and 7.10b).

**Table 7.9: Number of orphan visas issued in the US for children adopted from Europe, fiscal years 1991–2007 (peak years in bold)**

| State of origin | 1991[a] | 1996[a] | 2001 | 2002 | 2004 | 2006 | 2007 |
|---|---|---|---|---|---|---|---|
| Russia | < 50 | 2,454 | 4,279 | 4,939 | **5,865** | 3,706 | 2,310 |
| Ukraine | < 50 | 10 | **1,246** | 1,106 | 723 | 460 | 606 |
| Romania | **2,594** | 555 | 782 | 168 | 57 | 0 | 0 |
| Bulgaria | < 50 | 163 | **297** | 260 | 110 | 28 | 20 |
| Belarus | < 50 | <50 | 129 | 169 | **202** | 0 | 0 |
| Poland | 92 | 64 | 86 | 101 | **102** | 67 | 84 |
| Latvia | < 50 | **82** | 27 | 33 | 15 | 24 | 32 |
| Lithuania | < 50 | **78** | 30 | 21 | 29 | 14 | 27 |
| Hungary | < 50 | **72** | 13 | 21 | 8 | 10 | 10 |
| Total (9 states) | 2,686+ | 3,478 | 6,889 | 6,818 | 7,111 | 4,309 | 3,089 |
| All countries | 8,481 | 10,641 | 19.237 | 20,099 | 22,824 | 20,679 | 19,613 |
| 9 states as % | 32%+ | 33% | 37% | 35% | 33% | 21% | 16% |

*Note:* [a] 1991 and 1996 data list only top 20 states.

*Source:* US Department of State (2008)

**Table 7.10a: States sending most children to the US, Spain, France, Italy and EurAdopt agencies in 2004 (European states in bold)**

| US | Spain | France | Italy | EurAdopt |
|---|---|---|---|---|
| China | China | Haiti | Russia | China |
| **Russia** | **Russia** | China | **Ukraine** | Colombia |
| Guatemala | **Ukraine** | **Russia** | Colombia | South Korea |
| South Korea | Colombia | Ethiopia | **Belarus** | Ethiopia |
| Kazakhstan | Ethiopia | Vietnam | Brazil | India |
| **Ukraine** | India | Colombia | **Poland** | South Africa |
| India | Bolivia | Madagascar | Ethiopia | **Russia** |
| Haiti | Nepal | **Ukraine** | **Romania** | Thailand |
| Ethiopia | **Bulgaria** | **Latvia** | **Bulgaria** | Brazil |
| Colombia | **Romania** | Brazil | India | Bolivia |
| **22,884** | **5,541** | **4,079** | **3,402** | **4,204** |

**Table 7.10b: States sending most children to the US, Spain, France, Italy and EurAdopt agencies in 2007 (European states in bold)**

| US | Spain | France | Italy | EurAdopt |
|---|---|---|---|---|
| China | China | Ethiopia | **Russia** | China |
| Guatemala | **Russia** | Haiti | Colombia | Ethiopia |
| **Russia** | Ethiopia | **Russia** | **Ukraine** | Colombia |
| Ethiopia | **Ukraine** | Colombia | Brazil | South Africa |
| South Korea | Colombia | Vietnam | Vietnam | Thailand |
| Vietnam | Kazakhstan | China | Ethiopia | South Korea |
| **Ukraine** | India | Mali | **Poland** | India |
| Kazakhstan | Nepal | **Ukraine** | Cambodia | Vietnam |
| India | Bolivia | Thailand | India | Brazil |
| Liberia | Mexico | Brazil | Peru | Taiwan = Poland = |
| **19,613** | **3,648** | **3,162** | **3,420** | **2,881** |

*Source:* Data on states of origin from the central authorities of US, Spain, France and Italy and Euradopt Statistics for 2004 (Table 10a) and 2007 (Table 10b)

Statistics from EurAdopt[2] for 1993–2007 show that for member agencies the top 10 sending countries included only two European countries – Russia and Romania. In 1993, the top 10 were all from Asia or Latin America, with Colombia the most important source until 1998, since when China has sent most children. Romania was an important source from 1995 to 1999 and Russia from 1996 to 2006. Ethiopia has been one of the top 10 countries sending children throughout the period and was the second most important source of children in 2007 (Table 7.10b). In 2007, there were no European countries in the top 10 states of origin.

The impending accession of Bulgaria and Romania to the EU resulted in pressure on those countries to reduce the number of children sent, despite the fact that EU countries lead the way in receiving children and several of the new (2005) members such as Latvia, Lithuania and Poland continue to send many children. There is now clear evidence of the impact of these pressures on the total number of children sent by Romania since 2003 (see Table 7.11). Numbers have also fallen in Russia, Bulgaria, the Ukraine and Belarus, but Estonia, Hungary, Latvia, Lithuania and Poland all sent more children in 2006 than in 2003 (see Table 7.12).

## The movement of children within Europe, 2003–06

In order to provide an accurate picture of the current movement of children, this section will concentrate on a detailed analysis of the movement of children to and from 47 European states between 2003 and 2007. These are the 46[3] countries in the Council of Europe in 2003 and Belarus. The list includes three countries – Armenia, Azerbaijan and

**Table 7.11: Adoptions from Romania to 21[a] receiving states, 2000–05, ranked by number received by the five listed states in 2001**

| Receiving state | 2000 | 2001 | 2002 | 2003 | 2004 | 2005 |
|---|---|---|---|---|---|---|
| US | 1,119 | 782 | 168 | 200 | 57 | 2 |
| Spain | 583 | 373 | 38 | 85 | 48 | 3 |
| France | 370 | 223 | 42 | 17 | 16 | n/a |
| Italy | 23 | 173 | 40 | 70 | 119 | 0 |
| Ireland | 69 | 48 | 12 | 8 | 2 | 0 |
| **Total** | **2,478** | **1,813** | **413** | **421**[a] | **287**[a] | **15** |

Note: [a] All states listed in Table 7.5 and footnote a to that table, except Andorra and Cyprus.

Source: Data on states of origin in statistics provided by central authorities of the 21 receiving states (Selman, 2009)

Georgia – that are often classed geographically as Asian. Twenty-four of these were primarily receiving states (Table 7.1), but reliable annual data were not available for Austria, Cyprus, Liechtenstein, Monaco, San Marino and Slovenia. The data presented, therefore, concern a total of 18 European receiving countries (with partial data for Austria). Numbers of children sent to the 23 states of origin were estimated from the information on source of children from these 18 countries and five non-European states (see Selman, 2002, 2006, for a discussion of the accuracy of such estimates). Table 7.12 shows changes in total numbers sent by 15 European states of origin, including all those in the EU.

There are major differences among countries in the proportion received from or sent to other European states. Table 7.13 shows the

**Table 7.12: International adoptions from selected Eastern European states to 23 receiving states, 2003–07, ranked by number sent in 2003 (peak years in bold)**

| State | 2003 | 2004 | 2005 | 2006 | 2007 |
|---|---|---|---|---|---|
| Russia | 7,747 | **9,425** | 7,468 | 6,753 | 4,873 |
| Ukraine | **2,052** | 2,021 | 1,705 | 1,031 | 1,619 |
| Bulgaria[a] | **963** | 393 | 115 | 96 | 95 |
| Belarus | **656** | 627 | 23 | 34 | 14 |
| Romania[a] | **473** | 287 | 15 | 0 | 0 |
| Poland[b] | 346 | **408** | 378 | 362 | 359 |
| Lithuania[b] | 85 | **99** | 78 | 90 | 118 |
| Hungary[b] | 69 | 68 | 24 | 92 | **128** |
| Latvia[b] | 65 | 124 | 114 | **140** | 100 |
| Serbia | **59** | 49 | 16 | 14 | 16 |
| Slovakia[b] | 53 | **75** | 30 | 28 | 45 |
| Estonia[b] | 21 | 18 | 24 | 12 | **30** |
| Moldova | 30 | **65** | 66 | 34 | 62 |
| Czech Republic[b] | 18 | **34** | 27[c] | 25[c] | 20 |
| Albania | 14 | **27** | 20 | 25 | 15 |

Notes:

[a] Bulgaria and Romania joined the EU on 1 January 2007.

[b] These seven states joined the EU in May 2004 – for data provided by these 7 states to the ChildONEurope survey for the European Parliament see Selman et al (2009)

[c] Data from ChildONEurope survey suggest higher figures (53 and 35) for these years (Selman et al, 2009)

Source: Data on states of origin from statistics provided by central authorities of 23 receiving states with additional data from some EU states (Selman et al, 2009).

wide variation in the proportion of children going to eight European receiving countries from other members of the Council of Europe. Two of the smaller countries (Iceland and Luxembourg) received children only from outside Europe. Of the non-European receiving states, in 2004 Israel took children mainly (92%) from European countries (Belarus, Russia and the Ukraine) but also 11 from Guatemala while Australia took very few from Europe (none in 2003–04). The overall proportion of children received from other European countries falls steadily over the period. A similar wide variation was found in the sending countries (Table 7.14). The EU countries were most likely to send children to other European countries while the lowest proportion sent was found in Russia and the three European/Asian members of the Council of Europe, which sent children mainly to the US. Serbia/Montenegro and Croatia sent few children, all to other European countries in 2003. Although total numbers fell, the proportion of children sent to other European countries grew over the period, from 43% to 47%. For a fuller account of recent changes in the EU, including data from the nine EU states of origin, see Selman et al (2009).

**Table 7.13: Proportion of children adopted in Europe who came from other European states: selected receiving states, 2003–06, ranked by proportion from Europe in 2004**

| Receiving state | 2003 | | 2004 | | 2006 | |
|---|---|---|---|---|---|---|
| | Total number of adoptions | % from Europe | Total number of adoptions | % from Europe | Total number of adoptions | % from Europe |
| Ireland | 358 | 55 | 398 | 65 | 313 | 49 |
| Italy | 2,772 | 62 | 3,403 | 64 | 3,188 | 45 |
| Germany | 674 | 33 | 650 | 52 | 583 | 29 |
| Spain | 3,951 | 48 | 5,541 | 38 | 4,472 | 34 |
| **All Europe** | **16,898** | **34** | **19,502** | **32** | **16,553** | **25** |
| **All 23 countries** | **41,529** | **32** | **45,288** | **31** | **39,738** | **21** |
| France | 3,995 | 22 | 4,079 | 21 | 3,977 | 14 |
| Sweden | 1,046 | 20 | 1,109 | 16 | 879 | 11 |
| Norway | 714 | 6 | 706 | 4 | 448 | 6 |
| Netherlands | 1,154 | 2 | 1,307 | 2 | 818 | 4 |

*Source:* Central authorities of states listed

**Table 7.14: Proportion of children sent to other European states: selected sending states, 2003–06**

| State | 2003 | | 2004 | | 2006 | |
|---|---|---|---|---|---|---|
| | Number | % to Europe | Number | % to Europe | Number | % to Europe |
| Slovakia | 42 | 98 | 75 | 99 | 28 | 100 |
| Latvia | 65 | 77 | 124 | 86 | 140 | 83 |
| Poland | 345 | 72 | 408 | 74 | 362 | 81 |
| Ukraine | 2,052 | 60 | 2,021 | 60 | 1,031 | 49 |
| European states | 12,961 | 43 | 13,956 | 45 | 8,843 | 47 |
| All states of origin | 41,529 | 42 | 45,288 | 42 | 39,738 | 42 |
| Moldova | 30 | 20 | 65 | 29 | 34 | 56 |
| Russia | 7,746 | 30 | 9,425 | 36 | 6,752 | 42 |
| Armenia | 73 | 25 | 57 | 28 | 64 | 31 |
| Georgia | 156 | 2 | 32 | 6 | 9 | 0 |

*Source:* Data on states of origin from statistics provided by the central authorities of 23 receiving states

## Summary

We can see from the above tables that European countries now receive substantially more children than they send. Between 2003 and 2006, European receiving countries accounted for about 42% of all adoptions from abroad but the proportion of adoptions worldwide that involved children from Europe fell from 32% in 2003 to 21% in 2006. By that year, only 25% of adoptions to Europe were from other European countries. This is the result of a period in which Romania ended overseas adoption and a number of other East European countries reduced numbers significantly. The fall is most evident in Romania and Bulgaria, the two countries seeking membership of the EU during these years. However, several of the existing EU members from the former Eastern bloc – Estonia, Hungary, Latvia and Lithuania – actually increased the number of children sent over the same period (see Table 7.12). If we consider only those countries that were EU members in 2007, intercountry adoptions from these states in 2006 accounted for just 2% of the movement of children worldwide, while EU *receiving* states accounted for 40% of all intercountry adoptions in the same year.

# What has been the impact of intercountry adoption on the well-being of children in Europe?

In this section, I shall address a number of related issues, which impinge on current discussions about the future of intercountry adoption in Europe and especially within the EU (see, for example, Gibault, 2008; Lammerant and Hofstetter, 2008):

- What is the experience of the children adopted from outside Europe into European countries since the Second World War?
- What has been the experience of children adopted out of European countries?
- Has there been any difference in relation to children adopted to North America or Oceania in contrast to those adopted within Europe?
- Has the practice of intercountry adoption adversely affected the development of childcare, including in-country adoption, in sending countries?
- Has the growth of intercountry adoption discouraged receiving countries from developing special needs adoption for children within these countries?

## *What is the experience of the children adopted from outside Europe into European countries since the Second World War?*

There is now a substantial number of 'children' from Asia and Latin America who have grown up as European citizens – most still living in the West. The long tradition of overseas adoption in the Nordic countries and the Netherlands has resulted in a large body of research into such children, which extends to the experience of adoptees as adults (Hoksbergen, 1987; Saetersdal and Dalen, 1991; Verhulst, 2000).

Most of this research is positive, but early research in the Netherlands by Hoksbergen (1991, 2000) revealed that intercountry adoptees were five times more likely to be in residential care than native-born Dutch children and Dalen (1998) notes that in Scandinavia there is a substantial minority of adoptees who have major problems. A longitudinal study by Verhulst (2000) of children adopted in the Netherlands showed generally good progress but an increase in problem behaviour in adolescence. Further evidence for this is found in a study by Hjern et al (2002, 2004), which showed an increased risk of suicide in adopted people in their late teens and early twenties. Palacios et al (2006) have studied adoption disruption in Spain, where intercountry adoption has grown dramatically in the last decade. A detailed review of the outcomes for children adopted from overseas can be found in the work of Juffer and van IJzendoorn (2005, 2009) whose meta-analyses are interpreted as showing a 'massive catch-up in all developmental domains ... demonstrating that adoption as an alternative for institutional care is a very successful intervention in children's lives' (2009, p 187).

Issues of identity have been identified as a problem for older adoptees, especially in the Nordic countries where the number of people from minority ethnic groups was very small in the years when many children arrived for intercountry adoption. Even today, a majority of Koreans living in Denmark were adopted by Danish parents and Saetersdal and Dalen (1991, 2000) note some of the problems facing the Vietnamese adopted into Norway in the 1970s who as they reached adolescence sought to distance themselves from immigrants, the 'boat people' who arrived at the same time.

## What has been the experience of children adopted out of European countries? Has there been any difference in relation to children adopted to North America or Oceania in contrast to those adopted within Europe?

The children adopted to the US from war-torn Europe are now middle aged and yet there has been surprisingly little published research on them. There is, however a vivid account of one such adoption by Peter Dodds (1997), who was adopted in the US after being 'rescued' from a German orphanage in the 1950s, and articulates some of the problems not recognised by those who sent them away or who took them in. It is also often forgotten that many Finnish children moved to other Scandinavian countries during the Second World War; 70,000 to Sweden alone (Serenius, 1995).

There has been a substantial amount of research on the children adopted from Romania to Canada and the US (Haugaard et al, 2000). Most of this indicates positive gains, at least in the short term, and mirrors the experiences of children from Romania adopted within Europe (Rutter et al, 2000, 2009; Hoksbergen et al, 2002). There has been less research on children adopted from other European countries.

There have been suggestions of many problems associated with Russian children suffering from foetal alcohol syndrome and in the US some of these appear to have led to major reactions from the adoptive parents, with reports of a number who have killed their adopted children. Issues of adoption from Russia to Italy are dramatically highlighted in the 2005 Russian film, *The Italian*. The situation of children adopted from Russia to the UK is discussed by Farina et al (2004).

There has been less attention on children adopted from Poland and other countries joining the EU in 2005. This is urgently needed in relation to the growing placement of older children, children with special needs and sibling groups. Likewise, no studies have explored differences in outcomes for children adopted in contrasting receiving states.

### Has the practice of intercountry adoption adversely affected the development of childcare, including in-country adoption, in sending countries?

Concerns over child-trafficking and other irregularities in intercountry adoption from Eastern Europe have been expressed by several international charities during the last 20 years, especially in respect of adoptions from Romania (Defence for Children International, 1991) and Bulgaria (Save the Children UK, 2003).

It has also been argued that intercountry adoption has had a negative impact on the development of services for children in European states of origin. This has been most extensively argued in respect of Romania (Dickens, 2002, 2006; Post, 2007). These authors' findings mirror earlier concerns expressed by Sarri et al (2002) about the impact of high rates of intercountry adoption from Korea.

Chou and Browne (2008) have sought to extend this thesis to all European sending countries by presenting a Spearman rank correlation that shows a significant relationship between the proportion of all adoptions that are intercountry and the number of children in institutional care aged under three. However, the data used are flawed and the exclusion, due to lack of data on adoption, of two key countries – Poland and the Czech Republic – makes the finding suspect (Gay Y Blasco et al, 2008). The Czech Republic had many young children in residential care in 2003 (Browne, 2005) but a very low rate of intercountry and a preponderance of domestic adoption (Selman et al, 2009). Many children now sent for international adoption from Europe are older or have special needs and are hard to place domestically (Selman et al, 2009).

In 2008, Terre des Hommes published a study of six European receiving countries (Lammerant and Hofstetter, 2008, p 3) that is highly critical of some practices and calls for 'political measures by the receiving countries, individually and collectively, in the interests of children, especially within the framework of the Hague Conference on Private

International Law and the European Union' (p 3). A discussion in the European Parliament following the launch of the report revealed large differences concerning the future of international adoption in the EU, which are discussed further in a later section.

### Has the growth of intercountry adoption discouraged receiving states from developing special needs adoption for children within these countries?

The Terre des Hommes study was focused on European receiving states, which account for about 40% of all international adoptions (see Table 7.5). Although the US continues to be the main receiver of children in absolute numbers, the countries with the highest rate of international adoption standardised against population – Spain, Malta and the three major Scandinavian countries – are all from Western Europe (see Table 7.6). Among EU members, only Germany,[4] the UK and Portugal have a rate of less than one per 100,000 population. In recent years there has been a growing interest in the UK policy of encouraging domestic adoption as a solution to the failure of the care system, a policy shared with the US but not found in any other European country. Domestic adoption is rare in most European receiving countries (Selman and Mason, 2005; Selman et al, 2009) and this has been a trigger for childless couples in many of these countries to turn to intercountry adoption.

In their article, Chou and Browne (2008) argue that intercountry adoption also has a negative impact on children in receiving states. The authors accept that the correlation they find between international adoption and institutional care in receiving countries is 'open to question' (2008, p 47), but nonetheless assert that 'adopting healthy young children from abroad may distract attention from hard-to-place children within the receiving countries' (2008, p 47). The weak correlation shown is only made possible by the exclusion of the UK, Iceland, Slovenia and Norway, the European country with the highest rate of incoming intercountry adoption but the lowest level of children in institutions (see Gay Y Blasco et al, 2008). It seems likely that the impact of intercountry adoption varies between countries but many European countries are now reviewing their policies on domestic adoption of children with special needs.

# The position of the EU in intercountry adoption

Following the application for membership of the EU by Bulgaria and Romania, there seemed to be a growing feeling within the European Parliament that it was somehow inappropriate for a member country to be sending large numbers of children for intercountry adoption, despite the fact that many go to other European countries and member states receive some 40% of all children placed for international adoption. The pressure to end intercountry adoption from Europe was led by a determined campaign by Baroness Emma Nicholson, the European Parliament's special envoy for Romania from 1999 to 2005 (see Nicholson, 2006). As early as 1999, Romania was asked to reform its childcare system as a condition of membership and in 2001 to specifically reform its intercountry adoption laws, which were seen as incompatible with Romania's obligations under the UNCRC (Pereboom, 2005). In March 2004, the Parliament passed a further resolution, calling on Romania to undertake further reforms and expressing concern about the large number of children sent for international adoption by Bulgaria (Pereboom, 2005, p 18). In June 2004, Romania introduced a ban on international adoption other than by a child's grandparents, with the consequence that no intercountry adoptions have been recorded in recent years. In 2003, Bulgaria changed its laws so that intercountry adoption was allowed only after all other options had been explored and three domestic candidates had refused to accept the child offered to them. By 2006/07, adoptions from Bulgaria had fallen to less than 100 per year.

Nicholson's position was supported by the publication by Roelie Post (2007) of a diary, dedicated to Baroness Nicholson, which described eight years of work for the European Commission to help Romania reform its child welfare services. Post presented evidence of widespread corruption in a market 'where global politics and private interests compete with the rights of the child' and argued that there is no place or need for intercountry adoptions in Romania's reformed child protection system. Post also identified the emergence of a 'ferocious' lobby that wanted Romania to continue such adoptions. Led by parents' groups and adoption agencies in the US, the campaign also received backing from US House of Representatives (H.Res 578).

Following the end to international adoptions from Romania, the European Parliament seems to have had some second thoughts and Tannock (2006) has argued that many members are now lobbying the European Commission and the Romanian government to reopen adoptions. Pierre Moscovi, who took over from Emma Nicholson as the European Parliament rapporteur on Romania, has taken a very different stance on adoption from Romania and Members of the European Parliament (MEPs) have called on Romania to allow intercountry adoptions to take place 'where justified and appropriate'.

One key issue throughout has been the position of over 1,000 prospective adopters, whose adoptions were 'in the pipeline'. In February 2004, a petition was brought before the European Commission by a prospective adopter from Greece arguing that her adoption, which had been authorised, should be allowed as the matched child was 'left in deplorable conditions in a Romanian foster family'. In refusing the petition, the Commission welcomed the new Romanian legislation 'as a long awaited step to align Romanian law with ... the practice in EU members states' (European Parliament, 2006, p 2) and saw the suspension of the adoption as legal and a matter for the Romanian government alone. This position was reinforced by Olli Rehn, European Commissioner for Enlargement, who has ruled that the new legislation applies to all pending cases and that it is unlikely that any requests for completion will be accepted (Tannock, 2006).

Within the Parliament itself, there continue to be bitter divisions between those supporting the arguments of Nicholson and Post for an end to intercountry adoption from EU countries and French MEPs Claire Gibault and Jean-Marie Cavada, themselves adoptive parents, who argue for the resumption of intercountry adoption from Romania and Bulgaria to meet the interests of institutionalised children and 'the need to create an adoption procedure common to all European states and to encourage international adoption where there is no national solution' (Gibault, 2008). In May 2008, the European Parliament issued a call for tenders for a study of intercountry adoption in all 27 EU countries – the tender being awarded to ChildONEurope, which will report in early 2009 (see Selman et al, 2008).

## Unresolved questions

The discussion above still leaves many unresolved questions about the impact of intercountry adoption on children in Europe over the last 20 years:

- What are the implications of the reduction in level of adoptions from Romania and Bulgaria on the well-being of children in those countries?

- Why is there no concern over rising numbers of children adopted from other EU countries such as Poland, Latvia and Lithuania?
- Are there advantages in children moving shorter distances for intercountry adoption – for example within Europe – or between South and North America?
- What impact will the fall in supply of children have on competition between receiving countries in Europe and pressure to persuade sending countries to provide children for the growing number of waiting prospective adopters?

## Conclusion

The number of intercountry adoptions recorded worldwide has been falling since 2004 after a decade of continuous growth. The fall in numbers has been greater in Europe than in the US and within Europe has been greatest in Scandinavian countries and the Netherlands (Table 7.8). A major factor in this dramatic reversal has been the reduction in the number of children sent *from* Europe, although the impact of China's retrenchment has probably been more significant in total numbers (Selman, 2009).

One result of this largely unexpected change of direction has been that the number of people approved for intercountry adoption now far outstrips the number of children available. Prospective adoptive parents in France and Spain face a long wait for a child and many may never receive one. China's decision to end placements with single women means that this group will face particular difficulties. The fear is that this will bring out the market mechanisms that many have noted (Freidmutter, 2002) and lead to a trade in children, as agencies (and countries) seek new sources of adoptable children and the 'price' of such children rises or – as is already happening in Italy – prospective parents take on older children with potential problems for which they have not been prepared.

Although most research into the outcome of intercountry adoption is positive, showing a remarkable developmental 'catch-up' in children who had been in institutions (van IJzendoorn and Juffer, 2006; Juffer and van IJzendoorn, 2009), the findings from Hjern et al (2002) and others suggest considerable problems for a minority of those involved. Evidence of trafficking has led one commentator to express the fear that 'the recurrent cycle of scandal, excuse, and ineffective 'reform' will probably continue until intercountry adoption is finally abolished, with history labelling the entire enterprise as a neo-colonialist mistake' (Smolin, 2004, p 35). A recent article in the journal *Foreign Policy* (Graff,

2008) argues that many of the children involved are not orphans but stolen children 'laundered' (Smolin, 2007) for international adoption, which has become a trade (Kapstein, 2003) or an industry.

Much of the criticism is focused on US policy before ratification of the Hague Convention, but similar concerns are now expressed about intercountry adoption in Australia (Callinan, 2008; Rollings, 2008) and Europe (Lammerant and Hofstetter, 2008). While research seems to indicate that the outcome of international adoptions, including those from Romania, have been positive for most of the children involved, the impact of the practice on the many children not placed in overseas families remains unresolved. We should, perhaps, also ponder the words of Roy Parker in the conclusion to his devastating account of the 80,000 children shipped from Britain to Canada by Poor Law authorities and voluntary bodies between 1867 and 1917: 'One cannot help wondering how the convictions that are entertained today about the needs of vulnerable children and how these should be met might ….be judged 100 years from now' (Parker, 2008, p 293).

## Notes

1   The terms 'receiving State' and 'State of origin' are those used in the 1993 Hague Convention (see pp 139-40) for countries receiving or sending children for intercountry adoption.
2   EurAdopt is an organisation of European adoption agencies, predominantly from the Nordic countries and the Netherlands, with the gradual addition of selected agencies from Belgium, Italy, France and other European countries.
3   In 2003, Montenegro was still part of Serbia.
4   German numbers are probably too low as available statistics do not include 'private' adoptions (Selman et al, 2009).

## References

Altstein, H. and Simon, J. (1991) *Intercountry Adoption: A Multinational Perspective*, New York: Praeger.

Andersson, G. (1986) 'The adopting and adopted Swedes and their contemporary society', in R. Hoksbergen (ed) *Adoption in Worldwide Perspective*, Lisse: Swets and Zeitliger.

Bean, P. and Melville, J. (1989) *Lost Children of the Empire*, London: Unwin Hyman.

Callinan, R. (2008) 'Stolen children', *Time*, 21 August.

Carstens, C. and Julia, M. (1995) 'Legal, policy and practice issues for intercountry adoptions in the United States', *Adoption & Fostering*, vol 19, no 4, pp 26-33.

ChildONEurope (2006) *Report on National and Intercountry Adoption*, Florence: Istituto degli Innocenti.

ChildONEurope (2009: forthcoming) *International Adoption in the EU: Report to the European Parliament*, Florence: Istituto degli Innocenti.

Chou, S. and Browne, K. (2008) 'The relationship between institutional care and the international adoption of children in Europe', *Adoption & Fostering*, vol 32, no 1, pp 40-8.

Dalen, M. (1998) 'State of knowledge of foreign adoptions 1998', available at www.comeunity.com/adoption/adopt/research.html

Defence for Children International (1991) *ROMANIA: The Adoption of Romanian Children by Foreigners*, Geneva: DCI/ISS.

Dickens, J. (2002) 'The paradox of inter-country adoption: analysing Romania's experience as a sending country', *International Journal of Social Welfare*, vol 11, no 2, pp 76-83.

Dickens, J. (2006) 'The social policy contexts of intercountry adoption', Paper presented at the Second International Conference on Adoption Research, University of East Anglia, Norwich, 17-21 July.

Dodds, P. (1997) *Outer Search/Inner Journey: An Orphan and Adoptee's Quest*, Pyallup, Washington, DC: Aphrodite Publishing Company.

European Parliament (2006) *Notice to Members from the Committee on Petitions: Petition 0459/2005 by Teresa Afrataiou (Greek) on Actions of the Romanian Authorities in Halting Adoptions*, available at www.europarl. europa.eu/meetdocs2004_2009/documents/cm/615/615960/ 615960en.pdf

Farina, L., Leifer, M. and Chasnoff, I.J. (2004) 'Attachment and behavioural difficulties in internationally adopted Russian children', *Adoption & Fostering*, vol 28, no 2, pp 38-49.

Freidmutter, C. (2002) 'International adoptions: problems and solutions', Testimony before the House Committee on International Relations, 2 May, available at www.adoptioninstitute.org/publications/

Gay Y Blasco, P., McRae, S., Selman, P. and Wardle, H. (2008) 'The relationship between institutional care and the international adoption of children in Europe: a rejoinder to Chou and Browne', *Adoption & Fostering*, vol 32, no 2, pp 63-8.

Gibault, C. (2008) 'Towards a European adoption procedure', available at www.claire-gibault.eu/site/index.php?page=adoptionandhl=en_GB

Graff, E.J. (2008) 'The lie we love', *Foreign Policy*, November/December, pp 1-5.

Hague Conference (2005) *Responses to Questionnaire on the practical operation of the Hague Convention of 29 May 1993 on Protection of Children and Co-operation in Respect of Intercountry Adoption (Prel. Doc. No 1 of March 2005)*, The Hague: Hague Conference on Private International Law, www.hcch.net/index_en.php?act=conventions. publications&dtid=33&cid=69 (accessed 13 March 2009).

Hague Conference (2009) *Status Table for the Convention of 29 May 1993 on Protection of Children and Co-operation in Respect of Intercountry Adoption*, The Hague: Hague Conference on Private International Law, www.hcch.net/index_en.php?act=conventions.status&cid=69 (accessed 13 March 2009).

Halifax, J. (2006) 'Why are there so many international adoptions in France?', Paper presented at the Second International Conference on Adoption Research, University of East Anglia, Norwich, 17–21 July.

Haugaard, J., Wojslawowicz, J. and Palmer, M. (2000) 'International adoption: children from Romania', *Adoption Quarterly*, vol 3, no 3, pp 73-83.

Hayes, P. (2000) 'Deterrents to intercountry adoption in Britain', *Family Relations*, vol 49, no 4, pp 465-71.

Hjern, A., Lindblad, B. and Vinnerlung, C. (2002) 'Suicide, psychiatric illness and social maladjustment in intercountry adoptees in Sweden: a cohort study', *Lancet*, 2002, vol 360, pp 443-8.

Hjern, A., Vinnerljung, B. and Lindbald, F. (2004) 'Avoidable mortality among child welfare recipients and intercountry adoptees; a national cohort study', *Journal of Epidemiology and Community Health*, vol 58, no 5, pp 412-17.

Hoksbergen, R. (1987) *Adopted Children at Home and School*, Lisse: Swets and Zeitlinger.

Hoksbergen, R. (1991) 'Intercountry adoption coming of age in the Netherlands: basic issues, trends and developments', in H. Altstein and R. Simon (eds) *Intercountry Adoption: A Multinational Perspective*, New York: Praeger.

Hoksbergen, R. (2000) 'Changes in attitudes in three generations of adoptive parents', in P. Selman (ed) *Intercountry Adoption: Development, Trends and Perspectives*, London: BAAF, pp 295-314.

Hoksbergen, R., Dijkum, C. and van Stoutjesdijk, F. (2002) 'Experiences of Dutch families who parent an adopted Romanian child', *Journal of Developmental and Behavioral Pediatrics*, vol 23, no 6, pp 403-9.

Juffer, F. and van IJzendoorn, M.H. (2005) 'Behaviour problems and mental health referrals of international adoptees: a meta-analysis', *Journal of the American Medical Association*, vol 293, no 20, pp 2501-15.

Juffer, F. and van IJzendoorn, M.H. (2009) 'International adoption comes of age: development of international adoptees from a longitudinal and meta-analytical perspective', in G. Wrobel and E. Neill (eds) *International Advances in Adoption Research*, London: John Wiley, pp 169-92.

Kane, S. (1993) 'The movement of children for international adoption: an epidemiological perspective', *The Social Science Journal*, vol 30, no 4, pp 323-39.

Kapstein, E.B. (2003) 'The baby trade', *Foreign Affairs*, vol 82, no 6, pp 115-25.

Lammerant, I. and Hofstetter, M. (2008) *Adoption: At What Cost? For an Ethical Responsibility of Receiving Countries in International Adoption*, Geneva: Terre des Hommes.

Masson, J. (2001) 'Intercountry adoption: a global problem or a global solution?', *Journal of International Affairs*, vol 55, no 1, pp 141-6.

Nicholson, E. (2006) 'My position on inter country adoption', available at http://emmanicholson.info/work/my-position-on-inter-country-adoptions.html

Palacios, J., Sanchez-Sandoval, Y. and Leon, E. (2006) 'Intercountry adoption disruptions in Spain', *Adoption Quarterly*, vol 9, no 1, pp 35-55.

Parker, R. (2008) *Uprooted: The Shipment of Poor Children to Canada, 1867–1917*, Bristol: The Policy Press.

Pereboom, M. (2005 'The European Union and international adoption', Centre for Adoption Policy, available at www.adoptionpolicy.org/pdf/4-28-05-MPereboomTheEUandInternationAdoption.pdf

Post, R. (2007) *Romania – For Export Only: The Untold Story of the Romanian 'Orphans'*, Netherlands: EuroComment Diffusion.

Rollings, J. (2008) *Love Our Way*, Sydney: Harper Collins.

Rorbech, M. (1991) 'The conditions of 18- to 25-year-old foreign-born adoptees in Denmark', in H. Altstein and R. Simon (eds) *Intercountry Adoption: A Multinational Perspective*, New York: Praeger.

Rutter, M., O'Connor, T., Beckett, C., Castle, J., Croft, C. and Dunn, J. (2000) 'Recovery and deficit following profound early deprivation', in P. Selman (ed) *Intercountry Adoption: Developments, Trends and Perspectives*, London: BAAF, pp 107-25.

Rutter, M., Beckett, C., Castle, J., Colvert, E., Kreppner, J., Mehta, M., Stevens, S. and Sonuga-Barke, E. (2009) 'Effects of profound early institutional deprivation: an overview of findings from a UK longitudinal study of Romanian adoption', in G. Wrobel and E. Neill (eds) *International Advances in Adoption Research*, London: John Wiley.

Saetersdal, B. and Dalen, M. (1991) 'Norway: intercountry adoptions in a homogeneous country', in H. Alstein and R. Simon (eds) *Intercountry Adoption: A Multinational Perspective*, New York: Praeger.

Saetersdal, B. and Dalen, M. (2000) 'Identity formation in a homogeneous country: Norway', in P. Selman (ed) *Intercountry Adoption: Developments, Trends and Perspectives*, London: BAAF.

Sarri, R., Baik, Y. and Bombyk, M. (2002) 'Goal displacement and dependency in South Korean–United States intercountry adoption', *Children and Youth Services Review*, vol 20, pp 87–114.

Save the Children UK (2003) *Position Paper on International Adoption of Children from Bulgaria*, London: Save the Children.

Selman, P. (1998) 'Intercountry adoption in Europe after the Hague Convention', in R. Sykes and P. Alcock (eds) *Developments in European Social Policy: Convergence and Diversity*, Bristol: The Policy Press.

Selman, P. (2002) 'Intercountry adoption in the new millennium: the "quiet migration" revisited', *Population Research and Policy Review*, vol 21, no 3, pp 205–25.

Selman, P. (2006) 'Trends in intercountry adoption 1998–2004: a demographic analysis of data from 20 receiving states', *Journal of Population Research*, vol 23, no 2, pp 183–204.

Selman, P. (2009) 'From Bucharest to Beijing: changes in countries sending children for international adoption 1990 to 2006', in G. Wrobel and E. Neil (eds) *International Advances in Adoption Research for Practice*, London: John Wiley, pp 41–69.

Selman, P. and Mason, K. (2005) 'Alternatives to adoption for looked after children', Annex C, in *Adoption: Better Choices for our Children*, Edinburgh: Scottish Executive.

Selman, P., Moretti, E. and Brogi, F. (2009) 'Statistical profile of international adoption in the European Union', Chapter 1 in *International adoption in the European Union*, Final report to the European Parliament, 26 February 2009, Florence: Istituto degli Innocenti.

Serenius, M. (1995) 'The silent cry: a Finnish child during World War II and 50 years later', *International Forum of Psychoanalysis*, vol 4, pp 35–47.

Smolin, D.M. (2004) 'Intercountry adoption as child trafficking', *Valparaiso Law Review*, vol 39, no 2, pp 281–325.

Smolin, D.M. (2007) 'Child laundering as exploitation: applying anti-trafficking norms to intercountry adoption under the coming Hague Regime', *ExpressO*, available at http://works.bepress.com/david_smolin/4

Tannock, C. (2006) 'European parliamentarians break the Nicholson monopoly on intercountry adoptions', *Bucharest Daily News*, 8 March, www.charlestannock.com/pressarticle.asp?ID=1190

Textor, M.R. (1991) 'International adoptions in West Germany: a private affair', in H. Altstein and R. Simon (eds) *Intercountry Adoption: A Multinational Perspective*, New York: Praeger.

*The Italian* (2005) Russian film about an orphan due to be adopted in Italy who runs away to search for his mother, www.sonyclassics. com/theitalian/

Triseliotis, J. (2000) 'Intercountry adoption; global trade or global gift?', *Adoption & Fostering*, vol 24, no 2, pp 45-54.

UNICEF (United Nations Children's Fund) (1999) 'Intercountry adoption', *Innocenti Digest No 4*, Florence: UNICEF Innocenti Research Centre.

UNICEF (2000) *The State of the World's Children*, New York: UNICEF.

UNICEF (2003) *The State of the World's Children*, New York: UNICEF.

UNICEF (2006) *The State of the World's Children*, New York: UNICEF.

UNICEF (2007) *The State of the World's Children*, New York: UNICEF.

US Department of State (2008) 'Immigrant visas issued to orphans coming to the US 1990-2007', http://travel.state.gov/family/adoption/stats_451.html (accessed 29 March 2009).

Van IJzendoorn, M. and Juffer, F. (2006) 'The Emanuel Miller Memorial Lecture 2006: Adoption as intervention: meta-analytic evidence for massive catch-up and plasticity in physical, socio-emotional, and cognitive development', *Journal of Child Psychology and Psychiatry*, vol 47, no 12, pp 1228-45.

Verhulst, F.C. (2000) 'The development of internationally adopted children', in P. Selman (ed) *Intercountry Adoption: Developments, Trends and Perspectives*, London: BAAF, pp 126-42.

Weil, R.H. (1984) 'International adoptions: the quiet migration', *International Migration Review*, vol 18, no 2, pp 276-93.

## Appendix

Tables 7A and 7B provide adoption ratios and demographic data in 2004 for 24 European receiving states and 23 European states of origin (including the two countries – the Czech Republic and Portugal – defining themselves to the Hague Special Commission as 'both a receiving state and a state of origin').

Table 7A also includes comparative information on five non-European receiving states.

Table 7B has similar data for seven non-European states of origin.

**Table 7A: Intercountry adoptions in receiving states: adoption ratios (adoptions per 1,000 live births), GNI per capita and total fertility rates (TFRs) in 2004, in order of ratio for 24 European states and five non-European states**

| Receiving states 2004 | | | |
|---|---|---|---|
| Country | Ratio | GNI per capita (US $) | TFR |
| Norway | 12.8 | 52,030 | 1.8 |
| Spain | 12.4 | 21,210 | 1.3 |
| Sweden | 11.7 | 35,770 | 1.7 |
| Malta | 11.5 | 12,250 | 1.5 |
| Luxembourg | 9.3 | 56,230 | 1.7 |
| Denmark | 8.4 | 40,650 | 1.8 |
| Switzerland | 8.2 | 48,230 | 1.4 |
| Iceland | 7.0 | 38,620 | 2.0 |
| Netherlands | 6.9 | 31,700 | 1.7 |
| Italy | 6.4 | 26,120 | 1.3 |
| Ireland | 6.3 | 34,280 | 1.9 |
| France | 5.5 | 30,090 | 1.9 |
| Finland | 5.3 | 32,790 | 1.7 |
| Belgium | 4.2 | 31,030 | 1.7 |
| Austria | (1.14)[a] | 32,300 | 1.4 |
| Germany | 1.0 | 30,120 | 1.4 |
| UK | 0.5 | 33,940 | 1.7 |
| Cyprus | 0.3 | 17,580 | 1.6 |
| Slovenia | _[b] | 14,810 | 1.2 |
| Greece | _[b] | 11,098 | 1.2 |
| Andorra | 0.0 | _[c] | _[d] |
| Liechtenstein | _[b] | _[c] | _[d] |
| Monaco | _[b] | _[c] | _[d] |
| San Marino | _[b] | _[c] | _[d] |
| **Non-European receiving states** | | | |
| New Zealand | 6.4 | 20,310 | 2.0 |
| Canada | 6.0 | 28,390 | 1.5 |
| US | 5.5 | 41,400 | 2.0 |
| Israel | 1.7 | 17,380 | 2.8 |
| Australia | 1.5 | 26,900 | 1.7 |

Notes:

[a] Data on adoptions to Austria were incomplete.

[b] No data on adoptions in 2004 were available for these states.

[c] GNI $10,066+ per capita (State of the World's Children, 2006, Table 1).

[d] Total fertility rates in 2004 were not available for these states.

Source: Number of adoptions taken from statistics provided by the central authorities of the listed states; demographic and economic data for 2004 from State of the World's Children 2006 (UNICEF, 2005)

**Table 7B: Intercountry adoptions in states of origin: adoption ratios (adoptions per 1,000 live births), GNI per capita and total fertility rates (TFRs) in 2004, in order of ratio for 23 European states and the seven non-European states sending most children in 2004**

| States of origin | | | |
|---|---|---|---|
| | Ratio | GNI per capita (US $) | TFR |
| Russia | 7.7 | 3,410 | 1.3 |
| Belarus | 7.1 | 2,120 | 1.2 |
| Bulgaria | 6.3 | 2,740 | 1.2 |
| Latvia | 6.0 | 5,460 | 1.3 |
| Ukraine | 5.0 | 1,260 | 1.1 |
| Lithuania | 3.3 | 5,740 | 1.3 |
| Armenia | 1.7 | 3,720 | 1.3 |
| Slovakia | 1.5 | 6,480 | 1.2 |
| Moldova | 1.5 | 710 | 1.2 |
| Estonia | 1.4 | 7,010 | 1.4 |
| Romania | 1.2 | 2,920 | 1.3 |
| Poland | 1.1 | 6,090 | 1.2 |
| Hungary | 0.7 | 8,270 | 1.3 |
| Bosnia | 0.7 | 2,040 | 1.3 |
| Georgia | 0.6 | 1,040 | 1.4 |
| Croatia | 0.5 | 5,590 | 1.3 |
| Albania | 0.5 | 2,080 | 2.2 |
| Serbia and Montenegro | 0.4 | 2,620 | 1.8 |
| Azerbaijan | 0.2 | 950 | 1.8 |
| Macedonia | 0.22 | 2,350 | 1.5 |
| Turkey | 0.03 | 3,750 | 2.4 |
| **Both receiving and sending**[a] | | | |
| Czech Republic | 0.4 | 9,150 | 1.2 |
| Portugal | 0.08 | 10,441 | 1.5 |
| **Non-European states of origin sending most children in 2004** | | | |
| Guatemala | 8.1 | 2,130 | 4.5 |
| Haiti | 4.6 | 390 | 3.9 |
| Korea | 4.0 | 13,980 | 1.2 |
| Colombia | 1.8 | 2,000 | 2.6 |
| China | 0.8 | 1,290 | 1.7 |
| Ethiopia | 0.5 | 110 | 5.7 |
| India | 0.04 | 620 | 3.0 |

*Note:* [a] Countries stating that they were 'both a receiving state and a state of origin' in reply to questionnaire from Hague Conference (2005). In the Czech Republic there are many more children sent than received (Selman et al, 2009)

*Source:* Number of adoptions calculated from data on states of origin in statistical returns from central authorities of 23 receiving states with useable data listed in Table 7.1; demographic and economic data for 2004 from State of the World's Children 2006 (UNICEF, 2005)

# EIGHT

# Family income as a protective factor for child outcomes

*Ilan Katz and Gerry Redmond*

## Introduction

It is well established in the child development literature that children from materially deprived backgrounds have poorer outcomes than those from wealthy families (Hoff et al, 2002; Centre for Community Child Health Royal Children's Hospital, 2004; Richardson and Prior, 2005). There is now a significant body of literature on the relationships between indicators of material and social well-being on the one hand, and child outcomes on the other (Bor et al, 1997). The majority of studies compare families who are defined as poor with non-poor families (see, for example, Fergusson et al, 1994), or alternatively measure the average association between income or socioeconomic status (SES) and an outcome indicator (Haveman and Wolfe, 1994; Mayer, 1997). This academic focus on poor families reflects policy interest in the relationship between family poverty and children's outcomes, and intergenerational transfer of social and economic disadvantage. Underpinning much of this research, and associated policy interest, is the assumption that there is something specific about poverty that causes poor outcomes for children. Often, that 'something' is identified as an aspect of parenting, or parents' behaviour. Underlying this assumption, therefore, is the expectation of discontinuity between the behaviour, attitudes and relationships of poor families, and those found in the rest of society.

However, little research or theoretical attention has been devoted to the differences in outcomes among children who come from non-poor families. Yet differences in outcomes for children from high-income and middle-income households, for example, can also be significant. The purpose of this chapter is to use recent Australian data to explore these differences further. First, do children from high-income backgrounds have significantly better outcomes than children from middle-income backgrounds? And second, if better outcomes are found, what factors might explain this difference? In this analysis, we focus in particular on 'vulnerable' children – those with considerably less than average outcome scores across a range of measures. The question of differences in outcomes among children from middle- and high-income families has significant implications for our understanding of the relationship between material well-being and child outcomes, and how parenting influences that relationship, and for policy and practice relating to interventions to enhance developmental outcomes for young children. Moreover, by studying middle- and high-income children who have the best outcomes in the population, it may be possible to gain a deeper understanding of the factors that promote positive outcomes for all children.

Our main conclusion is that income does appear to make a difference to child outcomes after the impact of parenting is taken into account – but only for children with low-range outcome scores, and only where their parents have very high incomes – in the top 20% of household incomes in Australia. The analysis is divided into five parts. Some of the relevant literature on income and outcomes is considered in the next section. The following section discusses extrinsic and intrinsic factors that are commonly seen as governing the relationship between income and child outcomes. Then the data (from the Longitudinal Study of Australian Children) are summarised. Following this, some descriptive results are presented, and a more systematic explanatory analysis of the relationship between income and outcomes is developed. The results are then discussed and the final section concludes the chapter.

## Income, status and child outcomes

A large body of literature shows that children from low-income families have poor outcomes in comparison with children from higher-income families in all areas of development, that inequalities between the two groups increase over time, and that advantages and disadvantages are transmitted intergenerationally (Duncan and Brooks-Gunn, 1997; Feinstein et al, 2004). Research shows that the main reason for the differential outcomes between poor and non-poor children is that parents in different socioeconomic groups undertake the job of parenting differently. Both Hoff et al (2002) and Hill (2006) point out that differences in indicators of social and economic well-being are associated with differences in many parental beliefs, practices and attitudes, including the purposes of parenting and expectations of children's developmental trajectories. These beliefs and practices have in turn been linked to a number of different ways in which materially advantaged families differ from disadvantaged families, including access to material resources (DeGarmo et al, 1999; Duncan and Magnuson, 2003), levels of social capital (Coleman, 1988; Hoff-Ginsberg and Tardif, 1995) and parents' occupational conditions (Kohn, 1969; Luster et al, 1989; Hoffman, 2003).

However, this apparently straightforward relationship between parental material well-being and social status (whether measured in terms of socioeconomic status/socioeconomic position, class, income or wealth – henceforth we use the shorthand term 'family income') and child outcomes becomes rather complex when examined closely, presenting a number of challenges for research. The first of these relates to the fact that parenting style and practices are not the only differences between families in different socioeconomic groups. Poor families often differ from affluent families in their size, structure, geography and demographic characteristics, and all these factors are likely to have independent effects on children's outcomes. In addition, poorer parents are more likely to suffer from mental or physical illness or disability and misuse drugs and alcohol – again factors that influence child outcomes. A further complication is that these factors interact with each other, and it is therefore very difficult to disentangle the effects of material well-being or social status on parenting (and therefore child outcomes) from all these other factors (Berger, 2007).

A second challenge concerns the mechanisms through which family income impacts on parenting and child outcomes. Parenting is a complex process, which can be disaggregated into several component parts, including discipline, nurturance, education, socialisation and access to culture (Maccoby and Martin, 1983), each of which may have different impacts.

A third challenge, which is the main focus of this report, relates to the question of whether or not the relationship between family income, parenting and child outcomes is continuous across the range of family income indicators. Although it is consistently found that family income is related to child outcomes, this does not necessarily mean that the risk factors associated with poor outcomes for disadvantaged children are on a continuum, with a steady monotonic relationship between status, risk factors and child outcomes. Indeed, little of the vast body of research and theorising about the effects of family income on parenting and child outcomes explicitly addresses issues of continuity in the relationship between family income and child outcomes, simply because the focus is usually on poor or low-status children in comparison with non-poor or middle- and high-status children. Nonetheless, it is conceivable that there is not only a difference in outcomes between poor people and the rest of society, but also between the 'rich' and the 'middle class'.

If it is the case that outcomes for children vary across the entire range of family income, the policy implications are profound. Social policy on child development is largely premised on a division between 'the poor' and 'the rest', and is aimed at mitigating the effects of poverty. Underpinning this thinking is the concept of the *good-enough parent*, which was originally developed by the child psychiatrist Donald Winnicott (1964). This theory asserts that as long as the parent is in touch with the infant's feelings and needs, the infant will develop normally – Winnicott argued against parents trying too hard. The implication is that interventions should attempt to help parents become 'good enough', not to push them too hard. In terms of the risk/protective factors described below, Winnicott – and much of psychology and social policy that followed him – viewed poor parenting as a risk factor for child outcomes, but did not see exceptional parenting as a protective factor. But if the intention is truly to maximise the potential of every child, then we should look at those children who are doing best, rather than focusing on the worst performing or average, and we should try to find out what it is that facilitates their well-being. This has implications for overall aims for child development, and for targeting of services and benefits universally, or at particular groups.

## Extrinsic and intrinsic causation

There are two main perspectives that attempt to fill out the details on how family income impacts on child outcomes. The first of these is the *social causation (extrinsic)* perspective, which posits that the primary cause of substandard parenting and poor outcomes is the social circumstances of parents. Included under this heading are:

- parental investments;
- parental stress caused by economic disadvantage;
- a culture of poverty/underclass; and
- human, social and cultural capital.

The second perspective is the *social selection (intrinsic)* perspective, which attributes outcomes to the personal characteristics of parents:

- their personal backgrounds;
- genetic endowment.

Each of these six theories is briefly described below.

## Extrinsic explanations of social causation

*Parental investments* is the most straightforward theory – differences in outcomes between children in families with low family income and those in higher-status families are directly associated with the access to material resources that higher-status parents have, and which poor parents do not have, resources that allow higher-status parents to invest in their children's education and well-being (Haveman and Wolfe, 1994; Foster, 2002; Sammons et al, 2004). These resources include more nutritious food, educational toys and books, higher-quality daycare, extra tuition, out-of-school activities, superior healthcare, better housing and so on. However, the theory does not address the question of whether access to resources matters equally across all households. For example, it may be that once a certain level of investment is provided, marginal returns on further investments are minimal, or even negative (Foster, 2002). Nor does the theory say whether the investments themselves are the key factors in the child's development, or whether they are simply markers of other aspects of parenting and child development (Mahoney, 2000).

*Parental stress* is the predominant hypothesis linking poverty, parenting and children's outcomes. The theory asserts that parents living in deprived circumstances are under more stress than affluent parents, and that stress causes them to be less responsive, less consistent and more hostile towards their children than affluent parents (Elder et al, 1985; Bor et al, 1997; Conger et al, 1997; Ross and Roberts, 1999; Smith, 2004; Katz et al, 2007). One significant problem with the theory is that it is focused on the stress of poverty, while ignoring other reasons why stress levels might vary. For example, research shows that children themselves may be a cause of stress to parents, whatever their social and economic status, especially if their behaviour is challenging or they are disabled (Ghate and Hazel, 2002; Emerson et al, 2006).

The *culture of poverty/underclass* theory asserts that poor people (or a section of them) have developed different value systems and lifestyles from 'mainstream' society (Murray, 1990, 1996). In particular, they are less likely to be attached to the labour force, more likely to engage in antisocial behaviour and less likely to enter long-term partnerships. These attitudes are passed on to their children, and so the 'underclass' becomes more and more detached from mainstream society over generations. This theory has been challenged by many authors including Penman (2007) who argues that that there is little evidence that poor people in general (or even a significant section of poor people) have different values or aspirations from the rest of the population, or that they pass on these alternative beliefs or lifestyles to their children. Nevertheless, the notion of an 'underclass' has persisted in political discourse and the media (if not in academia). This theory applies to differences between poor and non-poor families and suggests a clear division in terms of parenting and child outcomes between the poor and the non-poor, rather than a monotonic relationship.

The theory of *human, social and cultural capital* in some ways mirrors the culture of poverty theory, but also offers a perspective on outcomes for all children, not just those from poor backgrounds. Human, social and cultural capital are considered to be analogous to economic capital in that they are resources that individuals (and families, communities and even nations) can accrue, and which can be used in order to achieve desired objectives (Bourdieu, 1986). Human capital is a resource that people accumulate in order to be more successful in the labour market. Social capital, on the other hand, refers to the networks of support and influence that individuals develop and are able to exploit in order to give and obtain support. Cultural capital refers to the body of knowledge, norms and values that parents pass on to their children. For example, one of the key resources that parents use is the language with which they interact with their children. In a rare example of research that focuses on the top half of the status scale, Hoff (2003) finds that the language and vocabulary used by mothers in middle and high socioeconomic groups differs from that used by mothers in lower social groups, and that children in the higher groups tend to develop a richer vocabulary.

### Intrinsic explanations of social causation

One example of an intrinsic explanation of the relationship between income, parenting and child outcomes relates to *parental characteristics*. The most prominent proponent of this theory is Susan Mayer (1997, 2002). She argues that simply raising parental income of children in low-income families, while keeping all other parental characteristics constant, will have little effect on any particular outcome. Mayer believes that the characteristics of parents that prevent them from participating effectively in the labour market also limit their parenting ability. These characteristics include mental ill-health, substance misuse, personality problems and so on, many of which are caused by parents' own experiences of inadequate parenting. This is a key point for the present study, since Mayer's argument is that money in itself (above a certain very low minimum) cannot buy better outcomes for children, but that parental characteristics can predict worse outcomes.

An alternative intrinsic explanation relates to *genetic endowment*. There is a great deal of evidence that genetics plays a significant role in many aspects of child development (Jensen, 1998; Hart et al, 2007; O'Connor and Scott, 2007; Van Hulle et al, 2007). Those parents who are genetically better endowed to be good parents may also have traits that facilitate their achieving high social and economic status. Thus, children of high-achieving parents may benefit from genetics in two ways: by inheriting better cognitive and other abilities, and by receiving better parenting from parents who are genetically endowed to be effective parents. However, the significance of genetic factors should not be overplayed, and evidence also exists that downplays the importance of genetics in influencing child outcomes (Duyme et al, 1999).

## Summarising theory on causation and child outcomes

The six theories examined in this section are relevant in different ways to the question addressed in this chapter. If parental stress is the main mediating factor that influences outcomes for children, then differences in parenting and child outcomes at any level of economic and social well-being should be explained by stress indicators. Alternatively, if lack of resources in itself is the major factor behind differences across the family income distribution, then income should explain these differences. However, this depends on the monotonicity of the relationship between status, parenting and outcomes. The culture of poverty theory in effect suggests that poor people (or a significant section of them) are different in several important respects from the non-poor, but has little to say on differences among the non-poor, who are all placed in the category of 'the mainstream'. Human, social and cultural capital theory suggests that outcomes steadily improve for children as their parents' social and economic status improves. This is the theory closest to the hypothesis that we test in this analysis, that is, that significant differences exist in outcomes between the children of middle-status parents and those of high-status parents. The final two theories discussed above – that differences in parenting and children's outcomes are mostly due to differences in personal backgrounds of parents, or alternatively to genetics – provide an antithesis to the theory underpinning this present analysis.

Although these two theories have to date focused only on comparing the characteristics of poor families with those of high-status families, given appropriate data both theories could potentially accommodate differences in outcomes for children across the whole socioeconomic spectrum. Our aim in the next section is to build a model that explores the validity of these six theories for a sample of four- to five-year-old Australian children.

## Data

The main data source used in this analysis is the Wave 1 'K' (four- to five-year-old) cohort of the survey *Growing Up in Australia: The Longitudinal Study of Australian Children* (LSAC). The purpose of LSAC is 'to provide the database for a comprehensive understanding of Australian children's development in the current social, economic and cultural environment, and hence to become a major element of the evidence base for policy and practice regarding children and their families' (Sanson et al, 2002, p v). The LSAC was launched in 2004, and will continue for seven years, with detailed information collected from responding families every two years until 2011. Data from two separate samples of children and their families are being collected, the first aged less than 12 months in 2003–04 (the 'B' Cohort), and the second aged four years in 2003–04 (the 'K' cohort). This analysis focuses only on the 'K' cohort. The main measures used in the analysis are described below, and are discussed in more detail in Redmond (2008).

### Child outcomes

The main measure of outcomes used in this analysis is the Composite Outcome Index derived by Sanson et al (2005). The Index is calculated from multiple direct outcome measures across three major domains – physical, social-emotional and learning. Distal measures, such as family circumstances or income, are not included in the Index. Within each of the three major domains that make up the Index, there are a total of 16 measures (including Body Mass Index, the Strengths and Difficulties Questionnaire, the Peabody Picture Vocabulary Test (PPVT) and the *Who Am I?* test). We tested the sensitivity of results to variations in the definition of outcomes, and found that they did not vary greatly from those given by the Composite Outcome Index. In this analysis we used the Index as a continuous score, but also examined differences and characteristics at the 10th, 25th, 50th, 75th and 90th percentile points of the Index distribution. Sanson et al (2005, p 22) note one limitation of the Index that may be important for this study: 'discriminability is stronger at the problem end than the positive end'.

## Indicators of social and economic well-being

In this analysis, we examined three different indicators: parents' income; socioeconomic position based on parents' income, education and occupation; and a geographical area-based indicator of socioeconomic advantage and disadvantage – the Social and Economic Index for Areas (SEIFA) index score (see Australian Bureau of Statistics, 2008), which is allocated to all postcode-sized districts in Australia. Relative rankings of households based on income, socioeconomic position and SEIFA scores were compared. Income and socioeconomic position were found to produce similar rankings: 55% of households were in the same or adjoining decile groups, while only 7% were five or more decile groups apart. In the case of the income and SEIFA rankings, however, only 41% of households were in the same or adjoining decile groups, while 16% were five or more decile groups apart, thus suggesting a lower concordance between these two indicators. Nonetheless, all three indicators produced similar results in the analysis, and hence only the results for one of them – parents' income – are reported here.

## Parenting variables

There is a considerable body of work that suggests that the relationship between family income and child outcomes is mediated by parental factors, and the LSAC contains data on a number of these factors, including 'background' variables such as education, and more direct measures of parental stress and parenting practice. Zubrick et al (2006) derive from these data for the 'K' cohort of LSAC a number of measures that are used in this present analysis, including:

- *life stress events*, where the main respondents were asked whether they or their partners had experienced a specific set of stressful events in the previous year;
- *community connectedness*, where the respondents were asked if they knew about the communities where they lived, and if they felt safe in them; and
- *psychological distress*, where respondents scaled themselves on a six-item measure of non-specific psychological distress.

In addition to these indicators, Zubrick et al (2006) also derived three composite indicators that more directly measured parenting practices:

- *parental warmth*, calculated from responses to six questions about feeling close to the child;
- *hostile parenting*, calculated from responses to questions on praising, disapproving of or punishing the child; and
- *parenting consistency*, calculated from responses to questions on how parents 'follow through' with instructions and warnings to the child.

### Sociodemographic characteristics

The LSAC questionnaire collects a wide range of information from parents and other sources on the demographic make-up of households, parents' education, occupations and incomes, housing and other indicators of social and cultural status and capital.

## Results

The first step in examining the relationship between income, parenting and outcomes was a descriptive analysis investigating whether income varied according to the level of outcome experienced by the child. The next step was an explanatory analysis, building a model that could explain the relationship between the two indicators, income and children's outcomes.

### Descriptive analysis

The data in Figure 8.1 suggest a fairly monotonic relationship between parental income and child outcomes, according to the Composite Outcome Index, which, as discussed above, represents an overall summary score of child outcomes at age four to five. The Figure shows where key percentile points for the Outcome Index lie within each decile group of household income. One in ten children in the bottom decile group of parents' incomes have Outcome Index scores below the p10 point (score = 81.8) for that bottom decile; and one in ten children in the top decile group have scores below the p10 point (score = 91.1) for that decile.

The Figure shows that percentile point scores of children's outcomes increase more or less monotonically across the decile groups as household

**Figure 8.1: Percentile scores on the Continuous Outcome Index, by decile group of household income**

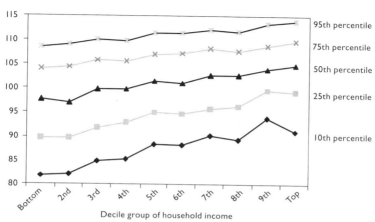

Source: LSAC Wave 1, authors' calculations

income rises. However, the Figure also shows that the difference in Outcome Index scores between the bottom and the top income decile groups is considerably smaller for children with high outcome scores than for children with low outcome scores, and that the range of scores (ignoring potential outliers) is wider at the bottom than at the top. In other words, households with higher incomes appear to have greater capacity to 'pull up' the Outcome Index scores of their most vulnerable children (if a low Index score can be seen as an indicator of vulnerability). Conversely, income appears to have rather less impact on the outcome scores of 'resilient' children (if children who score highly on the Outcome Index can be so described). This is indicated by the relatively flat slope on the p90 line, in comparison with the much steeper slope on the p10 line.

Figure 8.2 shows that most of the key differences are statistically significant. The vertical bars on this Figure represent 95% confidence intervals for the point estimates. Confidence intervals are widest around the p10 scores, and narrowest around the p50 scores. Differences in Outcome Index scores at p10 are not statistically significant in the top four household income decile groups. However, the differences between the top and the bottom income groups are significant at all levels. Differences are also significant at all levels of outcome score between the top two deciles and the 5th decile.

**Figure 8.2: 95% confidence intervals for Continuous Outcome Index scores, by decile group of household income**

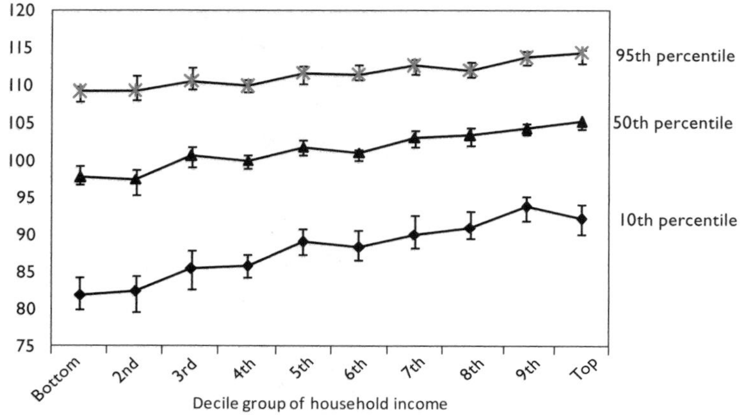

*Source:* LSAC Wave 1, authors' calculations

*Explanatory analysis*

As noted above, the relationship between income and the Composite Outcome Index is likely to be mediated by a number of factors. First, it is possible that the observed relationship between income and outcomes is fully explained by other factors that are associated with both income and outcomes, for example, parental stress, parenting practices or sociodemographic indicators. In order to test the relationship between household income and children's outcomes in the LSAC, we developed a simple, unidirectional causal model, illustrated by Figure 8.3. We modelled the impact of income, a range of sociodemographic characteristics, a number of parental stress indicators and three parenting practice indicators on children's Composite Outcome Index score (the elements in dashed boxes represent likely influences on child outcomes that we cannot observe with the LSAC).

This simple model goes some way towards examining the relationship between a range of inputs and outcomes, controlling for mediating factors such as parental stress and parenting practice. However, it does not explore in detail the interrelationships between explanatory variables (see, for example, Roosa et al, 2003; Conger and Donnellan, 2007). The approach taken in this analysis was to explore the complexity of relationships between incomes and child outcomes by comparing the impact of the explanatory variables on different parts of the distribution

**Figure 8.3: Simple causal model of determinants of child outcomes**

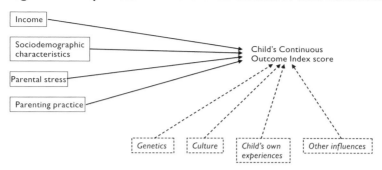

of child outcomes as measured by the Overall Outcome Index. Specifically, we examined how the impact of explanatory variables differs for children at around the 10th percentile of outcomes in comparison with children at the 25th, 50th, 75th and 90th percentiles. This approach, which relies on *quantile regression analysis*, represents an advance on analyses that dichotomise dependent variables (such as child outcomes) into 'low' and 'high', and those that investigate the impact of explanatory variables on the mean of an outcome indicator (see, for example, Haveman and Wolfe, 1995; Dooley and Stewart, 2004).

Table 8.1 shows how children with particular sociodemographic characteristics are distributed across quintile groups of both household income and Continuous Outcome Index scores. Given the positive relationship between these two variables shown on Figure 8.1, it is perhaps not surprising that sociodemographic variables tend to have more or less similar relationships with each of them. The following groups tend to have both higher household income and higher Continuous Outcome Index scores:

• children whose mothers have tertiary education,
• children whose mothers are aged 40 and over.

The following groups, on the other hand, have both lower household income and lower Outcome Index scores:

• children living in Indigenous households;
• children living in households where English is not the main language spoken at home;
• children whose mothers are aged 29 or under;
• children in lone-parent families.

**Table 8.1: Sociodemographic variables, by quintile group of household income and Continuous Outcome Index scores (%)**

| | | % all children | Lowest | 2nd | 3rd | 4th | Highest |
|---|---|---|---|---|---|---|---|
| | | | Quintile groups of household income and Continuous Outcome Index | | | | |
| Mother has tertiary education | Household income | 24.5 | 7.7 | 10.9 | 16.8 | 23.1 | 41.6 |
| | Outcome Index | | 12.0 | 17.3 | 17.6 | 23.2 | 29.9 |
| Mother has secondary education | Household income | 36.6 | 19.6 | 21.4 | 23.8 | 20.0 | 15.3 |
| | Outcome Index | | 19.3 | 19.3 | 21.7 | 20.2 | 19.6 |
| Indigenous household | Household income | 3.7 | 48.8 | 22.1 | 11.4 | 11.7 | 5.9 |
| | Outcome Index | | 38.1 | 21.3 | 17.5 | 17.3 | 5.8 |
| English not spoken at home | Household income | 14.1 | 33.3 | 21.8 | 16.0 | 12.1 | 16.7 |
| | Outcome Index | | 26.1 | 23.8 | 20.6 | 14.2 | 15.4 |
| Mother is aged 19-24 | Household income | 3.6 | 47.5 | 26.3 | 14.6 | 10.4 | 1.1 |
| | Outcome Index | | 30.0 | 27.7 | 20.4 | 10.7 | 11.3 |
| Mother is aged 25-29 | Household income | 13.4 | 33.4 | 27.1 | 18.9 | 14.7 | 6.0 |
| | Outcome Index | | 27.0 | 25.9 | 16.8 | 17.0 | 13.3 |
| Mother is aged 30-39 | Household income | 65.1 | 17.0 | 18.1 | 21.5 | 21.6 | 21.8 |
| | Outcome Index | | 18.5 | 18.7 | 20.6 | 20.7 | 21.5 |
| Mother is aged 40-55 | Household income | 17.8 | 17.3 | 18.3 | 16.6 | 20.2 | 27.6 |
| | Outcome Index | | 17.8 | 18.3 | 19.9 | 21.3 | 22.8 |
| Lone-parent family | Household income | 14.7 | 69.6 | 20.7 | 6.5 | 1.5 | 1.7 |
| | Outcome Index | | 32.1 | 24.0 | 16.3 | 14.9 | 12.7 |
| Step or blended family | Household income | 2.4 | 23.8 | 18.5 | 21.0 | 23.4 | 13.3 |
| | Outcome Index | | 18.4 | 19.2 | 26.1 | 27.8 | 8.5 |
| One or two children in the household | Household income | 58.9 | 17.4 | 16.8 | 18.6 | 22.0 | 25.2 |
| | Outcome Index | | 18.6 | 20.2 | 20.1 | 19.8 | 21.2 |
| Three or more children in the household | Household income | 41.1 | 24.5 | 23.8 | 22.1 | 17.2 | 12.4 |
| | Outcome Index | | 21.8 | 19.5 | 19.6 | 20.2 | 18.9 |
| Youngest child is aged 0-1 | Household income | 21.5 | 22.0 | 22.4 | 22.0 | 20.0 | 13.7 |
| | Outcome Index | | 21.2 | 21.1 | 20.6 | 18.5 | 18.5 |
| Youngest child is aged 2+ | Household income | 68.2 | 19.9 | 18.9 | 19.5 | 20.0 | 21.7 |
| | Outcome Index | | 19.6 | 19.6 | 19.7 | 20.3 | 20.8 |

*Source:* LSAC Wave 1, authors' calculations

Table 8.2 shows the relationship between indicators of parental stress and parenting practice, and quintile groups of household income. In most cases, there is a strong relationship between the parenting variables and household incomes – low-income households have poorer parenting scores. There are also notable differences between the 4th quintile of household income and the highest, in percentages for several other indicators, for example, for the experience of threatening events in the last year, and for parents' coping and psychological distress. There is also a marked difference between the 4th income quintile and the top group in percentages for the summary indicator, 'parent scored negatively on four or more parent stress or parenting practice indicators'.

### Table 8.2: Parental stress and parenting practice variables, by quintile group of household income and Continuous Outcome Index scores (%)

| | | % all children | Quintile groups of household income and Continuous Outcome Index scores | | | | |
|---|---|---|---|---|---|---|---|
| | | | Lowest | 2nd | 3rd | 4th | Highest |
| **Parent stress** | | | | | | | |
| Four or more threatening events in the past year | *Household income* | 19.4 | 31.8 | 24.5 | 17.8 | 15.1 | 10.8 |
| | *Outcome Index* | | 28.1 | 19.9 | 19.2 | 17.8 | 15.1 |
| Great difficulty of life at present | *Household income* | 9.8 | 30.1 | 25.9 | 18.9 | 15.9 | 9.1 |
| | *Outcome Index* | | 35.7 | 20.8 | 16.7 | 13.1 | 13.8 |
| Low level of support from family and friends | *Household income* | 24.4 | 20.8 | 18.5 | 20.2 | 18.4 | 22.1 |
| | *Outcome Index* | | 24.0 | 21.1 | 18.6 | 16.2 | 20.2 |
| Not coping well | *Household income* | 5.2 | 31.2 | 27.3 | 17.6 | 14.0 | 9.9 |
| | *Outcome Index* | | 44.4 | 23.7 | 15.7 | 8.6 | 7.6 |
| Low level of connectedness with community | *Household income* | 18.7 | 27.3 | 25.1 | 17.7 | 15.6 | 14.3 |
| | *Outcome Index* | | 26.7 | 23.3 | 20.0 | 16.6 | 13.6 |

*continued*

**Table 8.2:** *continued*

| | | % all children | Quintile groups of household income and Continuous Outcome Index scores | | | | |
|---|---|---|---|---|---|---|---|
| | | | Lowest | 2nd | 3rd | 4th | Highest |
| High level of psychological distress | *Household income* | 21.6 | 28.7 | 24.4 | 18.9 | 16.0 | 12.1 |
| | Outcome Index | | 36.5 | 20.8 | 16.7 | 14.6 | 11.4 |
| Parental practices | | | | | | | |
| Low level of parental warmth | *Household income* | 21.3 | 20.8 | 19.9 | 18.9 | 20.8 | 19.6 |
| | Outcome Index | | 26.2 | 24.6 | 19.2 | 15.8 | 14.2 |
| High level of parental hostility | *Household income* | 21.7 | 24.9 | 20.5 | 18.4 | 19.3 | 17.0 |
| | Outcome Index | | 39.2 | 23.9 | 17.2 | 12.2 | 7.5 |
| Low level of parental consistency | *Household income* | 23.0 | 30.6 | 23.1 | 18.2 | 15.0 | 13.1 |
| | Outcome Index | | 35.1 | 25.2 | 17.3 | 11.7 | 10.8 |
| Summary parenting score | | | | | | | |
| Parent scored negatively on four or more parent stress or parenting practice indicators | *Household income* | 10.4 | 32.0 | 27.0 | 17.4 | 14.0 | 9.6 |
| | Outcome Index | | 43.4 | 24.5 | 16.3 | 7.7 | 8.2 |

*Source:* LSAC Wave 1, authors' calculations

Table 8.3 shows coefficients for bivariate relationships between sociodemographic, parental stress and parenting practice indicators, and the children's Outcome Index scores. The Table shows both ordinary least squares (OLS) regression results and quantile regression results. Beta coefficients for OLS results are most valid for the mean of the Outcome Index. The extent to which the explanatory variables influence Outcome Index scores is for the most part low. For household income, $R^2$ is 0.0485 (meaning that income 'explains' about 5% of the variation in Outcome Index scores), although it increases to about 0.1 or more for parents' psychological distress, parent hostility and parent consistency. However, these statistics only describe the *overall relationship* between the explanatory variables and Outcome Index scores.

**Table 8.3: Ordinary least squares (OLS) and quantile bivariate regressions on Continuous Outcome Index**

| | N | OLS | | Quantile regression beta coefficients | | | | |
|---|---|---|---|---|---|---|---|---|
| | | Adj. Rsq | Beta | p10 | p25 | p50 | p75 | p90 |
| Log equivalised household income | 4595 | 0.049 | 3.192 | 5.896 | 4.520 | 3.516 | 2.435 | 1.783 |
| Mother's education | 4140 | 0.057 | | | | | | |
| Mother has tertiary education | | | 7.765 | 9.366 | 8.480 | 8.123 | 6.910 | 5.428 |
| Mother has post-school diploma/certificate | | | 6.639 | 8.097 | 8.969 | 7.047 | 5.485 | 4.811 |
| Mother completed year 11/has certificate | | | 4.052 | 4.177 | 4.348 | 4.351 | 3.837 | 3.712 |
| Mother completed year 10 | | | 1.954 | 1.40* | 2.01* | 2.247 | 2.309 | 1.450 |
| Indigenous household | 4878 | 0.011 | −5.562 | −7.688 | −6.224 | −5.587 | −4.328 | −4.315 |
| English not spoken at home | 4878 | 0.008 | −2.586 | −2.694 | −2.992 | −2.976 | −2.375 | −1.768 |
| Mother's age | 4878 | 0.018 | 0.255 | 0.280 | 0.288 | 0.258 | 0.227 | 0.251 |
| Lone–parent family | 4878 | 0.022 | −4.312 | −6.234 | −5.155 | −4.540 | −3.496 | −2.474 |
| Step or blended family | 4878 | 0.000 | −0.96* | −2.52* | −0.86* | −0.62* | −1.708 | −3.524 |
| Mother not married | 4878 | 0.028 | −3.979 | −0.582 | −4.657 | −3.801 | −3.226 | −2.774 |
| Number of children | 4878 | 0.002 | −0.523 | −0.087 | −0.664 | −0.550 | −0.424 | −0.457 |
| Age of youngest child | 4877 | 0.001 | 0.250 | 0.432 | 0.108 | 0.308 | 0.267 | 0.211 |
| Study child is at school or kindergarten | 4878 | 0.003 | 2.548 | 1.439 | 3.086 | 3.257 | 2.317 | 2.260 |

*continued*

**Table 8.3:** *continued*

| | N | OLS | | Quantile regression beta coefficients | | | | |
|---|---|---|---|---|---|---|---|---|
| | | Adj.Rsq | Beta | p10 | p25 | p50 | p75 | p90 |
| Number of threatening events in the past year (0-4, reversed) | 4821 | 0.010 | -0.730 | -1.221 | -1.007 | -0.479 | -0.474 | -0.574 |
| Life difficulty (0 = less difficulty) | 4119 | 0.027 | -5.562 | -9.840 | -7.274 | -4.777 | -3.214 | -2.253 |
| Support from family and friends (0 = more support) | 3778 | 0.007 | -1.963 | -3.290 | -2.450 | -1.682 | -0.485 | -0.815 |
| Coping (0 = coping well) | 4117 | 0.025 | -7.369 | -10.22 | -8.701 | -7.363 | -5.761 | -4.228 |
| Parents' connectedness with community (0 = high connectedness) | 4104 | 0.040 | -0.784 | -1.044 | -0.994 | -0.748 | -0.560 | -0.486 |
| Parents' psychological distress (0 = low distress) | 4111 | 0.102 | -0.839 | -1.212 | -1.008 | -0.784 | -0.649 | -0.518 |
| Parents' warmth (0 = high warmth) | 4876 | 0.029 | -0.613 | -0.641 | -0.612 | -0.701 | -0.592 | -0.499 |
| Parents' hostility (0 = low hostility) | 4875 | 0.122 | -1.455 | -1.818 | -1.717 | -1.429 | -1.281 | -1.060 |
| Parents' consistency (0 = high consistency) | 4872 | 0.098 | -0.910 | -1.290 | -1.094 | -0.896 | -0.694 | -0.512 |

*Note:* All beta coefficients are significant at $p<0.01$ except those asterisked.

*Source:* LSAC Wave 1, authors' calculations

Beta coefficients for quantile regression results give a different perspective, focusing on the relationship between the explanatory and dependent variables at particular points in the distribution of the Continuous Outcome Index. Figure 8.1 shows that the relationship between income and Outcome Index scores appears stronger at the 10th percentile of outcomes than it does at the median (or at the top of the distribution). The beta coefficients for quantile regressions at the 10th percentile in Table 8.3 show that the impact of income on Outcome Index scores diminishes greatly as we move up the distribution of outcome scores – from 5.896 at the 10th percentile (that is, a one-unit increase in log income would increase scores at the 10th percentile by about six points, or more than half a standard deviation), to 1.78 at the 90th percentile. A similar monotonic change in the impact of other variables is also evident. Indigenous status and lone-parent status impact on Outcome Index scores across the income distribution, but the impact is clearly strongest at the bottom. The relationship between parental stress and parenting practice indicators and outcomes is also for the most part monotonic. These show, for example, that the impact of parental psychological distress on outcomes is twice as strong at the 10th as at the 90th percentile of Outcome Index scores. One notable exception is parenting warmth, the impact of which appears to change little across Outcome Index scores.

Table 8.4 shows coefficients for multivariate relationships between sociodemographic, parental stress and parenting practice indicators and the child overall Outcome Index at age four to five. In this model, the impact of each explanatory variable on the child outcomes is calculated while holding all other variables constant. As with the bivariate analysis above, the Table shows both OLS regression results and quantile regression results. While Table 8.3 shows that all of the explanatory variables have a significant bivariate relationship with the Outcome Index, in the multivariate model most variables are no longer significant at the $p=0.05$ level. This suggests a high degree of correlation between the explanatory variables.

In the multivariate analysis, there are a number of explanatory variables that are significantly associated with outcomes. These include mother's education (although only at the lower levels), parents' connectedness with their communities, parental stress and parenting practices: parents' warmth towards their children, their hostile behaviour and their consistent behaviour. For most of these variables, the relationship is gradated – that is, their impact is stronger at the 10th percentile than at the 50th or 90th percentiles. Moreover, while income has a significant impact on child outcomes at the mean (this is what the OLS result shows), its impact is significant at the level of $p<0.1$ only at the 10th, 25th and 50th percentiles, and not in the top half of the distribution of child outcomes. In other words, income appears to matter for children with Outcome Index scores in the lower range, but not those with higher scores.

**Table 8.4: Ordinary least squares (OLS) and quantile multivariate regressions on Continuous Outcome Index**

| | OLS | Quantile regression percentile | | | | |
|---|---|---|---|---|---|---|
| | | 10th | 25th | 50th | 75th | 90th |
| Adjusted Rsq | 0.269 | 0.188 | 0.179 | 0.155 | 0.133 | 0.106 |
| Constant | 111.7 | 106.3 | 107.1 | 109.6 | 115.7 | 116.4 |
| | | | | | | |
| Log equivalised household income | 0.913* | 1.351‡ | 1.293* | 1.216* | 0.424 | 0.355 |
| Mother has tertiary education | 0.389 | 0.111 | 0.590 | 0.280 | 0.871 | 1.660 |
| Mother has post-school diploma/certificate | 1.206 | 2.764 | 2.216 | 0.425 | 1.677* | 1.794 |
| Mother completed year 11/has certificate | 2.457* | 3.139 | 3.224* | 2.335‡ | 2.587* | 2.438† |
| Mother completed year 10 | 3.106* | 3.258† | 3.477† | 2.549† | 3.398* | 3.870* |
| Indigenous household | −1.352 | 0.534 | −0.800 | −1.797 | −1.119 | −0.951 |
| English not spoken at home | −0.251 | −0.299 | −0.319 | −0.267 | −0.063 | −0.559 |
| Mother's age | 0.058 | 0.086 | 0.051 | 0.067 | 0.087‡ | 0.069‡ |
| Lone-parent family | −0.486 | 0.815 | −1.025 | −0.559 | −1.102† | −0.592 |
| Step or blended family | −1.756 | 0.244 | −2.420 | −2.109 | −1.851† | −2.429* |
| Mother not married | −0.537 | −1.729 | −0.157 | −0.309 | −0.203 | −1.046 |
| Number of children | 0.046 | −0.415 | 0.329 | 0.208 | 0.053 | 0.076 |
| Age of youngest child | 0.041 | −0.064 | 0.039 | 0.035 | 0.060 | 0.085 |
| Study child is at school or kindergarten | 0.772 | 1.753 | 1.199 | 0.989 | 0.929 | 0.658 |
| Number of threatening events in the past year (0-4, reversed) | −0.100 | −0.075 | 0.083 | −0.104 | −0.131 | −0.255 |
| Life difficulty (0 = less difficulty) | −0.246 | −0.534 | −0.701 | 0.280 | 0.777 | −0.134 |

*continued*

**Table 8.4: continued**

| | OLS | Quantile regression percentile | | | | |
|---|---|---|---|---|---|---|
| | | 10th | 25th | 50th | 75th | 90th |
| Support from family and friends (0 = more support) | 0.086 | −0.766 | 0.102 | 0.481 | 0.546 | 0.669 |
| Coping (0 = coping well) | −0.809 | −0.583 | −0.423 | −0.437 | −2.070† | −0.938 |
| Parents' connectedness with community (0 = high connectedness) | −0.277* | −0.533* | −0.444* | −0.272* | −0.150‡ | −0.006 |
| Parents' psychological distress (0 = low distress) | −0.435* | −0.632* | −0.465* | −0.399* | −0.381* | −0.315* |
| Parents' warmth (0 = high warmth) | −0.219* | −0.241 | −0.190‡ | −0.259* | −0.310* | −0.381* |

Table 8.5 explores further the impact of income on children's Outcome Index scores. The results for the multivariate model that are presented in this Table are identical to the results presented in Table 8.4, except that income is specified in terms of membership of decile groups. This model shows more clearly how the relationship between income and Outcome Index scores changes as household income increases. The beta coefficients for income deciles can be interpreted as the expected change in the Outcome Index score given an increase in household income from the lowest income decile group to the decile group in question. None of the beta coefficients for the 2nd, 3rd or 4th deciles of income are significant at $p<0.1$ in the OLS model, or in the quantile regression at any point in the distribution of Outcome Index scores. In other words, having household income in these decile groups is no different from having income in the lowest decile group as far as child outcomes are concerned, once other variables are controlled. From the 5th decile onwards, income starts to become significant both in the OLS regression and in the quantile regression for Outcome Index scores at the 10th percentile. Most notable, however, is the impact of high levels of household income (in the 9th and 10th decile groups) on outcomes at the 10th, 25th and 50th percentiles of the Outcome Index. This relationship is strongest at the 10th percentile, and fades out in the higher percentiles of the Outcome Index (it is not significant at $p<0.1$ at the 75th or 90th percentiles). This suggests that, when other factors are controlled, only the higher levels of income make a difference to Outcome Index scores, and then only where Outcome Index scores are low.

**Table 8.5: Ordinary least squares and quantile multivariate regressions on Continuous Outcome Index with income included as a categorical variable**

| | OLS | Quantile regression percentile | | | | |
|---|---|---|---|---|---|---|
| | | 10th | 25th | 50th | 75th | 90th |
| Adjusted Rsq | 0.270 | 0.192 | 0.182 | 0.157 | 0.136 | 0.109 |
| In 2nd decile of household income distribution | 0.399 | −0.804 | 0.975 | 0.749 | 0.393 | −0.135 |
| In 3rd decile of household income distribution | 0.185 | −0.843 | 0.893 | 0.589 | −0.283 | 1.783 |
| In 4th decile of household income distribution | −0.356 | 1.526 | −0.122 | −0.497 | −1.314 | −0.693 |
| In 5th decile of household income distribution | 1.595‡ | 3.245† | 1.634 | 1.602 | 0.236 | 1.379 |
| In 6th decile of household income distribution | 1.332 | 1.692 | 1.315 | 1.237 | 0.785 | 1.130 |
| In 7th decile of household income distribution | 1.696‡ | 3.279† | 2.158‡ | 2.123 | 1.278 | 1.337 |
| In 8th decile of household income distribution | 1.532‡ | 2.271 | 2.434† | 1.628 | 0.840 | 1.432 |
| In 9th decile of household income distribution | 2.417* | 4.005‡ | 3.024† | 2.372† | 1.004 | 1.013 |
| In top decile of household income distribution | 2.456* | 3.847† | 3.222* | 2.770* | 1.570 | 1.143 |
| Mother has tertiary education | 0.460 | −0.059 | 0.832 | 0.788 | 1.210 | 1.917 |
| Mother has post-school diploma/certificate | 1.242 | 2.384 | 2.464 | 0.765 | 1.707† | 1.882 |
| Mother completed year 11/has certificate | 2.442* | 3.086 | 3.394† | 2.785† | 2.886* | 2.702 |
| Mother completed year 10 | 2.953* | 2.883 | 3.599† | 3.002* | 3.540* | 3.938† |
| Indigenous household | −1.452 | 1.379 | −1.300 | −1.932 | −1.280 | −0.882 |
| English not spoken at home | −0.150 | 0.323 | −0.327 | −0.296 | 0.115 | −0.007 |
| Mother's age | 0.049 | 0.057 | 0.030 | 0.049 | 0.077‡ | 0.050 |
| Lone-parent family | −0.356 | 0.951 | −0.614 | −0.711 | −1.025 | −0.507 |
| Step or blended family | −1.747 | −0.375 | −2.559 | −2.171 | −2.230† | −3.286† |
| Mother not married | −0.377 | −0.632 | −0.195 | −0.010 | −0.022 | −0.736 |
| Number of children | 0.124 | −0.394 | 0.442 | 0.251 | 0.124 | 0.032 |
| Age of youngest child | 0.044 | −0.105 | 0.051 | 0.044 | 0.120 | 0.119 |
| Study child is at school or kindergarten | 0.650 | 1.495 | 0.950 | 1.313 | 0.995 | 0.893 |

*continued*

**Table 8.5:** *continued*

| | OLS | Quantile regression percentile | | | | |
|---|---|---|---|---|---|---|
| | | 10th | 25th | 50th | 75th | 90th |
| Number of threatening events in the past year (0-4, reversed) | −0.085 | 0.038 | 0.018 | −0.119 | −0.122 | −0.106 |
| Life difficulty (0 = less difficulty) | −0.259 | −1.531 | −0.159 | 0.406 | 0.921 | 0.066 |
| Support from family and friends (0 = more support) | 0.064 | −0.768 | 0.008 | 0.170 | 0.523 | 0.936* |
| Coping (0 = coping well) | −0.768 | −0.184 | −0.903 | 0.289 | −1.797 | −1.188 |
| Parents' connectedness with community (0 = high connectedness) | −0.282* | −0.522* | −0.420† | −0.255* | −0.128 | 0.011 |
| Parents' psychological distress (0 = low distress) | −0.432* | −0.643* | −0.465* | −0.400* | −0.379* | −0.336* |
| Parents' warmth (0 = high warmth) | −0.219* | −0.273‡ | −0.184‡ | −0.269* | −0.319* | −0.368* |
| Parents' hostility (0 = low hostility) | −0.925* | −1.195* | −1.177* | −0.981* | −0.734* | −0.490* |
| Parents' consistency (0 = high consistency) | −0.400* | −0.633* | −0.427* | −0.335* | −0.283* | −0.305* |
| Constant | 116.4 | 114.6 | 113.7 | 115.8 | 116.6 | 118.2 |

*Notes:* * significant at $p<0.01$; † significant at $p<0.05$; ‡ significant at $p<0.1$. All explanatory variables are interval level or dummy variables, except mother's education, where the 'base case' is 'mother completed less than year 10'.

*Source:* LSAC Wave 1, authors' calculations

## Discussion

Our main finding, that high income makes a significant and positive difference for children with very low outcome scores, is new, and potentially important. It offers an alternative interpretation to that of Susan Mayer's (1997) finding that, for the US, money is not the key determinant of outcomes for children. After testing the parental income–child outcome relationship in a number of ways, Mayer concluded that parents' income, over and above a certain basic minimum to ensure that children are decently clothed, fed and housed, has only a very small impact on children's outcomes. She did not attempt to identify in detail those characteristics that do influence child outcomes, other than to argue that:

[P]arental characteristics associated with their income influence children's well-being. We have no direct way of knowing what these characteristics are. Because they are associated with parents' income they must be correlated with characteristics valued by employers, such as social adjustment, skills, enthusiasm, dependability, and hard work. In today's economy, parents with less than their share of these characteristics cannot make enough money to support themselves unless they get outside help. The same characteristics are valuable to children. Without outside help, parents who rank low on these characteristics find it hard to create an environment conducive to children's success. (Mayer, 1997, pp 14-15)

The methods used in this present study are different from those used by Mayer (for example, she used longitudinal data, examined outcomes for older children and teenagers and focused on mean outcomes). Nonetheless, the findings in this analysis largely corroborate her findings. For most Australian four- to five-year-olds, income does not make a difference to their developmental outcomes. However, among children with below average outcomes, belonging to a family where parental incomes are in the top two deciles is associated with improved outcomes. For vulnerable children, therefore, high family income does matter.

There are three possible candidates from the above theoretical discussions on extrinsic and intrinsic causation that present themselves as explanations for this. First, and most obvious, is the investment theory – high-income parents are likely to invest more in their children than low-income parents (Haveman and Wolfe, 1994). This theory has generally been applied to older children or to children across the lifecourse. There is little in the literature specifically on the relationship between parental investment and development among vulnerable children with low range outcomes at any age. It is plausible that among this group, investments may make a particular difference.

Human, social and cultural capital explanations may also be relevant here. As Hoff (2003) argues, children in the higher groups tend to develop a richer vocabulary because their mothers use a richer vocabulary. Rowe (2008) states that this relationship between parent and child vocabulary is mediated by parental knowledge of child development. If parental knowledge of child development (not addressed in the LSAC) is one indicator of parental human, social and cultural capital, and closely related to parents' income (or education, which is closely related to income in the LSAC), then this may give substance to the view that the findings here are a reflection of that capital. However, this would not necessarily explain why they are only apparent among children of high-income parents, and only among children with low-range Outcome Index scores.

On the other hand, the (extrinsic) parental stress theory and the (intrinsic) theory of parental characteristics suggest a different interpretation – that the most significant relationship is between stress and parenting and outcomes, and not between income and outcomes. Support for this theory comes from the fact that the parental distress indicator, and all three parental practices indicators (warmth, hostility and consistency) (Table 8.5), are highly significant at all levels of child outcomes. However, the fact that the connection between these parental characteristics and outcomes is significant at all levels of outcomes, but the connection with income is not, suggests that income is important for children with low outcome scores, over and above the importance of parental stress and practice.

In summary, the quantile regression results in this analysis suggest that the benefits of wealth on outcomes may be more important for 'vulnerable' children (with low Outcome Index scores), than for the 'average' child. A number of questions remain. First, this finding needs to be substantiated with causal longitudinal models, which more clearly hypothesise the relationship between income and other explanatory variables over time. Second, the nature of the relationship between income and outcomes needs to be more thoroughly explored. For example, is there evidence in the LSAC or other data sources of greater spending by high-income families on vulnerable children, on extra education, medical treatment, remedial therapies or other development-related activities? This preliminary analysis shows that income, and high income in particular, may indeed have an independent impact on outcomes, but this finding needs greater substantiation.

## Conclusion

This chapter has examined a longstanding issue in the child development literature – the relationship between family income and child outcomes. However, rather than focusing on low-income families, this study has investigated the whole range of incomes. Our finding that high income appears to protect and support the development of vulnerable children with low-range Outcome Index scores is important, we argue, for understanding the protective factors leading to improved interventions to maximise the potential of all children. Material resources and services comprise the main levers available to governments for influencing outcomes, and if it can be shown that material resources (albeit only in significant quantities) can make a significant difference to child outcomes, then this is a policy that governments can pursue in seeking to help children develop their full potential. Already, the Australian government implicitly recognises that specialist interdisciplinary services might make a difference. Since 2004, Australians (including children) with special and complex health needs have been able to access a widened range of healthcare professionals through the Multidisciplinary Care Plan, allowing them up to five subsidised sessions or treatments a year. However further research is needed on who has been accessing these new services, what other services are being accessed by children with low-range Outcome Index scores and what impact these services have had. The results provided in this chapter give hope that, for some children at least, the impact may be positive.

It is important to acknowledge the limitations of this study. The most immediate of these is the fact that it was based only on one wave of data from one study. We are unable to show the precedents and consequents of the behaviour we are studying, and therefore are not able to comment on the causal directions of any of the associations we have found. It will be necessary to examine the consistency of results over time, as children develop and grow older. Feinstein et al (2004) show widening gaps with age, for children with both high and low initial Outcome Index scores. We will need to examine, as further waves of LSAC become available, whether the patterns uncovered here among Australian four- to five-year-olds remain evident as they grow older.

## References

Australian Bureau of Statistics (2008) *An Introduction to Socio-Economic Indexes for Areas (SEIFA)*, Cat. No. 2039.0, Canberra: Australian Bureau of Statistics, www.ausstats.abs.gov.au/ausstats/subscriber.nsf/0/D729075E079F9FDECA2574170011B088/$File/20390_2006.pdf

Berger, L.M. (2007) 'Socioeconomic factors and substandard parenting', *Social Service Review*, vol 81, no 3, pp 485-522.

Bor, W., Najman, J.M., Andersen, M.J., O'Callaghan, M., Williams, G.M. and Behrens, B.C. (1997) 'The relationship between low family income and psychological disturbance in young children: an Australian longitudinal study', *Australian and New Zealand Journal of Psychiatry*, vol 31, no 5, pp 664-75.

Bourdieu, P. (1986) 'The forms of capital', in J.G. Richardson (ed) *Handbook of Theory and Research in the Sociology of Education*, New York: Greenwald Press.

Centre for Community Child Health Royal Children's Hospital (2004) *Parenting Information Project Volume Two: Literature Review*, Canberra: Department of Family and Community Services.

Coleman, J.S. (1988) 'Social capital in the creation of human capital', *American Journal of Sociology*, vol 94 (suppl), pp S95-S120.

Conger, K.J., Conger, R.D. and Scaramella, L.V. (1997) 'Parents, siblings, psychological control, and adolescent adjustment', *Journal of Adolescent Research*, vol 12, no 1, pp 113-38.

Conger, R.D. and Donnellan, M.B. (2007) 'An interactionist perspective on the socioeconomic context of human development', *Annual Review of Psychology*, vol 58, no 1, pp 175-99.

DeGarmo, D.S., Forgatch, M.S. and Martinez, C.R.J. (1999) 'Parenting of divorced mothers as a link between social status and boys' academic outcomes: unpacking the effects of socioeconomic status', *Child Development*, vol 70, no 5, pp 1231-45.

Dooley, M. and Stewart, J. (2004) 'Family income and child outcomes in Canada', *Canadian Journal of Economics – Revue Canadienne D Economique*, vol 37, no 4, pp 898-917.

Duncan, G.J. and Brooks-Gunn, J. (eds) (1997) *Consequences of Growing Up Poor*, New York: NY: Russell Sage Foundation.

Duncan, G.J. and Magnuson, K. (2003) 'Off with Hollingshead: socioeconomic resources, parenting, and child development', in M.H. Bornstein and B.R.H. (eds) *Socioeconomic Status, Parenting and Child Development*, Mahwah, NJ: Lawrence Erlbaum Associates, pp 83-106.

Duyme, M., Dumaret, A.C. and Tomkiewicz, S. (1999) 'How can we boost IQs of "dull children"?: a late adoption study', *Proceedings of the National Academy of Sciences*, vol 96, pp 8790-4.

Elder, G., Van Nguyen, T. and Caspi, A. (1985) 'Linking family hardship to children's lives', *Child Development*, vol 56, no 2, pp 361-75.

Emerson, E., Graham, H. and Hatton, C. (2006) 'Household income and health status in children and adolescents in Britain', *European Journal of Public Health*, vol 16, no 4, pp 354-60.

Feinstein, L., Duckworth, K. and Sabates, R. (2004) *A Model of the Intergenerational Transmission of Educational Success: Wider Benefits of Learning Research Report, No. 10*, London: Centre for Research on the Wider Benefits of Learning.

Fergusson, D.M., Horwood, L.J. and Lynskey, M.T. (1994) 'The childhoods of multiple problem adolescents: a 15-year longitudinal study', *Journal of Child Psychology and Psychiatry*, vol 35, no 6, pp 1123-40.

Foster, E.M. (2002) 'How economists think about family resources and child development', *Child Development*, vol 73, no 6, pp 1904-14.

Ghate, D. and Hazel, N. (2002) *Parenting in Poor Environments: Stress, Support and Coping*, London: Jessica Kingsley Publishers.

Hart, S.A., Petrill, S.A., Deater Deckard, K. and Thompson, L.A. (2007) 'SES and CHAOS as environmental mediators of cognitive ability: a longitudinal genetic analysis', *Intelligence*, vol 35, no 3, pp 233-42.

Haveman, R. and Wolfe, B. (1994) *Succeeding Generations: On the Effects of Investments in Children*, New York: Russell Sage Foundation.

Haveman, R. and Wolfe, B. (1995) 'The determinants of children's attainments: a review of methods and findings', *Journal of Economic Literature*, vol 33, no 4, pp 1829-78.

Hill, N. (2006) 'Disentangling ethnicity, socioeconomic status and parenting: interactions, influences and meaning', *Vulnerable Children and Youth Studies*, vol 1, no 1, pp 114-24.

Hoff, E. (2003) 'Causes and consequences of SES-related differences in parent to child speech', in M.H. Bornstein and R.H. Bradley (eds) *Socioeconomic Status, Parenting and Child Development*, Mahwah, NJ: Lawrence Erlbaum Associates, pp 145-60.

Hoff, E., Laursen, B. and Tardif, T. (2002) 'Socioeconomic status and parenting', in M.H. Bornstein (ed) *Handbook of Parenting* (2nd edition, vol 2, Mahwah, NJ: Lawrence Erlbaum Associates, pp 231-52.

Hoff-Ginsberg, E. and Tardif, T. (1995) 'Socioeconomic status and parenting', in M.H. Bornstein (ed) *Handbook of Parenting, Vol. 2: Biology and Ecology of Parenting*, Hillsdale, NJ: Lawrence Erlbaum Associates, pp 161-88.

Hoffman, L.W. (2003) 'Methodological issues in studies of SES, parenting and child development', in M.H. Bornstein and R.H. Bradley (eds) *Socioeconomic Status, Parenting and Child Development*, Mahwah, NJ: Lawrence Erlbaum Associates, pp 125-44.

Jensen, A.R. (1998) *The G Factor*, Westport, CT: Praeger.

Katz, I., Corlyon, J., La Placa, V. and Hunter, S. (2007) *The Relationship between Parenting and Poverty*, York: Joseph Rowntree Foundation.

Kohn, M. (1969) *Class and Conformity: A Study of Values*, Homewood, IL: Dorsey.

Luster, T., Rhodes, K. and Haas, B. (1989) 'The relation between parental values and parenting behavior: a test of the Kohn hypothesis', *Journal of Marriage and the Family*, vol 51, pp 139-47.

Maccoby, E.E. and Martin, J.A. (1983) 'Socialization in the context of the family: parent–child interaction', in P. Mussen and E.M. Hetherington (eds) *Handbook of Child Psychology: Vol 4: Socialization, Personality, and Social Development* (4th edition), New York, NY: John Wiley.

Mahoney, J.L. (2000) 'School extracurricular activity participation as a moderator in the development of antisocial patterns', *Child Development*, vol 71, no 2, pp 502-16.

Mayer, S. (1997) *What Money Can't Buy: Family Income and Children's Life Chances*, Cambridge, MA: Harvard University Press.

Mayer, S. (2002) *The Influence of Parental Income on Children's Outcomes*, Wellington, New Zealand: Ministry of Social Development.

Murray, C. (1990) 'The British underclass', *The Public Interest*, vol 99, pp 4-28.

Murray, C. (1996) 'The emerging British underclass', in R. Lister (ed) *Charles Murray and the Underclass: The Developing Debate*, London: Institute of Economic Affairs, Health and Welfare Unit with *The Sunday Times*, pp 23-52.

O'Connor, T. and Scott, S. (2007) *Parenting and Children's Outcomes*, York: Joseph Rowntree Foundation.

Penman, R. (2007) 'Psychosocial factors and intergenerational transmission of welfare dependency: a review of the literature', in *Australian Social Policy 2006*, Canberra: Department of Community Services and Indigenous Affairs, pp 85-111.

Redmond, G. (2008) 'Using the LSAC to explore child development and well-being', Unpublished manuscript, Social Policy Research Centre, University of New South Wales.

Richardson, S. and Prior, M. (2005) 'Childhood today', in S. Richardson and M. Prior (eds) *No Time to Lose: The Wellbeing of Australia's Children*, Melbourne: Melbourne University Press, pp 1-35.

Roosa, M.W., Jones, S., Tein, J.Y. and Cree, W. (2003) 'Prevention science and neighborhood influences on low-income children's development: theoretical and methodological issues', *American Journal of Community Psychology*, vol 31, no 1-2, pp 55-72.

Ross, D.P. and Roberts, P. (1999) *Income and Child Well-Being: A New Perspective on the Poverty Debate*, Ottawa: Canadian Council on Social Development.

Rowe, M.L. (2008) 'Child-directed speech: relation to socioeconomic status, knowledge of child development and child vocabulary skill', *Journal of Child Language*, vol 35, no 1, pp 185-205.

Sammons, P., Sylva, K., Melhuish, E.C., Siraj-Blatchford, I., Taggart, B., Elliot, K. et al (2004) *The Effective Provision of Pre-School Education (EPPE) Project: Technical Paper 11: The Continuing Effects of Pre-School Education at Age 7 Years*, London: DfES and Institute of Education, University of London.

Sanson, A., Misson, S. and the Outcome Index Working Group (2005) *LSAC Technical Paper #2: Summarising Children's Wellbeing: The LSAC Outcome Index*, Melbourne: Australian Institute of Family Studies.

Sanson, A., Nicholson, J., Ungerer, J., Zubrick, S., Wilson, K., Ainley, J. et al (2002) *Introducing the Longitudinal Study of Australian Children*, LSAC Discussion Paper no 1, Melbourne: Australian Institute of Family Studies, www.aifs.gov.au/growingup/pubs/dp1.html

Smith, M. (2004) 'Parental mental health: disruptions to parenting and outcomes for children', *Child and Family Social Work*, vol 9, no 1, pp 3-11.

Van Hulle, C.A., Lemery-Chalfant, K. and Goldsmith, H.H. (2007) 'Genetic and environmental influences on socio-emotional behavior in toddlers: an initial twin study of the infant-toddler social and emotional assessment', vol 48, no 10, pp 1014-24.

Winnicott, D.W. (1964) *The Child, the Family, and the Outside World*, Harmondsworth: Penguin.

Zubrick, S.R., Smith, G.J., Nicholson, J.M., Sanson, A.V. and Jackiewicz, T.A. (2006) *Parenting and Families in Australia*, Canberra: Australian Government Department of Families, Community Services and Indigenous Affairs.

# NINE

# Managing shared residence in Britain and France: questioning a default 'primary carer' model

*Alexander Masardo*

## Introduction

The past 40 years have seen major shifts in the demographic constitution of families and households, in particular with regard to aspects of their formation and dissolution. A growing diversity in family forms has meant that increasing numbers of children are growing up in households that do not include both biological parents. Much of the research and policy interest surrounding these changes has focused on the growth in lone motherhood, where the ratio of lone mothers to lone fathers has remained remarkably consistent over many years, at roughly nine to one (Duncan and Edwards, 1999). As a result, in as much as fathers have been portrayed at all, they have been considered largely in their role as 'separated' or 'absent' fathers, living apart from their children. This focus has tended to mask the substantial differences that exist in the nature of their contact, care and residence arrangements, where many fathers endeavour to play an active and engaged role – emotionally and instrumentally – in the lives of their children, despite the parents' separation.

An increasingly favourable social and legal disposition towards the continuation of parent–child involvement, allied to notions of the welfare and 'best interests' of the child, has meant that despite the parents' separation '[t]he notion of a biological family which transcends individual household boundaries and in which children retain both parents in their lives … is a lived reality' (Neale et al, 1998, p 16). Not only are fathers involved in forms of ongoing and regular contact but also, for some, an arguably distinct model of post-separation family life in which both parents share the day-to-day care of the children can be discerned – 'shared residence'. Here, children reside with each parent for roughly equal amounts of time by alternating their home life across two households; in effect – for the children – a 'dual residence' (Maccoby and Mnookin, 1992; Neale et al, 2003).[1]

Definitions lack precision but generally involve upwards of 30% of the child's time throughout the year being spent in each household; usually designated by the number of overnight stays. Baker and Townsend (1996), for example, drawing on the American divorce literature, suggest that this 30-70 ambit of care is appropriate as a general rule, and Bradshaw et al (1999), in their seminal study of non-resident fathers, use a similar definition, setting a slightly lower minimum threshold of 104 nights over the year for the 'shared care' group they identify. While this spectrum of residence is in no sense a definitive guide as to what might constitute such arrangements, it nevertheless provides a useful framework within which to explore the intersection of resident and non-resident parenting.

Why is it important to do this? Because at present, parents are divided upon separation into two discrete entities – one 'with care' (the resident parent) and one without (the non-resident parent) – which results in the establishment of gendered roles of 'carer' and 'provider' (via child support). However, where the care and residence of the child is shared in more or less equal measure, a 'non-resident' status may not only be inappropriate in this instance, it may also lead to multiple levels of disadvantage, not only for the non-resident parent and their child but also for any other members of that household. As Giddens (1998, p 104) warns us: 'Exclusion is not about gradations of inequality, but about mechanisms that act to detach groups of people from the social mainstream'.

In many respects, a lone–absent or resident–non-resident parent dichotomy, which runs as an undercurrent within institutionalised social structures at practically every level, may be acting as just such a mechanism, serving to obfuscate the realities of a shared residence model of family life. Here, there exist two family units, indeed households, where neither parent is de facto 'lone' nor 'absent'; where both require recognition, perhaps for a variety of reasons, as legitimate family forms with concomitant needs. These needs may be particularly acute within low-income households and may, additionally, serve to discriminate against this model of family life taking place at all.

Although data on the actual prevalence of shared residence remains somewhat inconsistent and partial – given the non-comparability of studies, the disparity over definitions and the lack of data measures over time – there are indications that such approaches make up a significant proportion of those practised by separated families across many Western societies. Skinner et al (2007), in their international study of child support policy within 14 different countries, asked specific questions of national informants about 'shared care' – defined as being 'where the child spends roughly equal amounts of time living with each parent' (2007, p 3) – and found that, with the above caveats squarely in mind, reported levels varied from between 7% and 15%. Peacey and Hunt (2008), in their recent study of problematic contact after separation and divorce, found that between 9% and 17% of parents in the UK share the care of their child(ren) equally, or nearly equally, with the other parent. Also, Toulemon (2008), drawing on figures from the *ERCV* survey – the French part of the European Union Survey on Income and Living Conditions (EU-SILC) 2004 – tells us that a total of 12.2% of children whose parents live apart share their time between them and that, of the roughly equivalent number of children living in father-headed lone-parent families – a total of 11.9% – about half of these children are also spending some time living with their mothers. Overall, this could suggest that around 18% of French children of separated parents live in two residences.

The issue of shared residence has of late moved up the political agenda in a number of jurisdictions around the world, driven in some measure by an increasingly vociferous – and international – fathers' rights lobby (Rhoades and Boyd, 2004; Collier and Sheldon, 2006). Yet despite the substantial interest in the concept of shared residence this focus has generated, relatively little is known within the European literature about how it functions in practice; in particular, with regard to the relational and structural dynamics that exist in its negotiation and management. By *relational* I refer to the roles of and relationships between the various social actors involved; and by *structural* I refer specifically to the legal and policy frameworks within which it operates.

In the course of this chapter, I provide some insight into how these relational and structural dynamics are played out and, in this way, throw some light on an evolving *practice* that has received very little attention to date. In order to do this, I am going to draw on cross-national research funded by the Economic and Social Research Council (ESRC) that uses qualitative methodology to compare and contrast fathers' experiences of negotiating and managing shared residence in Britain and in France. I begin by briefly describing the methods employed in the study, outlining some of the central respondent characteristics and looking at the various patterns of care that have been adopted. I then provide some key findings from an analysis of the data, focusing on French law and policy to comment on UK debates and the challenges fathers face when parenting in this type of multi-residence situation.

## Methods

Between June 2005 and August 2006, qualitative (semi-structured) in-depth interviews were carried out with 20 British and 15 French fathers, who at the time of interview had at least one biological child under 19 years of age in a shared residence arrangement.[2] The main criterion for inclusion in the study was a minimum of 30% of the child's time spent resident with each parent over the year. Crucially, this definition meant that respondents included both officially resident as well as non-resident parents, thereby giving a clearer indication of what might be happening at this intersection. A qualitative approach was used primarily in order to capture these complexities and the multiple realities of this form of family life.

Participants were accessed using a snowball or 'network' sampling technique, which relies on the social contacts between individuals to trace additional respondents. Given that that there is no readily accessible sampling frame for the population of fathers with shared residence, this proved a more than adequate means of accessing participants. However, there are drawbacks to this type of sampling procedure. As Burton (2000, p 315) reminds us: 'Networks can tend to be homogenous in their attributes, rather than providing links to others who have different social characteristics'. As such, the findings are intimately linked to the issue of sampling bias. Nevertheless, a diverse range of experiences and perspectives have been brought to this study. In this short overview of the research findings, it should be borne in mind that it is not my intention to generalise these findings to the wider population of shared residence fathers or indeed families, rather it is to consider the challenges that individual respondents faced and the manner in which they approached certain obstacles as providing signposts for consideration.

On the whole, fathers in both groups were aged in their thirties and forties, were in paid employment and currently single. The only notable difference was that, in contrast to the majority of British fathers who had been previously married to their children's mothers, slightly more of the French respondents had been cohabiting. The number of children parents had and their ages at the time of separation also appear to have been strong contributory factors in facilitating such arrangements, as was the geographical proximity of homes. This was reflected in the fact that nearly all the children had been under the age of 11 when they first began alternating their residence, that respondents rarely had more than two children and that parents tended to live within a five-mile radius of each other – many of these within 'walking distance'.

Also of note was the high proportion of fathers claiming that the mothers had initiated the breakdown of the relationship. Although we do not have the mothers' accounts from which to compare these reports, they are significant nevertheless, since fathers would generally discuss the evolution of arrangements based on these terms. This could suggest that the manner in which these partnerships ended may have played a part in any consequent consideration and negotiation of care arrangements; specifically, with regard to the mothers' amenability towards shared residence.

Finally, the overwhelming majority of fathers in both sample groups claimed to have played a central role in the day-to-day care of their children prior to the parents' separation. This must lead us to ask whether shared residence is a more likely outcome where the father–child relationship has previously been imbued with high levels of active parenting. It is notable that strong care roles were reported regardless of whether subsequent arrangements had been made privately or through a legal dispute mediated through lawyers or the family courts.

## Parenting schedules and cycles of care

The parents in the study had adopted a variety of care patterns. In the main, these centred around a one- or two-week cycle of care that tended to be broken over holiday periods and according to the degree of flexibility parents demonstrated towards each other and towards their children's own wishes and needs. In order to summarise these, I have used a schematic representation over time in which each shaded block highlights the number of overnight stays the children make in each respective household, where M = with mother and F = with father. In addition, each week is shown diagrammatically as starting from Sunday.

*The one-week cycle*: Chris (Figure 9.1) provides us with an example of a one-week cycle of residence, where his two sons are with him from Wednesday until Saturday evening, and then spend Saturday evening until Wednesday morning with their mother.

**Figure 9.1: British respondent: Chris (aged 36) and Sue – Joel (aged 7) and Sam (aged 4)**

| M | M | M | F | F | F | M |
|---|---|---|---|---|---|---|
| Sun | Mon | Tue | Wed | Thurs | Fri | Sat |

*The two-week cycle*: Jacques (Figure 9.2) gives us an example of a two-week cycle of residence, where his children alternate their home life each week by spending every Friday evening until the following Friday evening resident with one parent.

**Figure 9.2: French respondent: Jacques (aged 44) and Mari-Lou – Julian (aged 12) and Sophie (aged 9)**

| Week 1 | | | | | | |
|---|---|---|---|---|---|---|
| M | M | M | M | M | F | F |
| Sun | Mon | Tue | Wed | Thurs | Fri | Sat |

| Week 2 | | | | | | |
|---|---|---|---|---|---|---|
| F | F | F | F | F | M | M |
| Sun | Mon | Tue | Wed | Thurs | Fri | Sat |

Variants of this alternate-weeks approach (*résidence hebdomodaire*) were practised by over a third of French respondents, making it by far the most common pattern of residence among this group. Other patterns in the French sample included a four-week cycle, where children would alternate between both homes every two weeks (*la quinzaine*), and a model of care known in the UK as 'nesting', where it is the parents who alternate their own residence to accommodate the child's one home. Where this occurred, it tended to take place in the initial stages following the breakdown of the parental relationship; in one instance, this model of care took place over a period of six months, in another for just over a year.

Parents in the French sample tended to adopt significantly longer blocks of time with their children than their British counterparts. While the most common arrangement among the French sample was an alternate-weeks pattern of care, in the British sample they were more often split into a series of shorter two-, three- or four-day blocks of residence. This could be explained, in part, by differences in attitude regarding the psychological well-being of the children: in the main, the French parents appeared desirous of avoiding the constant toing and froing for the children that shorter periods of residence would entail, while the British parents appeared more concerned about the effect that overly long absences from either parent would have on them. From what evidence there is available, these differences in the lengths of care patterns are also borne out in wider British and French research (cf Bradshaw et al, 1999; Moreau et al, 2004). While fathers revealed a great diversity within these cycles of care, not only in the days on which the changeovers occurred but also in their timing and logistics, in the main, they reflected the needs of all family members for consistency and a comprehensible rhythm.

Crucially, parenting schedules were not static, often evolving through their own dynamic and occasionally involving several different formulations over time; fathers varied in the lengths of time they had been separated from their former partners from two to 13 years. Respondents could also have separate arrangements for different children. Family recomposition, in particular, meant that some parents were subject to a series of parallel commitments and could have several residence arrangements running concurrently for different sets of children and/or stepchildren. Nevertheless, despite the dynamic nature of arrangements, which would often stem from a process of trial and error and in accordance with the changing needs and wishes of the various social actors involved, the levels of care and overnight stays children had with each parent tended to remain consistent across both sample groups – that is, shared in the sense of continuing to operate within the residence criterion used within the study. There were exceptions to this rule, for example, where a particular child had gone to live with one or other of their parents on a more permanent basis or where one parent had initially taken on the sole care of the child(ren) following parental separation and contact with the other parent had been minimal. For this small group of fathers and mothers (three and one respectively at six months post separation), these periods of solo parenting could play an important part of the overall picture of the factors that influenced the negotiation process and impacted in some measure on the way arrangements developed.

## Negotiating shared residence: personal histories

Two factors appeared to contribute, in particular, to the successful negotiation of shared residence between parents: first, a mutual respect for the other's parental role, which included a recognition that each would continue to play a central part in the children's lives; and second, an acceptance by both parents that their former partner now had a separate life and that any ongoing relationship between them would centre solely around the upbringing of the children. Nevertheless, despite a mutual acceptance of the involvement of the other parent in a care capacity, shared residence did not appear to require high levels of cooperative working among separated parents. This finding represents a major departure from hitherto taken-for-granted assumptions that shared residence is only established in the context of friendly co-parenting relationships. There was, however, clear evidence of two distinct patterns of parenting relationships that could be discerned among respondents: first, *cooperative co-parenting*, reflected in some form of working parental relationship; and second, *parallel* (or disengaged) *parenting*, where little or no communication took place between them, each essentially doing their own thing (see, for example, Maccoby and Mnookin, 1992).[3]

Fathers found that, in general, good communication between parents was healthy not only for practical reasons but also because it could also have a knock-on effect on their children's well-being. However, while more parallel parenting approaches could suggest greater underlying conflict or tension between parents that might act to militate against 'working' arrangements, for some parents it represented a useful means by which to facilitate shared residence through reducing the opportunities for flashpoints and thereby avoiding any potential conflict. In this sense, parents could be seen to be acting both rationally and responsibly, reducing any adverse effect of the parental relationship on the child and thereby acting in their children's best interests. In this context, we should be wary in conflating parental disengagement with conflict or indeed in assigning any underlying 'good' or 'bad' status to one approach over the other. Moreover, these approaches were not set in stone, with parallel parenting often leading to more cooperative parenting relationships over time, highlighting the need for a period of time – or 'bedding down' – within which parents could come to terms with the nature of events without setting themselves up in opposition to each other.

Other important and related aspects of the findings included striking a balance in the extent to which children would integrate the two halves of their home life. It appeared to be of particular importance to fathers that the children had a sense of ownership over their two worlds and that any integration should generally be led by the children themselves. This required that parents be open and responsive to their children's needs, which could change over time. Fathers also identified consistency in arrangements combined with an ability to be flexible where needed and remaining committed to establishing shared residence where it had not been in place from the outset.

Where fathers had repartnered and had additional children and/or stepchildren, they often identified a need to nurture the core biological family unit within the, now, wider one. Providing time and space for each genetic set of siblings to establish their own unique identity could act to dispel any sense their children might have of being 'visitors' in the household, where respondents' own children might spend less time resident with them than their new partners' children. The point was also raised that where two families had 'come together', having different arrangements for different sets of stepsiblings could also help to facilitate the arrangement, in the sense that the children were not constantly getting 'under each other's feet'. This was seen as healthy and thereby worked to sustain the arrangement. There was a general sense that relationships between these groups of children had to be handled with tact and care.

The levels to which children were actively engaged in decision making with respect to their care arrangements appeared to be minimal. This can be explained, in large part, by their very young ages at separation. However, fathers also claimed that children needed to feel included in the way events unfolded. The British sample revealed a greater willingness to let their children participate in decision making as they got older and talked of the potential need to reassess arrangements in light of their age and circumstances. However, while French fathers talked less about these issues, they were no less prepared to involve them in decision-making processes. It is also possible to speculate that the longer periods of residence that the children were subject to in the French sample, meant that more satisfactory arrangements had already been met, thus negating the need to alter them as they got older.

Given the highly individualised personal histories of respondents, an absence of any striking cross-national differences in the data with regard to the relational issues discussed here was not surprising. It should, however, act to draw our attention in greater measure to the similarities that have been drawn out from the fathers' narratives.

## Private agreements and legal proceedings

While three quarters of the British sample had arranged things privately, without recourse to lawyers or the family courts, the French sample was more evenly split.[4] However, many more fathers in the British sample indicated that they were unsatisfied with arrangements as they stood and that although they had been made privately, this did not mean that they had necessarily been worked out amicably or indeed that they had been in any way negotiated. These fathers tended to be those with weekend residence and were generally unhappy about their lack of involvement during the school week and in decision-making processes more generally.

Fathers felt vulnerable in ways they considered mothers did not have to. A particular concern fathers held was that the mothers of their children might decide to move away from the area, thereby making it difficult to maintain a shared residence arrangement. This vulnerability was often reflected in 'defensive measures' such as record keeping and in the desire for some form of concrete court order, which, they felt, could provide them with a sense of 'certainty' and security in the arrangements they made.

In terms of their awareness and understanding of their respective systems of family law, it became clear that the majority of respondents across both samples had felt unsure of their legal standing in relation to their children and had little knowledge of how any legal process might play out. Indeed, both parents could often have exaggerated perceptions of what could be achieved through legal means. While the group of British fathers who had used solicitors felt that these had generally been unhelpful, in particular, in terms of 'ratcheting-up the tension', those who had used *avocats* (lawyers) within the French sample were not as disparaging about them. However, several still found that they could be anything but helpful with regard to pursuing shared residence, often actively advising against it. The idea that shared residence was 'just not an option' among lawyers and the judiciary was prevalent in fathers' accounts across the board. Indeed, no shared residence orders were made through the family courts within the British context, even where such orders had been agreed on by the parents themselves.

A fine line appeared to separate those parents who managed to make arrangements privately from those who went to court. Fathers would invariably become involved in the legal process as a last resort. This was particularly the case where they felt that their children were being used as a point of control and that the fundamental rights of the children were not being respected. This would be reflected, for example, in no holiday contact, by imposing what they saw as unreasonable conditions on where and how they could see the children and in the arbitrary refusal of access.

Where parents do go to court, there appears to be a tendency to think of these cases as being somehow deviant. What fathers reveal in these accounts is that the key element in determining their approach appears to rest on whether or not a full and ongoing relationship with their children can be established. In this sense, many fathers who go to court vary very little from those who have made arrangements privately. More generally, while legal proceedings did not necessarily help respondents to increase their levels of contact with their children where this had become an issue, they nevertheless felt able to establish some certainty and control over their lives in respect of their relationships with their children.

Finally, a third 'conciliatory approach', exemplified in the process of family mediation, could also be identified in fathers' accounts. Despite highlighting a series of drawbacks associated with such approaches – for example, mothers refusing to attend or perceiving that the mediator had taken sides with the father – respondents nevertheless felt that this environment offered them a forum in which their voices and opinions were listened to and valued, and a venue in which they felt they were treated as equals. Some fathers appeared to find it helpful in enabling them to move on, in emotional terms, from past relationships and what, for many, had felt like a bereavement. This could feed into the way arrangements developed and thereby indirectly act to facilitate more shared care approaches.

## Shared residence and policy

Fathers in both Britain and France highlighted how the registered address of the child could vary according to the particular welfare mechanism or policy measure under consideration. In this sense, the 'official' residence of the child was dynamic and could be held by both parents simultaneously. For example, while one parent might receive family benefits, the other could be the resident parent for the purposes of their child's schooling or have their child registered at their address for the purposes of healthcare registration. Equally, as in the French case, tax breaks could be offset or 'traded off' against family allowances, making the official residence of the child both fluid and managed in light of certain, often complex, negotiations that were perceived to be of mutual benefit in the care and upbringing of the child. Where parents were able to negotiate to work their respective systems to their own advantage, this could facilitate the arrangement both directly and indirectly. However, where this was not possible, an administrative apparatus that was unable to accommodate the lived reality of families' lives could act to disadvantage the non-resident parent in a multitude of ways and thereby act to hinder the management of such arrangements.

Issues of housing and social security benefits emerged as particular dilemmas for fathers and, indeed, for mothers where they were the non-resident parent for the purposes of childcare recognition. Several respondents highlighted how a non-resident status could cause particular problems where they were either not in receipt of family allowances and/or had lost access to the family home, for example through a divorce settlement. Respondents also highlighted how non-resident parents on low incomes may find the practice of shared residence particularly hard where large families are concerned.

Very real issues of affordability appear to exist in relation to the practice of shared residence given the fact that suitable accommodation needs to be found by both parents. The receipt of benefits and child support maintenance can confer a profound advantage on the parent who is treated as the main carer. However, it is of note that over half of all respondents in both sample groups were not paying any maintenance and where they were this was often a nominal amount.

Finally, fathers' work practices appeared to enable them to prioritise family life over and above work commitments. Indeed, most fathers had actively tailored their employment patterns to suit their childcare responsibilities. Moreover, fathers were reluctant to use childcare facilities, preferring to care for their children personally where this was possible. Where the reverse was true and fathers worked their care arrangements around their working practices, this could lead to high levels of stress and act against the quality of care provided and consequently the shared nature of the care arrangement. Fathers appeared to prize being there in a care-role capacity above financial stability; which could often involve a certain amount of (financial) risk taking. For these fathers, a breadwinner role would appear to be a somewhat hollow exercise if not part and parcel of a broader family life. This must make us look again at notions that fathers' lives are centrally located in the public sphere.

Indeed, on this note, we should be mindful that the desire of parents to establish good contact arrangements with children in the wake of separation does not take place within a vacuum of care but rather within the context of a broader 'family life'. For the most part, whether parents have played a greater or lesser role in the day-to-day care of their children, they are, nevertheless, both part of a much broader social fabric that ties them into wider communities such as kin, school and friendship networks. What is at stake when parents separate is often more than a loss of day-to-day contact with their children. In addition, a whole host of other daily interactions that make up aspects of their social and psychosocial identities are called into question. The same may be said for children of separated parents relative to wider kin and friendship networks. As such, it may be useful to start thinking about post-separation care arrangements within these broader social contexts.

## Shared residence: a presumption or an option?

In France, the legal situation with regard to residence has recently changed with the introduction of *la loi du 4 mars 2002* reform of 'parental authority'. *Résidence alternée* (shared residence) is now an explicit option for separating parents within the French *Code civil* (Civil Code). The fact that it has been placed, symbolically, as the first option in a list of possible post-separation residence outcomes (Article 373-2-9, paragraph 1) is likely to influence the perceived reticence of judges to make such orders as well as the amenability of lawyers seeking such orders for their clients.

Since fathers' accounts within the French sample have, more often than not, depicted experiences that predate the 2002 reforms, it is important to contextualise the qualitative data and subsequent analysis in light of this change. While no presumption of shared residence exists, it is nevertheless now recognised within French family law as a legitimate option, challenging the very heart of post-separation family practices through explicitly questioning a 'default' primary carer model. Parents now have the right to ask specifically for shared residence as a preferred arrangement, even when one parent is not in agreement, with the judge able to order *un titre provisoire* (a trial period); the duration of which will, generally speaking, not exceed six months.

In addition, this option is now also supported through radical policy measures aimed at underpinning the notion of *coparentalité* (co-parenthood), which lies at the heart of the 2002 reforms: for example, through introducing a greater recognition of the housing needs of both separated parents; requiring parents to register the addresses of both parents at the start of each school year; modifying the legislation on *securité sociale* (national insurance) so that children may benefit from social health insurance through both parents, rather than a single allocation, as has been the case until recently; and culminating in the possibility of sharing *allocations familiales* (state allowance paid to families with dependent children) in cases of shared residence, the first payments of which were made in June 2007.

This now explicit option contrasts starkly with the infrequent use of shared residence orders within the British context and the emphasis that is placed squarely on private ordering alongside a primary carer model. By setting this option on an equal footing to a primary carer model, a 'no one size fits all' philosophy still prevails in France, yet simultaneously undercuts any discrimination that may exist against a shared residence model. This arguably allows for a period of 'bedding down' without setting parents in opposition to each other, for example by taking up opposing positions in order to establish themselves as the resident parent. It also sends a clear message that no one parent will automatically become the primary carer, which may lead to an increase in parents considering shared residence as a realistic option in France and, as a result, be less likely to embark on a dispute about residence. It is of note that recent figures from the French *Ministère de la Justice* reveal that a request for shared residence now represents one in ten of all contact and residence procedures concerning children (Moreau et al, 2004).

In France, debates around shared residence prior to the 2002 reforms were centred on whether it should be afforded the same legitimacy as other models of contact. In the British context, by contrast, recent debates have been framed in an altogether different way, instead centring around whether or not a presumption of shared residence should be made in law (DfES et al, 2004). Subsequently being rejected as 'impractical', framing the argument as a straightforward either/or solution to such a complex set of dilemmas has arguably not been helpful. Rather than addressing any long-term issues – or finding any long-term solutions – surrounding this practice, they have instead been bypassed, focusing instead on greater enforcement of contact orders, with the likely consequence of storing up problems for the future. As such, within the British context, shared residence is likely to remain something of a proverbial 'elephant in the room'.

In the British context, a shared residence model is not yet being considered as an acceptable addition to a residence–contact or 'primary carer' model, even where the differences between these modes of post-separation family life are becoming increasingly marginal in practice at the intersection of a resident–non-resident parent divide. In large part, this reluctance can be seen as due to the desirability of such arrangements being tied to high levels of cooperation between parents, which belies an assumption that shared residence will be difficult for adults (and their children) who do not conform to a very specific notion of a cooperative co-parenting ideal. However, as we have seen from an analysis of the qualitative data, such cooperative working is by no means a defining feature of shared residence families. Moreover, the rejection of such a model is also due to the overriding principle of non-intervention through private ordering, making the use of such orders somewhat moribund. At best, they will continue to be used in moderation, thereby specifically undermining what fathers themselves appear to wish for, namely a sense of legitimacy as equal partners in the upbringing of their children through the 'certainty' they feel such orders can bring.

It is not surprising, therefore, that of the total number of respondents in the British sample, of whom roughly one quarter had followed some form of legal proceedings, nowhere was an order for shared residence made, even in situations where parents had agreed to one. Rather, there were indications that consent orders – more usually associated with settling financial matters without the need to go to court – may be becoming more widespread with respect to the organisation of where a child is to live. A preference for consent orders over shared residence orders (where they are not imposed) is likely to mask the levels to which parents are desirous of shared residence and the extent to which de facto shared residence is taking place. In this instance, the infrequent use of such orders may be acting to influence not only the perceptions of the variety of family professionals engaged in such matters, for example legal advisers and welfare officers, but also parents themselves.

It is also likely, in the British context at least, that any moves towards the sharing of benefits in cases of shared residence will continue to prove highly controversial and problematic. The issue does not exist solely within a vacuum of care or indeed welfare. If benefit-sharing were facilitated further, it may not only require levels of expenditure that may be deemed unacceptable, but any government introducing such measures would run the risk of being accused of providing perverse economic incentives for families to separate.

## Conclusion

Within this chapter, my intention has been to provide the reader with a clearer picture of the ways in which shared residence manifests itself and identify areas of complexity within which such practices are becoming established. Key findings from an analysis of qualitative cross-national data have been outlined that point to some of the main challenges of parenting in this type of multi-residence situation. While it has been fathers' narratives that have been privileged within the research and consequent analysis, their accounts nevertheless hold wider purchase.

There are likely to be consequences for the lives of children and those charged with their care. Shared residence clearly relies on certain material conditions being met. Where this proves difficult, issues of child poverty and exclusion loom large and will need addressing. Where a resident–non-resident parent dichotomy lies at the heart of policy management, this may be particularly challenging. Such a division can act to discriminate against those currently managing shared residence as well as those families that would wish for such an arrangement but are prevented from doing so by the structural barriers such a divide creates.

A growth in such practices will require a refiguring of the ways in which traditional notions of carer and provider are conceived within law, policy and practice alike. Such a model may require a new approach that affords some recognition of the childcare needs of both parents, thereby legitimising families on a needs criterion rather than whether or not they hold a primary carer status, which at present can act to support one family group while simultaneously disenfranchising another. It becomes important, therefore, that attention is paid by policy makers and through research into such arrangements, thereby challenging the boundaries that may unwittingly discriminate against a shared residence model of family life as a viable option for separating families. Drawing on the French policy experience could help to cast some light on the policy challenges ahead.

**Notes**

[1] This definition is used here in its most generic sense. There are also instances in which it is the parents who alternate their own residence around the child's one home.

[2] Two (unstructured) pilot interviews were carried out beforehand in order to ground the direction of the research and develop the topic guide. These interviews were subsequently included in the analysis.

[3] Maccoby and Mnookin (1992) have identified four post-separation parenting relationships: cooperative, conflicted, disengaged and mixed.

[4] The analysis here refers to the total numbers of fathers involved in each process relative to residence and contact only, and not in respect of divorce proceedings and/or financial issues.

## Acknowledgements

This chapter is based on findings from doctoral research funded by the Economic and Social Research Council. For further information, please contact ssmfam@bath.ac.uk. The author wishes to thank Karen Rowlingson, Jane Millar, Christine Skinner and Jane Batchelor for their advice and support.

## References

Baker, A. and Townsend, P. (1996) 'Post-divorce parenting – rethinking shared residence', *Child and Family Law Quarterly*, vol 8, no 3, pp 217–27.

Bradshaw, J., Stimson, C., Skinner, C. and Williams, J. (1999) *Absent Fathers?*, London: Routledge.

Burton, D. (ed) (2000) *Research Training for Social Scientists*, London: Sage Publications.

Collier, R. and Sheldon, S. (2006) *Fathers' Rights Activism and Law Reform in Comparative Perspective*, Oxford: Hart Publishing.

DfES (Department for Education and Skills), Department for Constitutional Affairs and Department for Trade and Industry (2004) *Parental Separation: Children's Needs and Parents' Responsibilities*, Cm 6273, London: The Stationery Office.

Duncan, S. and Edwards, R. (1999) *Lone Mothers, Paid Work and Gendered Moral Rationalities*, Basingstoke: Macmillan.

Giddens, A. (1998) *The Third Way: The Renewal of Social Democracy*, Cambridge: Polity Press.

Maccoby, E.E. and Mnookin, R.H. (1992) *Dividing the Child: Social and Legal Dilemmas of Custody*, Cambridge, MA: Harvard University Press.

Moreau, C., Munoz-Perez, B. and Serverin, É. (2004) 'La résidence en alternance des enfants de parents séparés', *Études et Statistiques Justice 23*, Paris: Ministère de la Justice.

Neale, B., Flowerdew, J. and Smart, C. (2003) 'Drifting towards shared residence?', *Family Law*, vol 33, December, pp 904–8.

Neale, B., Wade, A. and Smart, C. (1998) *'I Just Get On With It': Children's Experiences of Family Life following Parental Separation or Divorce*, Working Paper 1, Leeds: Centre for Research on Family, Kinship and Childhood, University of Leeds.

Peacey, V. and Hunt, J. (2008) *Problematic Contact after Separation and Divorce?: A National Survey of Parents*, London: One Parent Families/Gingerbread.

Rhoades, H. and Boyd, S.B. (2004) 'Reforming custody laws: a comparative study', *International Journal of Law, Policy and the Family*, vol 18, pp 119-46.

Skinner, C., Bradshaw, J. and Davidson, J. (2007) *Child Support Policy: An International Perspective*, Research Report No 405, London: The Stationery Office.

Toulemon, L. (2008) *Two-Home Family Situations of Children and Adults: Observation and Consequences for Describing Family Patterns in France*, Paris: Institut national d'études démographiques (INED), available at http://epp.eurostat.ec.europa.eu/pls/portal/url/ITEM/4EC0934EBE3225ECE0440003BA9322F9

# Strategic challenges in child welfare services: a comparative study of Australia, England and Sweden

*Gabrielle Meagher, Natasha Cortis and Karen Healy*

## Introduction

Comparative welfare research now acknowledges that social services, as well as social security systems, define welfare states (Bambra, 2005; Jensen, 2008). In the child welfare field, cross-national studies offer critical insight into the goals, priorities and logic of welfare systems; differences in institutional structures and boundaries; and differences in the roles and characteristics of professionals, managers and service users in contemporary welfare states (Hearn et al, 2004; Hetherington, 2005). Interview methodologies enrich these approaches, linking stakeholder preoccupations and perspectives to cross-national analyses of system priorities and design (Hetherington, 2005).

This chapter draws on interview data from three study countries to map the strategic challenges confronting child welfare systems and to explore differences in the responses of these systems to the common challenges. Data were collected in Australia, England and Sweden as part of a bigger project seeking to understand the links between the characteristics of the workforce in child welfare services and the quality of service outcomes. The premises of the broader study were as follows. First, social services such as child welfare are primarily constituted by interpersonal interaction. Second, and following from the first, the characteristics of the workforce and the organisational contexts that shape and constrain their practice will be critical determinants of the quality of services for users. The three countries were chosen because two – England and Australia – have historically shared a common approach to child protection, focusing on targeted intervention to prevent abuse and neglect in an otherwise weakly developed system of public supports for parents and children characteristic of liberal welfare states. In both countries, however, there has been much reform activity in the child welfare sector in recent years, with many initiatives aimed at early intervention and gesturing towards more universal support for families. The third – Sweden – offers a useful contrast because child welfare services are embedded in a more universalistic system of support for parents and children, characteristic of social democratic welfare states.

The findings contribute to understanding the difficulties facing child welfare systems of different types – and give some insight into why reform is hard to achieve. Interviews with participants in child welfare systems (in this chapter, senior and local managers and policy workers, as well as researchers) provide some insight into the day-to-day experience of structural features of those systems. The complex and diverse impacts of one transnational force in the governance of rich democracies – New Public Management – can also be explored.

## Child welfare system characteristics

The child welfare systems in the study countries arise out of fundamentally different traditions (Gilbert, 1997; Hessle and Vinnerljung, 1999; Wiklund, 2006), as noted earlier. This section gives a brief overview of the structure of, and recent developments in, the system in each country as background to the analysis of strategic challenges that follows.

In *England*, child protection laws, policies and guidance are set nationally, but administered locally, through the referral, assessment, placement, review and planning processes of local authorities. The voluntary sector also plays a significant role in service delivery, particularly of family support and foster care placement services (Sellick and Howell, 2004). At the time of the interviews, central government was implementing ambitious plans to expand, reorganise and renew children's services (Fawcett et al, 2004; Garrett, 2008; Winter, 2008), as part of its social inclusion agenda. New legislation (the 2004 Children Act, based on the Green Paper *Every Child Matters*; DfES, 2004) increased the roles and responsibilities of local authorities in response to high-profile child deaths (Laming, 2003; DfES, 2004), specifying goals of achieving outcomes for all children (not just those in need); creating the Children's Commissioner post; and obliging authorities to improve coordination and strengthen their preventative capacity by 'joining up' processes and practices (NSPCC, 2007). Supporting initiatives include the introduction of a Common Assessment Framework for children and the Children's Index, which – controversially – aims to establish a comprehensive database of all children in England (Parton, 2006; Garrett, 2008). Despite the universalising aspirations of the Change for Children programme under the new Children Act, however, the tension between a child welfare/family support orientation on the one hand, and the child protection/statutory investigation orientation characteristic of child welfare systems in English-speaking countries on the other, has not been resolved and may actually be exacerbated under the legislation (Munro and Calder, 2005; Platt, 2006, p 271).

At the same time that the 2004 Children Act put children firmly on the policy agenda, the children's services *workforce* attracted significant policy attention (DfES, 2005), reflecting recognition that quality, stable human resources were integral to the sector's capacity to fulfil the national vision (Gupta and Blewett, 2007). Social work has been the principal profession in child welfare work in England, and one element of the policy response to developing the children's workforce, linked to the workforce goals in the broader agenda of 'modernising social services', has been the replacement of a diploma-level qualification for social work with a degree (Moriarty and Murray, 2007). However, another element of the Change for Children programme has been the introduction of a 'lead professional' to act as a single point of contact for families. This person need *not* be a professionally trained social worker, although social workers will probably maintain their role as the lead profession in statutory child protection services (Garrett, 2008, p 276).

In *Australia*, child welfare is primarily the responsibility of the eight state and territory governments. Thus, the child welfare system is fragmented across jurisdictions, with differences in legislation, policy, intake, investigation and case management processes between the states and territories (Bromfield and Higgins, 2005). The statutory child protection services, which are the traditional focus of Australian child welfare systems, are provided within the public sector, while non-governmental, often church-based agencies deliver most family support, and some foster and residential care services, under contract to governments. The federal government and many municipal governments also directly fund some family support services, so that many non-governmental organisations (NGOs) put together their budgets from several diverse funding sources. Overall, Australia lacks a national framework for the coordination of child welfare services and policy (although the newly elected federal government is beginning to develop one; FaHCSIA, 2008) and, within jurisdictions, service provision is split across government (statutory work) and non-governmental (preventative and treatment work) sectors, with NGOs funded through several (often poorly coordinated) state and federal programmes.

Children, children's services and the children's services workforce were not on Australia's policy agenda in the overarching and determined way seen in England at the time of the interviews. However, as in England, reviews and inquiries into child protection in the two states studied had resulted in several departmental reorganisations, as well as some new reporting and investigation requirements, the appointment of Children's Commissioners, and new funding commitments including significant workforce expansion (Ainsworth and Hansen, 2006). As part of this reform process, governments are giving increasing attention, if not concerted strategic coordination, to early intervention, but as in England, tensions between early intervention and forensic child protection remain significant. Unlike in England and Sweden, social work is not the principal profession in child welfare services. Indeed, there is *no* principal profession in child welfare, with statutory child protection workers drawn from a range of occupations, and family support offered by a mix of professional, paraprofessional and volunteer workers.

In *Sweden*, child welfare services are delivered by the 290 municipal social services departments, under national 'framework' legislation, which reflects commitments to women's and children's rights and social justice. This configuration leaves much more room for local policy development and professional discretion than in the English system, which seems, on the surface, to be structurally similar. Accordingly, Swedish child protection services are not defined as strictly as in the English and Australian systems. Although professionals working with children have long been required to report suspected child abuse and neglect, and children at risk can be removed from their parents by court order (Sundell et al, 2007, pp 182-3), the focus of the child protection dimension of the Swedish system is less on substantiation of alleged parental malfeasance and more on providing supportive services to remediate at the family level (Wiklund, 2006, p 43). Children do not need to be formal child welfare 'cases' to access supports; there are generally more resources available to assist families; and parents rarely lose custody of their children (Khoo et al, 2002, 2005). Overall, this tends to result in a less punitive, less stigmatised and more therapeutic approach to child welfare practice, with less acute systemic tensions between child protection and family support orientations than are evident in England and Australia. The Swedish model of child welfare also engenders a more varied workload for the professionals, almost all social workers, who deliver services. Non-governmental or voluntary sector organisations play a limited role in the Swedish system (Lundström, 2001), although there has been noteworthy growth in for-profit provision of residential care services, especially for troubled adolescents (Sallnäs, 2005; Johansson et al, 2008), who are defined as in need of child welfare interventions rather than subject to criminal justice institutions (Sundell et al, 2007, p 183), as they would more likely be in English-speaking countries. Although system stability rather than upheaval characterises the Swedish child welfare system at the macro level, within municipalities, organisational restructuring, typically in the direction of functional specialisation, has been undertaken in the vast majority of social service departments in recent years (Bergmark and Lundström 2007, pp 62-3). The implications of this development for social workers' daily practice remain to be established.

## Methodology

In 2004-06, interviews were conducted with child welfare managers, policy analysts and researchers in the three study countries. The aim was to learn from those with systemic (researchers, policy analysts) and organisational (managers) perspectives. A purposive sampling method was used to recruit these key informants and 69 interviews were conducted between July 2004 and June 2005 (see Table 10.1). There were 74 interviewees in total, as five interviews were with two respondents.

The distribution of respondents between categories differs between countries for two reasons. First, there are structural differences between

**Table 10.1: Institutional location of key informants (number of interviews)**

| Country/ institution | Government | Non-governmental organisation/union | University | Total | Dates |
|---|---|---|---|---|---|
| Australia (two states) | 23 | 13 | 0 | 36 | July to December 2004 |
| England (primarily London and the North of England) | 8 | 4 | 5 | 17 | January to March 2005 |
| Sweden (Stockholm and one provincial city) | 10 | 1 | 5 | 16 | April to June 2005 |

the child and family welfare systems in the study countries – for example not-for-profit organisations play a very significant role in Australia. Thus, documenting a comprehensive range of perspectives required a different sample structure for each country. Second, as the authors are researchers in the child and family welfare field in Australia, there was no need to draw on other researchers to gain an 'outsider's' systemic perspective, so resources could be devoted to interviewing system 'insiders'. (Australian respondents also outnumber those from England and Sweden, because the authors' location in Australia increased access to local informants.)

A semi-structured interview (lasting 45–90 minutes) was conducted with each informant. The interview schedule included questions about:

- strategic challenges in the child and family welfare system in general and with the workforce in particular;
- perceptions of the educational and professional preparation of frontline practitioners;
- opportunities and constraints in providing training and supervision for frontline practitioners; and
- the role of foster carers in child welfare systems.

This chapter reports on respondents' perceptions and analyses of the wide range of challenges facing child and family welfare systems; other outcomes from the project have focused on education and training (Healy and Meagher, 2007) and recruitment and retention problems (Healy et al, 2009). The interview data were analysed thematically, to identify commonalities and differences between informants' accounts of strategic challenges in each country.

## Strategic challenges

Informants' accounts point to the complex interactions between social, regulatory, organisational, workforce and professional factors, impacting on child welfare service delivery in each country.

### Social problems and the increasing caseload

In each country, systems were straining in response to increasing caseloads, increasingly complex social problems or both. In England, informants perceived problems of mental health, child behaviour and cultural diversity to strain system capacity. At the same time, the children's rights agenda was heightening emphasis on service entitlement and access:

> 'The children's human rights agenda is very firmly on the agenda within childcare policy in the UK now in a way it wasn't certainly, definitely wasn't 10 years ago. So there is a different understanding of children having rights, and therefore we have to support those rights and deliver services in a way that will make sure that they're getting their entitlements.' (#50, government researcher, England)

In Australia, informants spoke of the increasing numbers of children coming to authorities' attention. Their views are corroborated by official statistics, which show child protection notifications doubling nationwide in the five years to 2005-06, in part because of the introduction of mandatory reporting, and increasing proportions of children entering out-of-home care (SCRCSSP, 2001; SCRGSP, 2006). At the same time, client families were perceived to bring with them more complex problems of drugs, family violence and disability, problems with which child welfare workers may be poorly equipped to deal (Hayden, 2004). Further, systems were struggling to develop appropriate ways to address extreme levels of disadvantage in Indigenous populations. Past policies of forced separation and relocation and entrenched disadvantaged (HREOC, 1997; de Maio et al, 2005) mean that Indigenous children remain almost five times more likely to be the subject of a substantiation than other children, and six times more likely to be in out-of-home care (AIHW, 2007).

In Sweden, economic and political pressures, combined with an increasing complexity of social problems, were challenging system capacity. The police and the courts were reportedly referring increasing numbers of young people to child welfare services, reacting to politicians' and media calls to take tougher action against youth crime. At the same time, managers were facing increased scrutiny from politicians to find less costly solutions. Behavioural problems, problems associated with drugs and alcohol, and the use of residential care for high-needs adolescents were raising costs, sometimes precipitously:

> 'The youngsters who take the drugs, they have maybe problems in their families and their schoolwork is a mess and so on, and then they come into the circle of social welfare system.... Some of those young people, they can't fix it at home. The social services

have to take them and put them in foster care or in a treatment centre ... and in this last three, four years, it has increased very much, young people going to treatment centres. So I think [the municipality] paid about 25 millions two or three years [ago] for that type of treatment. Now it's about 60 millions.' (#66, manager, local authority, Sweden)

In addition, addressing need among new groups of immigrants concentrated in urban centres raised further challenges of service capacity, culturally appropriate service provision and workforce diversity.

Further, the thinning of Sweden's traditionally comprehensive system of health- and education-based social supports (under budgetary strain) meant that increasing numbers of families were channelled to child welfare. However, while informants considered Swedish child welfare systems to be strained, administrative data equivalent to England's child protection register or Australia's notification records were not available to corroborate this. These data are not collected and reported uniformly across the municipalities, and child protection interventions are not always distinguishable from services, and so are difficult to count (Hessle and Vinnerljung, 1999).

Indeed, dealing with young people with high needs, who required out-of-home care, was recognised as a very significant problem by informants in all three countries – not least because of the rapidly ballooning costs involved:

'[I]n the out of home care area in particular, so stuff around the high-needs kids as we call them, that's a big [challenge], because that's sucking out resources not necessarily very effective, very costly, so developing different models, and different service models for kids and young people is a big thing.' (#23, government senior manager, Australia)

One English informant identified this problem in the context of her account of the way the local authority would find resources for meeting the inevitably greater demand for services that would arise from the new universalising orientation of the new Children Act:

'[O]ur aim is to shift resources from highly intensive, highly intrusive services that cost an arm and a leg. Well, for example, out-of-authority placements: every local authority is bearing a huge burden of paying for specialist placements because they can't deal with children with challenging behaviour in-house and it's costing [this local authority] something like five million quid. The whole of Children's Services' budget is £4 million, so it's mad.... So that the long-term aim is to shift that back up into primary mental health work.' (#49, senior manager, local authority, England)

## Organisational challenges: joined-up working versus decentralisation

Tensions around levels of centralisation and decentralisation, and the devolution (or otherwise) of power, were evident in each country. In England, challenges related to the capacity of systems to cohere and centralise in line with the national reform agenda and principles of 'joined-up government'. In Australia, challenges related to the division of resources and responsibility between the government and non-governmental sectors, in the context of a system fragmented by jurisdiction. In Sweden, the decentralised system was criticised by some informants for being unable to deliver consistent interventions, especially in the face of uneven political and economic pressures.

English interviewees accepted the thrust of the national reform agenda for children's services. Most referred back to defining legislation and policy guidance, welcoming the leadership and associated resourcing. The agenda for service integration was largely welcomed, with interviewees critical (after the high-profile death of Victoria Climbié) of the impact of fragmented service delivery and professional practice:

'Because the workforce is fragmented, they fragment the needs of children and young people.' (#49, local authority manager, England)

But while the service integration agenda was welcomed, it also presented a major strategic challenge for the sector. Informants identified a series of dilemmas in attempting to translate New Labour's ambitious priorities of joined-up thinking and joined-up policies into joined-up frontline processes and practices. At one level, this related to models of partnership between local authorities and the voluntary sector. Some local authorities felt that they lacked a tradition of collaboration with the voluntary sector, while in the non-governmental sector, under-resourcing was felt to preclude small agencies, including minority specific services, from coordinating with others. Larger NGOs voiced concerns about their ability to continue to work with other services, as funding from large initiatives, such as the Children's Fund and Sure Start, dried up.

Like their English counterparts, Australian informants lauded reviews and inquiries for helping clarify priorities and expand early intervention, but, in the statutory sector, they criticised government responses for focusing on destabilising departmental and management restructures; and for expanding the workforce with large intakes of inexperienced staff – an issue further discussed later. Compared with the national strategic vision evident in England, reviews and restructures in Australia had not seemed to have established impetus for coordination and collaboration across jurisdictions and sectors. Rather, among Australian informants, key issues of joined-up working tended to focus on the relationship between government and NGOs in child welfare. This is not surprising, given the major role that NGOs play in service provision. Purchaser-provider models, under which most public–NGO sector relationships are organised, were core concerns, both in terms of resource levels and the nature of partnerships. Some NGO interviewees saw increasing divisions between (statutory) investigation and (non-governmental) family support as evidence that government agencies were strategically divesting themselves of responsibility, expecting (traditionally independent) NGOs to fulfil government policy goals by performing therapeutic work with families with complex needs, but without sufficient resources to support it. As government agencies consolidated the shift from models of 'funding' services to models of 'purchasing welfare outputs' (see DoCS, 2001), NGO managers struggled to ensure that service specifications didn't compromise their independence:

> 'More and more we are asked to perform the duties of a government agency. So it's about having a good, effective, collaborative partnership with government, but at the same time retaining our identity.' (#22, NGO director, Australia)

Issues of joined-up working among agencies highlight significant differences between the Swedish system on the one hand and the Australian and English systems on the other – for obvious structural reasons related to the relative roles of the public and voluntary (and private) sectors.

Yet some Swedish informants did express concern about some structural issues. A core set of challenges that they identified relate to the highly decentralised structure of Swedish child welfare services. Despite being comparatively well resourced (with, for example, two social workers often assigned to each case, and good access to professional supervision), some informants perceived economic pressures to be compromising the consistency of service delivery. Without a strong centralising child welfare authority, political pressure to contain budgets was uneven. With no requirement to provide preventative services, economic pressures were reportedly causing some municipalities to streamline their focus on the more serious problems, like sexual abuse, and in areas with weaker economies, thinning institutional supports (such as social workers in schools) was observed to divert families to child welfare and compound pressures on child welfare departments' caseloads.

Some Swedish respondents were concerned that lack of an active central authority precluded effective regulation across the municipalities. The lack of system-wide administrative data was also perceived to limit the research and evaluation necessary for accountability. One significant development over the previous decade had been the growing extent to which residential care for children and young people has come to be provided by private, for-profit organisations, from which municipalities purchase 'beds'. In the relatively decentralised environment, there are few controls on the homes. This means that a highly differentiated set of institutions has emerged across the country, and it was difficult for municipalities to see what they were getting for the very significant outlays they were making on this form of care (see also Sallnäs, 2005).

Underlying these informants' critique of the decentralised system were ethical concerns about ensuring consistency for service users across the municipalities. Some informants called for a more interventionist role for central government on the grounds of equalising access and ensuring consistent intervention methods and practice standards across the municipalities. However, decentralisation still demonstrated some of the benefits that justified its introduction, for example the capacity to respond to local needs in locally determined ways. One informant, a service manager from a regional centre in Sweden, explained how the politicians and senior managers in the municipality had responded to the steeply rising cost of residential care for young people by calling for a collaborative process of programme development, with no funding cuts, to generate a new model for care of young people at risk. Further, the call for more national steering is not universal, and there is considerable debate about the role and efficacy of nationally developed practice guidelines in social interventions (see, for example, Bergmark, 2007, on guidelines in drug and alcohol treatment).

### Accountability: top down and bottom up

Further challenges relate to increases in the regulation of frontline child welfare practice, as governments and agencies in England and Australia introduced increasingly demanding and bureaucratic processes to manage risk. Informants' responses further highlight the impact of New Public Management (NPM) on the child welfare systems in these countries. In Sweden, the concept of accountability so central to NPM had an entirely different inflection.

English informants expressed concern about accountability requirements affecting priorities in the distribution of organisational resources and of personnel efforts. Performance measurement practices overall were perceived to divert resources from service delivery. Moreover, the performance information required by central oversight agencies was perceived to prioritise procedural efficiency over outcomes for families.

For managers and professionals, risk management processes, aimed ostensibly at both protecting organisations and workers and making them accountable, were onerous. Workers were struggling to document their compliance to protocol, and to enter and maintain required management information. Overwhelmingly, procedures and paperwork were perceived to change the nature of local authority child welfare work, with informants describing day-to-day work as increasingly standardised, administrative and focused on coordination and brokerage rather than direct work of therapy, support and advocacy:

> 'The social work role has become more of a coordination and administrative role than an agent of individual change with clients or customers.' (#37, local authority manager, England)

In Australia, too, procedures designed to provide accountability were considered onerous and insufficiently directed at what matters to families and those who help them. Among NGO informants, the performance reporting designed to ensure accountability in purchaser–provider relationships was felt to burden rather than support staff, and to skew organisational priorities, especially for small NGOs cobbling together small amounts of funding from several sources; in organisations lacking the management skills to comply; and where outputs and outcomes were most difficult to measure. In the statutory (government) sector, reporting was similarly burdensome, and some informants felt that performance measures were guided more by crisis avoidance (including industrial harmony, keeping out of the newspaper, avoiding scandals over child deaths and public complaints) than service quality.

Whereas accountability in English-speaking countries was understood as ensuring that procedures were in place to guide and monitor behaviour from the top down, Swedish informants' accountability concerns were more likely to focus on ensuring that practice is based in the best professional knowledge. Among Swedish informants, accountability was framed more as an issue of professional ethics than as a managerial imperative or a means of managing risk to politicians' or organisational leaders' reputations. Service provision without an evidence base was seen as unethical, and evaluation was not presented as a way to account upwards to managers, funders or central oversight agencies, but rather as a way to improve professional knowledge and tools; overall to:

> 'make social services more open and transparent for clients, for parents, for children.' (#61, government policy officer/researcher, Sweden)

Several Swedish informants at the national level expressed concern about the evidence underpinning practice in child welfare work and the long-term effects of various interventions on children, especially out-of-home care. Academics highlighted difficulties in developing an evidence base, and in ensuring that child welfare practitioners were trained to base interventions on sound research evidence. Informants called for a stronger research orientation, especially for interventions involving adolescents, where potential to do harm was seen to be strong.

Informants in Australia considered performance management and professional supervision to be either ad hoc or squeezed out by resource pressures in both statutory and non-governmental sectors. In the statutory sector, statistical information such as assessment clearance rates and complaints were compelling performance management and workload allocation processes to encroach on, and overshadow, professional supervision. Similarly, in England, supervision was perceived as largely reinforcing managerial priorities over professional guidance, mentoring and emotional support. In combination with the highly bureaucratised accountability systems, supervision was criticised for priorities of 'keeping organisations safe' and prioritising timely assessments and meeting targets:

> 'Supervision has become a form of performance management so that staff aren't actually able to reflect on cases in the way

they might have been able to do in the past.' (#50, government researcher, England)

In England, increased regulation and oversight in general was perceived to dampen job satisfaction in local authorities, contributing to the workforce problems that were impeding national policy implementation. With public scrutiny and regulatory requirements undermining professional discretion and morale in the statutory sector, experienced workers were observed to flee from investigatory roles to rapidly growing opportunities in the non-governmental sector, like family support:

> 'The job has become increasingly in the public eye. It's also becoming increasingly bureaucratic, and driven by performance targets within agencies, which are handed down by government. There's a tendency to make the job more to do with form filling and ensuring that certain kinds of reports and so on are completed in particular set timescales and these kinds of things. And it may well be that the inherent sort of satisfaction of doing the job has been undermined by bureaucratisation of the work. There's a kind of – almost a vicious circle here that sort of arises that government doesn't trust people to do the job. Therefore, it tries to control the level of work with checklists, forms, various kinds of measures of performance and that these make the job less satisfying to do and therefore people drift away from the job and so on, and the standard of the workforce may be undermined.' (#52, NGO researcher, England)

In Sweden, social workers were not subject to the same level of management oversight affecting child welfare workers in other countries, particularly in England. Whereas in England, top-down policies and procedures (and a burdensome level of associated administrative work) were felt to reflect a lack of trust and culture of blame, some Swedish informants felt that more detailed structuring of social work processes could improve child welfare systems, giving clarity to workers and clients rather than degrading the work. One informant, who had worked in child welfare social work in both England and Sweden, expressed aspirations for aspects of UK structures to be combined with Swedish practice:

> '[In England,] there's lots of paperwork, it's more like social assistant work. You do paperwork, filing, answer telephones, look

in filing cabinets.... In Sweden, you're more like a social worker ... I would like to have the UK structure and the Swedish way of doing social work, where the social worker can take responsibility and do good work in the families....' (#68, practitioner and manager, government sector, Sweden)

There are moves towards increasing central direction of social work practice in Swedish municipalities, and one intervention initiated at the national level has been a project to adapt the English 'Looking-After Children' practice framework for use in child welfare. However, some informants who had participated in this project were concerned to avoid what they perceived as England's 'mistakes'; specifically the top-down requirements for paperwork that detracted from workers' capacity to address family needs. In the pilot programme, researchers worked collaboratively with social workers to develop a documentation system that, in the researcher-informant's account, social workers came to welcome as a constructive support rather than as a bureaucratic imposition offering little to practitioners. It seems that the participatory and consultative process of introduction, which contrasts sharply with the top-down imposition of reporting technologies in Australia and England, may have contributed to the more positive reception this new technology received in Sweden. Meanwhile, the tradition of supportive professional supervision also remains strong. Most respondents reported that child welfare practitioners in most Swedish social services departments had access to regular supervision aimed at enabling reflection on cases and at supporting workers to manage their own responses to their work.

Despite these positive aspects of the less bureaucratic approach to management in Sweden, some informants perceived that the decentralised organisation of Swedish child welfare led to managerial challenges: specifically, a lack of central monitoring, coordination and guidance. As one informant described in relation to residential care:

'[I]t's too loose, nobody is governing it. You do as you wish. There's too little control and inspection and steering.' (#54, university researcher, Sweden)

Further, some informants based in universities and government research organisations were not confident that the kind of quasi-therapeutic supervision widely used by child welfare departments was effective. However, its inclusion in the working life of child welfare social workers suggested a more supportive environment than is experienced in England

and Australia, where such opportunities were less available, especially in the statutory sector.

### Workforce challenges

Two key workforce challenges are experienced in all three study countries. First, are retention and turnover problems, which are serious in Australia and England. Although these problems are not quite so acute in Sweden, retention is still a recognised and significant problem (Tham and Meagher, 2008; Healy et al, 2009). Second, and related, is the problem of a concentration of relatively inexperienced or novice practitioners in the frontline of child welfare work. In all three countries, respondents spoke about the stresses and strains of statutory child welfare work, when children may be removed from their parents, as a significant reason why child welfare workers, who may be young and inadequately prepared for the work, leave to find gentler work in other fields. Many of the challenges at the organisational and regulatory/accountability levels have impacts on the workforce and on professional identity and development in child welfare systems, especially in England and Australia.

In England, turnover and vacancy rates were reportedly high in many local authorities and in the NGO sector:

'[T]he major issue is attracting and retaining people in this area of work that is not highly valued and that carries high risk.' (#44, NGO manager, England)

Relaxed staffing standards were observed to create more problems:

'[T]hey went through a phase of saying, "well, if it's got a pulse, we'll recruit it".... It was just so shortsighted because actually a bad social worker is worse than no social worker at all, because they create chaos and havoc.' (#49, local authority manager, England)

In part, informants traced recruitment and retention difficulties to the unpleasant nature of child welfare. Child protection work was perceived to have a 'short shelf life', with experienced workers routinely lost to more 'pleasant' work in the third sector:

'You can do it [local authority work] for two years, three years, perhaps four or five years, but you'd be fairly burnt out after that.... [It's] the nature of the work, the pressures of doing both the volume of child protection investigations and the emotional nature of child protection investigations ... the third sector could be seen as a gentler, safe, firm, more caring, more responsive location for a professional with three, four or five years' experience.' (#45, researcher, England)

In response, English local authorities increasingly depended on temporary staff, many from overseas. Yet, as documented by others (Hoque and Kirkpatrick, 2008), hiring agency staff could exacerbate problems. High wages stripped social workers from local authorities and raised their staffing costs, while facilitating a churning of workers throughout the sector:

'If they're not enjoying it in an authority they can ask their agency to find them somewhere else. So local authorities and child protection particularly are really fighting in a limited market of social workers out there. I think you can see the knock-on effect.' (#48, manager, government sector, England)

English informants also recognised that the push for integrated services meant fundamental change for the workforce:

'Because it [Every Child Matters] is a joined-up approach to childhood, the knock-on effect is that we need a joined-up workforce.' (#45, researcher, England)

Informants raised concerns about the implications for relationships between various welfare professionals as policies, procedures and practice became integrated. Informants pointed to the potential for conflict over professional values, identities, practices and skills; the risk that social workers' status might be undermined by professionals with a more 'scientific' evidence base in multidisciplinary teams; and that social work skills and tasks might come to focus on coordination over clinical practice:

'I think the role has become much more a childcare "broker" in some ways rather than the direct work. It's about finding other people to come in and do certain things like the therapeutic work, and so people are becoming deskilled....' (#48, manager, government sector, England)

In Australia, as in England, statutory agencies were plagued by costly and disruptive recruitment and retention problems. Experienced frontline professionals were generally difficult to recruit and retain, especially outside the metropolitan areas, where workers were observed to stay months rather than years:

> '[T]he maximum we get here is 18 months. And that's because we won't transfer people under 18 months. They'd be gone if it didn't take that long.' (#16, manager, statutory sector, Australia)

Informants explained general workforce shortages in terms of:

- the structural problem of a wide geographic divide between professional and client populations;
- the emotionally and physically exhausting nature of child protection work;
- the demanding legislative and community knowledge and personal characteristics required;
- the lack of organisational support or career pathways; and
- the adversarial nature of the work and personal risk it involves.

As one government manager observed, workers end up:

> 'worn out emotionally, they get attracted to other jobs with the same pay but less stress, they become unhappy and disillusioned with the system, they feel unsupported.... [In investigation and assessment teams] there's generally an unrelenting workload, the work always has an element of urgency attached to it, there are risks involved in terms of decision, but there are also personal risks. And I think because there is this fear of failure and what will it mean if I make a wrong call or make a wrong decision and a young person gets harmed?' (#20, manager, statutory sector, Australia)

For the Indigenous workers, who are seen as integral to culturally appropriate service delivery, informants traced recruitment difficulties to a justifiably low regard for child protection authorities, after generations of forced removals.

To solve workforce problems, statutory agencies in Australia were offering improved salaries and conditions in centralised recruitment drives. Yet these proved short-term solutions, resulting in large numbers of inexperienced new recruits being sent to the front line, putting pressure on training and supervisory resources and risking compromising services to clients:

> 'I find myself at the moment, as a manager probably carrying more risk than I've ever carried in terms of inexperienced staff, new staff…. [T]here needs to still be the resources there that allow area offices to do their work, and allows people to get the experience on the job, so to speak, but that allows for a steady stream of people coming through instead of these big intakes, so that you're getting people trained in a much more gradual way, and you're not throwing them in the deep end, which is what's happening now.' (#14, manager, statutory sector, Australia)

Individual managers were attempting to organise workloads in ways that accounted for both client need and staff experience, but with inadequate resources for professional supervision and planning, new workers were being 'thrown in' or 'dumped with' rather than 'guided into' child welfare work. The absorption of new workers by large government recruitment drives were flowing on to the non-governmental sector, with agencies scrambling to recruit staff as service provision reached crisis point, challenging standards across the sector:

> '[W]e've got to take what we can get, and we can't get enough of them. People are coming in through all sorts of doorways. Many of them are working out okay, but it's not really ideal. The level of knowledge of skill and professionalism is well below what we would want to see for our sector.' (#35, chief executive officer, NGO peak body, Australia)

Unlike in England where temporary agency staff were used to respond to shortages, Australian responses centred on the use of paraprofessional workers, also perceived as a risky solution:

> '[T]hey're making decisions in cases without the evidence, without the framework, because people have let them do it for years. But I have seen some outcomes that aren't good for children and families that we've allowed that to happen because of lack of staff or lack of training of these workers … that puts them in a real difficult position and puts our whole case for accountability at risk. And

so to me, it's just because we don't have the people – that we're grabbing people.' (#9, manager, statutory sector, Australia)

In England and Australia, there is also some contestation over what kind of personnel should be delivering child welfare services. In both countries there has been increased recognition of the need for professionally qualified workers – in England, with the introduction of the social work degree, and, in one of the states studied in Australia, with the introduction of a policy mandating a minimum of a degree-level qualification for entry-level statutory child welfare workers.

A minority of informants disagreed that professional qualifications were necessary – some Australian informants emphasised the value of life experience and personal qualities, and spoke about what they saw as the good work done with families by lay practitioners, especially in family support. More common was the response that professional qualifications are not enough, and that experience and/or advanced specialised training was ideal. In England, the establishment of a post-qualifying childcare award has been a crucial part of the children's workforce development strategy (Gupta and Blewett, 2007), and informants from both government and NGO sectors reported prioritising funding to enable staff to undertake this further education. In Australia, there is not a central profession in the child welfare field – social workers are employed alongside psychologists, social scientists, nurses, teachers and others. Some respondents believed that this undermined the capacity to build a sound and supportive professional identity in the sector. In England, challenges of building professional identity were seen as more likely to arise from interprofessional working in the 'joined-up' system.

In Sweden, workforce problems were not as acute as in Australia and England, and workers were not so overloaded that illness and training could not be covered. Salaries were considered relatively low overall, but some areas were reportedly increasing salaries to attract new recruits. Whereas child welfare was previously the domain of experienced workers, vacancies were, like in Australia and England, increasingly being filled by new graduates. To promote retention and ensure quality service delivery, informants recommended:

- ensuring sufficient staff numbers at the front line;
- balancing new and experienced staff to ensure training, supervision and mentoring;
- continuing to fund external professional supervision (separated from management supervision) as an essential human resource strategy;

- ensuring autonomy for social workers; and
- developing specialist career paths and 'competence ladders'.

Further, there is no evident challenge to the role of social work as the central profession, and a social work degree as the basic qualification for most positions, in Swedish child welfare, although some larger child welfare departments might also employ a psychologist or another specialist, according to one informant, a researcher. However, several informants believed that there was a need for further training to support competent child welfare practice, and efforts to do so depended on resources at the municipal level.

## Discussion

Although the challenges in each of the study countries are not the same, child welfare systems in each show some sign of strain (see Table 10.2). Perceptions of increasing calls on the child welfare system because of broader social problems were evident in all three countries, as were reports of the particular challenges of caring for difficult adolescents, on whom there was very significant expenditure for residential placement.

**Table 10.2: Summary of key strategic challenges**

|  | Policy | Regulatory | Organisational | Workforce/ professional |
|---|---|---|---|---|
| England | National coherence | Regulatory burden, proceduralisation. | Promoting joined-up working | Shortages, status, agency staff |
| Australia | Coordination | Contracting, performance measures | Collaboration, resourcing | Turnover, status, supervision, role of paraprofessionals |
| Sweden | Decentralisation | Accountability to clients, evidence-based practice | Decentral-isation | Novices at the front line, advanced training |

Informants also pointed to some common dilemmas, including, at the policy level, how to balance support for families with surveillance and protection, and what role child welfare should play among broader structures of social support. Considered an intrinsic problem for child welfare systems (Cameron and Freymond, 2005, pp 13–14), striking a balance between monitoring, controlling, protecting and supporting children and families remains a challenge in each of the countries. In Sweden, the challenge is to maintain a preventative focus, in the context of pressure to cut costs, while systems in Australia and England are struggling to increase their capacity to prevent harm. In England, the refocusing process remains hotly contested. Some argue that the agenda has shifted too strongly towards prevention, leaving problems in child protection systems unresolved (Munro and Calder, 2005). Others have argued that, despite policies and rhetoric of early intervention, child protection remains dominant, with managers and practitioners reluctant to fully refocus because of the adverse publicity and recrimination associated with child protection 'mistakes' (Platt, 2001; Spratt, 2001; Hayes, 2006). As such, the impact of refocusing may be exaggerated, as early intervention processes remain focused on policing child protection risk, albeit with more covert surveillance and higher levels of engagement with families (Spratt and Callan, 2004).

At the regulatory level, common challenges emerged in ensuring service quality and accountability without stifling professional autonomy, and ensuring that practice accords with solid evidence of what works. The impact of the 'all-purpose' set of doctrines associated with NPM (Hood, 1991) placed common pressures on resource discipline and accountability, although rising regulation and oversight shaped child welfare in each country in different ways. Managerialism is manifest in Swedish child welfare primarily in the form of increased political scrutiny over child welfare costs; in England as tensions between top-down surveillance and target setting, and the logic of professional service (Hernes, 2005); and in Australia as tensions around purchaser–provider structures and performance indicators. In Sweden, the diffusion of NPM policies is not uniform between social care sectors. Purchaser–provider splits are widespread in elder care (Blomqvist, 2004) but apparently limited to residential care in the child welfare field.

Organisationally, governments' use of departmental restructures to manage the politics of child welfare was a common feature. Australian and English systems were facing challenges of interagency, intersectoral and interprofessional collaboration, problems that may be intrinsic in attempts to join up government by merging previously separate processes and professional systems (Pollitt, 2003; Horwath and Morrison, 2007). While the need for multi-agency, multidisciplinary working in health, education and social services has been documented in research, child welfare lacks evidence as to the likely effectiveness of joined-up working (Sloper, 2004). With uncertain results, the joining-up process underpins challenges in practice and professional cultures, as well as in organisation. Sets of professionals are bound by different ethical codes and those from different agencies are accountable to different management structures, underpinning conflict between professional opinion and managerial authority, and between joint decision making and lead agency accountability (Harlow and Shardlow, 2006). Moreover, financial restraint encourages agencies to streamline and focus only on primary objectives, undermining their capacity to coordinate with others (Harlow and Shardlow, 2006). A further constraint is the turnover of social work personnel and the use of temporary agency personnel, which can disrupt interagency relationships (Harlow and Shardlow, 2006, p 67).

At the workforce level, problems recruiting and retaining skilled staff were compromising quality and blowing out cost, pushing Australian and English systems to crisis point. For child welfare professions in these countries, the burden of risk management and managerial oversight underpins new sets of problems. Processes seeking to promote uniformity and ensure appropriate interventions were found to increase the administrative content of the work, and to undermine professional discretion, independence and integrity, contributing to professional dissatisfaction and turnover.

These developments raise tensions between, on the one hand, guidance and reduction of risk for professionals and organisations, and, on the other, services to families. As others have also found in England, the domination of social work with tools to promote consistency, and administrative tasks such as data input into management information systems, while recognised as necessary, can detract from time for relationship building and professional discretion (Munro and Calder, 2005; Gupta and Blewett, 2007; White et al, 2008).

The findings suggest that although there are some common challenges in the three study countries, their underlying structures and orientations shape and constrain the directions in which policy and practice develop. Constraints seem more pressing in Australia and England, where structured tensions between statutory and supportive work are most entrenched, and where the social work profession is not centrally positioned and supported.

## Acknowledgements

We would like to thank the informants to this study, who gave us their time and considerable insight. We would also like to thank Rhondda Hollis, who assisted ably with transcription. The Australian Research Council funded the project (DP0344988).

## References

AIHW (Australian Institute of Health and Welfare) (2007) *Child Protection Australia 2005–06*, Child Welfare Series no 40, Cat no CWS 28, Canberra: AIHW.

Ainsworth, F. and Hansen, P. (2006) 'Five tumultuous years in Australian child protection: little progress', *Child and Family Social Work*, vol 11, no 1, pp 31-41.

Bambra, C. (2005) 'Cash versus services: 'worlds of welfare' and the decommodification of cash benefits and health care services', *Journal of Social Policy*, vol 34, no 2, pp 195-213.

Bergmark, A. (2007) 'Guidelines and evidence-based practice', *Nordic Studies on Alcohol and Drugs*, vol 24, no 6, pp 589-99.

Bergmark, Å. and Lundström, T. (2007) 'Unitarian ideals and professional diversity in social work practice – the case of Sweden', *European Journal of Social Work*, vol 10, no 1, pp 55-72.

Blomqvist, P. (2004) 'The choice revolution: privatization of Swedish welfare services in the 1990s', *Social Policy and Administration*, vol 38, no 2, pp 139-55.

Bromfield, L. and Higgins, D. (2005) 'National comparison of child protection systems', *Child Abuse Prevention Issues Paper 22*, Melbourne: National Child Protection Clearinghouse, Australian Institute of Family Studies.

Cameron, G. and Freymond, N. (2005) 'Understanding international comparisons of child protection, family service and community caring systems of child and family welfare', in G. Cameron and N. Freymond (eds) *Towards Positive Systems of Child and Family Welfare: International Comparisons of Child Protection, Family Service, and Community Caring Systems*, Toronto: University of Toronto Press, pp 3-26.

de Maio, J., Zubrick, S., Silburn, S., Lawrence, D., Mitrou, F., Dalby, R., Blair, E., Griffin, J., Milroy, H. and Cox, A. (2005) *The Western Australian Aboriginal Child Health Survey: Measuring the Social and Emotional Wellbeing of Aboriginal Children and Intergenerational Effects of Forced Separation*, Perth: Curtin University of Technology and Telethon Institute for Child Health Research.

DfES (Department for Education and Skills) (2004) *Every Child Matters: Change for Children*, London: The Stationery Office.

DfES (2005) *Children's Workforce Strategy: Consultation Document*, London: The Stationery Office.

DoCS (Department of Community Services) (2001) *Purchasing: A Partnership Model*, Position paper, Ashfield, New South Wales: Partnerships and Communities Directorate, DoCS.

FaHCSIA (Department of Families, Housing, Community Services and Indigenous Affairs) (2008) *Australia's Children: Safe and Well: A National Framework for Protecting Australia's Children*, Discussion Paper for Consultation, Canberra: FaHCSIA.

Fawcett, B., Featherstone, B. and Goddard, J. (2004) *Contemporary Child Care Policy and Practice*, Basingstoke: Palgrave.

Garrett, P. (2008) 'How to be modern: New Labour's neoliberal modernity and the Change for Children programme', *British Journal of Social Work*, vol 38, no 2, pp 270-89.

Gilbert, N. (ed) (1997) *Combatting Child Abuse: International Perspectives and Trends*, New York, NY: Oxford University Press.

Gupta, A. and Blewett, J. (2007) 'Change for children? The challenges and opportunities for the children's social work workforce', *Child and Family Social Work*, vol 12, no 2, pp 172-81.

Harlow, E. and Shardlow, S. (2006) 'Safeguarding children: challenges to the effective operation of core groups', *Child and Family Social Work*, vol 11, no 1, pp 65-72.

Hayden, C. (2004) 'Parental substance misuse and child care social work: research in a city social work department in England', *Child Abuse Review*, vol 13, no 1, pp 18-30.

Hayes, D. (2006) 'Rebalanced and refocused social work practice?', *Child Care in Practice*, vol 12, no 2, pp 97-112.

Healy, K. and Meagher, G. (2007) 'Social workers' preparation for child protection: revisiting the question of specialization', *Australian Social Work*, vol 60, no 3, pp 321-35.

Healy, K., Meagher, G. and Cullin, J. (2009) 'Retaining novices to become expert child protection practitioners: creating career pathways in direct practice', *British Journal of Social Work*, vol 39, no 2, pp 299-317.

Hearn, J., Pösö, T., Smith, C., White, S. and Korpinen, J. (2004) 'What is child protection? Historical and methodological issues in comparative research on lastensuojelu/child protection', *International Journal of Social Welfare*, vol 13, no 1, pp 28-41.

Hernes, T. (2005) 'Four ideal-type organizational responses to New Public Management reforms and some consequences', *International Review of Administrative Sciences*, vol 71, no 1, pp 5-17.

Hessle, S. and Vinnerljung, B. (1999) *Child Welfare in Sweden: An Overview*, Stockholm University, Department of Social Work, Edsbruk: Akademitryck AB.

Hetherington, R. (2005) 'Learning from difference: comparing child welfare systems', in G. Cameron and N. Freymond (eds) *Towards Positive Systems of Child and Family Welfare: International Comparisons of Child Protection, Family Service, and Community Caring Systems*, Toronto: University of Toronto Press, pp 27-50.

Hood, C. (1991) 'A public management for all seasons', *Public Administration*, vol 69, no 1, pp 3-19.

Hoque, K. and Kirkpatrick, I. (2008) 'Making the core contingent: professional agency work and its consequences in UK social services', *Public Administration*, vol 86, no 2, pp 331-44.

Horwath, J. and Morrison, T. (2007) 'Collaboration, integration and change in children's services: critical issues and key ingredients, *Child Abuse and Neglect*, vol 31, no 1, pp 55-60.

HREOC (Human Rights and Equal Opportunity Commission) (1997) *Bringing Them Home: Report of the National Inquiry into the Separation of Aboriginal and Torres Strait Islander Children from their Families*, Sydney: HREOC.

Jensen, C. (2008) 'Worlds of welfare services and transfers', *Journal of European Social Policy*, vol 18, no 2, pp 151-62.

Johansson, J., Andersson, B. and Hwang, C.P. (2008) 'What difference do different settings in residential care make for young people? A comparison of family-style homes and institutions in Sweden', *International Journal of Social Welfare*, vol 17, no 1, pp 26-36.

Khoo, E., Hyvonen, U. and Nygren, L. (2002) 'Child welfare or child protection: uncovering Swedish and Canadian orientations to social intervention in child maltreatment', *Qualitative Social Work*, vol 1, no 4, pp 451-71.

Khoo, E., Nygren, L. and Hyvönen, U. (2005) 'Resilient society or resilient children? A comparison of child welfare service orientations in Sweden and Ontario, Canada', in J. Flynn, P. Dudding and J. Barber (eds) *Promoting Resilience in Child Welfare*, Ottawa: University of Ottawa Press.

Laming, Lord H. (2003) *The Report of the Inquiry into the Death of Victoria Climbié*, London: The Stationery Office.

Lundström, T. (2001) 'Child protection, voluntary organizations, and the public sector in Sweden', *Voluntas: International Journal of Voluntary and Nonprofit Organizations*, vol 12, no 4, pp 355-71.

Moriarty, J. and Murray, J. (2007) 'Who wants to be a social worker? Using routine published data to identify trends in the numbers of people applying for and completing social work programmes in England', *British Journal of Social Work*, vol 37, no 4, pp 715-33.

Munro, E. and Calder, M. (2005) 'Where has child protection gone?', *The Political Quarterly*, vol 76, no 3, pp 439-45.

NSPCC (National Society for the Prevention of Cruelty to Children) (2007) 'An introduction to child protection legislation in the UK', Child Protection Factsheet, www.nspcc.org.uk/Inform/resourcesfo rprofessionals/InformationBriefings/ChildProtectionLegislationUK PDF_wdf48953.pdf

Parton, N. (2006) '"Every Child Matters": the shift to prevention whilst strengthening protection in children's services in England', *Children and Youth Services Review*, vol 28, no 8, pp 976-92.

Platt, D. (2001) 'Refocusing children's services: evaluation of an initial assessment process', *Child and Family Social Work*, vol 6, no 2, pp 139-48.

Platt, D. (2006) 'Investigation or initial assessment of child concerns? The impact of the refocusing initiative on social work practice', *British Journal of Social Work*, vol 36, no 2, pp 267-81.

Pollitt, C. (2003) 'Joined-up government: a survey', *Political Studies Review*, vol 1, no 1, pp 34-49.

Sallnäs, M. (2005) 'Vårdmarknad med svårigheter: om privata aktörer inom institutionsvården för barn och ungdomar' [A care market with problems: on private entrepreneurs in residential care for children and youth], *Socialvetenskaplig tidskrift*, vol 12, no 2-3, pp 226-45.

SCRCSSP (Steering Committee for the Review of Commonwealth/ State Service Provision) (2001) *Report on Government Services 2001*, Canberra: AusInfo.

SCRGSP (Steering Committee for the Review of Government Service Provision) (2006) *Report on Government Services 2006*, Canberra: AusInfo.

Sellick, C. and Howell, D. (2004) 'A description and analysis of multi-sectoral fostering practice in the United Kingdom', *British Journal of Social Work*, vol 34, no 4, pp 481-99.

Sloper, P. (2004) 'Facilitators and barriers for co-ordinated multi-agency services', *Child: Care, Health and Development*, vol 30, no 6, pp 571-80.

Spratt, T. (2001) 'The influence of child protection orientation on child welfare practice', *British Journal of Social Work*, vol 31, no 6, pp 933-54.

Spratt, T. and Callan, J. (2004) 'Parents' views on social work interventions in child welfare cases', *British Journal of Social Work*, vol 34, no 2, pp 199-224.

Sundell, K., Vinnerljung, B., Löfholm, C.A. and Humlesjö, E. (2007) 'Child protection in Stockholm: a local cohort study on childhood prevalence of investigations and service delivery', *Children and Youth Services Review*, vol 29, no 2, pp 180-92.

Tham, P. and Meagher, G. (2008) 'Working in human services: how do experiences and working conditions in child welfare social work compare?', *British Journal of Social Work*, Advance Access, published online 11 March 2008, doi:10.1093/bjsw/bcm170.

White, A., Hall, C. and Peckover, S. (2008) 'The descriptive tyranny of the common assessment framework: technologies of categorization and professional practice in child welfare', *British Journal of Social Work*, Advance Access, published 16 April 2008.

Wiklund, S. (2006) 'Signs of maltreatment: the extent and nature of referrals to Swedish child welfare agencies', *European Journal of Social Work*, vol 9, no 1, pp 39-58.

Winter, K. (2008) 'Recent policy initiatives in early childhood and the challenges for the social work profession', *British Journal of Social Work*, Advance Access, published 15 April 2008, doi:10.1093/bjsw/bcn051.

# Part Three
Rescaling social policy

# ELEVEN

# Governance at a distance? The turn to the local in UK social policy

*Andrew Wallace*

## Introduction

It has been noted that the concept of governance has been both underused as a tool of analysis and underresearched as a set of practices by social policy scholars (Daly, 2003). In response, this chapter will argue that governance can provide a useful framework for understanding recent shifts in the organisation and delivery of welfare in the UK. 'Governance' is a nuanced process open to various interpretations and enactments (Davies, 2005) and in this chapter the focus is on its contribution to the rescaling of social policy through processes of spatialisation and localisation, which increasingly structure welfare activities around the sociopolitical lifeworlds of local territories (Lowndes and Sullivan, 2008). The chapter regards the drive towards the self-governance of neighbourhoods as a genuine, if contradictory, strategy of UK governing practice. However, it is mindful of the contributions of the critical governance literature, which contends that processes of 'localisation' are occurring alongside a deepening of the control of the central state (Davies, 2005) and of those who point out that a rhetoric of self-governance often struggles to translate into meaningful local autonomy (Marinetto, 2003). However, the main thrust of the chapter is that localised governance is an unstable but genuine goal of government policy justified with reference to a set of assumptions about the 'active' civic community. This generates some problems for those 'on the ground' who are invited participants within the nexus of self-governance (Taylor, 2007). This is not the same as arguing that governance is a deliberate means of control on the part of the central state (see, for example, Raco and Imrie, 2000). Self-governance, it is argued here, is a top-down driven process, but one that the New Labour government has attempted to shape and implement according to a particular model of the local-social. The chapter will begin by sketching the current localising impulse apparent in the rhetoric of both main UK political parties. The chapter shares Daly's (2003) belief that governance as an explanatory concept allows us to map some of the continuities in recent political debates and illustrate how the Labour and Conservative Parties have outlined similar critiques of centralised policy practice. The chapter will continue by examining the raft of recent measures under consideration or implemented by the UK government designed to hybridise local governance and place 'communities in control' (DCLG, 2008). It then proceeds with a brief analysis of localised self-governance. Daly (2003, p 125) has argued that the concept of governance is state-centred and tends to 'frame change … in terms of a rearticulation of the state rather than originating in society'. However, this chapter will argue that there is a more fluid relationship between governance and the social than she allows and suggest that the character and assumptions that underpin self-governing communities are shaped by particular assumptions about excluded urban space and idealised conceptions of communitarian citizenship. The article argues that present in this relationship is a significant conceptual blind spot that generates a set of tensions and problems for the realities of self-governance. The chapter will draw on some of the author's own research findings to reflect on some of these tensions and briefly consider what this has meant 'on the ground' for participant groups and the tensions inherent in current and future welfare strategies.

## From government to self-governance

The shift from government to governance is thought to refer to a recalibration of the role and standing of the state and the forging of new sets of relationships with markets and civil society in sustaining social development (Kooiman, 1999, Stoker, 2000). This is often analysed as an epochal change signifying the rescaling of government from a hierarchical and unitary system of control towards greater devolution, decentralisation and dispersal of power and resources to a plurality of subnational and/or non-state actors (Swyngedouw, 2005; Taylor, 2007), although some have questioned its novelty as a recent development (Somerville, 2005). A central feature of governance is that the negotiation and delivery of welfare programmes and the meeting of collective goals across a variety of policy domains such as healthcare, criminal justice and regeneration is said to be localised (Amin, 2005), while the central nation–state 'steers' or 'enables' from a distance. An important aspect of this form of governance is that it relies on an active and engaged public sphere as a 'partner' in directing and implementing policy (Barnes et al, 2003). Public engagement and empowerment is often framed spatially, drawing in neighbourhoods, communities and resident citizens as well as various assemblages of local partnerships and networks as key actors in circuits of self-governance that operate through shared geographic and institutional spaces. In what is portrayed as a decisive break with post-war convention, spatialised localities such as neighbourhoods are constructed as exterior sociocultural territories drawn into policy-making spheres of influence and 'enabled' to generate and direct their own trajectories (Lowndes and Sullivan, 2008). These territories tend to be conceived as a resource for the broader governance project and stand in counterpoint and as an important corrective to the excesses of both state and market. They are constructed as consensual and generative partners, assumed to contribute to a shared political agenda in which both the central and the local come together, to pursue (under a New Labour government) a 'third way' or 'one nation' project of economic prosperity and social justice (Davies, 2005) and what Newman (2001, p 142) calls 'a new social settlement' in which there is a transition in civic relations and the generation of ethical citizenship. This new settlement is facilitated by the creation of 'invited spaces' 'beyond the state' (Swyngedouw, 2005) through which hybridised governance is configured and civic engagement is realised. New forms of governing have been deployed to simultaneously address vertical pressure for more entrepreneurial and responsive solutions to local policy challenges while enhancing the horizontal 'capacity' of local spaces to take responsibility for their own affairs and to repair the fabric of neighbourhoods and broader civic life. In addition to this instrumental role and in the spirit of consensus and order, empowered spaces are thought to be imbued with the necessary 'capacity' to sustain ethical projects, which reorder civic space through the cultivation of individual responsibility and strengthening of the collective (Imrie and Raco, 2003). In turn, this generates positive social resources that can tackle barriers to 'liveable' neighbourhood space and a cohesive civil society. As far as the main political parties are concerned, a spatialised construct of 'community' continues to 'people' UK governmental practice (Clarke, 2003, cited in Hughes, 2007) and is intrinsic to the remapping of civic relations and the building of a cohesive polity. Rhetorically, the concept of individual and community empowerment sits neatly alongside 'ownership', 'control' and 'choice' to fuse together a narrative of self-governance tailored for an age in which the certainties of governing through the state have been corroded by the supposed enlightenment of the citizen-consumer and the alleged failures of 'welfare liberalism' (Schofield, 2002).

## Political interpretations of governance

While the transformation from government to governance is amenable to different interpretations (Bevir and Rhodes, 2003) and cannot be considered a new concept or development per se, the tenor of recent UK policy announcements and debates suggests that, politically, governance has hardened into a distinct form, appropriated to symbolise the modernising 'newness' of both Labour and Conservative Parties in the UK (Clarke and Glendinning, 2002, p 42). The is evident from how both political parties have competed to be seen as the authentic champions of pluralist models of public service provision underpinned by an ethic of civic practice. Both favour the use of the private sector and quasi-markets, but have increasingly softened the edges of their pro-market thinking by claiming it as only one part of a mixed economy of welfare provision and presenting the amorphous 'third sector' as a soothing balm in social policy design uniquely placed to deliver 'personalised' services (for example, DWP, 2008). In addition, the notion of governing 'beyond the state' appears to have gained significant normative traction as a signifier of progressive, 'post-bureaucratic' statecraft and is aligned with a transformation in the conditions and parameters of social and political citizenship. Both the New Labour government and the Conservative opposition under David Cameron have often constructed governance as a downward, localising process and committed themselves to devolving power to spatially defined agencies whether they are local communities or voluntary neighbourhood organisations. This has resulted in a formulation of individual citizen empowerment wherein profound social and political expression is thought to be best furnished within a familiar, local and 'strong' neighbourhood unit (Lowndes and Sullivan, 2008). Both parties have constituted this as an ethical liberation from state dominance and paternalistic welfare – a purer form of citizenship where decisions can be considered, contested and owned by stakeholders.

In terms of the actual policy practice of the two parties, New Labour has, from its initial years in power. been keen to embrace a governance model as a means of achieving 'third way' ends of modernised public services, civic renewal and the reformulation of social citizenship

(Newman, 2001). For New Labour, governance has also included steps to engage citizens in local 'partnership' regeneration strategies designed to hybridise local policy making and strengthen the capacity of neighbourhoods to achieve vibrant and sustainable futures (Atkinson, 2003). In particular, it has been used as a mechanism for governing socially excluded neighbourhoods, implying that the management strategies of the central state were no longer tolerable or possible in such areas. For example, the New Deal for Communities (NDC) sought to challenge interweaving problems of poverty, crime, inadequate services and a weak social infrastructure generating a passive or fatalistic civic milieu. The NDC is a 10-year investment programme in 38 of the poorest localities in England committed to working with local neighbourhood organisations as well as local businesses and the wider voluntary sector to regenerate local services and facilities while reinvigorating cultures of community responsibility and social entrepreneurship. Neighbourhoods selected for NDC status were deemed by central government as able to participate closely or manage the interface between local policy and practice and to some degree develop into self-governing entities. It is here that the spatialised and localised nature of New Labour's governance model is evident – as a means for delivering transformations in the socioeconomic, cultural and political infrastructure of the neediest areas.

Civic renewal and community empowerment have been consistent themes of New Labour social policy with the creation of various policy units within the central state apparatus in Whitehall designed to promote this agenda. These included the Social Exclusion Unit, the Active Community Unit and the Civic Renewal Unit, each producing reports and strategies on how to further devolve decision making and stimulate the involvement of citizens in their local areas. This culminated in the symbolic installation of the Department for Communities and Local Government (DCLG) in 2006, which replaced the Office of the Deputy Prime Minister and has responsibility for intensifying the localism and empowerment agenda. Latterly, possibly in response to Conservative incursions in this policy area, there has been a ratcheting up of the government's governance aspirations and a desire to devolve power and responsibility 'further and faster' (Blears, 2007). First, the DCLG published *Strong and Prosperous Communities: The Local Government White Paper* in March 2006 (DCLG, 2006a). This was followed by another White Paper in July 2008: *Communities in Control: Real People, Real Power* (DCLG, 2008). Both of these set out new arrangements for more 'responsive' public service delivery and plans to improve investment in community organisations. These documents were spliced in 2007 by a Green Paper produced by the newly minted Ministry of Justice – *The Governance of Britain* (Ministry of Justice, 2007) – in which Gordon Brown's accession in 2007 was heralded by proposals to create a 'more participatory democracy' in which citizens, communities and charities are empowered to become 'fully engaged in local decision-making' (Ministry of Justice, 2007, p 49). Taken together, it is clear that, rhetorically at least, the New Labour government has expended much energy developing a model of governance that seeks to tighten the citizen–state relationship. This both is a means of 'modernising' policy delivery and contains distinct claims about the consensual nature of the 'community' (Davies, 2005) and the responsibility of citizens to be active in the civic labour that underpins community self-governance. Hazel Blears (2008, p iii) has commented:

> With the right support, guidance and advice, community groups and organisations have a huge, largely latent, capacity for self-government and self-organisation. This should be the hallmark of the modern state: devolved, decentralised, with power diffused throughout our society.

One of the key narratives of the Conservative Party under the leadership of David Cameron has been that the vectors of political debate are largely no longer economic, but social. The dominance of a neoliberal capitalist settlement has meant that political parties must turn the bulk of their attention to solving problems spanning the interpersonal and the social. They must focus on delivering 'GWB – general well being' as well as GDP (Gross Domestic Product) and offer remedies for the 'broken' British society (Centre for Social Justice, 2006). Unsurprisingly perhaps, given the post-materialist analysis, solutions to the fragmented social have thus far tended to be morally and culturally prescriptive rather than structural or redistributive. Allied to this narrative, and in spite of the efforts outlined earlier of the New Labour government to embrace a decentralising agenda, has been a desire to dismantle the legacy of what is perceived as New Labour's statist welfarism by embracing a model of the post-bureaucratic state in which public service professionals are set free from the yoke of demoralising performance management, public services are increasingly provided by market or third sector organisations and the 'frontiers' of civil society are 'rolled forward' to enhance the responsibility of 'big citizens' (Cameron, 2007). Governance and its properties of hybridity and institutional reform are central to these narratives offering as they do both a normative critique of the over-weaning central state and a means of strengthening societal bonds through increased personal and civic responsibility. As with Labour, governance is constructed as a pragmatic and revitalising arrangement embossed with a prescriptive model of citizenship in which aggregations of the public are expected to contribute to a transformative project of self-government. However, where Labour tends to stress the benefits of governance for creating an ethical communitarianism, the Conservatives appear to place more emphasis on investing in individuals and communities as a way of offering a challenge to the institutional and cultural dominance of the state – in other words, constituting the territories and networks of civil society as the driver of political and cultural change in the post-bureaucratic era.

## Communities in control

The concept of governance is a useful way of understanding how the UK central government is constructing new institutional and discursive spaces in which policy is conceived and administered. It provides us with a lens to examine the increased investment in self-governing spatialised territories and the 'active citizenship' that supports such self-reliance. There is not space here for a fulsome analysis of recent policy developments in these areas, so this section will focus on providing a flavour of how recent policy announcements are contributing to what can be described as a rescaling of aspects of welfare.

As we have seen, an important aspect of governance for New Labour is the need to enhance the capacity of individual and neighbourhood actors to self-manage local problems (Newman, 2001, p 36). The most recent government policy statements regarding the empowerment of local communities and neighbourhood organisations have begun to specify how this might be done in practice. *Communities in Control: Real People, Real Power* (DCLG, 2008) offers a multidimensional empowerment agenda designed to recalibrate the relationship between citizens and the state and challenge some of the perceived obstacles to greater citizen freedom and more responsive government. It emphasises the need to devolve power and resources to regional and local levels in order that democratic engagement can be revitalised, local information flows opened up and greater ownership of local services facilitated:

> [The White Paper] … aims to pass power into the hands of local communities. We want to generate vibrant local democracy in every part of the country and to give real control over local

decisions and services to a wider pool of active citizens. (DCLG, 2008, p 1)

The White Paper builds on the work of previous documents – *Strong and Prosperous Communities* (DCLG, 2006a) and *An Action Plan for Community Empowerment: Building on Success* (DCLG, 2007) – in attempting to describe why active citizenship and community empowerment is desirable and what substantive policy innovations will furnish these cornerstones of self-governance. Its central narrative attempts to situate New Labour as an ally of the individual citizen rather than the 'producer' interests of the bureaucratic state:

> We do not think that only an enlightened and altruistic class of political leaders and administrators can deliver what is good for people. We trust people to have the common sense and ingenuity to run their own affairs and to be the authors of their own destiny. (DCLG, 2008, p 13)

The document outlines some initiatives designed to harness this 'ingenuity' and facilitate neighbourhood self-governance. These include greater use of information and communication technology and community media to encourage information sharing among local citizens and an ability to monitor local trends such as neighbourhood crime statistics and the quality of local services (such as local policing). The White Paper also has a commitment to expand participatory budgeting – where citizens are included in local government funding decisions – renewal of pilot schemes beyond the current cohort and ensure that it is used by all local authorities by 2012 (DCLG, 2008, p 68). Other measures include the opportunity for citizens to establish community councils where they feel existing local authorities too distant or disconnected from their neighbourhood, particularly within large urban areas (DCLG, 2008, p 71). It also states a commitment to a greater role for citizens in the commissioning of local services. It is argued that this commissioning role will occur through 'personalised' budgets where individual citizens can purchase service packages tailored to meet their own needs, by delegating service delivery to social enterprises and cooperatives or by directly involving people in the commissioning decisions of statutory agencies (DCLG, 2008, p 74). The White Paper also includes measures to encourage 'community leadership' through the launch of a new £7.5 million 'Empowerment Fund', which, between 2008 and 2011, will provide financial leverage for voluntary sector organisations working with local communities in trying to encourage social entrepreneurship and greater community control and influence over local decision making (DCLG, 2007). There are also commitments to establish an Asset Transfer Unit to increase the transfer of assets such as leisure facilities to local communities where possible; to develop a framework to support the development of additional Community Land Trusts; and to set up a Social Enterprise Unit to encourage the adoption of social enterprise models in reforming local services (DCLG, 2008).

At a performance management level, the White Paper contains a range of pledges that reinforce some of the announcements from *Strong and Prosperous Communities* (DCLG, 2006a). These will include new Local Area Agreements (LAAs) – which embody multi-agency targets and clarify local delivery responsibilities (DCLG, 2008, p 16) to be set out in a 'Sustainable Community Strategy'. From 2009, LAAs will contain an explicit 'Duty to Involve' both citizens and statutory agencies and will have a responsibility to consult individuals or groups on policies and decisions that may affect them. Indeed, the government advises that at the local level there should be a 'comprehensive approach to community engagement rather than isolated consultation events, and Local Strategic Partnerships should ensure a cross-section of the community is involved' (www.idea.gov.uk/idk/core/page.do?pageId= 6908743#contents-9). Comprehensive Area Assessments will be used from 2009 to collectively performance-manage local organisations. The criteria of these assessments will be partly informed by consulting local service users on the quality of services, and residents on the quality of life in their neighbourhood. Agencies will also be examined for the level and quality of their public engagement (DCLG, 2008, p 94). Through the construction of these measures, we can see how government is drawing in citizens, communities and third sector organisations – both towards community building and as a 'means' of government (Rose, 1996) in a bid to restructure welfare institutions through mechanisms of participation, stakeholding and decision making.

As noted earlier, the concept of governance allows us to observe the respatialising of welfare that has occurred under New Labour, where the empowerment of individuals tends to be understood as most effective within a 'strong' geographical community. Neighbourhood spaces are constructed as the locus of individual and collective action where power can be effectively and safely devolved. Self-governance works by enabling communities to flourish through the establishment of programmes and funding streams, which will enhance not only their capacity for self-determination, but also their 'liveability' and quality of social networks.

This has intrinsic benefits for neighbourhoods, but, according to the White Paper, it also has benefits for wider society through the creation of opportunities for shared dialogue and cultural exchange, which transcend and stabilise difference:

> [Community empowerment can] ... support more cohesive and integrated communities. As individuals engage with their neighbours, with community groups and local decision makers on how to tackle shared concerns, there is more interaction between people of different backgrounds and more emphasis on shared goals. (DCLG, 2008, p 22)

For New Labour, key components of this vision of the empowered community are effective networks of social capital generated by neighbourliness and volunteering:

> [T]he familiar, often mundane everyday meetings between neighbours in the street or at the school gate, are very important in generating well-being. Strong social networks, good community spirit and a local sense of belonging and place, are foundations for confident healthy communities. (DCLG, 2008, p 21)

The communitarianism that underlies this approach is a well-known aspect of New Labour's theory of the social (see, for example, Imrie and Raco, 2003). Recent policy documents illustrate that 'strong communities' continue to be viewed as delivering an instrumental benefit by enabling the restructuring of welfare arrangements and offering a challenge to state power as well as being social goods in themselves by securing individuals in responsible local contexts. To equip communities for this new role, government argues for community development techniques to be brought to bear on localities and citizens:

> A profound change is taking place in public understanding of how society is governed.... Modern developments are too complex, fast-moving and diverse to be micro-managed from the centre.... So the shift to an enabling role requires a complex, paradoxical, partial transfer of power and responsibility ... community development helps people and public institutions respond to this transformation by creating additional avenues for participation. (DCLG, 2006b, p 8)

*Communities in Control* (DCLG, 2008) sets out commitments to a range of initiatives designed to generate and furnish well-rounded communities and active citizenship. Volunteering, including mentoring and befriending, are identified as requiring further support as well as funding for community 'development' and 'leadership'. Voluntary organisations are to receive assistance through a new Community Builders fund with the Grassroots Grants programme supporting smaller groups. In addition, New Labour has been unstinting in promoting 'respect' and community safety as a key factor in enhancing the liveability of neighbourhoods, thereby safeguarding their capacity to self-govern. Therefore, strategies to identify 'antisocial' and problematic groups within spatialised territories relates directly to wider concerns about the transformation of neighbourhoods. The existence of non-compliant groups has to be tackled because they represent a threat to the fabric of the cohesive community and undermine claims of localities to be 'in control'. Therefore, a crucial facet of self-governance as noted in both *Communities in Control* and the recent Casey review of policing (Cabinet Office, 2008) is that 'decent' local people are empowered to challenge or eradicate troublesome elements in their midst. Increasingly, this is achieved through processes of neighbourhood management and public involvement in policing, both of which enable residents themselves to sanitise and 'tame' the community that they inhabit (Stenson, 2007).

Overall, it is possible to argue that recent policy announcements including the *Communities in Control* White Paper express a commitment to a fairly radical decentralisation of power to citizens and local non-state agencies and it seems clear that there is a substantive shift towards embedding some aspects of welfare more in the sociopolitical lifeworlds of local territories. We should of course be mindful of the critics of governance who would view 'localism' as an ephemeral discourse or a strategic retelling of government by which communities are made 'calculable' and can be more deeply regulated (Raco and Imrie, 2000). Furthermore, there are legitimate concerns raised by scholars who point to the centralising tendencies of successive New Labour governments, which would appear to undermine and constrain any move towards local empowerment (Marinetto, 2003). Therefore, the shift towards governance that is the premise of this discussion must be viewed as an unstable, somewhat contradictory recalibration subject to new techniques of surveillance and performance management by the central state. This locates the empowered citizen/community, through which governance is valorised, within complex governing terrain in which autonomy can be both enhanced but also mediated through new matrices of control.

Nonetheless, this chapter maintains that a commitment to a rescaling of social policy is in evidence and argues that this is underpinned by a particular set of assumptions about the local-social that raises important questions about how it is being practised on the ground and how citizens handle their new-found status as 'partners' or 'co-producers' of welfare within such terrain. The final section will address some of these questions, focusing specifically on how the meaning and shape of governance, as conceived by policy makers and politicians, undermines opportunities for the exercise of effective citizen power.

## Analysing community self-governance

Until now, this chapter has sought to argue that we are witnessing an attempt by the central state in the UK to draw in spatial territories and their inhabitants as co-producers of institutional, social and cultural change. This can be understood as a feature of governance where the apparatus of policy decision making and implementation is rescaled to subnational levels (Stoker, 2000). This is designed to reform or 'modernise' governing practice and reinvigorate civic space as a locus of policy innovation, collective expression and cultural meaning. However, it has been made clear that this is an uneven, contradictory process. This section of the chapter moves on to explore some issues around the material impact of governance on citizens, and to think more broadly about how governance can be used to analyse the reconstruction of the institutional and cultural arrangements of welfare. This involves challenging Daly's (2003, p 125) suggestion that governance only 'frames change ... in terms of a rearticulation of the state' and will draw on some illustrative findings from my own research in an NDC neighbourhood. This was a study designed to explore the complexities and challenges involved in regenerating poor neighbourhoods and involved interviewing a broad sample of residents and stakeholders within the area over the course of one year. Interviews took an individual semi-structured form in addition to some focus groups where appropriate and examined residents' feelings and perceptions of the regeneration process and of their community more generally.

It was noted earlier that a common feature of the policy agendas of both main political parties is that they solidify the importance of place and belonging. For example, Daly (2003) has described this as a 'respatialisation' of welfare in which policy constructs the citizen as having allegiances to particular community norms and values, replacing society as the locus of 'collective existence'. Similarly, Massey (2004) has referred to 'geographies of responsibility' in which the identities of 'active' citizens – particularly for those residents in poor neighbourhoods – are increasingly configured as place bound. While localised governing practice may rely on transforming complex 'places' into governable 'invited spaces' (Taylor, 1999), it is apparent that neighbourhood self-governance is foremost a responsibility for the defence and reproduction of place and *spatially rooted* cultures of self-reliance and civic participation. This is important because it indicates that while territories have been drawn in as objects of new welfare governance arrangements – through localised decision making often linked with anti-exclusion and empowerment projects – governance as a framework for devolution and partnership is infused with assumptions about the non-hierarchical, place-bound, 'local' nature of 'community' as well as a presumption towards the presence of an active, consensual citizenry. In this instance, governance is a useful analytic tool for observing how the assumed (or mythologised) properties and dynamics of 'organic' civic space have been incorporated into the reframing of welfare practice. This would suggest a more fluid relationship between governance and 'the social' than Daly (2003) allows as the very nature of this practice is infused by particular representations of the extra-territorial 'civic' and intimations about the breadth of responsibilities that society can bear. The meanings of 'devolution' and 'empowerment' present in documents like *Communities in Control*, whether they are prescriptive or presumptive, contain a variety of suppositions about the composite 'otherness' of the social, with a focus on how the 'citizen' and the 'community' can be harnessed to reform or ameliorate the problematics of state-governed societies. Governance, therefore, as imagined and practised in the UK, can be considered to be embedded within discourses of not only state, but also social transformation. This is not to characterise governance as an ethical, normative project per se, but rather that it embodies a set of distinct beliefs about the social on which policy draws. This process can be unpacked in three interlinking ways.

First, we can situate the turn to 'localism' within recent political and policy debates, which have tended to evoke and emphasise the associational and mutual 'esprit de corps' of the local cooperative and local community. These images have underpinned attempts to construct an ideal type for citizen involvement in public service innovation that transcends state management and control.[1] Here we have the spirit of the sociospatial unit mobilised as the wellspring of a shift in the modus operandi of modern governance. The concept of 'social entrepreneurship' is an attempt to harness this spirit of collaborative civic endeavour to challenge the sterility of state bureaucracy and offer a more wholesome and authentic alternative.

Second, in their narratives of social breakdown and repair, both the government and the opposition have seized on the idioms and textures of idealised civic and spatial forms to develop a vision of localised governance as contributing to a therapeutic communitarianism where the identities and needs of individual citizens are integrated and managed within local 'communities'. Government's job is to enable the growth of networks of partnership, support and self-reliance in order that positive cultural norms can be sustained and social order upheld by the collective. Devolution to communities is a secure and productive context in which to empower individuals due to the alleged immanent social properties possessed by 'strong' communities (Day, 2006; DCLG, 2008).

Third, we can situate the assumptions underpinning governance of cooperative, responsible communities not just in spatial or social terms, but also in an analysis of the active citizenship that is said to sustain the 'community', but extends into wider political and cultural struggles. In other words, localised governance is framed partly by a calculation that citizens have proven over time that they want greater control over their lives and will disrupt 'traditional' governing practices to achieve it. Therefore, government can and should provide opportunities for individual and collective self-help and expression. For example,

> Our history is punctuated by great struggles for democracy ... the Rochdale families who took control over the food they bought by creating the first co-operative ... to the Chartists who marched in their thousands at Kersal Moor.... Ours is a government committed to greater democracy, devolution and control for communities. We want to see stronger local councils, more co-operatives ... more people becoming active in their communities as volunteers, advocates and elected representatives. (Blears, 2008, p iii)

If we consider this indicative, we can argue that the rhetorical contours and meanings of local governance and post-bureaucratic citizenship are infused to some extent by a powerful narrative of popular civic activism and the active community. The increased emphasis by policy makers on resident participation derives not only from the experience of 'failed' (prescriptive therefore unresponsive) policies, but also from a desire to incorporate citizen voices within the fabric of policy itself. The notion of an active citizenry has been appropriated and internalised by new governance strategies that transform citizens into 'partners' and 'stakeholders'. However, there is a clear tension in assuming a clamour for government-mandated avenues of empowerment. Furthermore, assumptions of consensus and pliability in neighbourhoods leaves local managers trying to manage conflict and resistance that policy makers either did not anticipate (Davies, 2005) or did anticipate, but thought they had strategically circumvented (Wallace, 2007). Furthermore, while Hazel Blears makes a seemingly valid point about popular struggle, it is one that succeeds in maintaining a fictitious historical distance between government and resistance. Indeed, as one might expect, one of the effects of greater local involvement and the rhetoric of empowerment is not only that it can invite previously excluded actors to participate in policy frameworks, but also that it can be a lightning rod for generating competing claims and grassroots struggles around the control of resources and identities at the local level, to some degree destabilising policy practice. It does not necessarily draw the sting of querulous citizenship, especially if the process of community governance is one that residents find difficult to negotiate or engage with. In the course of my own fieldwork in an NDC neighbourhood I met some residents who felt genuinely empowered by the process while others felt that they were viewed as ill-equipped or were marginalised:

> 'When I used to work, I used to work in an industry that was run by the unions, but I used to work in an environment which worked together with management and, basically, my behaviour or me saying 'that's not right' was looked upon as a good thing. I wasn't seen as a maverick.' (Jim, male, aged 21-60, resident)[2]

The marginalisation this resident felt may reflect the lack of preparedness on the part of the NDC partnership for an assertive or angry local citizenry and a tendency to assume pliant local residents who would be grateful of the opportunity to participate (Craig et al, 2004, p 230) and who would practise a brand of consensual community politics (Davies, 2005). This is a striking presumption of passively obedient rather than 'active' citizenship. There were further examples of residents pursuing a sense of empowerment in resistance to or in spite of the NDC process. For example, local residents sought to mobilise and manipulate the 'community ownership' rhetoric of the NDC programme to resist the demolition and sale of land to private developers around their estates – a cornerstone of the NDC strategic plan for the area. As one resident noted:

'But the thing is, they [the local authority] never consulted us because they were buying this land with this plan anyway in mind 'cos the council know what they want to do.... New Deal are meant to come here to look after us ... at the end of the day we [local residents] are the main thing about New Deal ... it's meant to be New Deal for Communities, but it is new deal for councils here in a big way.' (Jim, male, aged 21-60, resident)

What ensued was a period of intense campaigning from some residents, including a poster campaign and the organisation of a resident survey to challenge the findings of the official NDC public consultation:

'What happened up here, they wanted to knock down 30-odd pit houses, most of them privately owned, but they were having none of it ... they did the same surveys we did and the last survey came back "we don't wanna go", so they couldn't get them out 'cos I find if you stick together they can't get you out never mind what they say.' (Jim, male, aged 21-60, resident)

The result of this resistance to the NDC development plan was that this one terraced street was 'saved' from demolition and, in an ironic twist, the chief executive of the NDC appeared in a group photograph with some residents of the street and praised their efforts in an article in the NDC newsletter, claiming that the campaign was proof that NDC was a resident-driven programme. Needless to say, the vast bulk of the redevelopment process proceeded in spite of local opposition. An example such as this could be used to illustrate either the resistance and instability bred by localised governance or how popular protest can be absorbed into the decision-making repertoires of policy managers. Either way, it is clear that in spite of the explicit commitment of government to 'empower' and 'include', participants in governance spaces do not experience these invitations in a straightforward manner and can challenge or influence policy directions on their own terms. This is a pattern that has been repeated across several NDCs (McCulloch, 2004; Davies, 2005).

In the case of NDC, it is claimed that some partnerships have been 're-regulated' by central government if compliance between the NDC and local residents has proved unachievable, leading to policy failure (Davies, 2005, p 326). In my own experience, this did not seem to be the case. As described earlier, the NDC partnership – ostensibly an alliance of government, market and community actors – tended to neutralise and absorb challenges locally, avoiding any obvious loss of autonomy back towards central government. This may have reflected the predominance of the local authority over this particular NDC and its ability to overcome local intransigence and pursue its strategic agenda. For example, an NDC programme manager I interviewed characterised the local authority as exhibiting an 'old Labour paternalism', which was 'rife', and who was going along with the NDC 'reluctantly' because 'it is another pot of cash to be doled out' (Kerry, female, aged 21-60, NDC staff member). This organisational dominance by the local council was a view shared by many residents, although some were more likely to blame a culture of apathy on the part of local people and pointed to the lack of local involvement in NDC processes:

> 'I suppose more could be done [to involve people], but what do you do more? You've got a newsletter that comes out, people are told where meetings are, time of meetings have been changed from afternoon to evenings back to afternoons ... I mean, like I say, information is put out, information is produced. All the meetings are open, anybody can attend. I think it's just the way of the world unless it affects you, that little bit where you live, you don't actually get your bum into action do you?' (Mary, female, aged 21-60, resident and NDC board member)

However, another local resident and NDC board member was more constructive in his analysis:

> 'I am not wanting to make these people [residents] middle class, but I want to give them the confidence that they can play a ... that, you know, just because the city council says it is going to happen, doesn't mean you can't change it. Historically they have not had those skills because constantly they have been disabled by the process.' (Nick, male, aged 21-60, resident and NDC board member)

Clearly, each NDC has its own idiosyncrasies, but it would seem that in this area the way in which self-governance was operationalised in practice not only assumed a pliant local citizenry, but also represented a continuation of institutional dominance on the part of the local authority. Therefore, for people like Nick, the goal of empowerment was overcoming that dominance, rather than working in 'partnership' per se. Whereas the NDC demanded consensus, many residents sought a renegotiation of an entrenched power relationship – one that they thought had compounded the exclusion of the area and its residents over time:

> '[B]ecause we had apathy in this area and no one got involved right, they [the council] just took over. I'm sorry to say but it's the way we are … we've had that many bad dealings with the councils, they ask us why we don't come to meetings 'cos we sit there … for two or three hours to talk about base targets blah blah blah…. But when the money came in this area, the council knew what to do, started moulding it the way they wanted it because we've always suffered this apathy or this non-involvement … because we've been shit on for years and years, so you know, they ask why don't you get involved, what's the fucking point? You don't listen to us anyway when we get involved. (Jim, male, aged 21-60, resident)

Comments such as Jim's invite us to consider the degree of congruence between the ethic of partnership that permeates so much welfare policy discourse and the material reality that citizens in many poor neighbourhoods inhabit. In particular, it emphasises how social action is conditioned and structured by experiences of exclusion and neglect that are bound to impinge on people as they contemplate or engage in local 'invited spaces'. As successive scholars have noted, there is a serious question mark around the reframing of welfare citizenship as a resource of the 'community' and how individuals manage that process (Dinham, 2005; Taylor, 2007; Turner, 2007; Wallace, 2007). In particular, there are concerns about self-governance being infused with assumptions about the cooperative spirit of the spatial 'community' and the extent to which this is a locus or form of experience that citizens identify with, understand or want to engage with (Amin, 2005). Localised governance problematises how we protect and advance the well-being of citizens because it translates welfare into a sociospatial product structured by 'correct' expressions of social action, the identification by citizens with specific territorial realities and an ability or willingness to collaborate with the state. This seems to occur without much attention paid to the structural or interactional contexts mitigating both the practice and the ethical justification of self-governance. In particular, it invites us to consider the social and political relations that constitute spatialised civic spaces and the extent to which these are an appropriate foundation for a reorganisation of welfare. There is a need to recognise and map the context, complexities and nuances of the sociospatial units that are being annexed as agents in the production of post-bureaucratic welfare and to move towards a politics of spatialised social policy that can offer some perspective on the meaning and impact of recent governance innovations. Localised governance can and does provide opportunities for many, but a more robust analysis is needed of attempts to create sustainable social and political configurations in conditions of material disadvantage and neglect.

## Conclusion

This chapter has attempted to deploy 'governance' as a framework to understand the localising and spatialising of social policy. It argued that we are witnessing a growing belief in the need to devolve and decentralise power to local territories and civic groups. This is evinced by the narratives of recent political debates around welfare and citizenship and the recent policy announcements of the New Labour government. Empowering local neighbourhoods is increasingly considered a vital tool in the reframing of government and the ordering of civil society. However, it was noted that this is a complex process that does not always translate into greater autonomy for citizens. The main argument here was that this failure to translate into meaningful opportunities is rooted in the construction of governance as shaped by a set of assumptions about the alleged consensual, cooperative and active nature of civic spaces. It was suggested that this creates tensions and difficulties for localised governance in practice because there are failures to consider the complexities of local spaces and the experiences that shape a propensity to self-govern. In other words, the rhetoric of government policy might fail, not because there is a continued desire to control citizens per se, but because there is a lack of understanding of how self-governance will be managed and deployed by those citizens. Finally, it suggested that this might signify a shift towards a depoliticising of welfare in which an awareness of context and constraint on individual action is increasingly sidelined as welfare is redefined as a local sociospatial product in which social relations are depoliticised and transformative horizons are narrowed.

**Notes**

¹ Both parties have evoked this, but perhaps the most striking recent example is the Conservative cooperative movement, set up in 2007 and mooted to be able to run local services such as schools if and when the party takes power (see www.conservativecoops.com).

² Data come from a study in an NDC neighbourhood in Northern England, funded by the Economic and Social Research Council (grant number 030-2002-01758). The fieldwork was undertaken in 2004. Names used are pseudonyms, followed by gender, age range and status of the respondent.

**References**

Amin, A. (2005) 'Local community on trial', *Economy and Society*, vol 34, no 4, pp 612-33.

Atkinson, R. (2003) 'Addressing urban social exclusion through community involvement in urban regeneration', in R. Imrie and M. Raco (eds) *Urban Renaissance? New Labour, Community and Urban Policy*, Bristol: The Policy Press.

Barnes, M., Newman, J., Knops, A. and Sullivan, H. (2003) 'Constituting "the public" in public participation', *Public Administration*, vol 81, no 2, pp 379-99.

Bevir, M. and Rhodes, R.A.W. (2003) *Interpreting British Governance*, London: Routledge.

Blears, H. (2007) 'Empowering people', Press Release, London: Department for Communities and Local Government, www.communities.gov.uk/news/corporate/516935

Blears, H. (2008) 'Introduction', in Department for Communities and Local Government, *Communities in Control: Real People, Real Power*, London: The Stationery Office.

Cabinet Office (2008) *Engaging Communities in Fighting Crime*, London: Cabinet Office.

Cameron, D. (2007) Speech to the Royal Society of Arts, www.guardian.co.uk/politics/2007/apr/23/conservatives.davidcameron

Centre for Social Justice (2006) *Breakdown Britain*, London: Centre for Social Justice.

Clarke, J. (2003) 'New Labour's citizens: activated, empowered, responsibilised, abandoned?', *Critical Social Policy*, vol 25, no 4, pp 447-63.

Clarke, J. and Glendinning, C. (2002) 'Partnership and the remaking of welfare governance', in M. Powell, C. Glendinning and K. Rummery (eds) *Partnerships: A Third Way Approach to Delivering Welfare?*, Bristol: The Policy Press.

Craig, G., Taylor, M. and Parkes, T. (2004) 'Protest or partnership? The voluntary and community sectors in the policy process', *Social Policy and Administration*, vol 38, no 3, pp 221–39.

Daly, M. (2003) 'Governance and social policy', *Journal of Social Policy*, vol 32, no 1, pp 113–28.

Davies, J. (2005) 'Local governance and the dialectics of hierarchy, market and network', *Policy Studies*, vol 26, nos 3-4, pp 311–35.

Day, G. (2006) *Community and Everyday Life*, Oxford: Routledge.

DCLG (Department for Communities and Local Government) (2006a) *Strong and Prosperous Communities: The Local Government White Paper*, London: The Stationery Office.

DCLG (2006b) *The Community Development Challenge*, London: The Stationery Office.

DCLG (2007) *An Action Plan for Community Empowerment: Building on Success*, London: The Stationery Office.

DCLG (2008) *Communities in Control: Real People, Real Power*, London: The Stationery Office.

Dinham, A. (2005) 'Empowered or over-powered? The real experience of local participation in the UK's New Deal for Communities', *Community Development Journal*, vol 40, no 3, pp 301–12.

DWP (Department for Work and Pensions) (2008) *No One Written Off: Reforming Welfare to Reward Responsibility*, London: The Stationery Office.

Hughes, G. (2007) *The Politics of Crime and Community*, Basingstoke: Palgrave Macmillan.

Imrie, R. and Raco, M. (2003) 'Community and the changing nature of urban policy', in R. Imrie and M. Raco (eds) *Urban Renaissance? New Labour, Community and Urban Policy*, Bristol: The Policy Press.

Kooiman, J. (1999) 'Socio-political governance: overview, reflections and design', *Public Management*, vol 1, no 1, pp 67–92.

Lowndes, V. and Sullivan, H. (2008) 'How low can you go? Rationales and challenges for neighbourhood governance', *Public Administration*, vol 86, no 1, pp 53–74.

Marinetto, M. (2003) 'Who wants to be an active citizen? The politics and practice of community involvement', *Sociology*, vol 37, pp 103–20.

Massey, D. (2004) 'Geographies of responsibility', *Geografiska Annaler, Series B: Human Geography*, vol 86, no 1, pp 5–18.

McCulloch, A. (2004) 'Localism and its neoliberal application: a case study of West Gate New Deal for Communities in Newcastle upon Tyne, UK', *Capital and Class*, vol 83, pp 133-65.

Ministry of Justice (2007) *The Governance of Britain*, London: The Stationery Office.

Newman, J. (2001) *Modernising Governance: New Labour, Policy and Society*, London: Sage Publications.

Raco, M. and Imrie, R. (2000) 'Governmentality and rights and responsibilities in urban policy', *Environment and Planning A*, vol 32, pp 187-204.

Rose, N. (1996) 'Governing "advanced" liberal democracies', in A. Barry, T. Osborne and N. Rose (eds) *Foucault and Political Reason*, London: UCL Press.

Schofield, B. (2002) 'Partners in power: governing the self-sustaining community', *Sociology*, vol 36, no 3, pp 663-83.

Somerville, P. (2005) 'Community governance and democracy', *Policy & Politics*, vol 33, no 1, pp 117-44.

Stenson, K. (2007) 'Framing the governance of urban space', in G. Helms and R. Atkinson (eds) *Securing the Urban Renaissance*, Bristol: The Policy Press.

Stoker, G. (ed) (2000) *The New Politics of British Local Governance*, Basingstoke: Macmillan.

Swyngedouw, E. (2005) 'Governance innovation and the citizen: the janus face of governance-beyond-the-state', *Urban Studies*, vol 42, no 11, pp 1991-2006.

Taylor, M. (2007) 'Community participation in the real world: opportunities and pitfalls in new governance spaces', *Urban Studies*, vol 44, no 2, pp 297-317.

Taylor, P. (1999) 'Places, spaces and Macy's: place–spaces tensions in the political geography of modernities', *Progress in Human Geography*, vol 23, no 1, pp 7-26.

Turner, A. (2007) 'Bottom-up community development: reality or rhetoric? The example of Kingsmead Kabin in East London', *Community Development Journal*, published online 15 October 2007, doi:10.1093/cdj/bsm047.

Wallace, A. (2007) '"We've had nothing for so long that we don't know what to ask for": New Deal for Communities and the regeneration of socially excluded terrain', *Social Policy and Society*, vol 6, no 1, pp 1-12.

# TWELVE

# Spatial rescaling, devolution and the future of social welfare

*Michael Keating*

## The bounded state

The European welfare state has rested since its inception on an explicit or implicit model of the bounded nation-state. Common nationality underpins social solidarity and provides a rationale for redistribution. State boundaries lock in actors, notably capital and labour, bind their fate together, and encourage them to engage in social dialogue. Similarly, rich and poor regions are bound together, and inter-territorial redistribution is part of a national circulation of wealth, which benefits all. A strong and centralised state can mobilise resources for welfare programmes and redistribute both among individuals and across territories. These features are being transformed in the process of spatial rescaling, which is creating new levels of action above and below the state, in the form of globalisation and European integration on the one hand, and regional devolution on the other. At the same time, the relationship between state and market is changing. Some people have argued that the demise of the nation-state means that the welfare state is also in peril as wealthy actors and territories can desolidarise with their poorer compatriots. A closer analysis, however, shows that rescaling may allow the re-emergence of solidarity at new levels. New policy instruments may also be appropriate in the new conditions.

To elaborate, the European nation-state is a set of spatial boundaries enclosing a number of linked systems. One is the national economy. Of course, economic systems have never corresponded entirely with states and there has always been interdependence, stronger in some eras than in others. Yet transactions have always been greater within than across political borders and governments have, with greater or lesser success, pursued macro and microeconomic policies at the state level, extracting taxes and regulating economic behaviour. The nation-state has also corresponded, to a greater or lesser extent, with a common culture and identity, often built by the state itself through education and other socialisation policies and through shared historical experiences. It is a set of institutions for policy making, regulation and representation of citizens, although political systems themselves may vary in their details and be more or less centralised. Since the 20th century, it has formed the basis for the welfare state.

The coincidence at the nation–state level of the functions of economic regulation and social welfare has had important consequences for the evolution and development of the welfare state. It has meant that social welfare can be sold both for its own sake as a contribution to equity, and more instrumentally as a way of enhancing productivity by improving health, education and life chances. Such welfare outputs are thus both private goods for their beneficiaries, and public goods, contributing to the economy as a whole, in particular business firms. The existence of state boundaries and the difficulty of firms in escaping these meant that they could be taxed to pay for these goods and were unable to free-ride. It also meant that the representatives of capital and labour operated within the same borders, providing incentives to social compromise, whether in the form of fully fledged corporatism or more limited social pacts, or just acquiescence in governmental welfare policies. The broad responsibilities of national governments ensured that all interests had an incentive to participate in the policy process, opening the agenda of politics. The linking of economic policy to social welfare is captured in the expression 'Keynesian welfare state'. This is a curious expression since Keynesianism was a macroeconomic strategy compatible with any welfare model, but it does capture the essence of what governments were seeking to achieve in the fields of economic regulation and social policy.

The 'nation' side of the formula refers to a common sense of identity, which may sustain the *demos* necessary for democracy, as J.S. Mill (1972) insisted and whose absence is blamed for the failure to democratise the European Union (EU) and other supranational spaces. It may also underpin a willingness to engage in redistribution. David Miller (1995) and others have argued that nationality can be defended on precisely these grounds, against other liberals and social democrats, who have tended to disapprove of it. It is well known that people are more likely to feel solidarity with co-nationals and redistributive social policy and collective provision may in turn help consolidate shared national identity. T.H. Marshall's (1992) famous account of citizenship draws on similar ideas, tracing the evolution of civil, political and then social citizenship within the nation-state. In Marshall's time, just after the Second World War, the concept of the nation-state as the framework for these three dimensions of citizenship was so strong and pervasive as to escape notice and Marshall himself seems to have taken it for granted. Despite living in a multinational state (the UK), he failed to mention national complexity and, like so many English writers, confounded the UK with England as a unitary nation-state.

The Keynesian welfare state also had a strong territorial dimension. Part of this was implicit, in the form of automatic stabilisers that insured against asymmetrical shocks. In less technical language, this means that when there were bad times in one part of the country, additional spending flowed there through unemployment payments and other welfare benefits, while less taxation was extracted. More explicitly, regional policies transferred resources from wealthy to poorer regions. Regional policy had a threefold objective, which explains its political support. Economically, it sought to bring into production idle resources in peripheral regions, thus enhancing national output and correcting for market imperfections. In this sense, it was seen as a temporary measure to integrate these regions into national economies, after which they could look after themselves. Socially, it was the territorial expression of national solidarity, since transfers were massively greater than anything contemplated by way of aid to poorer nation-states. Politically, it helped sustain support for the state in regions with secessionist tendencies or which were sources of other forms of discontent. It could be sold as in the interests of all. Poorer regions gained development. Rich regions benefited from the relief of inflationary pressures and infrastructure congestion and gained markets for their goods. The national economy gained from increased production and mobilising unused labour and resources.

The Keynesian welfare state was thus associated with political and social centralisation. A unitary demos created a rationale for redistribution and social solidarity. Centralised institutions and policies mobilised resources on a state-wide basis for redistribution. Territorial cohesion accompanied social cohesion through centralised and top-down regional policies. Even in federal states like Germany, there was a trend to uniformity and coordinated policies and against territorial divergence.

It was widely believed by the 1970s that the task of national integration in Western European states was largely complete. Territorial cleavages were seen as a legacy of the past, rapidly being transcended in the course of modernisation. Functional integration, in the economy and social systems, together with the nationalisation of political parties and political competition and the welfare state were, it was thought, strongly homogenising forces. A similar type of reasoning, in the form of neo-functionalism, underpinned thinking about European integration, seen as proceeding from economic integration to political and social integration. Other analyses, however, pointed to the persistence of territorial politics. The expression 'nation-state' concealed the multiple forms of identity within plurinational states (Keating, 2001). Territorial differentiation was not merely a left-over from an earlier era, but was reproduced in modern industrial society (Tarrow et al, 1978) and even within the most unitary of nation-states. Integration was not a unidirectional process and states had a continued task in territorial management (Keating, 1988). Indeed, some of the very policies intended to integrate territories into national space had the effect of raising the salience of territory and inviting citizens and interest groups to articulate their demands in a territorial framework. Governments also found themselves continually forced to address the question of mechanisms for delivering national policies on the ground, through reform of local and regional government and administration. While they usually sought to depoliticise the question by presenting it as a purely technical one linked to managerialism and efficiency, the political implications soon emerged. For example, during the 1960s, governments made wide use of quasi-corporatist institutions for regional development, involving government, business, trades unions and experts, seeking to promote growth, which it was assumed would be in the interests of all. Yet different growth strategies have their own winners and losers and policies emerging bottom-up in the regions did not also chime with the priorities of the centre. Territorial politics has, however, taken on a new significance since the 1990s, in the context of global and European-level change.

## Spatial rescaling

In recent years, there has been a lot of talk about deterritorialisation, the end of territory and a borderless world. At first sight, the argument is plausible. Economic systems no longer correspond to national boundaries, capital is mobile on a global scale and goods and services, although not yet labour, flow freely. National governments have lost much of their capacity for economic and social regulation. Even culture is to a degree globalising, while individualism is said to be eroding older attachments and identities. Within Europe, this process is deeper, with the effects of the internal market in dismantling barriers to movement of goods, services, capital and labour and the disappearance of much of the apparatus of physical borders in the Schengen area.

Yet at the same time there is a process of re-territorialisation, as functional, cultural and institutional spaces are re-bounded in different ways. The literature on spatial rescaling and the new regionalism (Storper, 1997; Keating, 1998; Scott, 1998; Brenner, 2004) shows how different systems are reconstituting at new scales, which, unlike in the ideal type of the nation-state, do not always correspond with each other. The drivers of this are functional, notably to do with economic restructuring; political; and institutional.

European integration may be seen as an instance of globalisation but it is not global in reach and can also be seen as a new form of boundary-building at the continental level. Within the EU, however, integration is eroding economic boundaries, while leaving state borders and the boundaries of welfare systems largely intact. A great deal of economic policy is now determined at this level, including monetary policy, the parameters of fiscal policy, competition and regulation. This has serious implications for the national welfare state since firms can now move freely to escape national social obligations and taxes and have less incentive to engage in national social compromises. Europe has also curtailed states' ability to manage their spatial economies. On the one hand, diversionary policies telling firms that they cannot invest in prosperous regions and must go to poorer ones are ineffective when they have the option of leaving the country altogether. On the other hand, European competition laws strictly limit the investment incentives available in the form of state aids, reducing the ability of states to manage their spatial economies or ensure territorial solidarity.

This coincides with important changes in the geography of development and in our understanding of it, which have revealed the growing importance of sub-state spaces. Old-style regional policies were based on the assumption that territory, in itself, is not an important factor in development. Some territories might have raw materials or be nearer to markets and thus favoured, but these advantages could be corrected through investment incentives, transport links and telecommunications. Under the principle of comparative advantage, all parts of the national territory could be given a role in the national division of labour, so maximising national output. In our times, territory might seem to have become even less important, as the economy has moved beyond physical production towards knowledge-based activities, and transport systems and communications have been revolutionised. Yet what we are seeing is, in many ways, the reverse. Territorial concentration appears greatest precisely in those industries, like financial services or computer software, that depend most on electronic communication and least on the old-style factors of production. The literature now emphasises the importance of territory, not as mere physical space or a constraint on mobility, but as a social system, with its own institutions, traditions and practices.

The argument is complex and there are many versions of the new regionalism in economic development. Some emphasise transaction costs as the key element, noting how informal communication and learning are important in modern, high-technology sectors and how spatial proximity facilitates these. Others are more culturally embedded, pointing to local and regional values and customs, solidarities and the modernisation of traditions from earlier eras. All, however, note the importance of locality and region in economic development and the rise of regional economies. For some, regions should be seen not merely as spaces of production but also as production systems, with their own internal logic (Crouch et al, 2001). The emphasis of policy has shifted from 'hard' factors such as infrastructure and financial incentives towards 'soft' factors such as education, training, research, development and innovation, and the promotion of entrepreneurship and social learning. The cultural and institutional factors that give some regions an advantage are summarised in the concept of 'social capital'. This points us in the right direction, showing how the social construction of a region influences policy processes and outcomes. Too often, however, it is used as a single summary indicator to distinguish virtuous from benighted regions (as in Putnam, 1993). In so doing, it suppresses the real policy choices to be made at the regional level.

It is increasingly recognised that there is no contradiction between sub-state regionalism and either globalisation or European integration. On the contrary, they represent two sides of spatial rescaling, both of them eroding the old nation-state. Indeed, the word 'regionalism' is used to describe both supra-state and sub-state spaces, although, coming from international relations on the one hand, and political science and sociology on the other, proponents do not always employ the same underlying conceptual apparatus. It is further argued that these twin processes pitch the new production systems in competition with each other to advantage on a continental and global scale. This is not uncontested (Lovering, 1999). Many economists would argue that only firms, not regions, compete. Yet the idea of interregional competition now informs policy at both national and European levels, while regional and local politics often revolves around who can best enhance competitive advantage. The result is a certain neo-mercantilism, as regions are portrayed as competing for absolute advantage rather than, as in the old model, occupying complementary niches in a world marked by comparative advantage. This has further undermined old national regional policies as the emphasis has switched to what regions can do to help themselves. Regional policy has, in consequence, been decentralised from the state to the regions themselves.

This has raised fears of an increase in spatial inequalities, as the better-off regions are able to build on their advantages in both infrastructure and social capital. There may also be an increase in intraregional inequality, as those individuals and sectors best equipped for international competition are able to demand favourable treatment as the price of staying put. Regions lacking in inherent advantages will seek to retain and attract capital by cutting costs and social overheads and, wherever allowed, giving costly incentives to investors, thus reducing the amount available for social programmes. This is the famous 'race to the bottom', as regions and localities competitively seek to cut the costs of doing business and emphasise the narrowly economic against the social and the environmental. Such a race to the bottom is visible in the US, where both states and cities are exposed directly to market forces without the intermediation of a national welfare state. Critics have worried that it could operate at the European level, as states seek to be competitive within the European single market, although there is not a lot of evidence for this in practice. It is also predicted to be a result of decentralisation within states.

It is not only economic systems that have rescaled. Political identities have recomposed at multiple levels. There is little evidence of an emerging European identity, except among selected occupational and population groups. Below the state, however, we are seeing revived and new territorial identities, often based on existing cultures and institutions. Historic nations have re-emerged and national minorities been mobilised. So just as the state is problematised by rescaling, so is the nation. New and emerging nationality and national minority movements have engaged with supranational integration and now are likely to place their demands in a European context (Keating, 2004). The growth of these competing territorial identities, it is feared, will undermine 'national' identity at the state level and thus endanger an important factor in national solidarity. If citizens no longer see each other as co-nationals, they will be less willing to share with them.

## Rescaling government

As functional systems have rescaled, so have systems of economic and social regulation. European integration in the form of the EU represents an evolving system for regulating matters that have migrated to the supra-state level and require a common response. There are constant arguments about the nature of this level and what it should ideally be. These pitch intergovernmentalists, who want to protect the nation-state, against supranationalists, who want to create a more unified European space; and those seeing Europe as a mere market against those who favour a more social vision.

There has also emerged a sub-state level of regulation at the regional or 'meso' level, which now exists in all the large and some of the small states of the EU, as states seek to master the process of change at that scale. Often this involves a rationalisation of tasks being performed at the regional level by agencies of various sorts. Another motive is to respond to demands for democratisation and responsiveness. A third responds to emerging and re-emerging sub-state identities in regions and historic nations. Regional government takes a variety of forms, from the functionally restricted form in France, where regions are mainly responsible for planning and investment programming, to general multi-purpose systems in Spain and the devolved nations of the UK, countries that are now quasi-federal in their constitutional make-up.

Regions are being constituted as new spaces in various senses. They are functional spaces, defined by economic criteria, which, in the European single market, do not necessarily correspond to state boundaries but may be sub-state or trans-state spaces. They are institutional spaces, defined by new institutions of government of various types. In some cases, they are spaces of identity and belonging, resting on cultural affinity or historic tradition. Regions may be political spaces, in the sense that citizens appraise social and economic issues with regard to their impact on the region and not just the state as a whole, and that political parties campaign in a regional framework. They may be spaces for civil society, to the extent that groups and social movements mobilise on a regional basis and frame their demands in regional terms. These various meanings of region may coincide, in which case we get a strong regionalism. In other cases, they may follow different boundaries, creating tensions and arguments over the definition of regional space. In others again, there may be a weak territorial articulation of function or political demands and little organisation of space. Even in the stronger cases, regions remain weakly bounded spaces compared with the old nation-state, with porous and often contested boundaries. The building of the region itself and the delineation of its boundaries and meaning themselves are often matters of political contestation, since they will influence the distribution of power and resources.

The process has been widely described as a move from territorial government to multilevel governance in which power has been pulled up, down and outwards from the state, and in which policy is the outcome of bargaining among actors located in networks rather than of purposive action by government (Hooghe and Marks, 2001; Bache and Flinders, 2004). This is an extremely vague concept, which often seems to cover everything and nothing. It is most often used to contrast the present-day world with an imagined world of the ideal-type centralised nation-states, which was never more than an aspiration. It also neglects the key issues about solidarity, redistribution and identity that provided the normative underpinning for the nation-state as an ideal-type. This perhaps explains why it has been taken up by bodies such as the European Commission and the World Bank, in search of legitimation but lacking in the traditional attributes of states or a democratic mandate. Nor does multilevel governance contain a concept of level or scale, allowing us to address the rescaling debate. It represents politics as socially disembedded, with the units of analysis being the organisation rather than the social group. So multilevel governance may represent a threat to the welfare state as a reality, if we are moving away from government to a world of autonomous actors, in which the most powerful will win; or that it can provide a rationale for those wishing to undermine the welfare state by denying any social basis to politics.

In so far as spatial rescaling follows a functional logic, it is likely to produce a disarticulation of functions previously linked at the level of the nation-state. Market regulation is the task of European and, to some degree, global institutions. Market-making in the form of economic development promotion is increasingly regional and local. Market-correction, in the form of the welfare state, remains largely at the national level. It is feared that this separation will undermine the welfare state (Bartolini, 2005) and there is indeed a strong argument here. Business and the better off are no longer confined to national spaces, reducing their incentive to engage in social compromises including paying taxes. Macroeconomic and social policies can no longer be taken together. Regions and localities, lacking regulatory powers, are constrained to bribe businesses to invest. Powerful interests can go 'venue-shopping', taking their concerns to that level that is more likely to be favourable, while the least powerful are confined to one level. They can also threaten to relocate physically. Since capital tends to be more mobile than labour, this may build in an advantage for business.

Fears have been expressed that governmental decentralisation will itself lead to a breaking up of the unitary welfare state, which rested so heavily on centralised institutions and policies. Even where regions have few of the main welfare state functions, with most explicitly redistributive policies retained at state level, there are redistributive implications in competitive regionalism. While economic development is presented as a non-zero-sum game, at least within the region, since it is about generating new resources that can be used for all, in practice any economic development strategy has winners and losers. Rapid economic growth involves restructuring and typically entails an increase in social inequality.

## Governance to government

Functional change, however, is not everything, since alongside functional restructuring we are seeing changes in politics and institutions, themselves adjusting to new spatial scales. Governance, understood as loosely connected networks responding to functional needs, is almost inevitably faced by challenges. Yet it is not so easy to separate the economic from the social by locating them at different scales. Losers insist on politicising issues, while states and political movements seek to rationalise by formalising mechanisms of regulation. The response is often to build new institutions that are multifunctional and can integrate policy domains. There are also demands that such institutions be open and accountable. Hence the move to regional government. Demands arise for the reintegration at both supra-state and sub-state levels of the social with the economic dimensions of policy. This is also apparent at the European level, hence the repeated demands for a social dimension to European integration to match the competitive market thrust and for stronger mechanisms for controlling the market and for supranational institutions of accountability and representation. Governance thus becomes the forerunner to government at new scales (Goetz, 2008).

Where regional government is multifunctional, it is forced to balance economic, social and environmental considerations. Multifunctional government also draws in a wider range of actors and interests, broadening the political agenda and the policy community. Where government is elected, depoliticisation is impossible and again the agenda is broadened to include social and other concerns. So regional government is a very different creature from governance, if the latter is seen as a loosely regulated and pluralistic order of agencies and actors. The stronger the form of regional government and the wider its functions, then the stronger the functional boundary that is built around the region, locking in interest groups including capital, labour and social activists. These can no longer venue-shop by taking their concern to another level if they are losing out locally, and so have to engage in politics at the regional level. Since capital is generally more mobile than labour, business interests have usually been in a stronger position to opt out of local and regional social compromises, but this is a variable, depending on the strength of the regional government and the need of business for a territorial footing. There are few signs of regional corporatism to correspond to the strong national agreements of the past, but there is a possibility of weaker forms of concerted action and social compromise.

Europe has developed some mechanisms to regulate the disparities that emerge from the single market and the protagonism of regions. Since the 1980s, competition policy has been tightened and extended to the regional level, limiting the subsidies that can be paid to investors in the pursuit of economic development. This is sometimes resented by regions and seen as a constraint on their autonomy, but generally works in favour of poorer regions, who would otherwise consistently be outbid by wealthy ones in the competition for inward investment and would have to divert scarce resources from social and other programmes to match the incentives offered elsewhere. This is what happens in the US, where it is the poorest states and cities that offer the largest subsidies to private corporations. Europe also has the Structural Funds, now the second largest item in its budget, which are explicitly redistributive on a territorial basis. Their rationale is similar to that of national regional policies in the Keynesian era, to integrate poorer regions into the single market rather than to sustain them through welfare. While large in absolute terms, the Structural Funds are tiny in comparison with national welfare spending, but do help to sustain a commitment to pan-European solidarity. Recent reforms have shifted the balance of spending to the new member states of Central and Eastern Europe, but an element of universalism is preserved in order to sustain support for the policy; so all member states get something back from the funds.

Some observers have distinguished between a 'low road' and a 'high road' to regional development. On the low road (which is essentially the race to the bottom), the emphasis is put on reducing costs, including taxes, social overheads and environmental and other regulation in order to attract business. This strategy is practised widely in countries with less

well-developed welfare states, including Ireland and many countries of
Central and Eastern Europe. It has been advocated elsewhere, including
Scotland, where some wish to emulate Ireland's low tax policies. Such
a strategy deprives governments of revenues needed for social policies
and can be self-defeating even in narrowly economic terms, since social
investment, including in health and education, as well as infrastructure,
are key factors in modern development. The high road, by contrast,
is a high-cost strategy involving extensive public investment in order
to raise the skills and capacity of the region to compete in advanced
economic sectors. The Nordic countries provide examples here. What
is not possible is the strategy advocated by some politicians in the UK,
including the Scottish National Party, of combining the Irish low level
of taxation with the high Nordic welfare spending. The argument that
tax cuts will attract so much investment that they will pay for themselves
is an illusion reminiscent of Reaganomics in the 1980s, which led to
financial disaster.

New thinking on both regional development and welfare provides
another way to resolve the dilemma. There is a strong emphasis nowadays
on human capital and skills, as well as social capital, as key elements in
successful regions. These can bridge the division between economic
and social policy. Similarly, active labour market policy provides a link
between welfare policy and economic development. There is a trend
across Europe to devolve training policy to the regional level and to link
it both to welfare and to development. European policies, transmitted
through the Structural Funds as well as the Lisbon Agenda, encourage
this.

There is a wide variety of regional development strategies in Europe,
corresponding more or less closely to these ideal-types, and we can
identify a number of factors that influence the balance between purely
market-driven and more socially inclusive forms of development. One
is the constitution of regional government or administration itself. In
some cases, the regional level consists of narrowly defined functional
bodies dedicated to economic development. England is an example,
where the development agencies are, moreover, dominated by the
representatives of business, with only appointed, weak and soon-to-
be abolished assemblies to balance them. A somewhat more inclusive
model were the regional development councils of the 1960s in the UK
and other European countries, which were quadripartite bodies drawn
from business, trades unions, central and local government and outside
experts. The idea was to have bodies that could focus strategically on the
task of development and be detached from local government, with its

distributivist concerns. In practice, the effort to depoliticise economic development and detach it from other issues could never work, since the choices to be made are inherently political and policies will always mobilise political and social actors in favour or against. The same lesson was learnt with the English Urban Development Corporations in the 1980s, which were eventually forced to take on social and environmental concerns, despite their initially narrow remit.

The scale and form of meso-level government also affects the collective identities underpinning social solidarity. As noted above, the traditional welfare state depended on both the institutional boundaries of the nation-state and the affective aspects of national identity, which underpin solidarity. Another concern about decentralisation and welfare is that, in so far as social solidarity is attached to the nation, it can only be realised at that level. Once we move upwards to Europe or downwards to the region, solidarity is lost (Segall, 2007). This argument rests on the old conflation of nation and state and the assumption that any other spatial level is a violation of the natural affinity of these two terms. There is also the suggestion that state-level solidarity is praiseworthy, while solidarity at other levels is mere selfishness. So regional devolution is seen as a way for rich regions to look after themselves, while European solidarity is achieved at the expense of the developing world. What these criticisms miss is the point that the nation-state is itself a partial and spatially limited form, which has no intrinsic moral status. So anybody criticising regional-level solidarity on grounds of selfishness could logically support only global-level redistribution, not the nation-state.

There remains the argument that, empirically, social solidarity is greater at the level of the nation-state because it rests on shared nationality and that, imperfect and partial though this is, it is the best that we have. There may be some truth in this argument. For example, Germany has transferred vast resources to its eastern regions, while its aid to Central and Eastern Europe is a great deal more modest. There may, on the other hand, be cases where the sub-state level is more solidaristic, an argument that has been made in the case of Quebec (Noël, 1999) and Scotland. Indeed, welfare and social solidarity may be used precisely in the cause of region-building or stateless nation-building in the way it was used by nation-states in the 20th century (McEwen and Moreno, 2005). There is not a lot of evidence on social solidarity at the sub-state level, and what we have is drawn from separate surveys asking different questions. It does appear, for example, that in Scotland solidarity is increasingly seen on a Scottish scale, with Scots finding more in common with a fellow Scot from another class than with a non-Scot from the same class. Class, generally, is a poorer indication of support for redistribution. Indeed, one of the forces driving the devolution movement in the 1990s was a concern to defend the welfare state in Scotland from Conservative attacks. This was not because Scots were more pro-welfare than English people. Surveys show rather small differences (Rosie and Bond, 2007). Rather, it was because nationality in Scotland was used to force institutional change to entrench the welfare settlement, while such a territorial theme was not available in England.

There is a wide variety of region-building projects across Europe, with varying institutional configurations and social and economic contents. There has not been a systematic comparison of social policies at the regional level but we know of some initiatives that started at the regional level. The minimum income policy in Spain, for example, was initiated in the Basque Country before spreading to the other autonomous communities. A similar trend occurred in France in the 1980s. This suggests a 'race to the top' as regions compete to demonstrate their social concerns and gain the support of citizens for regions as institutions as well as for the winning parties. Welfare state restructuring is also taking a more regionalised form. In Belgium, Germany, Italy, Spain and the UK, there are significant territorial differences in models of service delivery, emphasising traditional public sector mechanisms or forms of private delivery and New Public Management. It seems that, where possible, regions are redefining their own 'deserving poor', with different priorities for population groups and more, or less, universal coverage. There are experiments in regionalised pensions or supplementary pensions, which interact with European norms about transferability in complex ways (Ferrera, 2006).

## Conclusion

Spatial rescaling in Europe has transformed the relationship among territory, identity, functions and institutions. The old welfare state ideal, built on shared social citizenship, strong central institutions and social compromises, may be threatened by the territorial delinking of functions, institutional decentralisation and a weakening of social and territorial solidarities (Bartolini, 2005). There is a danger of a race to the bottom, but this is not an inevitable result of rescaling, but a political choice built on a particular representation of the world. The portrayal of regions as engaged in a zero-sum competition for advantage may be built on elements of reality but is also a political construction by those, like Ohmae (1995) who wish to use this argument to undermine the welfare state. To seek to rebuild the old welfare state on its old foundations in the face of the changes we are experiencing would be a recipe for failure. Yet we can find new forms of social solidarity at new levels and scales and new forms of social compromise. This requires that regional devolution and decentralisation be seen not merely as technical management reforms or a search for a one-best-way to structure government but as profoundly political. The link between the economic development function at the regional level and the politics of social inclusion is critical here and the challenge is to find models of regional development, in a competitive Europe, that are socially inclusive. There is equally a need to explore the possibilities for a more social Europe. If this cannot be based on the strong affective solidarity of the old nation-state model, it might nonetheless be seen as the necessary counterpart to market-making at the supranational level. As in the old nation-state, there may also be an economic case for redistribution, as in the Structural Funds model, which is presented as a contribution to economic growth. There is also an argument for larger levels of solidarity to deal with shocks, which seems to require as large an area as possible for mutual insurance. The welfare state, therefore, is not dead, but it needs to be rescaled to take account of the rescaling of economic and political systems.

## References

Bache, I. and Flinders, M. (eds) (2004) *Multi-Level Governance*, Oxford: Oxford University Press.

Bartolini, S. (2005) *Restructuring Europe: Centre Formation, System Building and Political Structuring between the Nation-State and the European Union*, Oxford: Oxford University Press.

Brenner, N. (2004) *New State Spaces: Urban Governance and the Rescaling of Statehood*, Oxford: Oxford University Press.

Crouch, C., le Galès, P., Trigilia, C. and Voelzkow, H. (2001) *Local Production Systems in Europe: Rise or Demise?*, Oxford: Oxford University Press.

Ferrera, M. (2006) *The New Boundaries of Welfare*, Oxford: Oxford University Press.

Goetz, K.H. (2008) 'Governance as a path to government', *West European Politics*, vol 31, no 1 and 2, pp 258-79.

Hooghe, L. and Marks, G. (2001) *Multilevel Governance and European Integration*, Lanham, MD: Rowman & Littlefield.

Keating, M. (1988) *State and Regional Nationalism: Territorial Politics and the European State*, Brighton: Wheatsheaf.

Keating, M. (1998) *The new regionalism in Western Europe: Territorial restructuring and political change*, Cheltenham: Edward Elgar.

Keating, M. (2001) *Plurinational Democracy: Stateless Nations in a Post-Sovereignty Era*, Oxford: Oxford University Press.

Keating, M. (2004) 'European integration and the nationalities question', *Politics and Society*, vol 31, no 1, pp 367-88.

Lovering, J. (1999) 'Theory led by policy: the inadequacies of the "new regionalism"', *International Journal of Urban and Regional Research*, vol 23, pp 379-90.

Marshall, T.H. (1992) *Citizenship and Social Class*, London: Pluto.

McEwen, N. and Moreno, L. (eds) (2005) *The Territorial Politics of Welfare*, London: Routledge.

Mill, J.S. (1972) *On Liberty, Utilitarianism, and Considerations on Representative Government*, London: Dent.

Miller, D. (1995) *On Nationality*, Oxford: Oxford University Press.

Noël, A. (1999) 'Is decentralization conservative?', in R. Young (ed) *Stretching the Federation: The Art of the State in Canada*, Kingston: Institute of Intergovernmental Relations, Queen's University.

Ohmae, K. (1995) *The End of the Nation State: The Rise of Regional Economies*, New York, NY: Free Press.

Putnam, R. (1993) *Making Democracy Work: Civic Traditions in Modern Italy*, Princeton, NJ: Princeton University Press.

Rosie, M. and Bond, R. (2007) 'Social democratic Scotland?', in M. Keating (ed) *Scottish Social Democracy*, Brussels: Presses Interuniversitaires Européennes/Peter Lang.

Scott, A. (1998) *Regions and the World Economy: The Coming Shape of Global Production, Competition, and Political Order*, Oxford: Oxford University Press.

Segall, S. (2007) 'How devolution upsets distributive justice', *Journal of Moral Philosophy*, vol 4, no 2, pp 257-72.

Storper, M. (1997) *The Regional World: Territorial Development in a Global Economy*, New York, NY: Guilford Press.

Tarrow, S., Katzenstein, P. and Graziano, L. (eds) (1978) *Territorial Politics in Industrial Nations*, New York, NY: Praeger.

THIRTEEN

# Rescaling emergent social policies in South East Europe

*Paul Stubbs and Siniša Zrinščak*

## Introduction: situating South East Europe

It is far from clear where South East Europe begins and ends. It is as much, if not more, a geopolitical construct as it is an identifiable geographical space. It may best be conceived as an emergent subregional space, more ascribed by outside forces rather than celebrated as a region from within. These ascriptions are, themselves, contradictory and somewhat Janus-faced, with a rather pejorative construction of the Balkans, only slightly amended in the European Union's (EU) notion of the Western Balkans (former Yugoslavia minus EU member state Slovenia and plus Albania), standing in some tension with an idea that the countries of the region are next in line for EU membership. These tensions relate to real political processes, which tend to fuse and confuse the border between truly 'domestic' and truly 'international' policy processes, between a status of 'rejoining Europe' or remaining as one of 'Europe's others'. At times, nation-state building processes have led to a scramble for positioning regarding what has been termed 'Euro-Atlantic integration' in which countries and territories seek to out-do their neighbours in meeting broad conditionalities for EU and NATO membership. At other times, quite specific political choices have led to rather idiosyncratic developmental paths being pursued, producing new hybrid political economies merging a rather clientelistic 'crony capitalism' (Bičanić and Franičević, 2003) with the existence of authoritarian nationalisms and parallel power networks (Solioz, 2007). Sometimes, both tendencies appear to co-exist in a rather uneasy relationship not easily challenged by a rather crude 'stick-and-carrot' approach from the EU and other regional players (Bechev, 2006).

The wars and conflicts since 1991, and the reconstitution of various states, mini-states and territories with a rather complex relationship to each other, indicate how political, social, cultural, economic and institutional arrangements have been profoundly destabilised, and subnational, national and regional scales and their interrelationships are still heavily contested (Deacon and Stubbs, 2007; Clarke, 2008). The complexities of governance arrangements in the region certainly stretch the logics of a 'multilevel governance' approach popular within Western European political science, although whether or not this stretching reaches 'breaking point' is contested (see Stubbs, 2005; Bache et al, 2007). The complexities of state fragmentation and state-building consequent upon the wars of the Yugoslav succession remain unfinished.

In this chapter, we explore emergent social policies in South East Europe, broadly including Albania, Bosnia-Herzegovina, Croatia, Kosovo, Macedonia, Montenegro and Serbia, noting some commonalities but, perhaps, above all, emphasising their diversities. At one extreme, Kosovo is still a semi-protectorate with a new EU Rule of Law Mission and an EU Special Representative in situ following a contested declaration of independence on 17 February 2008. Bosnia-Herzegovina also has an EU civil and military mission and still has an Office of the High Representative, overseeing extremely complex governance arrangements, consequent upon the Dayton Peace Agreement, with politicians in one entity – *Republika Srpska* (RS) – frequently asserting their right to independence and some politicians in the other entity – the Federation of Bosnia-Herzegovina (FBH) – urging the abolition of entities and a more unitary state. At the other extreme, Croatia has candidate status for EU membership and, unlike Macedonia which has the same status, has made significant progress in accession negotiations. The Kosovan and Bosnian examples certainly suggest that governance issues in the region go way beyond technical questions of 'coordination'. In addition, the continued role of a plethora of supranational and transnational agencies in South East Europe means that there is no path dependency in terms of Europeanisation, and that questions of supranational agency competition, and of diverse strategic interests and alliances, also need to be addressed.

It is also the case that, with the exception of Albania, all the emerging nation-states and territories from the former Yugoslavia share, in broad terms, a common social policy legacy. Much of this dates from the Yugoslav period, with the Socialist Federal Republic of Yugoslavia (SFRY) after 1945 marked by modernisation linked to industrialisation and mass urbanisation, mass literacy, and universal education and healthcare. Later innovative participatory self-management went alongside a recognition of the need for professional social workers in deconcentrated Centres for Social Work (CSWs) to manage social problems and engage in local social planning. Despite this, there is a danger of overstating the homogenising nature of Yugoslav socialism. For much of the period, tensions between dual social structures existed and were exacerbated by political events, particularly in the crisis period of the mid to late 1980s. One dualism was between industrial workers and small farmers and the second between those in the most developed northern republics – Croatia and Slovenia – and those in the underdeveloped Southern republics and autonomous provinces – Bosnia-Herzegovina, Macedonia and, particularly, Kosovo. In parts of former Yugoslavia, which fell within the Austrian-Hungarian Empire, the legacy of Bismarckian social insurance systems also should not be ignored.

This chapter begins by examining the broad contours of contemporary sociopolitical economies in the region before addressing the role of international actors in broad-brushstroke terms. Three interlinked themes are then discussed in turn: labour markets; pensions; and poverty and social exclusion. A concluding section summarises the arguments, explores the social dimension of emerging regional and subregional processes, and suggests a number of fruitful avenues for further research.

## Social, political and economic conditions in South East Europe

The wars of the Yugoslav succession and the turbulence in Albania in the 1990s undermined and eroded welfare legacies, with rather dramatic consequences in terms of economic and social conditions. At the same time, public perceptions of the achievements of pre-war welfare settlements continued to play a role in a kind of conservative nostalgia for those arrangements even in the context of transition. In a sense, the uneven impact of wars, restructuring and the transition paradigm have produced greater diversity in terms of the political economies of the region. Figure 13.1 shows data on Gross Domestic Product (GDP) per capita in 2004 for the countries of the region and Kosovo plus Turkey compared with the-then EU-25, Romania and Bulgaria. While Croatia, at one extreme, has a GDP per capita of almost 30% of the EU-25 average, most of the other countries in the region hover around or just below 10% of the average, and Kosovo is barely 4%.[1]

**Figure 13.1: Nominal GDP per capita, 2004 (euros)**

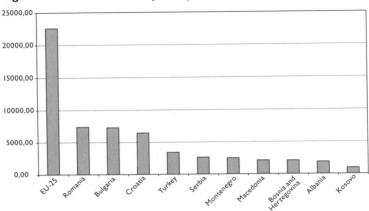

Source: Eurostat: European Union, Candidate and Potential Candidate Countries webpage

Table 13.1 shows, however, that growth rates have been impressive since 1996 and, in particular, since 2000, although part of this is related to the catastrophic reductions in GDP in the early 1990s, with figures from the United Nations Children's Fund (UNICEF) suggesting that GDP per capita at constant 2000 US dollar (USD) rates did not recover to 1990 levels until 1997 in Albania, 2002 in Croatia and in Macedonia they have still not recovered (UNICEF, 2007). While figures for Bosnia–Herzegovina and Serbia and Montenegro are not available for the early 1990s, the delay in returning to 1990 levels is likely to be even later given the extent of the war in Bosnia–Herzegovina and the crisis conditions and hyperinflation in Serbia and Montenegro. Indeed, the Economics Institute of Belgrade calculates that, in real terms, GDP in Serbia in 2007 was still only 68% of its 1989 level, recovering from a low of 41% in 1993 (Bajec et al, 2008, p 2).

Aggregate figures are in danger of masking growing subnational regional inequalities within South East Europe and, in particular, growing disparities between capital cities, other large urban areas and rural hinterlands. In Croatia, the ratio of per capita GDP between the capital Zagreb and the poorest county was almost exactly 3:1 in 2002 (UNDP Croatia, 2006, p 30), with a similar ratio observable in Kosovo between the capital Prishtine and the poorest municipality (UNDP Kosovo, 2004, p 26), with a spread of life expectancy by municipality of some 10 years (2004, pp 27–8). Bosnia–Herzegovina and Serbia also

**Table 13.1: Key economic indicators, South East Europe, 2006, unless stated otherwise**

| | Albania | Bosnia-Herzegovina | Croatia | Macedonia | Serbia & Montenegro | Bulgaria | Romania |
|---|---|---|---|---|---|---|---|
| GDP per capita (current USD) | 2,825 | 2,924 | 9,649 | 3,052 | 4,220 | 4,089 | 5,579 |
| Growth average (1996–2006) | 5.0 | 9.2 | 3.9 | 2.4 | 2.2 | 3.6 | 2.5 |
| Growth average (2000–06) | 5.3 | 5.1 | 4.7 | 1.7 | 5.1 | 5.1 | 6.0 |
| Fiscal balance (% GDP) | −3.2 | 2.6 | −3.1 | −0.6 | −1.5 | 3.2 | −0.8 |
| Foreign direct investment (% GDP) | 3.7 | 4.6 | 7.8 | 5.6 | n.k. | 12.7 | 9.8 |
| Government expenditure (% GDP) | 27.8 | 48.6 | 48.8 | 35.3 | n.k. | 38.3 | 31.1 |
| External debt (%) GDP | 20.8 | 52.2 | 89.0 | 38.4 | 62.1 | 80.4 | 32.4 |

*Source:* Kathuria (2008, p 2)

have significant regional inequalities and significant differences between urban and rural areas.

With the exception of the Albanian communities in Albania, Kosovo and Macedonia, the region is marked by rather dramatic demographic ageing of the population. When this is combined with high unemployment, low activity rates and low rates of contributions as a result of the grey economy and the number of workers registered as receiving only minimum wages, there is a significant erosion of contributory insurance-based welfare systems. In terms of health systems, again with the partial exception of Albania, the legacy of well-developed, if over-medicalised, universal health systems in the context of high public expectations of 'health for all' have actually heightened the funding crisis as systems have been unevenly affected as a result of 'locked-in' expenditures, particularly in terms of hospitals and medical technologies. Emerging evidence from surveys points to increasing inequalities in access to healthcare facilities, to treatment, to appropriate medicines and to quality care, by income, by region and by ethnicity. Research in Croatia, showing trends that may well be common throughout the region, suggests that lower-income groups, the unemployed, returnees, those in rural areas and Roma minorities have significantly worse health outcomes, live further from the nearest health facility and use fewer preventive services than the rest of the population (Šućur and Zrinščak, 2007). In addition, informal marketisation throughout the region and the increasing use of out-of-pocket payments, also seem to affect poor and excluded groups more than others, who are also overrepresented in the group of people who for one reason or another lack basic health insurance.

In terms of governance, it is certainly the case that 'normal' social policy is rendered difficult in the context of disrupted governance arrangements and the existence of what have been termed 'parallel power networks' (Solioz, 2007, p 80) based on the interweaving of formal and informal social practices and a circularity of elites in politics, business and, in some cases, organised crime, working through patronage. Corruption and perceptions of corruption are high throughout the region, with trust in key institutions low. In addition, as noted above, 'state-building', while in danger of technicising the complex social and political engineering that is being attempted in parts of the region, remains unfinished and leads to a reframing of social policy in terms of discourses of security, refugee return and democratisation (Deacon and Stubbs, 2007). In addition, notwithstanding the Yugoslav legacy of public provision through a network of CSWs, there is now enormous diversity in the scaling of social welfare with Bosnia having an over-decentralised system and Croatia an over-centralised one.

## A crowded arena: international actors and the making of social policy in South East Europe

A bewildering array of international actors and their representatives, likened to a 'crowded playground' (Arandarenko and Golicin, 2007, p 182), some of whom wear more than one face, all compete to shape the social policy of the region. This has major implications for transparency and ownership, with some countries' social affairs ministries confused and disempowered in these processes (Deacon et al, 2007, p 226). Indeed, it is not unknown for different donors to be working with different ministries on similar themes, from divergent perspectives, at the same time. In this crowded arena, social policy choices can become somewhat arbitrary, with significant policy shifts depending on a particular constellation of external consultants and ministers working in the absence of any public political discourse or debate. While this is particularly visible in protectorates or semi-protectorates such as Kosovo and Bosnia-Herzegovina, it has a wider resonance.

In addition to the presence of the World Bank, the International Monetary Fund, the EU and the United Nations agencies including the United Nations Development Programme (UNDP), the International Labour Organisation (ILO) and UNICEF, the region is marked by a proliferation of actors, some of which are completely new and largely incomparable with any other bodies elsewhere, and all of which contribute, explicitly or implicitly, to a complex arena of policy advice, project implementation and strategic alliance-building in social policy, largely shielded from public or even research scrutiny. Bilateral donor agencies, notably the UK's Department for International Development (DFID), the Swedish International Development Cooperation Agency (SIDA) and the United States Agency for International Development (USAID), also play a role but are joined by a very wide range of international non-governmental organisations (INGOs) and emerging international consultancy companies (ICCs). Together with a growing number of 'freelance' consultants, these knowledge workers form interlocking transnational knowledge networks, which may operate in many sites but, when they do cohere in national and subnational spaces, invariably have ties to local intermediaries capable of 'getting things done' (Lendvai and Stubbs, 2008).

An historical analysis of these actors suggests that a little discussed legacy in terms of social policy is that of humanitarianism as a result of the encounter between international actors more used to working in developing country settings and a conflict region with relatively high levels of human development and sophisticated and longstanding social welfare infrastructures. In the name of non-political humanitarian interventions, then, local structures became subordinated to, and mere distribution hubs of, the international aid apparatus, tending to work with emerging new, often professionally led, service-oriented local NGOs rather than with governmental bodies. In some ways, the mistrust that existed between state and non-state actors, and the tendency within international interventions to micro-ise and projectise (see Tendler, 2002) further contributed to a situation in which the region was seen by international actors more through the lenses of social development and post-conflict reconstruction than in terms of 'social sector' reforms (Deacon, et al, 2007, p 233). Certainly, the fact that emergency relief agencies operated through international and local NGOs, often subcontracted to provide services on a micro scale, tended to encourage the formation of a parallel system with little integration or functional relationship to a well-established system of public services through the network of CSWs.

The World Bank has, arguably, not had such a strong and pervasive role in the region as it may have had elsewhere in Central and Eastern Europe. It is true that a broad 'structural adjustment' framework can be found in a variety of reform projects and programmes, with loans and conditionalities co-existing with rather partial advice on policy choices. It is also true that the World Bank's early involvement and investment in strategic alliances with policy makers, researchers, local think-tanks and other key policy brokers schooled in the World Bank's methods, statistical techniques and broad policy orthodoxies occurred in the region. A number of 'neoliberal' think-tanks and researchers operate in the region, leading to 'a circular process between the knowledge (the World Bank) produces and the audiences that legitimise that knowledge' (St Clair, 2006, p 77).

Notwithstanding these facts, there are a number of complex countertendencies at work limiting the World Bank's role and, certainly, mitigating against the smooth reproduction of neoliberalism. Crucially, the lack of strong state partners both committed to and able to work with international institutions is important. In addition, by the time conditions allowed for greater World Bank influence, there had been something of a 'turning of the tide' (Deacon, 2005) in terms of challenges to 'one size fits all' safety-net thinking. Perhaps even more importantly, an emerging Europeanisation challenged, at least implicitly, some of the World Bank's prescriptions, particularly in candidate countries where the EU's profile has recently shifted from a post-conflict reconstruction agenda to more European understandings of social protection and social inclusion. As the cases of labour market policies, pensions, and poverty and social exclusion show, however, it is the unpredictability of policy advice and the possibility of resistance and complexity that describes most accurately social policy making in the region.

## Jobless economic growth: labour market policies

Concerning basic labour trends, South East European countries stand in clear contrast not only to the EU-27 but also to other post-communist Central European countries, now EU member states. With some minor exceptions, the South East European countries have lower activity rates, much lower employment rates, significantly higher unemployment rates and, in some cases, extremely high long-term

unemployment rates. However, there are also notable differences among
South East European countries. Croatia has recently come much closer
to the EU-27, if only in terms of basic labour market characteristics.
What is of particular interest is the striking fact that, in general terms,
notwithstanding prolonged economic growth, there are few signs of
improvement elsewhere. In Montenegro and Serbia between 2000 and
2006, the employment rate fell and the unemployment rate rose. In
other countries, although data are sometimes unreliable, similar broad
trends occurred, albeit more inconsistently with periodic rises and falls.
High long-term unemployment rates show the structural nature of
employment stagnation (Table 13.2). The South East European countries,
including Croatia, also share similarities in terms of key groups, with a
low share of female employment, and low employment rates for both
younger and older workers. For example, the female employment rate
was 57.3% in the EU-27 in 2006 compared with 49.4% in Croatia, the
highest in South East Europe, 24% in Bosnia-Herzegovina, and only
11.8% in Kosovo.

**Table 13.2: Main labour market indicators, South East Europe**

| | Economic activity rate | | Total employment rate | | Total unemployment rate | | Total long-term unemployment rate | |
|---|---|---|---|---|---|---|---|---|
| | 2000 | 2006 | 2000 | 2006 | 2000 | 2006 | 2000 | 2006 |
| Albania | 66.2 | 57.8[a] | 55.0 | 49.7[a] | 16.8 | 14.1[a] | – | – |
| Bosnia-Herzegovina | – | 51.3 | – | 35 | 39.73 | 31.1 | – | 28.4 |
| Croatia | 62.2 | 62.6 | 51.3 | 55.6 | 17.0 | 11.1 | 9.1 | 6.7 |
| Kosovo | – | 52.3 | – | 28.7 | – | 44.9 | – | 41.1 |
| Macedonia | 59.7 | 62.2 | 40.3 | 39.6 | 32.2 | 36.0 | 26.9 | 31.1 |
| Montenegro | 60.35 | 49.9[a] | 38.46 | 34.8[a] | 19.26 | 30.3[a] | – | – |
| Serbia | 68.2 | 63.56 | 59.2 | 49.85 | 13.3 | 21.0 | 9.9 | 17.0 |
| EU-27 | 68.6 | 70.3 | 62.2 | 64.5 | 8.7 | 8.2 | 4.0 | 3.7 |

*Note:* [a] 2005.

*Source:* Eurostat: European Union, Candidate and Potential Candidate Countries webpage

The wars and profound political and economic crises are obviously
causally related to the very unfavourable employment situation
(Arandarenko, 2004, pp 31-2). In a way, the South East European
countries mirror the employment situation in the whole of post-
communist Central and Eastern Europe in the 1990s (Nesporova,

2002), with the crucial difference being that there has not yet been the initially steady, subsequently significant, improvements that occurred there. Even when the wars ended, transition was delayed in parts of the region, for example in Serbia where a populist economic policy within an authoritarian polity sought to preserve formal rights and postpone necessary reforms (Arandarenko and Golicin, 2007).

In a number of other ways, South East European labour markets remain qualitatively different from their Central and Eastern European neighbours. A recent European Training Foundation (ETF) report (Fetsi, 2007) points to the significance of informal, unstable and precarious employment rendering traditional labour market indicators and Labour Force Survey data somewhat unreliable, as many people have developed lifestyle and survival strategies that involve switching between 'multiple employment statuses' (Fetsi, 2007, p 10). The report notes the existence of three unstable labour market statuses: those in informal agricultural employment, often a buffer for those who cannot find formal employment; the unemployed; and 'others' consisting mainly of so-called 'discouraged workers' who are not classified as unemployed or studying. These three groups represent around 40% of the working population in Bosnia-Herzegovina, 25% in Albania and 20% in Serbia, so that high labour market mobility is less an indication of a well-functioning labour market, and more of the rise of precarious labour markets (Sansier, 2006; Fetsi, 2007). High labour market segmentation, with a core of well-protected workers covered by social security schemes, and a significant group of peripheral workers with less secure contracts, and limited or no social security coverage, is a reality in South East Europe (Račić et al, 2005; Nesporova, 2008), and likely to remain so for a longer period. Such a pattern is not unknown in other European countries, particularly those that are more liberal and Southern European, but in South East Europe the level of segmentation seems much higher and the consequences more acute.

The post-Yugoslav countries inherited unemployment insurance and a range of employment institutions from the socialist period that had to be further adapted to new circumstances. Again, this process started relatively late, with the main reforms, generally changes in labour laws and the slow introduction of active labour market policies, not occurring until after 2000. Albania, which did not have unemployment insurance, introduced it through a 1993 law. In the context of massively rising unemployment, reforms restricted the right to unemployment benefit and reduced its value throughout South East Europe (see Arandarenko and Golicin, 2007; Gerovska Mitev, 2007; Ymeraj, 2007; Matković, 2008).

Changes in labour laws, usually framed by the policy advice of the IMF and the World Bank, sought to 'liberalise' labour markets, reducing the supposed 'rigidity' of labour contracts and seeking to construct a more dynamic labour market. Change has been piecemeal, uneven and slow, and very far from a sweeping liberalisation in the field of labour rights. This is due, in large part, to a combination of poor institutional capabilities, an awareness of the political price of pursuing reforms, and the rather different context and conjuncture that reformers encountered in South East Europe.

## Is privatisation a solution? Reforming pension systems

The pattern in terms of pension reforms also differs in some respects from the general picture in other post-communist countries in Central and Eastern Europe. Radical pension reform, in which a public pension system is subject to the introduction of significant voluntary and compulsory private elements, was a main feature of pension reforms throughout Central and Eastern Europe, becoming, after Latin America, a new receptive site for an emerging pension orthodoxy (Müller, 1999, 2003; Orenstein, 2005). Slovenia and the Czech Republic, whose pension systems could build on more favourable transition circumstances, without the financial pressure of rising pension costs, were the exceptions that proved the rule in terms of the crucial role of the World Bank in influencing pension reforms (Müller, 2002).

Again, while South East European countries show a different trend, the diversity of reform outcomes must be emphasised. Table 13.3 shows the division between 'young' countries, such as Albania and Kosovo, 'old' countries, such as Bosnia-Herzegovina, Croatia and Serbia, and 'intermediate' countries, that is, Macedonia and Montenegro. All of the former countries of Yugoslavia, except Kosovo with its Albanian majority population, have entered the process of demographic ageing, much as in EU member states. In terms of expenditures, the situation is somewhat more diverse, but all countries except Albania, Bosnia-Herzegovina and Kosovo are facing the burden of high expenditures. In addition to demographic processes, the political and economic situation, reflected in overall economic restructuring, low employment and high unemployment, and in particular in terms of the costs of wars and the post-conflict consequences, including commitments to war veterans, have contributed to the fiscal unsustainability of pension systems in the region.

**Table 13.3: Old-age dependency ratio and pension expenditures[a]**

| Country | People aged 65 or over as share of total population | | Pension expenditures as % of GDP |
|---|---|---|---|
| | 2000 | 2006 | Around 2004 |
| Albania | – | 8.62 | 4.2 |
| Bosnia-Herzegovina | – | 14.09[b] | 3.9 (FBH) 4.6 (RS) |
| Croatia | 16.4 | 16.94 | 12,35 |
| Kosovo | 5.5 | 7.1 | 2.5 |
| Macedonia | 9.97 | 11.14 | 10.7 |
| Montenegro | 11.32 | 12.73 | 13 |
| Serbia | 16.11 | 17.21 | 12 |
| EU-27 | 15.6 | 16.8 | 12,1[b] |

Notes:

[a] As information on expenditures in non-EU countries in Sansier's paper is based on different country reports, it is not always easy to identify the exact year of information on expenditures.

[b] 2005.

Source: Eurostat: European Union, Candidate and Potential Candidate Countries webpage for old-age dependency ratio and pension expenditures for EU-27; Sansier (2006) for other pension expenditures

The countries of the former Yugoslavia inherited a Bismarckian type of pension system, which can be traced as far back as the end of the 19th century when some parts of the former Yugoslavia belonged to the Austrian–Hungarian Empire (Puljiz, 2007). After the Second World War, the system was fully established, based on contributions formally paid by employees and employers although in a state-owned economy that part of the contribution usually paid by employers was actually paid by the state, with benefits calculated on the base of paid contributions. Although the system was completely controlled by the state, it was public and Pay As You Go.

As in other post-communist countries, the World Bank led the reforms proposing a multi-pillar system, where the first pillar would remain public although much reduced, along with the introduction of new compulsory and voluntary-funded schemes. In reality, the timing and sequencing of reforms, the actual reform paths and the overall impact of the World Bank's advice differed significantly in South East Europe compared with other post-communist countries. In the context of widespread political instability and economic uncertainty, Croatia began to implement the pension privatisation plans pushed by the World Bank as early as the mid-1990s, at the same time as, for example, in Poland and Hungary, although the new, multi-pillar system was only finally in place in 2002

(Stubbs and Zrinščak, 2006, 2007; Puljiz, 2007). The same multi-pillar system was implemented in Macedonia in 2006 (Gerovska Mitev, 2007), while in other countries in the region (Albania, Bosnia-Herzegovina, Montenegro and Serbia), irrespective of World Bank advice, pension systems were reformed but not privatised (Sansier, 2006; Arandarenko and Golicin, 2007; Ymeraj, 2007). Indeed, such cases demonstrate how reform of the public system can effectively reduce expenditures, the main driver of change in any case, without the need for funded pillars in circumstances where both the market economy and state institutions function improperly, and where basic social trust is absent.

The Kosovo story is completely different, but again shows the importance of the prevailing political and economic conditions and the nature of the state-building process. Kosovo as a kind of internally administered protectorate, breaking all ties with Serbia, abandoned completely the inherited system and even the pension rights that could be claimed from the Serbian Pension Fund (Cocozzelli, 2007). Thus, under external influence, not only from the World Bank but also from USAID, the new system was designed and implemented from scratch in 2001, consisting of a mandatory basic or social pension and an individual savings pension, and two optional supplementary employer and individual pension schemes. The basic pension is paid to all permanent residents over the age of 65 regardless of work and contribution history, at a rate of €40 per month. Under political pressure, from 2008 onwards, those who can prove a minimum of 15 years of pensionable insurance contributions receive an extra €35. After its separation from Serbia and in the context of newly initiated economic liberalisation, Montenegro has also started preparations for more radical pension reform, in part as a result of an alliance between external actors and domestic neoliberal think-tanks, showing the continued possibility of experimentation in smaller and newer states in the region. Pension reform issues remain ongoing throughout the region with the World Bank continuing to focus on options to reduce benefits, raise retirement ages and/or raise contributions in the public pillar.

## Absence from the public agenda: poverty and social exclusion

Approaches to poverty and, latterly, social exclusion in the region also bear the hallmark of World Bank influence in terms of measurement and policy prescriptions with EU-compatible relative poverty statistics not yet gathered routinely. Tables 13.4 and 13.5 show absolute poverty lines using the same Purchasing Power Parity (PPP) (Table 13.4) and using consumption basket lines, which vary considerably across the region (Table 13.5), as reported in a number of recent studies. The studies suggest some reduction in absolute poverty in the context of economic growth but high rates, still, in Albania, Bosnia-Herzegovina and Kosovo.

Again, national aggregate statistics do not show significant and increasing regional disparities. Indeed, it has been argued that:

> Poverty is concentrated in a distinct band encompassing Kosovo and its immediate surroundings: north and northeast Albania, southern Serbia and northern Macedonia (as well as) ... Western Serbia and, within Bosnia-Herzegovina, *Republika Srpska*. (DFID, 2004, p 4)

**Table 13.4: Poverty and economic vulnerability rates, South East Europe, 2002–04 (%)**

|  | Year | USD 2.15 PPP per day | | | USD 4.30 PPP per day | | |
|---|---|---|---|---|---|---|---|
|  |  | Poverty rate P0 | Poverty depth P1 | Poverty severity P2 | Poverty rate P0 | Poverty depth P1 | Poverty severity P2 |
| Albania | 2002 | 24 | 5 | 2 | 71 | 28 | 14 |
| Bosnia | 2004 | 4 | 1 | 0 | 27 | 7 | 3 |
| Bulgaria | 2003 | 4 | 1 | 0 | 33 | 9 | 4 |
| Macedonia | 2003 | 4 | 1 | 0 | 24 | 7 | 3 |
| Romania | 2003 | 12 | 3 | 3 | 58 | 19 | 9 |
| Serbia and Macedonia | 2002 | 6 | 1 | 1 | 42 | 12 | 5 |

*Source:* World Bank (2005, table 2 in Annex)

**Table 13.5: Those living below administrative, official or absolute poverty lines (%) and adult monthly equivalent (€)**

|  | Matković (2006) | | | SPSI (2008) | | | |
|---|---|---|---|---|---|---|---|
|  | Year | Rate | Extreme | Year | Rate | Extreme | Adult monthly equivalent (€) |
| Albania | 2002 | 25.0 | 4.7 | 2005 | 18.5 | 3.5 | 40.00 |
| Bosnia | 2001 | 19.5 | 0 | 2004 | 17.8 | 0 | 94.72 |
| Montenegro | 2002 | 9.4 | 0 | 2006 | 11.3 | 0 | 144.68 |
| Serbia | 2002 | 10.6 | 2.4 | 2007 | 6.6 | 0.3 | 109.40 |
| Kosovo | 2000 | 50.0 | 12.0 | 2005/06 | 45.1 | 16.7 | 43.00 |

*Sources:* As shown

As the report notes, these areas have traditionally lagged behind and, it could be added, benefit least from the fruits of recent economic growth. It seems that traditional rural poverty is now joined by new urban poverty and by poverty in war-affected areas. Vulnerable groups are fairly consistent throughout the region, including lone-parent households; refugees and displaced persons; minorities, particularly Roma; larger families and those with young children; people with disabilities not resulting from war; and, albeit rather more unevenly, older people, particularly those without a pension.

Notwithstanding emerging evidence that child benefits can be a useful contribution to the fight against poverty, neither Albania nor Kosovo has child benefit schemes, although one of Kosovo's social assistance schemes is available only to those capable of work if they have young children. Elsewhere, there has been no change from a legacy of means-tested benefits with coverage and rates varying considerably. Social assistance schemes are mainly administered by social workers in CSWs or local officials and do not always perform well in terms of poverty alleviation with low coverage.

Less often discussed are social services, which, again with the exception of Albania and partly Kosovo, are still too weighted towards residential care at the expense of community-based services provided by non-state actors. Residential care is problematic less in terms of absolute rates, which are much lower than those in Bulgaria and Romania, and more in terms of quality and appropriateness of care, which is too often long term and remote from centres of population. The general exclusion of people with disabilities in the region, their lack of access to formal labour markets, and problems faced by children with disabilities in accessing mainstream education are also pronounced. In addition, true social planning and the provision of adequate social casework services is missing in the region, with CSWs in need of reform and modernisation of skills. In Bosnia-Herzegovina, municipalities and, to an extent in the Federation of Bosnia-Herzegovina, cantons (a regional tier of government) are the only actors involved in financing social protection, leading to huge disparities of benefits.

Strategic documents, often produced with the support of international actors, are uneven, sometimes contradictory and overlapping, with poor coordination and extremely poor monitoring and evaluation. In Croatia and, to an extent, elsewhere, the influence of the World Bank is beginning to be challenged by increased EU interest, focusing on strategy development, statistical alignment, consultation with stakeholders and improved horizontal and vertical coordination. In this context, the World

Bank favours experimentation as in recent policy advice in Macedonia to introduce certain kinds of conditional cash transfer schemes tying social assistance benefits to desired behavioural outcomes such as school or health clinic attendance, based on experience in Latin America.

## Conclusions

In terms of social policy, the region has experienced a series of complex de- and re-territorialisations of welfare in which the existence of refugee and displaced populations and a complex pattern of forced migration and uneven return; contiguous and other diasporas involved in sending significant remittances home; various kinds of 'enclave welfare' in which spatially concentrated ethnic groups develop separate welfare arrangements; and all manner of cross-border claims and entitlements all co-exist and are rather weakly regulated. In addition, the wars, ethnicised nationalisms and economic restructurings have had significant social consequences that have impacted on the region as a whole, albeit unevenly in different subregions. These developments have exacerbated the differences within the region that were already present before transition. Crucially, the wars, the growth of ethnicised nationalism and political authoritarianism, and the existence of competing state-building projects have undermined further any common legacies that may have existed from the past. Above all, the nature of citizenship claims as a basis for claiming social rights has been fundamentally altered, with new exclusions co-existing with a reconstitution of ethnicised solidarities.

The region is also marked by the presence of a vast army of transnational organisations vying for position and influence and bringing explicit or implicit social policy advice from elsewhere, often confusing rather than clarifying the nature of policy choices, frequently technicising political questions, and rendering policy processes unaccountable and non-transparent. Domestic policy resistance, subversion or simply inertia also plays a part, of course, leading to unfinished and hybrid reforms, rather than 'coherent implementations of a unified discourse and plan' (Clarke, 2004, p 94). Until recently, the region has been seen by international agencies through the lenses of development and post-war reconstruction, thus bringing to the area a development discourse and practice combined with emergency interventions that have reconfigured what is understood in terms of social policy. In Table 13.6, we attempt to summarise the key international actors, the social policy issues they focus on, as well as issues of the scaling of social welfare and the nature of the welfare mix.

**Table 13.6: Summary of social policy issues and influences in South East Europe (as at 15 December 2008)**

| | Main international actors | EU status | Key social policy issues and policies | Scale | Welfare mix |
|---|---|---|---|---|---|
| Albania | IFIs | PCC | Grey economy and emigration<br>Rural and new urban poverty and ill-health<br>Social assistance | Increasingly decentralised | State and local state still dominates but INGO/local NGO provision emerging |
| Bosnia-Herzegovina | IFIs; OHR; others | PCC | Governance of social policy very poor<br>Exclusion of minorities<br>'Captured' social policy | Highly decentralised | Local state dominates with parallel local NGO provision |
| Croatia | EU | CC (with negotiations) | Pension reform (three pillar)<br>Flexible labour markets<br>Linking social assistance and social services | Largely centralised | State dominates with parallel local NGO sector and emerging private sector |
| Macedonia | EU; IFIs | CC (no negotiations) | High and structural unemployment<br>New conditionalities on cash transfers | Mixed but decentralised for political reasons with weak capacity for social policy planning | Mixed but dominated by state and local state |
| Montenegro | IFIs | PCC | Pension reform<br>Linking social assistance and social services | Centralised | State dominates with parallel INGO and local NGO provision |
| Serbia | IFIs | PCC | Pension reform; holistic deinstitutionalisation strategies<br>Targeted social assistance | Mixed but absence of true regional policies | Local state dominates with parallel local NGO provision |
| Kosovo | Others | PA | Safety net minimal system with some discussion of insurance-based system in future | Centralised but proposed decentralisation for political reasons | Local state dominates with parallel INGO provision |

*Notes:* CC = Candidate Country; IFI = international financial institution; INGO = international non-governmental organisation; NGO = non-governmental organisation; OHR = Office of the High Representative; PA = Partnership Agreement; PCC = Prospective Candidate Country for the EU.

The belated and still rather limited influence of the EU in the region, with only Croatia having any realistic chance of membership in the short or even medium term, is also relevant in terms of the failure to develop a true Europeanisation of social policy. While in Croatia, strategies for tackling poverty and social exclusion, and employment policies, are beginning to be framed in terms of accession, this is not the case elsewhere. For much of the region, the EU's heavily bureaucratised external assistance agenda, and its various aid and reconstruction programmes, bear at best only a passing connection to social policy issues. All of the countries of the region are members of the Council of Europe, with the exception of Kosovo, so that regular reporting on obligations arising from the European Social Charter, and responses from the Council's Committee of Experts, has the potential to align social policy processes in South East Europe with broader European values and perspectives, although these tend to be paper exercises with little real impact.

New structures are emerging, notably a Regional Cooperation Council (RCC), replacing the Stability Act for South Eastern Europe, and meant to be more explicitly focused on regional ownership. Although only recently formed, the Council appears to be adopting a rather technical-bureaucratic approach, promoting cooperation between nation-state actors, neglecting non-state actors, policy entrepreneurship and, indeed, networking. Its choice of initial areas to focus on also seems limited, combining an over-economistic emphasis on development with a political concern with security issues, leaving little room for social policy as traditionally understood. While coordination between the relevant parts of the European Commission, the Council of Europe and the RCC could provide a more consistent set of messages regarding social policy for the region, the shifts needed within each organisation would, however, need to be enormous, in the context of noted 'turf wars' and different kinds of organisational cultures. Consistency of message would, in any case, not necessarily provoke consistent response in a context where there is still little appetite for regional cooperation by policy makers.

Studying South East Europe requires an understanding of 'scale' as socially and politically constructed, so that social policy making becomes both trans-local and consolidated in particular constructed *locales*. The rescaling of social policies in the region has been quite profound but also extremely varied and is almost nowhere based on any policy discussion, much less decision about the optimal scale for different kinds of benefits and services. Similarly, while non-governmental organisations said to constitute a new 'civil society' are everywhere present, modes of incorporation within emergent welfare settlements are extremely complex and contested. The entire space is little researched, with huge data gaps and inconsistencies, a lack of accurate population figures in parts of the region and little investment in building analytical and policy-making capacity for a progressive social policy. Above all, the relationship between national identity, state-building, citizenship, war and humanitarianism, and complex governance arrangements, appear likely to be the key themes through which the social policies of this region will need to be researched in the future.

## Note
[1]  Eurostat only has GDP per capita in Purchasing Power Standards (PPS) for Croatia and Macedonia. These suggest that Croatia has 52.0% of the EU-27 in 2006 and Macedonia 28.2% (Eurostat, 2008).

## Acknowledgements
This work was supported by the Ministry of Science, Education and Sport of the Republic of Croatia, through two scientific projects: 'Socioeconomic aspects of unemployment, poverty and social exclusion' (002-0022469-2462) and 'Social cohesion indicators and the development of the Croatian social model' (066-0661686-1432).

## References
Arandarenko, M. (2004) 'International advice and labour market institutions in South-East Europe', *Global Social Policy*, vol 4, no 1, pp 27-53.

Arandarenko, M. and Golicin, P. (2007) 'Serbia', in B. Deacon and P. Stubbs (eds) *Social Policy and International Interventions in South East Europe*, Cheltenham, UK, and Northampton, MA: Edward Elgar, pp 167-86.

Bache, I., Geddes, A., Lees, C. and Taylor, A. (2007) 'Multi-level governance in South East Europe (SEE) – institutional innovation and adaptation in Croatia, Greece, Macedonia and Slovenia', Paper presented to the UACES Conference, Portsmouth, September, available at www.shef.ac.uk/content/1/c6/08/18/80/UACES_paper_final. doc

Bajec, J., Krstić, G. and Pejin-Stokić, L. with Penev, G. (2008) *Social Protection and Social Inclusion in the Republic of Serbia*, Report for the European Commission, Directorate General on Employment, Social Affairs and Equal Opportunities, Belgrade: Economics Institute, available at http://ec.europa.eu/employment_social/spsi/docs/social_inclusion/2008/study_serbia_en.pdf

Bechev, D. (2006) 'Carrots, sticks and norms: the EU and regional cooperation in Southeast Europe', *Journal of Southern Europe and the Balkans*, vol 8, no 1, pp 27–43.

Bičanić, I. and Franičević, V. (2003) *Understanding Reform: The Case of Croatia*, GDN/WIIW Working Paper, Vienna: Vienna Institute for International Economic Studies, available at www.wiiw.ac.at/balkan/files/GDN_UnderstandingReform_Croatia.pdf

Clarke, J. (2004) *Changing Welfare, Changing States: New Directions in Social Policy*, London: Sage Publications.

Clarke, J. (2008) 'Governance puzzles', in L. Budd and L. Harris (eds) *eGovernance: Managing or Governing?*, London: Routledge.

Cocozzelli, F. (2007) 'Kosovo', in B. Deacon and P. Stubbs (eds) *Social Policy and International Interventions in South East Europe*, Cheltenham, UK, and Northampton, MA: Edward Elgar, pp 203-20.

Deacon, B. (2005) 'From "safety nets" back to "universal social provision": is the global tide turning?', *Global Social Policy*, vol 5, no 1, pp 19–28.

Deacon, B. and Stubbs, P. (2007) 'Transnationalism and the making of social policy in South East Europe', in B. Deacon and P. Stubbs (eds) *Social Policy and International Interventions in South East Europe*, Cheltenham, UK, Northampton, MA: Edward Elgar, pp 1-21.

Deacon, B., Lendvai, N. and Stubbs, P. (2007) 'Conclusions', in B. Deacon and P. Stubbs (eds) *Social Policy and International Interventions in South East Europe*, Cheltenham, UK, and Northampton, MA: Edward Elgar, pp 221-42.

DFID (Department for International Development) (2004) *Regional Assistance Plan for the Western Balkans 2004/5 – 2008/9*, London: DFID, available at www.dfid.gov.uk/Pubs/files/rapwesternbalkans.pdf

Eurostat website, http://epp.eurostat.ec.europa.eu/portal/page?_pageid=1090,30070682,1090_33076576&_dad=portal&_schema=PORTAL

Fetsi, A. (ed) (2007) *Labour Markets in the Western Balkans: Challenges for the Future*, Turin: ETF, available at www.etf.europa.eu/web. nsf/pages/EmbedPub_EN?OpenDocument&emb=/pubmgmt. nsf/(WebPublications%20by%20themeR)/F624E6A60F073F75C12 5728F002FFCF0?OpenDocument

Gerovska Mitev, M. (2007) 'Macedonia', in B. Deacon and P. Stubbs (eds) *Social Policy and International Interventions in South East Europe*, Cheltenham, UK, and Northampton, MA: Edward Elgar, pp 130-48.

Kathuria, S. (ed) (2008) *Western Balkan Integration and the EU: An Agenda for Trade and Growth*, Washington, DC: World Bank, available at http://siteresources.worldbank.org/ECAEXT/Resources/ publications/454763-1213051861605/balkan_ch1.pdf

Lendvai, N. and Stubbs, P. (2008) 'Assemblages, translation, and intermediaries in South East Europe: rethinking transnationalism and social policy', *European Societies*, forthcoming.

Matković, G. (2006) 'Overview of poverty and social exclusion in the Western Balkans', in *Stanovništvo*, no 1, pp 7-46, available at www. komunikacija.org.yu/komunikacija/casopisi/stanov/XLIV_1/01/ download_gb

Matković, T. (2008) 'Politika zapošljavanja i nezaposlenost' [Employment policy and unemployment], in V. Puljiz, G Bežovan, T Matković, Z. Šuæur and S. Zrinščak (eds) *Socijalna Politika Hrvatske* [*Croatian social policy*], Zagreb: Pravni fakultet u Zagrebu.

Müller, K. (1999) *The Political Economy of Pension Reform in Central-East Europe*, Cheltenham, UK, and Northampton, MA: Edward Elgar.

Müller, K. (2002) 'Beyond privatisation: pension reform in the Czech Republic and Slovenia', *Journal of European Social Policy*, vol 12, no 4, pp 293-306.

Müller, K. (2003) *Privatising Old-Age Security: Latin America and Eastern Europe Compared*, Cheltenham, UK, and Northampton, MA: Edward Elgar.

Nesporova, A. (2002) 'Why unemployment remains so high in Central and Eastern Europe', *ILO Employment Paper 43*, Geneva: ILO.

Nesporova, A. (2008) 'Comparative overview of labour market characteristics: South Eastern Europe and the EU', Power Point Presentation, available at www.imo.hr/europa/conf/agenda/nesporova. ppt

Orenstein, M. (2005) 'The new pension reform as global policy', *Global Social Policy*, vol 5, no 2, pp 175-202.

Puljiz, V. (2007) 'Hrvatski mirovinski sustav: korijeni, evolucija i perspective' [The Croatian pension system: origins, evolution and perspectives], *Revija za Socijalnu Politiku*, vol 14, no 2, pp 163-92.

Račić, D., Babić, Z. and Podrug, N. (2005) 'Segmentation of the labour market and the employee rights in Croatia', *Revija za Socijalnu Politiku*, vol 12, no 1, pp 45-65.

Sansier, F. (2006) *Regional Assessment Report on Social Security Issues*, Strasbourg: Council of Europe, available at www.coe.int/t/dg3/sisp/Source/SISP(2007)ExpRepFinIssFS.doc

Solioz, C. (2007) *Turning Points in Post-War Bosnia: Ownership Process and European Integration* (2nd edition), Baden–Baden: Nomos.

SPSI (Social Protection and Social Inclusion) (2008) Reports on Social Protection and Social Inclusion in the Western Balkans, available at http://ec.europa.eu/employment_social/spsi/studies_en.htm#western_balkans

St Clair, A. (2006) 'Global poverty: the co-production of knowledge and politics', *Global Social Policy*, vol 6, no 1, pp 57-77.

Stubbs, P. (2005) 'Stretching concepts too far? Multi-level governance, policy transfer and the politics of scale in South East Europe', *Southeast European Politics*, vol 6, no 2, pp 66-87.

Stubbs, P. and Zrinščak, S. (2006) 'International actors, "drivers of change" and the reform of social protection in Croatia', Paper presented at the ISA World Congress, Durban, South Africa, July.

Stubbs, P. and Zrinščak, S. (2007) 'Croatia', in B. Deacon and P. Stubbs (eds) *Social Policy and International Interventions in South East Europe*, Cheltenham, UK, and Northampton, MA: Edward Elgar, pp 85-102.

Šućur, Z. and Zrinščak, S. (2007) 'Differences that hurt: self-perceived health inequalities in Croatia and the European Union', *Croatian Medical Journal*, vol 48, no 5, pp 653-68, available at www.cmj.hr/2007/48/5/17948951.htm

Tendler, J. (2002) *Why Social Policy is Condemned to a Residual Category of Safety Nets and What to Do About It*, Geneva: UNRISD.

UNDP (United Nations Development Programme) Kosovo (2004) *The Rise of the Citizen: Challenges and Choices*, Human Development Report, Pristina: UNDP.

UNDP Croatia (2006) *Unplugged: Faces of Social Exclusion in Croatia*, Human Development Report, Zagreb: UNDP.

UNICEF (United Nations Children's Fund) (2007) *TransMONEE Database*, Florence: ICDC.

World Bank (2005) *Growth, Poverty and Inequality: Eastern Europe and the Former Soviet Europe*, Washington, DC: World Bank, available at http://siteresources.worldbank.org/INTECA/Resources/complete-eca-poverty.pdf

Ymeraj, A. (2007) 'Albania', in B. Deacon and P. Stubbs (eds) *Social Policy and International Interventions in South East Europe*, Cheltenham, UK, and Northampton, MA: Edward Elgar, pp 187-202.

# Index

Note: Departments, organisations and initiatives in index headings refer to the UK unless otherwise specified.

## C

New Deal for Communities
(NDC) and local governance 6,
249, 259-62
New Labour
anti-poverty strategy 23-4, 26
child poverty pledge 21, 22, 23,
25
education policy and reforms
49-64
emphasis on paid work 41-2
national childcare strategy 38, 41
limitations 42-3
NHS policy and reforms 70-81,
82-3
turn to local governance 245-64
New Public Management and
child welfare services 226, 236
New Town Corporations in
Scotland 89-90
Newman, J. 247
Next Step Reviews *see* Darzi, Ara
NHS *see* National Health Service
(NHS)
NHS Act (1946) 69
NHS Constitution 76-7
*NHS Plan, The* 70
Nicholson, David 80
Nicholson, Baroness Emma 154,
155
non-governmental organisations
(NGOs)
and child welfare services
accountability 226
'joined-up' working 223-4
international NGOs and South
East Europe 289, 300-1
Nunn, Thomas Hancock 110
nursery education and child
outcomes 38

**O**

O'Connor Don, the 110
Ohmae, K. 280-1
older people and poor relief 113,
114, 116, 118, 119

Organisation for Economic Co-
operation and Development
(OECD) PISA study 61
outdoor relief and Poor Law 113-
14, 117, 118, 119
overcrowding in Scotland 88, 90,
91, 92, 93, 96, 97

**P**

Palacios, J. 150-1
parental choice of schools 58
parenting
and family income and child
outcomes 168-9
'good-enough parent' concept
170
parental characteristics 171,
172-3, 175-6
parental investment 170, 171,
190
parental stress 170, 171, 173,
181-5, 191
and policy 38
*see also* childcare; shared residence
arrangements
parenting contracts 52
Parenting Orders 52
Parker, Roy 157
part-time employment
and women 36-8
disadvantages 44-5
participatory budgeting 252
participatory democracy and local
governance 250
partnership working
child welfare services 223-4
and local governance 247, 249,
253, 259-62
and patient choice 77-8
passive welfare 30
patient choice and NHS reform
71-2, 77-8
Patten-MacDougall, James 110
Paull, G. 44
pauper funerals 114

pay gap and women's part-time
work 45
'payment by results' (PBR) 71
Peacey, V. 199
Penman, R. 172
Pension Credit 14, 20, 21, 22, 23,
25
pensions
and benefits level 20
private contributions 14, 20
reforms in South East Europe
293-5
Pensions Act (2007) 22, 23
performance management
and child welfare services 226-
30, 236
and local governance 253
and NHS 74, 75
and health inequalities 78-9
implementation and evaluation
79-81, 82-3
'payment by results' reform 71
*see also* testing in schools
personal budgets 72, 252
'personalisation' agenda 72, 248
Phelps, Rev. Lancelot Ridley 110,
121, 122
Piachaud, D. 22
Plato 124
'polyclinics' proposal 75
Poor Law Commission reports 3,
109-26
poor relief system and Poor Law
12, 109-26
'deserving' and 'undeserving'
poor 101, 120
in practice in Edwardian era
116-23
and social theory 123-5
population concerns in postwar
Britain 33, 34
'positive welfare' 67-8
positive health 67, 68-9, 70, 82
Post, Roelie 154, 155
'postcode lottery' and health 75, 76

poverty
and Beveridge's freedom from
'want' 11-26
'rediscovery of poverty' debate
17-18
and housing for poor in Scotland
91-3, 95-7, 104
measurement of poverty
and benefit levels 22, 25
New Labour 'equivalised'
poverty level 21, 22
and rescaling social policy in
South East Europe 295-8
*see also* family income and child
outcomes; poor relief system
and Poor Law
Powell, Enoch 35, 98
practice-based commissioning 73
Presbytery of Glasgow report 92
prevention: positive health and
policy 68-9, 70, 82
Primary Care Trusts (PCTs)
and commissioning process 73,
79
and patient involvement 72-3
performance evaluation 80
performance on health inequality
78
and 'polyclinics' proposal 75
'primary carer' model and shared
residence 198, 209-11
'primary poverty' measure 12, 17
private sector
and child welfare services 225
and council house building 96-7
hospitals and patient choice 71-2
pension contributions 20, 23
privatisation and 'Right to Buy'
87, 103
and social insurance 14, 20
professional freedom in education
accountability and testing in
schools 53-7
postwar education 49-50
professionalisation and child
welfare workforce 234

provider plurality in health service
73
Provis, Sir Samuel 110
Public Assistance 111, 113
Public Assistance Institutions 111
public engagement *see* local
governance
public health and policy 69, 70,
79, 82
public sector
creation of jobs 34, 35
and part-time work for women
37
post-war professional freedom
49–50
purchaser–provider model and
child welfare services 224, 225,
236

## Q

Quelch, Henry 121

## R

*Raising Expectations and Increasing
Support* (White Paper) 42
Rathbone, Eleanor 29
recession and employment levels
26
redistribution and nation-state 268,
276, 279, 281
and regional policy 269
Regional Cooperation Council
(RCC) in South East Europe
300
regional development policies
278–9, 280
regional devolution and welfare 6,
267–81
implications for government
274–80
'race to the bottom' danger 273,
277–8, 280
'race to the top' outcomes 280
*see also* local governance
regulation

and child welfare services 225,
226–30, 236
and NHS 74
*see also* accountability
Rehn, Olli 155
Reid, John 80
rent relief 101
rescaling *see* spatial rescaling and
social policy
resistance and local governance
259–61
'respect' agenda and New Labour
255
'respectable' working-class families
as council tenants 87, 89–90,
90–1, 92–3, 94–5, 97, 104
Richards, Mike 76
'Right to Buy' policy 87, 103
rights
children's rights 220–1
and responsibilities: educational
contract 52
Robinson, Sir Henry 110
Rose, M.E. 115
Rousseau, Jean-Jacques 124
Rowe, M.L. 190–1
Rowntree, B.S. 12, 17
Royal Commission: *Report on
the Housing of the Industrial
Population of Scotland* 93
Royal Commission on Equal Pay
35
Royal Commission on the
Housing of the Working Classes
91
Royal Commission on the NHS
69
Royal Commission on the Poor
Laws 109
Royal Commission on the
Population 33
Rutter, M. 54

# S

treatment of women
  as dependants 30, 33-4, 43-4
  lone mothers 38-41, 42, 43
  welfare-to-work and its
    limitations 41-6
and freedom from 'want' 11-26
  contemporary developments
    21-5
  discretionary additions 19-20
  employment and 'want' 18-19
  entitlement levels 13-15
  and 'rediscovery of poverty'
    debate 17-18
  variation in levels of benefit
    19-21, 22, 24, 25
  and 'withering safety net'
    expectation 16-17
and shared residence
  arrangements 207-8, 209, 211
in South East Europe 297-8
Social Security Advisory
  Committee 42
social selection: family income and
  child outcomes 170-1, 172-3
social services
  in South East Europe 285, 297
  wartime expansion 36-7
  *see also* child welfare services
solidarity and regional devolution
  279-80, 281
South East Europe and rescaling
  social policy 6-7, 283-301
  geopolitical constructions 283-5,
    298
  intervention of international
    agencies 288-301
  labour market policies 290-3
  socioeconomic conditions 285-8
  Yugoslav legacy 284-5
spatial rescaling and social policy
  5-7, 243-305
  local governance 245-64
  and regional devolution 267-81
  in South East Europe 283-301
special needs *see* children with
  special needs
'squalor' 3, 87-105

Standard Assessment Tests (SATs)
  50, 53-7
state
  and turn to local governance
    245-6, 246-8
  *see also* centralised government;
    nation-state and levels of
    welfare
Statutory Sick Pay 20
Stevens, Simon 80
Stirling, Scotland: council housing
  89, 94-5, 96-7, 103
Stone, Deborah 11
stress: parental stress and child
  outcomes 170, 171, 173, 181-5,
  191
Sumner, John Bird 113
supervision and child welfare
  services 227-8, 229
Supplementary Benefits 14, 16-17,
  19-20
  and 'rediscovery of poverty'
    17-18
Supplementary Benefits
  Commission 40
supply-side economic theory 32
supply-side reforms in health
  services 71-3
Sure Start programme 38
Sutherland, K. 80
Sweden
  child welfare services 5, 215-37
  independent sector for education
    59, 61

# T

Tannock, C. 154-5
tax credits 19, 22, 24, 25-6, 38, 44
Taylor, Matthew 79-80
teacher assessment as SATs
  alternative 55
'teaching to tests' 55-6
tenements and Scottish council
  housing 88, 89, 91
Terre des Hommes study 152-3